PRAISE FOR VOLUME ONE:

"These daily reflections from Alistair Begg are simple but profound, short but meaty, challenging but encouraging. They offer truth for all of life, truth to consecrate a life, truth to transform a life. Together, they make an ideal devotional resource for individuals, couples, and families alike."

TIM CHALLIES, Blogger; Author, *Visual Theology* and *Epic*

"Here speaks a pastor who knows both his Bible and his people. He not only understands the Scriptures but lovingly applies them like medicine for the soul. These daily devotions will do that. They will help you get to know the Bible better and how it fits together. They will stretch your mind with deep, bracing theology expressed with accessible clarity. They will warm and nourish your heart because they breathe the beauty of Christ. I have been struck by the freshness and variety of the devotions, from every part of the Scriptures, and by the pastor's heart that beats through them. There is rich nourishment here for the soul, the fruit of many years of mining the Scriptures and caring for people."

CHRISTOPHER ASH, Writer-in-Residence, Tyndale House, Cambridge, UK; Author, *Zeal Without Burnout* and *Married For God*

"In this rich resource, Alistair Begg provides what we've come to expect from him—solid biblical truth presented with clarity, winsomeness, and a focus on the person and work of Christ."

NANCY GUTHRIE, Host, Help Me Teach the Bible podcast; Author, *Even Better Than Eden* and *Saints and Scoundrels*

"The discipline of daily Bible-reading is one that is always in danger of become routine or a chore. That is where a good devotional guide can be helpful in keeping the familiar stories and teachings of Scripture fresh and thought-provoking. Alistair Begg has produced one such volume. Like Spurgeon's *Morning and Evening*, this is not a guide to extended passages of Scripture but a series of reflections on particular verses touching particular aspects of the faith. Each one is designed to make the Christian think more clearly, love God more fervently, and act in ways that are more godly. For those looking for a book that will reinvigorate their devotions, this book might well be it."

CARL R. TRUEMAN, Professor of Biblical and Religious Studies, Grove City College, PA; Author, *The Rise and Triumph of the Modern Self*

"A good daily devotional is a wonderful aid to a daily habit of reading and meditating on Scripture. And this one, as you would expect from Alistair Begg, is pure gold. With the skill of a spiritual surgeon, he carefully dissects both the Scriptures and our hearts. A daily devotional dose of wisdom from one of the finest preachers of our time. How could this possibly be anything but life-giving nourishment for the mind and heart?"

DEREK W.H. THOMAS, Senior Minister, First Presbyterian Church, Columbia, SC; Teaching Fellow, Ligonier Ministries; Chancellor's Professor, Reformed Theological Seminary

"I found these daily devotions by Alistair Begg to be a huge help to daily Bible reading—a critical barometer of our spiritual health. Time and again I was made to think freshly about a passage and then given another chapter which made me reflect more deeply on the verses that the commentary had opened up. A very timely gift to aid discipleship in the church."

RICO TICE, Senior Associate Minister, All Souls Langham Place, London; Founder, Christianity Explored Ministries; Author, *Faithful Leaders* and *Honest Evangelism*

"If you are looking for wise and perceptive guidance to help you see and experience the deep impact of God's words in Scripture, you will love this devotional. Each day's reflection is a gem, focusing the light of the chosen Scripture text onto our thinking, our affections and our behaviour. I cannot imagine it being read without benefit!"

JOHN WOODHOUSE, Former Principal of Moore Theological College, Sydney, Australia

"These devotions will help you praise when you are celebrating, will comfort you when you are struggling, will encourage you when you are doubting, and will be a balm when you are hurting. Each day, Alistair points to the glory and goodness of God as He reveals Himself to us in His word. Whoever you are, there is rich treasure for you in this book."

KEITH & KRISTYN GETTY, Hymn Writers; Founders of Getty Music and the Sing! Conference

TRUTH FOR LIFE

365 DAILY DEVOTIONS

VOLUME TWO

ALISTAIR BEGG

2

Truth For Life Volume Two: 365 Daily Devotions

Published by:
The Good Book Company

thegoodbook.com | thegoodbook.co.uk
thegoodbook.com.au | thegoodbook.co.nz | thegoodbook.co.in

Published in association with the literary agency of Wolgemuth & Associates.

Cover design by Faceout Studio, Molly von Borstel
Design and art direction by André Parker

ISBN: 9781784987688 | Printed in India

INTRODUCTION

Welcome to the second volume of this Truth For Life devotional. If you have already enjoyed Volume One, then you will be familiar with this Introduction, and might like to move straight on to January 1st's devotional. If, on the other hand, these are the first Truth For Life devotionals you've picked up, then do read on…

God's word is a glorious gift. Our Father has given it to us in order that we might know His Son and that we might live in the power of His Spirit, in obedience to His truth.

It is worth pausing to consider this reality: when we read the Bible, we're dealing with the words of the Creator of the universe, spoken to His creation. It is impossible for us to understand ourselves, our world, or anything else without His word. As we read a newspaper, as we try to make sense of our society, and as we look to our history and to our future, it is the Bible we need if we are to get a handle on it all. God's word is the truth that you and I need to navigate every day of this life, and to point us to the one in whom we find the life that really is life.

So in this devotional, by far the most important words on each page are the ones at the top, just under the date and title. Those are the words of the living, reigning, eternal God. My aim in the comments below those divinely inspired words is simply to explain them, to encourage you from them, and to reflect on how they inspire and equip us to enjoy living for Christ in every area of our lives. God's word says of itself that it is able to "make you wise for salvation through faith in Christ Jesus" and that these God-breathed words are "profitable for teaching, for reproof, for correction, and for training in righteousness, that the man of God may be complete, equipped for every good work" (2 Timothy 3:16-17).

This is a *daily* devotional, because man does not live by bread alone but by every word that comes from the mouth of God (Matthew 4:4). That is, God's word sustains us each day and is as necessary to our spiritual health as food is to our physical health. On some days you may find reading God's word a delight, and on other days it may be done more out of duty, but every day it is essential. Think of it like exercise. If you're a runner, there are times when you're running around the track and it feels amazing; and there are others when it feels like an effort and you need to push on and push through. Most of us will not tumble out of our beds each morning thinking how fantastic our time in God's word is going to be. If we approach the Scriptures thinking that we need to be stirred as we read them, or that we ought to "get a blessing" whenever we open them, then we will either be intermittent or disappointed Bible readers. There will be times of delight and excitement and feeling something as you read and meditate on God's word—but do not worry if those times do not come every day, or even most days. Make a commitment to turn to the Bible every day (and if you realize you have fallen out of the habit of doing so, simply jump back in), for God's word is living and active, and it will be going to work in you in ways far deeper and more profound than your feelings can intuit.

And the Scriptures will—or they should—make a difference to our minds, to our hearts, and to our lives. Therefore, at the bottom of each devotion you will see three icons: . These are a prompt to say to yourself, *Now that I have read and considered these verses…*

- *how is God calling me to think differently?*
- *how is God reordering my heart's affections—what I love?*
- *what is God calling me to do as I go about my day today?*

It may be that God's word does not speak to all three of those areas each day; but learning to ask yourself these questions will ensure that you are open to what God's Spirit may be saying about your mind, heart, and life. And they will be helpful prompts to pray in response to what you have read, too.

Beside those icons you will see a passage that is linked in some way to what we have been considering; if you have time, turn up that passage and enjoy going deeper into God's word. I have also found it very profitable to read through the whole of the Scriptures from start to finish in a year, and so, at the very foot of each page, you'll see a Bible-reading plan that enables you to do just that.

God's words are the words that we need. And so I am praying for you: that, in taking you to those words each day, this book would be life-changing for you, God's beloved child, as His Spirit works through His word to show you His Son. Why not make that your prayer too? You could begin each day by using the words of my friends Keith Getty and Stuart Townend and praying:

Holy Spirit, living breath of God,
Breathe new life into my willing soul.
Let the presence of the risen Lord
Come renew my heart and make me whole.
Cause Your word to come alive in me;
Give me faith for what I cannot see,
Give me passion for Your purity;
Holy Spirit, breathe new life in me.[1]

1 Keith Getty and Stuart Townend, "Holy Spirit, Living Breath of God" (2005).

JANUARY 1

THE GOD OF HOPE

"May the God of hope fill you with all joy and peace in believing, so that by the power of the Holy Spirit you may abound in hope." ROMANS 15:13

We find ourselves at a period in history when it is easy to question hope in the midst of worldly peril. While even a brief study of centuries past would remind us that our age is not the worst, darkest, most evil age that has ever been experienced, with our limited perspectives we are apt to grow concerned, distracted, and anxious. We would do well to read the apostle Paul's words as an indirect prayer for our daily lives: that the God of endurance might grant us encouragement in times of fear and uncertainty by filling us with all joy and peace.

The book of Romans, Paul's greatest theological treatise, was written to a diverse congregation in Rome made up of Jews and Gentiles, men and women, and rich and poor, all of varying levels of spiritual maturity. As he reached the end of his glorious letter, Paul wanted to call them to live confidently as people marked by a distinct and abounding hope.

We find such hope simply by knowing our God. He is our God of hope for two reasons.

First, it is God who generates hope *in* us. His word "was written for our instruction" (Romans 15:4) so that we might think about and learn from His unchanging trustworthiness. Hope, endurance, encouragement, and peace are not commodities outside of ourselves; rather, in giving us Himself, dwelling in our hearts by His Spirit, God gives us all these things, which well up from inside.

Second, He is also the *object* of our hope. The prophet Jeremiah said in the midst of his own dreadful circumstances, "The Lord is my portion ... therefore I will hope in him" (Lamentations 3:24). The psalmist agreed when he wrote in response to the disheartening circumstances that surrounded him: "My flesh and my heart may fail, but God is the strength of my heart and my portion forever" (Psalm 73:26). In other words, it doesn't matter how long difficulty lingers in our lives; if we have God, He is ours for eternity, and He is enough for eternity.

The God whom we meet in Scripture is therefore the God of hope—a hope that is neither superficial nor fleeting. Our enduring Savior stands the test of time.

When you face a crisis, you quickly discover where your hope is placed. If your faith rests on the promises of God, then your hope will be grounded in those promises, and it will not be disappointed. It will abound through all the trials of life. It doesn't matter what fear parades before your eyes; you can know beyond a shadow of a doubt that your God, who brought the world into being and brought you from death to life, preserves it and sustains you by His power.

It is in God alone that true hope can be found. And it is in looking to Him that we find ourselves filled with all joy and peace—today and every day, on into eternity.

PSALM 46

JANUARY 2

THE PROPHETIC WORD

"A great prophet has arisen among us!" LUKE 7:16

By nature, we do not see any beauty in Jesus. Of our own accord we do not declare that Jesus is wonderful, that Jesus is beautiful, that Jesus is incomparable. Left to ourselves, we are in utter darkness, having rejected what God has made obvious to us.

Spiritual darkness, noted the 17th-century Puritan Thomas Watson, is worse than natural darkness, yet "natural darkness affrights," whereas "spiritual darkness is not accompanied with horror" and "men tremble not at their condition; nay, they like their condition well enough."[2] We love darkness rather than light because the inclination of our hearts, and of our deeds, is actually evil (John 3:19-20).

Is there any light for our darkness? Is there any freedom from our bondage to self? The answer, of course, is an emphatic yes—namely, in the person of Jesus Christ! And as we consider how it is that Christ brings light and life, by God's grace we are moved all over again to praise Him as wonderful, as beautiful, and as incomparable.

Consider, for example, how Jesus is the greatest and final prophet (Hebrews 1:1-3). God's sending of His prophets, and finally His Son, represents an implicit judgment on us, since it is our shortcomings that make prophets necessary. We are by nature ignorant of God. We need divine help in order to grasp life's most important truths.

Old Testament prophets were anointed and sent by God to speak into the people's ignorance and blindness. These prophets, however, only *spoke* the word of God. When God came to us in the person of Jesus, He came *as* the Word of God, to speak into our ignorance, to unstop our deaf ears, and to open our blind eyes. Here is the greatest of the prophets.

We find in the Gospels that as Jesus began His ministry, He was almost immediately viewed as a prophet. So it was that following the raising of the widow of Nain's son, the people responded, "A great prophet has arisen among us!" Similarly, in John 6, when the 5,000 were fed, the response was "This is indeed the Prophet who is to come into the world!" (John 6:14). Indeed, Jesus Himself acknowledged this role when, in Luke 4, He pointed out in Nazareth that "no prophet is acceptable in his hometown" (Luke 4:24).

Jesus came as the very Word of God. And so, in Him, the prophetic word has found its fulfillment, and in Him we discover the ultimate expression of truth—the truth contained not only in His teaching but also in His person. We need Jesus to teach our hearts, to dispel our darkness, to reach us in a way that no one else can. Until He teaches us, we will never learn about Him. Until we see Him as the Word of God, we will never be wise for salvation. But when this greatest of the prophets speaks truth to our hearts, we say, "This is truth"—and we praise the one who is all truth as our wonderful, beautiful, incomparable Teacher and Savior.

2 PETER 1:16-21

2 "Christ's Prophetic Office" in *A Body of Divinity* (Banner of Truth, 2015), p 169.

JANUARY 3

LIFE AT LOW TIDE

"Be gracious to me, O Lord, for I am languishing; heal me, O Lord, for my bones are troubled. My soul also is greatly troubled. But you, O Lord—how long?" PSALM 6:2-3

Have you ever felt like your life is at low tide? Perhaps you feel that way now. Sometimes we sense that we no longer have the spiritual vitality we once did. Either our own sins or sins committed against us have sapped our strength. Dark clouds seem to overshadow our faith. What was once a devoted zeal has become a distanced formalism, and what we used to enjoy we now merely endure. Such feelings may barely register at first. The waters seem to recede slowly. But the next thing you know, you look down and see the bare ocean floor. The ship of your faith has run aground.

When David wrote Psalm 6, his soul was at low tide. He was stuck in despair, saying, "I am weary with my moaning" (Psalm 6:6), and "My eye wastes away because of grief" (v 7). David's experience shows that it is not abnormal for us as believers to feel overwhelmed by sin, be it our own or that committed against us.

But hope for a higher tide remains.

David pleads for God to be gracious to him: "Turn [and] deliver my life," he asks (Psalm 6:4). Living this side of the cross, we know the ultimate source of that deliverance for which David pleaded. There on the cross is mercy without measure. At Calvary, God canceled the record of our sins and shamed our spiritual enemies (Colossians 2:14-15). Yes, Christ's cross confronts us with our guilt and brings us to our knees—but the grace and mercy that God lavishes on us there also stands us on our feet. The God who encounters our hardened hearts is the same God who grants us repentance (2 Timothy 2:25) and liberates our lips to praise Him.

Because of Christ, God hears all our weeping and despair (Psalm 6:8)—and if we have come to know and love His mercy, then we can claim with David, "The Lord has heard my plea; the Lord accepts my prayer" (v 9). We come to Him. We cry to Him. We commit ourselves to Him. No matter how low we are, how guilty we feel, or how hurt by the actions of others we may have been, God can still turn our mourning into dancing and clothe us with gladness (Psalm 30:11).

God doesn't guarantee that the tide will come rushing back as soon as we cry out to Him. But hope is never far away for those who trust in the Lord. One day—whether today or the first day of our eternity with Him—we will know complete healing of our souls and bodies and, ultimately, an end to all our troubles. God's timing may be mysterious to us. But the tide will come in and all our troubles will be swept away. The cross declares it.

PSALM 6

◇ Bible Through The Year: Genesis 7–9; Romans 3

JANUARY 4

FROM PRECEPTS TO PROMISES

"This is the covenant that I will make with the house of Israel after those days, declares the Lord: I will put my laws into their minds, and write them on their hearts, and I will be their God, and they shall be my people." HEBREWS 8:10

The law of God is a masterpiece, revealing our deep guilt and, at the same time, graciously teaching unholy people how to approach a holy God in worship. Its instructions form a carefully assembled tapestry; if one thread is pulled, the entire thing unravels.

This means that there are no small matters in the law. When we break a single command, we become guilty of violating the entire thing. James tells us this frankly: "For whoever keeps the whole law but fails in one point has become guilty of all of it" (James 2:10). The law is not like a pile of stones, from which you can take one stone away and still have a heap. Rather, it is like a sheet of glass: a single crack compromises the whole thing. Why? Because God's law is no arbitrary set of rules and regulations; it is an expression of the character and nature of our perfect and pure God of glory.

When you add this all together, it amounts to a terrifying reality. How can we ever hope to measure up to such a high standard? And yet, for those who know Christ Jesus by faith, the law no longer condemns us. The Son of God fulfilled God's law Himself so that His people no longer have to face His wrath. We have escaped God's just penalty on our sins through Jesus' death on the cross and resurrection from the dead. Now the law does not remain outside of us; it is written upon our hearts. Now the Spirit of God who wrote it there goes to work to transform us so that we gladly accept its duties and obligations. In Christ we are not only saved from the penalty for not keeping the law; we also have the resources to keep the law as never before.

Imagine a thief who walks into a church on Sunday, sees a list of the Ten Commandments, and trembles in fear at the words "You shall not steal" (Exodus 20:15). He or she repents of that sin and receives the offer of new life in Christ. From then on, when they read that command, it means something different. The prohibition, "You *must* not steal," has become a promise: "You *will* not steal."

This is the case for everyone who calls on Jesus as Lord. What sins are you particularly struggling against or giving in to? By the Spirit, you have all the resources to obey your Father, looking to the law neither as a ladder to heaven nor as a source of condemnation but as a guide to life. Armed with this hope, you can battle against your sin with the confidence that comes from Christ's great victory.

ROMANS 8:1-6

JANUARY 5

THE CONSEQUENCES OF LAZINESS

"The desire of the sluggard kills him, for his hands refuse to labor. All day long he craves and craves, but the righteous gives and does not hold back."
PROVERBS 21:25-26

The book of Proverbs is an intensely practical book. It reminds us that a godly life is lived out in the everyday events of our journey. As Derek Kidner writes, "Its function in Scripture is to put godliness into working clothes."[3] In many ways, Solomon's writings are both immensely profitable and distinctly uncomfortable.

One lesson that Proverbs teaches us is the consequences of laziness. The biblical text uses the word "sluggard" to refer to a lazy person. It's not a contemporary word, but it *is* a suitable word—one that describes a habitually inactive person whose lifestyle is framed by indolence and dormancy.

The sluggard, we learn, is hinged to his bed (Proverbs 26:14). This could mean that the person rises from bed after lunchtime or simply that they make little or no progress in their daily work. They don't like to be approached directly or to be held accountable. When asked, "Will you do this?" they resent the follow-up question: "*When* are you planning to do it?"—or, in the words of Proverbs 6:9, "How long will you lie there, O sluggard? When will you arise from your sleep?" They never actually refuse to do anything, but they put off tasks bit by bit. They deceive themselves into thinking that they'll "get around to it," but minute by minute, they allow opportunity to quietly slip away.

In Proverbs 12:27, Solomon also tells us that "whoever is slothful will not roast his game, but the diligent man will get precious wealth." In other words, a lazy person does not finish what they start. But we, as followers of Christ, are called to a kind of perseverance that, as we work unto the Lord, will reap a harvest in due season if we do not give up (Galatians 6:9). As we remain accountable in Christian community, we can help each other see our blind spots so that the excuses we make for our lazy behaviors don't become larger issues of self-indulgence.

The real tragedy of the sluggard's life is that laziness is not an infirmity but a sin. Contemporary culture drives many on a quest for an overabundance of so-called leisure. But believers can set a radically different example. God created us to work with a purpose: that we may let our light shine before others so that they may see our good works and give glory to our heavenly Father (Matthew 5:16). The best adventure you can have is found along the pathway of goodness and duty. The greatest reward is not in leisure and ease and ducking out but in giving and giving and not holding back. How will that shape your approach to your day, and your tasks, today?

PROVERBS 6:6-19

3 *Proverbs: An Introduction and Commentary*, Tyndale Old Testament Commentaries (Tyndale, 1968), p 35.

JANUARY 6

COMMUNICATING LOVE

"Being affectionately desirous of you, we were ready to share with you not only the gospel of God but also our own selves, because you had become very dear to us." 1 THESSALONIANS 2:8

There is no greater communication of love than proclaiming the gospel of God. Such a love forfeits lesser benefits—being well thought of, meeting the expectations of others, holding a prestigious title, enjoying a comfortable life, and so on—for the sake of making the good news of Jesus known. Not that those blessings can't be given to us by God, but they are not primary.

Notice that Paul and his missionary partners sought to share both the gospel *and* themselves. The gospel is best communicated within a loving friendship. But a loving friendship is not the same as gospel communication. No one declares the gospel passively; it must be actively shared.

And so we see that while Paul labored to build strong relationships, he also "proclaimed to [the Thessalonians] the gospel of God" (1 Thessalonians 2:9). The word "proclaimed" in this verse denotes the action of a herald, who declares what is given to him to say. A herald's job is not to make things up, to respond to all the felt needs of those around them, or to make people feel good; it is to stand up and to speak up.

If you are a gospel believer, you are a gospel herald. The only question is: How effective a herald are you? We cannot replace the God-given message of the cross with our own views. If we get caught up in the desire to impress others, then we will quickly neglect what's most important. We are meant to go into the throne room of the King, to receive His message, to enter our little spheres of influence, and to share what He has said—nothing more and nothing less. As John Stott writes, "Every authentic Christian ministry begins here, with the conviction that we have been called to handle God's Word as its guardians and heralds. We must not be satisfied with 'rumors of God' as a substitute for the 'good news from God.'"[4]

Some of us, then, need to love others enough to spend time with them, serving them and demonstrating that we are for them, so that we might love them by sharing the gospel of love with them. Others of us, though, need to use the friendships and networks we already enjoy as bridges for the gospel. What will gospel-sharing love for others look like for you, in the place and among the people God has set you today? Whatever the answer, remember this: there is no better way you can love and care for others than to tell them the good news of Jesus Christ.

2 CORINTHIANS 5:16-21

4 *The Message of 1 and 2 Thessalonians*, The Bible Speaks Today (InterVarsity, 1991), p 68.

JANUARY 7

TRUTH YOU CAN TRUST

"Sanctify them in the truth; your word is truth." JOHN 17:17

Post-Enlightenment, rationalist, materialist culture has cooked up all sorts of enticing solutions to mankind's greatest questions and dilemmas. We're told that science has already delivered a deathblow to religion, and any talk of God or the Bible is dismissed as a superstition of a bygone age. Christian faith is regarded as a leap into the dark—a leap into intellectual oblivion.

One of the great challenges to faith in Christ, then, is whether we will take God at His word and be satisfied with what He says. In our cultural milieu, it's good for us to periodically ask ourselves: "Do I believe the Bible? Am I actually prepared to trust what it says?"

We can have confidence in the testimony of Scripture for all kinds of reasons. We can consider the undeniable integrity of its manuscripts, its historical reliability down to the details of its claims, or even the way it has engendered faith across cultures for nearly two thousand years. But there's actually a reason that's even more fundamental than these or other defenses we could muster: the most essential reason we submit ourselves to the authority of Scripture is because it is a necessary consequence of our submission to the lordship of Christ. Our Lord Jesus Christ believed the Bible; therefore, so do we. He acknowledged the authority of God's word; therefore, so do we.

In His High Priestly Prayer on the night before He died, Jesus prayed to His Father, "Sanctify them in the truth; your word is truth." Notice that there are no qualifications here. According to Jesus, God's word simply *is* truth. So then, the pressing question becomes, *Do I believe Jesus?* And if I believe Jesus, then I believe the words Jesus spoke. Therefore, I accept what He taught about the Scriptures. Therefore, I embrace the Bible, just as He did.

If you have tasted and seen the goodness of Jesus Christ, then refresh your resolve to cherish God's word daily. In our confused and conflicted world, nothing will steady your life like the truth of the Scriptures. Doubtless, some will try to convince you that embracing the Bible is equivalent to taking a blind leap into the dark. But the truth is that when you read the Scriptures in faith that it is God's word and that every word is therefore true, you'll find it to be a lamp to your feet and a light to your path (Psalm 119:105).

PSALM 12

JANUARY 8

REGULAR REMINDERS

"Now I would remind you, brothers, of the gospel I preached to you, which you received, in which you stand, and by which you are being saved, if you hold fast to the word I preached to you—unless you believed in vain." 1 CORINTHIANS 15:1-2

The good news of the gospel can so easily be forgotten or taken for granted. If we begin to feel that we need to go beyond it, or we find it irrelevant in our lives or affections, we should be concerned, not complacent. Just as young children need regular reminders to keep them from forgetting what they need to remember, we need to recall routinely the transforming power of Jesus Christ in human hearts.

Why? Because the gospel is not just the way *in to* salvation but the way *of* salvation; it is not only the ABC of the Christian life but the A to Z. It is the word to which we must "hold fast."

As Paul describes it in 2 Corinthians 4:3, life without the gospel is like living with a veil covering our eyes: we are blinded by our own sin, by our pursuit of comfort or doing "enough" good, or even by our own theology or religious adherence. This clouded vision is common to all mankind; by nature, we all face a No Entry sign at the gate of heaven. The road is flooded, and there is apparently no way through. But the gospel, the glorious news, is this: there is one who stands ready to clear the way. In His living, dying, and resurrection, Jesus lived the life we can't, died the death we deserve, and conquered death once and for all so that all who believe can have a relationship with God.

On the day we first understood the full weight of this—the day when God's grace opened our clouded eyes, unplugged our ears, and softened our hardened hearts—we could run no other way than toward Him, crying, "Save me!" As the old hymn says:

Long my imprisoned spirit lay
Fast bound in sin and nature's night;
Thine eye diffused a quickening ray,
I woke, the dungeon flamed with light;
My chains fell off, my heart was free;
I rose, went forth, and followed Thee.[5]

Now, having run to Him as the gospel bids us, we need to remain with Him as the gospel reminds us. So, where does the gospel find you today? Are you living in this freedom? Or are you still occasionally living as though imprisoned, trying, trying, trying with all your might to find the freedom only Christ gives?

To the Christian, the gospel is and must be as water in a dry land. It is the priceless, payment-free water that the Lord Jesus offers—it is the water of life (Revelation 21:6). Be sure to rehearse to yourself the simple gospel today, and every day, so that it never grows cold to you and so that you live in the freedom that Christ died to win for you.

2 CORINTHIANS 4:1-6

5 Charles Wesley, "And Can It Be, That I Should Gain?" (1738).

JANUARY 9

SPIRITUAL PARALYSIS

"Woe to her who is rebellious and defiled, the oppressing city! She listens to no voice; she accepts no correction. She does not trust in the Lord*; she does not draw near to her God."* ZEPHANIAH 3:1-2

Some Christians walk straight toward spiritual paralysis. It's never something we choose. No one consciously opts for stagnation and impairment. But there is a path down which disaster awaits. What could cause this sort of malady and wreak this havoc on a soul?

Such a devastating debility is often caused by hearing the voice of God in His word but then disobeying Him. It's like looking Him straight in the face through Scripture but choosing to ignore Him. It is to be confronted with truth from your Creator and to claim, as His creature, to know better.

In the prophet Zephaniah's day, the Spirit of God confronted the people of God with "woe"—with a warning of captivity and bondage. The "oppressing city" was Jerusalem itself—the city of God's people. What was true for Jerusalem in a physical sense will be true of us in a spiritual sense if we refuse to listen to the voice of God and accept no correction from Him. There can be no blessing, no life, and no vitality where His word is neglected or disobeyed.

It is wise, then, to ask ourselves some difficult questions, rather than assuming that these kinds of warnings are only for others. Has God been speaking to you about a sinful habit in your life that you've decided you will hold on to and not break? Has He been speaking to you about a holy habit that you should establish, and you know that you should but you never actually do so? Has He been speaking to you about an apology that needs to be made, but in your pride you are avoiding doing this? Has He been speaking to you about a reconciliation that needs to take place with a loved one in your physical family or in the family of God?

Thankfully, God always receives His children with open arms when we turn to Him and heed His voice again. "If we confess our sins, he is faithful and just to forgive us our sins and to cleanse us from all unrighteousness"—all on account of Christ (1 John 1:9). When we are humble enough to listen to His voice and put our trust in Him, then we enjoy the experience of nearness to God once more. How is the Spirit prompting you as you read this passage today? There's no better time than now to step off the path to spiritual paralysis and find grace in the arms of your Savior.

ZEPHANIAH 3:1-17

JANUARY 10

TRUTH AND LOVE

"You are witnesses, and God also, how holy and righteous and blameless was our conduct toward you believers. For you know how, like a father with his children, we exhorted each one of you and encouraged you and charged you to walk in a manner worthy of God, who calls you into his own kingdom and glory."
1 THESSALONIANS 2:10-12

There is no doubt that Paul's life and work changed the world. But what moved him, stirred him, and grounded him?

His first letter to the Thessalonian church gives us wonderful insights into what made Paul tick. He was clearly committed to truth and love—to the truth of God's word and to a love for God's people. These two coexisted in and drove forward his ministry. Paul knew that neither can outweigh the other without causing great harm. Truth without love is harsh and can result in a ministry that is motivated by personal gain. Love without truth is rootless and results in a ministry that departs from the gospel.

Paul was not interested in prestige, wealth, or popularity. He simply wanted to see fellow believers "walk in a manner worthy of God." He longed to see spiritual maturity.

In Paul's thinking and writing, walking worthy of God means living in the awareness that we have been adopted into God's kingdom by grace. We can build no other kingdom. We must not strive to establish an empire of our own or of our church or of our ministry, nor focus on success or reputation. More than any attachment to an individual or institution, our greatest concern must be to see in our own lives, and in the lives of men and women around us, a devotion to Jesus Christ—a commitment to holding to His truth and living with His love.

John the Baptist exemplified this humility when he proclaimed of Christ, "He must increase, but I must decrease" (John 3:30). He knew he was simply a servant of the Lord, receiving only what was "given him from heaven" (v 27) and nothing else. The best man at a wedding does not bring attention upon himself or want the bride for himself but rather rejoices in the groom's joy. In the same way, our great excitement must be in Christ pursuing and winning His bride, the church—whether He uses us in some significant way or not.

As you make decisions, as you respond to setbacks, as you care for others, as you serve in ministry, is your greatest desire simply to "walk in a manner worthy of God"? Is it to be a person of both truth and love? Let it be said of you, as it could be said of Paul, that you loved God's truth and that you truly loved God's people.

EPHESIANS 4:1-6

JANUARY 11

TURNING THE OTHER CHEEK

"You have heard that it was said, 'An eye for an eye and a tooth for a tooth.' But I say to you, Do not resist the one who is evil. But if anyone slaps you on the right cheek, turn to him the other also. And if anyone would sue you and take your tunic, let him have your cloak as well." MATTHEW 5:38-40

These words of Jesus are familiar, but they are also very challenging, and we ought to be very careful not to strip them of their impact by immediately trying to qualify them in a thousand different ways. Yet we also need to be sure to understand what is *not* commanded here. These verses don't advocate some kind of apathetic passivity, although they're pressed in that way by some. So how *should* we interpret what Jesus said?

It's always important to compare Scripture with Scripture. The instruction given here is for interpersonal relationships; it's not given to determine the role of the state either in warfare or in the execution of justice (Romans 13:1-7). The key is to distinguish between the temptation we face to enact personal vengeance and the duty we've been given to uphold both God's glory and the rule of law. Jesus doesn't want us to be unconcerned about issues of truth, righteousness, or justice. But He also doesn't want us to be driven by a desire to protect our own rights or to pursue personal revenge.

David understood this distinction when he called down curses on people in the imprecatory psalms (for example, Psalm 5:10). He was not seeking to execute personal vengeance. Rather, he was looking at God's glory and majesty and at the wholesale rebellion of the culture and saying to God, *Please, for the glory and honor of Your name, deal with these circumstances.*

Similarly, although Paul wrote that we should never avenge ourselves (Romans 12:19), he, too, recognized the separation between retaliation and matters of civil justice. In Philippi, he and Silas were accused of unlawful actions and dragged away to jail. Acts 16 records how, when the magistrates tried to release them quietly, "Paul said to them, 'They have beaten us publicly, uncondemned, men who are Roman citizens, and have thrown us into prison; and do they now throw us out secretly? No! Let them come themselves and take us out.'" Then "the police reported these words to the magistrates, and they were afraid when they heard that they were Roman citizens" (Acts 16:37-38). They were afraid because they knew what they had done was illegal. Yet there was no sense of personal vengeance in what Paul did. Rather, he was upholding the rule of law.

We will be helped as we keep in mind this distinction between personal retaliation and matters of civil justice. We need the humility to trust God for justice in our interpersonal relationships and the courage to promote righteousness and the glory of His name and the integrity of the rule of law. But the challenge still stands: without ignoring justice, we are to seek to bless those who have hurt us and to share with those who have taken from us. What might that look like for you?

ROMANS 12:13-21

JANUARY 12

EMBRACING OUR LIMITATIONS

"When I applied my heart to know wisdom ... then I saw all the work of God, that man cannot find out the work that is done under the sun." ECCLESIASTES 8:16-17

We all like to have answers. In life's endless uncertainty, and especially when the world or our own personal circumstances feel chaotic, we long for surety. Just think of all the experts to whom we look for guidance: medical experts, social experts, political experts, and so on. Yet while the proliferation of experts may be unique to our day, the quest for certainty is not. In every age, humans have searched for some kind of rhyme or reason to make sense of the grand events of history and the experiences of their individual lives.

We find an ancient example of this quest in the Old Testament book of Ecclesiastes. Its writer shares with us his attempts to understand "all that is done under heaven," applying his heart "to know wisdom and to know madness and folly" (Ecclesiastes 1:13, 17). Yet in the end, he concludes that "man cannot find out the work that is done under the sun." Most people arrive at the same conclusion without so much effort—all we need is enough time to live our lives and to observe the world around us. The wise response to this truth is to humble ourselves and live by the light of God's word. In other words, we acknowledge that while God does not permit us to know all we might want to know, He has given us all we need. Genuine humility admits, and even embraces, this limitation.

If we were to behold the fullness of all of God's activity and purposes, it would be like looking up directly into a very bright sun. The light we are meant to live by is revealed in Scripture. It is the word of God that lights our path: "The unfolding of your words gives light; it imparts understanding to the simple" (Psalm 119:130). It may not light all our surroundings, but it does light the way ahead—if we will walk in trust and obedience.

Rather than busying ourselves with what cannot be known, we need to come to the Scriptures humbly, expectantly, and consistently, so that we might discover the light it provides. We won't understand life entirely, but we may understand it sufficiently, and so sing with William Cowper:

Deep in unfathomable mines
Of never-failing skill,
He treasures up His bright designs
And works His sovereign will.[6]

This view of life under the sun is what will enable us to increasingly trust that God will, in His own time and in His own way, bring perfect order out of seeming confusion. He will use all of our circumstances to complete all of His purposes for all of eternity.

ECCLESIASTES 8

6 William Cowper, "God Moves in a Mysterious Way" (1774).

JANUARY 13

THE OLDEST CHRISTIAN CONFESSION

"At the name of Jesus every knee should bow, in heaven and on earth and under the earth, and every tongue confess that Jesus Christ is Lord, to the glory of God the Father." PHILIPPIANS 2:10-11

From very early on, while the church has stood on the firm foundation of God's word, she has also looked to the support structure, as it were, of her creeds and confessions to faithfully summarize the core tenets of the Christian faith. Perhaps you have recited the Apostle's Creed or the Nicene Creed, or maybe you have made use of the Westminster Confession of Faith to aid your understanding of a particular point of doctrine.

The historical nature of such creeds and confessions demonstrates how the Christian faith has held its ground over time. For example, the Nicene Creed reaches all the way back to AD 325, when the earliest version was adopted at the Council of Nicaea. Seventeen hundred years is quite a shelf life! But it is not the oldest confession, for there is one that reaches back even earlier, to the earliest days of the church. It's only three simple words: *Jesus is Lord*.

This earliest confession can be found throughout the New Testament, in places such as Romans 10:9, 1 Corinthians 12:3, and Philippians 2:11. In making such a statement, the early Christians said a great deal about the identity of Jesus Christ. In the Old Testament, God identifies Himself with four Hebrew letters, equivalent to YHWH in English, which some pronounce "Yahweh." This divine name is rendered in our English Bibles most often as LORD, with small caps. When the Hebrew version of the Old Testament was translated into Greek, nearly all the occurrences of Yahweh—over 6,000 of them—were rendered with the Greek term for "Lord," *kurios*. So to say "Jesus is Lord" is not just to call Christ *Master* but to affirm that He is fully and completely *God*.

While some try to argue that the New Testament never really identifies Jesus as God, nothing could be further from the truth. To confess Him as Lord is really to call Him Yahweh. He is not just a teacher or healer or miracle-worker but God in the flesh.

This earliest confession demands some reflection from us: *Do I really confess, with my life as well as my lips, that Jesus is Lord? Do I really believe that He has total claim over my life and every right to command my allegiance and obedience? Do I really accept that He knows better than me and that I may hold nothing back from Him?*

"Jesus is Lord," then, is no trite statement. But it is not a terrifying one, either. For this Lord is kind and good, "merciful and gracious, slow to anger, and abounding in steadfast love and faithfulness" (Exodus 34:6). His love means that before He sat on His heavenly throne, He hung on a wooden cross. Since He is Lord, He can always ask for your all—and since He loves you, you can give it joyfully.

So what will you confess today?

EXODUS 34:1-10

JANUARY 14

FORGETTING GOD

"Stand still that I may plead with you before the LORD concerning all the righteous deeds of the LORD that he performed for you and for your fathers. When Jacob went into Egypt, and the Egyptians oppressed them, then your fathers cried out to the LORD and the LORD sent Moses and Aaron, who brought your fathers out of Egypt and made them dwell in this place. But they forgot the LORD their God." 1 SAMUEL 12:7-9

Many of our problems arise when we forget to remember.

As the prophet Samuel thought he was drawing toward the end of his time of ministry and prepared to bid farewell to Israel, he wanted the people to consider how immensely good God had been to them. (Samuel would, as it turned out, have many more years of ministry ahead, as God called him first to warn and then to pronounce judgment on King Saul.) God's grace and provision had been revealed to Israel over and over—and yet, though they had been warned on a couple of occasions, "Take care lest you forget the LORD your God" (Deuteronomy 8:11), they had turned their back on Him, revealing their fickleness. In fact, throughout the generations of the judges, of whom Samuel was the last, Israel "forgot the LORD their God" and instead served false gods (Judges 3:7).

Years later, the Preacher of Ecclesiastes would write, "Remember also your Creator in the days of your youth" (Ecclesiastes 12:1). This means more than remembering that there *is* a Creator. It means to dwell upon the very "Godness" of God. The Israelites failed to remember Him; in fact, they chose to forget, for it was inconvenient for them to consider God in all His holiness and all His might. And Samuel's message in response was essentially this: *You're not thinking!*

But even though the people forsook Him and forgot His righteous deeds, God didn't abandon them. He never does abandon His own. Every time, in His mercy, He showed Himself to be righteous in His dealings and gracious in His salvation of and patience with His people.

We must be careful not to judge the Israelites too harshly. God has been abundantly gracious to us as well—and, at times, we also have chosen to forget Him. Whenever we deviate from the narrow path, whenever we seek to slip out from underneath our almighty King's jurisdiction, we are failing to remember who God is and what He has done for us: that He has buried us in baptism and raised us to newness of life (Romans 6:4).

If you are in Christ, you are no longer the person you once were. You have been made a member of a people who will last forever. So when you face temptation, stop for a moment and remember your Creator. Contemplate the goodness and holiness of God, both in history and in your own experience, and thank Him for His abounding mercy as He deals with you. Don't forget to remember.

JUDGES 3:7-11

JANUARY 15

OUR RESURRECTION HOPE

"If Christ has not been raised, your faith is futile and you are still in your sins. Then those also who have fallen asleep in Christ have perished ... But in fact Christ has been raised from the dead." 1 CORINTHIANS 15:17-18, 20

Questions surrounding death and dying have faced mankind ever since the fall: "What will happen when I die? Will I go somewhere when I die, or is this it? Is there any significance to my life? What does it all mean?"

All of Scripture is timelessly relevant, and it provides answers to these questions. Paul, for example, addresses the issues of resurrection and eternal life in 1 Corinthians 15. Without the resurrection, he says, our faith would be in vain. Our salvation would be false, for we would still be living in sin. Death would prove to be stronger than God. Jesus' claims would be untrue: He would not be Lord, and He would not be returning. History would have no goal or purpose, and the human race would be going nowhere.

Since that's the "reality" in which unbelievers live, it's no wonder there is so much angst in our world! But the Christian can say, "Hey, not so fast! Don't say that history is going nowhere and all is meaningless! Consider the resurrection." We believe Christ rose from the dead and promises each of His followers full resurrection—not a resurrection only of soul but one of body *and* soul (1 Corinthians 15:42-49).

John Locke, the 18th-century British philosopher, wrote of Christ's resurrection that it is "truly of great importance in Christianity; so great, that his being, or not being the Messiah, stands or falls with it."[7] It is the resurrection that proves that Jesus is who Scripture claims He is, the resurrection that seals our salvation, and the resurrection that transforms our lives. You can visit the burial sites of Buddha's ashes, Muhammad's body, and Gandhi's urn, but the tomb of Jesus of Nazareth is an empty one. Belief in the resurrection is the narrow gate through which we enter, and it's the only one that leads to life (Matthew 7:13-14). All our hope hangs on this fact: Jesus is alive!

Because of this hope, we can say that this life is not all there is; it is simply the appetizer, the first course. Shadows fall on our greatest successes on this earth. We lose loved ones. We're confronted by sin. Even our best days leave us longing for something more. But the fact is that we are only preparing for a day yet to come, when these former things will pass away and the new, resurrected kingdom will come. The resurrection of Jesus is what gives purpose to all you do today, and comfort in all your trials, and hope for all your tomorrows.

REVELATION 1:9-18

7 "A Second Vindication of the Reasonableness of Christianity" in *The Works of John Locke, in Nine Volumes* (Rivington, 1824), 6:341-42.

JANUARY 16

WHY THE OLD TESTAMENT MATTERS

"Whatever was written in former days was written for our instruction, that through endurance and through the encouragement of the Scriptures we might have hope." ROMANS 15:4

While we may understand the importance of God's word for our lives, we might also wonder, deep down, why we should study Old Testament stories. What can modern people gain from such a study? Why not focus on the New Testament and the stories of what Jesus and His apostles did and said?

Here is the answer: these ancient segments of history are significant not just for the biblical characters or for Israel but also for you and me—and, indeed, for the entire world! Such a sweeping claim may sound like hyperbole. But if we approach our study of the Bible with certain convictions in mind, we will begin to understand and be convinced, as the apostle Paul was clearly convinced, that the Old Testament was written for us, that it was written to instruct, and that it gives us hope.

The first conviction is that there is unity to the Bible, from creation in Genesis to the new creation in Revelation. In between is the record of humanity's fall and the chaos and brokenness of the universe that flowed from it. Through it all, we discover the story of redemption and the plan and purpose of God to put together a people of His very own. We need to read the whole of that story, from start to finish.

The second conviction guiding our study of God's word is that this biblical unity exists not because it is a collection of religious documents but because it is the word of God, written by men who "spoke from God as they were carried along by the Holy Spirit" (2 Peter 1:21). We need to read all of what God has chosen to tell us.

Thirdly, there is the conviction that we need our Bibles to understand human history, our own little histories, and our place within history. Much of what is happening within us and around us does not make sense apart from an understanding of human nature and God's sovereignty at work as revealed in Scripture.

Finally, we hold the conviction that the Bible, including the Old Testament, is a book about Jesus. If we take our eyes from Jesus, then we don't just lose our way around the universe; we also lose our way around the Bible. The Old Testament points us to Christ, prepares us for Christ, and shows us pictures of Christ. One of the questions we ought always to be asking is "How does this record of things show me good news about Jesus Christ?"

With these convictions in mind, we can have confidence as we study the Old Testament that it is instructive. But not only that: it is full of hope, for it shows us our Savior. The more we read the parts of the Old Testament as books written by God, through His Spirit, about His Son, the more we grow in hope, in understanding, and into the likeness of our Savior.

2 TIMOTHY 3:12-17

JANUARY 17

TO BE CONTINUED

"... Proclaiming the kingdom of God and teaching about the Lord Jesus Christ with all boldness and without hindrance." ACTS 28:31

When I was growing up, I watched television programs in the comforting assurance that they would reach a timely and logical conclusion. Whether it was *Bonanza*, *The Dick Van Dyke Show*, or *Perry Mason*, I could be sure that there would be a resolution to the plot. It was a bad show when the plot *didn't* resolve and the dreaded phrase appeared at the bottom of the screen: "To be continued..." In a similar way, the plot in Acts is left unresolved, and we are left with the realization that the full story is yet to be completed.

In writing the book we know as Acts, its author, Luke, wasn't composing a biography of the apostle Paul. Rather, he was demonstrating the power of the Holy Spirit to spread God's word in the world through a variety of individuals in the unfolding story of human history. He wasn't encouraging readers to create their own endings but inviting them to be a part of the continuing story.

The final word in the Greek text of the book of Acts is *akolytos*, which means "unhindered." This is in step with what Paul wrote during his second imprisonment: "I am suffering, bound with chains as a criminal. But the word of God is not bound!" (2 Timothy 2:9). In other words, Acts concludes but the action continues. Acts is the beginning of the story, a story of the work of God's Spirit, through His church, that sweeps into our world and up to our time.

In fact, the unfolding story of redemption, in which we find ourselves, actually begins much earlier than Acts 1. We catch one of our first glimpses when God promised Adam and Eve that one of their family would crush Satan and undo the effects of their sin (Genesis 3:15); we see another when the Lord told Abraham, "In your offspring shall all the nations of the earth be blessed" (22:18). The Father's plan was always that He would give to His Son the nations as an inheritance (Psalm 2:8). This is an all-encompassing promise worthy of our life, and even our death.

Your life is wrapped up in this amazing story. The same Spirit that powerfully worked in the book of Acts is still at work today. The extension of the gospel message—that Jesus is the long-promised King and the much-needed Savior—did not conclude with Paul in Rome, nor when it arrived at your doorstep. God is still telling it, and His people are still called to share it, unhindered. Whether you give your life to doing that as a missionary overseas or you seek each day to make Christ known among your family, friends, coworkers and neighbors, God wants you to be involved in the greatest story of the ages, which will be told throughout eternity. What would you rather spend your life doing than writing a line in this great, unfinished story?

PSALM 2

JANUARY 18

WHO DOES WHAT?

"His divine power has granted to us all things that pertain to life and godliness, through the knowledge of him who called us to his own glory and excellence, by which he has granted to us his precious and very great promises, so that through them you may become partakers of the divine nature, having escaped from the corruption that is in the world because of sinful desire. For this very reason, make every effort to supplement your faith with virtue, and virtue with knowledge." 2 PETER 1:3-5

A question often arises in the mind of Christians as we grow in Christ: Who's doing what? What is God's role, and what is ours? The question gets at the paradox we see in Scripture, where in various places we are told two messages that seem to be in conflict: first, that we are to work hard in our Christian lives, and second, that God is the one providing resources for such labor.

This verse is one example of this apparent paradox. One one hand, Peter writes that God's "divine power has granted to us all things that pertain to life and godliness." In other words, He has given us everything we need to follow Jesus. But then, a few lines later, Peter directs his readers to "make every effort." God has supplied what we need, and yet we are still to put in the effort.

In Colossians 1:29, Paul similarly describes his ministry labors as "toil" and "struggling." There is little doubt that Paul worked hard for the cause of Christ. But how did he do this? He tells us that his toil and struggle was done "with all [God's] energy that he powerfully works within me." Paul's toil was genuine, *and* it was fueled by Christ Himself.

Similarly, in Philippians 2:12, Paul tells us to "work out your ... salvation." This is a call to real effort to stay on the narrow way. Yet Paul continues by saying, "It is God who works in you."

If we are going to honor and heed the call to labor that these passages describe, we must remember that God has accomplished our salvation for us; and now, rather than leaving us to our own devices, He continues to be constantly at work within us so that we have the will and the power to do what pleases Him.

We should avoid the erroneous thinking that responds to passages like these by concluding either that we contribute something to our salvation or that we have no need to work hard as we journey toward our heavenly home. Instead, we need first to acknowledge that we contribute nothing to salvation other than the sin from which we need to be saved, and then at the same time embrace the truth that our walk with Christ must be the single most significant aspect of our lives.

What, then, is a faithful response to biblical calls such as this? It is to strive for holiness and pray for growth. It is to follow Christ, and when we stumble and sin, to confess and repent and keep going. You must toil if you are to find yourself a citizen in the new creation; but toil you will because His divine power gives you everything you need in order to do so. When you stand with Jesus, you will not say, "What a good person I was!" You will declare, "What a great and mighty God I serve!"

COLOSSIANS 1:24 – 2:3

JANUARY 19

INCORRUPTIBLE COUNSEL AND COMFORT

"I bless the Lord *who gives me counsel; in the night also my heart instructs me."*
PSALM 16:7

Most of us receive constant counsel, seemingly from everywhere. Everyone, every book, every social-media feed is trying to tell us precisely what will make us happier and more fulfilled. Hopefully, some of the input into our lives is godly and biblical. If we're honest, though, some of it we could probably go without.

But what if, instead of soundbites and social media, we could go straight to the fount of inexhaustible wisdom? What if we could receive counsel from the one who Himself needs no counsel?

This is exactly what David receives in Psalm 16: "I bless the Lord who gives me counsel."

How do we access this counsel? One of the greatest gifts God gives us is the counsel of His heart through the sufficiency of His word. Did God leave anything out of His book that we need to make it from here to eternity? Is there any unwise guidance, or are there any mistakes? No, never! God is the pre-eminent counselor. His words are wisdom without end. Not only that but when you pray, you never get His voicemail. There's never a time when you can't speak with Him.

God offers wise counsel, and in this we find real comfort. David declares, "Because he is at my right hand, I shall not be shaken" (Psalm 16:8). Elsewhere, Asaph prays, "I am continually with you; you hold my right hand. You guide me with your counsel" (73:23-24). It's as if we are children crossing a busy street, and our Father is holding our hands as we cross. Those cars zipping by sure can be intimidating—but with God at our side, what have we to fear?

God will guide us by His hand on the path of life; He will not abandon us. We can rejoice securely in Him (Psalm 16:9-11). We know this with certainty because our Lord Jesus Christ, who went before us to the grave, was raised to new, incorruptible life (Acts 2:25-32), and He is the firstfruits of all who trust in Him (1 Corinthians 15:20).

The path Christ trod is the same way God now leads you along. You, too, must take up your cross and follow your Lord (Matthew 16:24). You, too, will struggle and even endure pain. But through it all, you will never have to go without your Father's wise counsel. Be sure to turn to it. You will never be without His real comfort. Be sure to rest in it. You are never out of reach of His strong hands. Be sure to remember it.

PSALM 16

JANUARY 20

SAVED FROM THE FEAR OF DEATH

"Since therefore the children share in flesh and blood, he himself likewise partook of the same things, that through death he might destroy the one who has the power of death, that is, the devil, and deliver all those who through fear of death were subject to lifelong slavery." HEBREWS 2:14-15

Death is not an appealing subject to consider. We don't like to think about how it might be that our bodies and minds will fail us. Driven by a fear of dying, well-meaning people spend vast sums of money in attempts to put off their end and find meaning in life. But even the best attempts can't answer life's essential questions: Who am I? Where am I from? Where do I go when I die?

This is nothing new. Adam and Eve did the same thing in Genesis 3 when they listened to the false hope of Satan's seductive lie welcoming sin and death into the world: "You will not surely die … you will be like God" (Genesis 3:4-5). We continue to believe the same lie. We try to be like God, longing to construct our own meaning and aiming to live forever. But death continues to hold terror for us, enslaving us in fear. When signs of old age emerge, when illness sets in, when the funeral procession passes by, we're reminded that our false hopes have no substance. We must find true answers.

Everybody bases their hope on *something*. Let us base ours on the enduring strength and authority of God's word. When we want to run away from troubling thoughts and crippling fears, let us run to the foot of the cross, where Jesus delivered "all those who through fear of death were subject to lifelong slavery." Why did Jesus come? "The reason the Son of God appeared was to destroy the works of the devil" (1 John 3:8). By Christ's death and resurrection, He drowned out the seductive voices of false hope, He took all our sin and rebellion and made our record clean, and He delivered us from all fear—even the fear of death itself. In taking our sins from us, Jesus has taken away Satan's voice. There is nothing left for him to accuse us of, and there is nothing left to stand between us and the presence of God forever.

Death should therefore hold no fear for the Christian. As Paul writes, "If you confess with your mouth that Jesus is Lord and believe in your heart that God raised him from the dead, you will be saved" (Romans 10:9). Saved from what? Saved from sin, from judgment, from the terrors of death and hell, from fear of the grave—and saved for all eternity. This is the eternal life that the world longs for but can never find. It is not an escape *from* death but an escape *through* death—and it is the reason that Jesus left heavenly glory and became a human like me and you, and the reason that He died a criminal's death.

When you are tempted to base your hope in the things of this world and are blinded by tempting lies, or when you find yourself considering aging, frailty, and death with a rising fear, tell yourself, "Jesus has destroyed the one who has the power of death. Jesus has delivered me from the fear of death." Learn to see death as it truly is and you will be able to see life as it truly is for all God's children: eternal, free, and full of joy.

ACTS 7:54-60

JANUARY 21

OUR GREAT INSTRUCTOR

"Teach me, O Lord, the way of your statutes." PSALM 119:33

There is something truly special about learning from a master teacher: an expert in his or her chosen field. Many graduate students select their universities based on the opportunity to work with esteemed professors in their desired specialties. But have you considered that as Christians we have the opportunity and the privilege to learn daily from our Master Teacher, as His Spirit works in our hearts through His word? His instruction is comprehensive, and He promises to do the teaching Himself, with the Bible as our guide. And even better, He does so as an instructor who is also a Father, taking a personal interest in the welfare of His children.

God's instruction is vital. It is vital for beginners in the Christian life. We begin as infants, unaware of God's ways and dealings and consequently unaware of truths about ourselves. But when we become new creations, we cease to take pride in our own opinions, to live for ourselves, or to regard Christ from a worldly point of view (2 Corinthians 5:12-17). We become ready to hear what God says instead of telling Him what we think. By grace, we learn to see clearly.

God's instruction is also vital for those who are confused. The Bible tells us that we are wayward and foolish people. When the apostle Paul wrote to Timothy, he warned that among his congregations there would always be those "led astray by various passions, always learning and never able to arrive at a knowledge of the truth" (2 Timothy 3:6-7). Only through the Holy Spirit is it possible for us to spiritually mature instead of drifting like children from one idea to another.

His instruction is also vital for the forgetful—and however long we may have been Christians, we are easily forgetful! That's why the Bible tells us again and again to *remember.* Paul urged Timothy to "remember Jesus Christ" (2 Timothy 2:8). Jesus urged His disciples to "remember Lot's wife" (Luke 17:32), who looked and turned back. Ecclesiastes calls out to us, "Remember also your Creator in the days of your youth" (Ecclesiastes 12:1). Indeed, the ministry of teaching and preaching is essentially a ministry of reminders—and so are our daily personal devotional times.

Charles Spurgeon once said, "He who has made you his child, will put you to school, and teach you until you shall know the Lord Jesus as the way, the truth, and the life."[8] When we read or listen to Bible teaching, we participate in a divine dialogue and begin to experience deep-seated heart change. In our core, we know that holy instruction is taking place—we are being instructed by the very one who inspired the book whose pages we are studying. This is what God enables His servants to do. What an opportunity, and privilege, it is to open His word, anticipate the work of His Spirit, and pray, "Teach me, O Lord, the way of your statutes"!

PSALM 119:1-8

8 "Bit and Bridle: How to Escape Them," *The Metropolitan Tabernacle Pulpit 37*, no. 2190, p 101.

JANUARY 22

POWER IN WEAKNESS

"A thorn was given me in the flesh, a messenger of Satan to harass me, to keep me from becoming conceited. Three times I pleaded with the Lord about this, that it should leave me. But he said to me, 'My grace is sufficient for you, for my power is made perfect in weakness.'" 2 CORINTHIANS 12:7-9

Difficulties, disappointments, failure, and weakness are all inevitable in life. But have you ever considered the possibility that these limitations may be the key to usefulness in the service of Christ? We often find ourselves saying or thinking something like "If I wasn't like this, or if my circumstances were different, or if I was healthier or in better shape, *then* God could and would better use me." It is easy to wish we could be someone we're not, instead of believing what the Bible says: that God formed us purposefully, divinely, and intricately in our mother's womb and has overseen each of our days since then (Psalm 139:13), making and molding each of us as a unique individual.

When we doubt our worth, Satan is quick to encourage us to question the integrity of God's character and promises. Indeed, Paul calls his weakness, his thorn in the flesh, a messenger from Satan. Why? Because Satan had used it to bring about doubt in Paul: *Why you, Paul? Why didn't Peter have this thorn? Wouldn't your ministry be more effective without it? God's not coming through for you, is He?* But our heavenly Father knows best, and He is painting on a far bigger canvas. His purpose is not to make our journey through life pleasurable or to make all our dreams come true. His purpose for us is far grander: to conform us to the image of His Son, Jesus Christ.

John Berridge, an 18th-century preacher, observed, "A Christian never falls asleep in the fire or in the water, but grows drowsy in the sunshine."[9] We grow too comfortable, too self-reliant, when life is easy and our strengths are apparent. And so God graciously gives us thorns to wake us up.

When God told Paul, "My grace is sufficient for you, for my power is made perfect in weakness," He didn't change Paul's pain. He changed his perspective. Paul was able to quit focusing on his weakness and begin appreciating the gift that came through it: Christ's own strength. The thorn suddenly became a rose: something redemptively given instead of something only unwanted. God makes even Satan's insinuations work for our good, causing us to turn to Christ in childlike and prayerful dependence upon His promises.

The things about ourselves that we want to run from, hide from, or cover up are the very things that could suddenly open the door to phenomenal ministry. Have you considered this truth? Have you considered the possibility that your limitations, your disappointments, and your weaknesses are not detriments to effectiveness but true assets, as they bring you to lean on His strength? Do not see your weakness as an obstacle to serving God but as an opportunity for it.

2 CORINTHIANS 4:7-18

9 John Berridge to Samuel Wilks, Everton, August 16, 1774, in *The Works of the Rev. John Berridge,* ed. Richard Whittingham (Simpkin, Marshall, and Co., 1838), p 396.

JANUARY 23

SOVEREIGN OVER SUFFERING

"His disciples asked him, 'Rabbi, who sinned, this man or his parents, that he was born blind?' Jesus answered, 'It was not that this man sinned, or his parents, but that the works of God might be displayed in him.'" JOHN 9:2-3

Sometimes God has something better for us than an answer to our questions.

When Jesus' disciples saw "a man blind from birth" (John 9:1), they asked the probing question: *Who is to blame?* Yet Jesus' answer indicates that the disciples were asking the wrong question. Rather than looking for someone to blame for the blind man's state, they needed to learn a lesson about God's sovereignty over suffering.

Their assumption was that sin and suffering are intimately connected. This assumption is generally true. Genesis 3 makes clear that it was the entry of sin into the world that disrupted the goodness of the world. All the thorns and thistles—the disharmony, mayhem, illnesses, and everything else—are a consequence of Adam and Eve's disobedience. Yet while the disciples' assumption is understandable, their belief that there was a connection between the sin and the sufferings of a particular individual put them on shaky ground.

It is encouraging to know that two millennia ago those closest to Jesus had questions about suffering. We, too, face these questions when the news from the doctor is the opposite of what we had hoped for, and perhaps most acutely of all when our loved ones face pain that we cannot remove. We face them, too, as we talk with those in our community.

When we search the Scriptures, we see that even though there is a cost to be paid for our sin, the suffering we experience is not the form of payment. God's word doesn't introduce us to a deity on a deckchair who is indifferent to our pain. Rather, it directs us to a God on a cross, who understands rejection, pain, and grief at the deepest level because He has experienced those things. Not only that, but He did it for us. He has "borne our griefs and carried our sorrows" (Isaiah 53:4) and, in bearing the crushing weight of our sin on Himself, has made it so that "this light momentary affliction is preparing for us an eternal weight of glory beyond all comparison" (2 Corinthians 4:17). The same Jesus who gave the man born blind his sight (John 9:6-7) has given you, born in sin as you are, your salvation. We may not understand why God leads us along the paths that He does in this life, but we have an eternity of pain-free joy in His presence to see how, through all of it, He was guiding us toward our heavenly home.

Have you been through something so difficult that it has caused you to lose your bearings? Have your circumstances left you looking for someone to blame? God suffered and died for you, and He has promised never to leave you nor forsake you (Hebrews 13:5). He is not surprised by your situation or your struggle. He might not give you answers right now, but He has given you the cross, which assures you that there is no length to which He will not go to for your eternal good. Come to Him with all of your pain and confusion, and He will give you rest.

JOHN 9:1-11

JANUARY 24

HIDDEN WITH CHRIST

"You have died, and your life is hidden with Christ in God." COLOSSIANS 3:3

One of Satan's main schemes for attacking believers is accusation (Revelation 12:10). As the father of lies (John 8:44), he will use anything within his arsenal of demonic devices to cause Christians to feel condemnation—though the truth, of course, is that "there is … now no condemnation for those who are in Christ Jesus" (Romans 8:1).

So how are we to stand firm in Christ when the Accuser tempts us to despair? When he whispers, "Would a Christian really think that?" or "How could a Christian ever do that?" what will we say? Should we point out that last week was a very good week or that this Bible reading or that prayer time ought to offset our guilt?

Surely, any good thing in our life is an evidence of God's grace at work. But no list of good works will ever assuage the Accuser. Our best response is to confront the Evil One head-on and tell him that Jesus bore our sins in His death, He rose to victory, and we are now united to Him and all His benefits by grace and through faith. We certainly want to live in a way that demonstrates real, active, vibrant faith; however, the most important thing about us isn't what we do but who we are in Christ. "You have died, and your life is hidden with Christ in God," says Paul. It is "Christ in you" who is "the hope of glory" (Colossians 1:27).

In the fight for faith, the issue is always the gospel. We must ask ourselves, "Have I come to entrust myself to Christ? Have I admitted who He is, who I am, and why I need Him? Is my hope in Jesus and what He has done for me, and not in any way in what I do for Him?" If we can answer yes, then we can confront the devil's lies and insinuations with the gospel. So, when the Accuser comes to you and suggests that you are not really a Christian, not really saved, not really forgiven—and he will!—take refuge in the finished work of your Lord on your behalf. Jesus has already won the victory. Therefore, hidden in Him, His triumph is now yours, and not one of Satan's schemes can change that glorious truth.

COLOSSIANS 3:1-4

JANUARY 25

SAINTS IN CHRIST

"Paul and Timothy, servants of Christ Jesus, to all the saints in Christ Jesus who are at Philippi..." PHILIPPIANS 1:1

What is meant by the word "saint"? How does one become a saint? What role do saints play in the church?

While there are certainly individuals in church history who have been strikingly effective and particularly used by God, in the language of the New Testament there is no basis for titling someone "Saint So-and-So" while the rest of us are called by our ordinary names. Biblically, saints are not a special group of outstanding Christians who have done something peculiarly pious. Saints are normal Christians who follow Jesus.

"Saint" is simply the New Testament word used to describe every believer. In the introductions to Paul's letters, he frequently addressed the recipients as "saints." The word means "set-apart ones" or "holy ones," and all Christians are those who have been set apart *from* what they once were in sin and set apart *for* Christ. They are His treasured possession—His saints.

And if you are in Christ, so too are you.

The key to becoming a saint, then, is not building up a résumé of good deeds; it is being "in Christ Jesus." The Bible says that by nature, we are "in Adam," and unless we are placed into Christ, we remain in Adam and will die in our sins (1 Corinthians 15:22). Jesus came to do all that Adam failed to do and undo all that Adam did in the fall. People are brought from their experience in Adam to a new experience in Christ by His atoning death on the cross. Paul puts it this way: "If anyone is in Christ, he is a new creation. The old has passed away; behold, the new has come" (2 Corinthians 5:17).

Here is the real question about sainthood: not "Am I in church?" but "Am I in Christ?" It's good to be "in church," but just as someone can be "in a garage" and not become a car, someone can be "in church" and not be a Christian. If we are not in Christ, we are still the same old stuff—religiously painted up and spiritually interested, perhaps, but fundamentally unchanged.

Are you in Christ? If so, then you are a saint! All the benefits and blessings of being in Christ Jesus accrue to you, and you have the privilege of living for Him. Paul's addressing of ordinary Christians as saints stood as a reminder to them: *This* is what you are, and this is what you should live as. You are different. You are not to be like the world. You are His. Rejoice today, this moment, if He has set you apart for Himself, and live in freedom to the praise of His glory.

EPHESIANS 1:1-14

JANUARY 26

HE WILL CARRY YOU

"Fear not, for I am with you; be not dismayed, for I am your God; I will strengthen you, I will help you, I will uphold you with my righteous right hand."
ISAIAH 41:10

The story is told of a pastor who was moving his study to his new home—and therefore had to relocate his library of hundreds of books. But he was not without help. He had brought his four-year-old son along with him to carry some materials up the stairs. Not wanting to overtax the boy's small frame, this father had given his son a sheaf of papers and a couple of magazines to bring up. But as the pastor was coming back down the stairs, having just deposited a tall stack in the study, he heard his boy crying halfway up the stairs.

He rushed over to his little boy and found him struggling with a huge, oversized concordance. The father said to the son, "I never gave you this to struggle with. I never meant for you to carry such a heavy thing by yourself!" He then picked up his boy, picked up his boy's problem, and carried them both up the stairs.

How often we struggle with so much that God never gave us to carry on our own! We decide that we'd rather worry about this or fret about that, when God is not asking us to bear any of our burdens alone. Our Father desires that we cast all our anxieties on Him (1 Peter 5:7). Whether it is directly through the work of His Spirit or whether it is through the burden-sharing love of His people (Galatians 6:2), He wants to take you and your problems and carry both.

Picture that pastor picking up his son and his son's burden. Isaiah presents us with just such a picture of our God: one who is not only willing but also fully able to help us in our time of need. We have no cause for worry, fear, or dismay. He has committed Himself to strengthen and uphold us. He promises, "Even to your old age I am he, and to gray hairs I will carry you. I have made, and I will bear; I will carry and will save" (Isaiah 46:4).

What burdens are you carrying today? You have a God who is always near and infinitely strong. He will help you. He will carry you. All you have to do is ask Him.

ISAIAH 41:5-16

JANUARY 27

LEAVING MATTERS IN GOD'S HANDS

"Now Sarai, Abram's wife, had borne him no children. She had a female Egyptian servant whose name was Hagar. And Sarai said to Abram, 'Behold now, the LORD has prevented me from bearing children. Go in to my servant; it may be that I shall obtain children by her.' And Abram listened to the voice of Sarai." GENESIS 16:1-2

Life is difficult, and living as a Christian does not mean we are spared those difficulties. As we face illness, unemployment, heartache, broken relationships, and other challenges, we are confronted by this fundamental question: Will we walk the path of faith or will we try to take matters into our own hands?

Abraham was a man who was just like us—he experienced both triumph and failure in his walk of faith. God had promised to make his family a nation and to bless the world through someone from that nation (Genesis 12:1-3). Though childless, elderly Abraham and his wife, Sarah, would have their "very own son" who would be their heir (15:4). Abraham "believed the LORD, and he counted it to him as righteousness" (v 6).

But after years and years of waiting, Abraham's faith wavered. Presumably, on a monthly basis, their hopes would rise and collapse—and with every passing month and year, Sarah grew older, sadder, and more impatient. So it was that they reached a crisis of faith. They knew that God is real, that God is all-powerful, and that God had *promised* them a son, but they also knew they didn't yet *have* a son. Would they allow the questions of their hearts to overturn their faith or would they allow their faith to overturn the questions of their hearts?

The verses above narrate the sorry conclusion: they took matters into their own hands, and the solution that they adopted was self-effort. In their doubting and despair, Sarah ordered Abraham to sleep with her maidservant, Hagar, in hopes of bringing about the promised child, and Abraham complied.

It was the wrong decision. Doubting that God would keep His promise, they instead sought to bring it about by their own (immoral) actions. They made their decision based on expediency. They didn't ask, *What is right?* They asked, *What will work?* They allowed pragmatism to be their guide over and against faith—and in doing so, they brought about more suffering, more pain, and more heartache for themselves and for Hagar. They thought that intervening would simplify things; instead, it complicated everything.

Whenever we set faith aside and apply self-effort, we complicate our lives. Whenever we seek to take things into our own hands and make our own plans instead of trusting God to keep His promises, we end up with chaos and heartache. Faith and waiting go hand in hand. Do not lose heart as you sit in life's waiting rooms. It is always right to wait *upon* God, and it is always right to wait *for* God. In what area of your life do you need to live this out today?

JOB 1:13-21

JANUARY 28

THANKFUL, PRAYERFUL, JOYFUL

"I thank my God in all my remembrance of you, always in every prayer of mine for you all making my prayer with joy, because of your partnership in the gospel from the first day until now. And I am sure of this, that he who began a good work in you will bring it to completion at the day of Jesus Christ."
PHILIPPIANS 1:3-6

Our prayers tell us a great deal about ourselves and about our view of those around us.

Paul and the Philippian believers enjoyed a partnership grounded in the gospel. Theirs wasn't a static fellowship based on a little bit of common belief. Rather, it was a deepening friendship that blossomed as they continued "striving side by side for the faith of the gospel" and to "work out" their salvation "with fear and trembling" (Philippians 1:27; 2:12). The Philippians' lives were marked by progression both in their relationship with Paul as their servant *and* their relationship with Christ as their Savior. Because of this partnership, Paul could be thankful, prayerful, and joyful.

If a church is to grow spiritually, the relationships among its people must be those of genuine thankfulness. Such gratefulness shouldn't depend upon the perfection of others; we are all far from perfect. Indeed, our imperfections should fuel our prayers for each other! Even so, true, heartfelt thankfulness allows fruitful ministry to continue.

Paul's partnership was reflected in Paul's prayers. As he prayed for the Philippian believers, his prayers were comprehensive: "... in every prayer of mine *for you all*." He didn't just pray for those who were doing well or those who were in his inner circle; he prayed for *everyone*. We need to do the same! Indeed, if we pray for those who are often hardest to pray for, we will discover that they can actually become some of our best companions. We may even think they have changed, only to discover that *we* have changed, simply because we added prayerfulness to thankfulness.

Joyfulness comes as we partner in prayer with each other. Inevitably, some prayers involve pain. Our hearts ache as we get under the burden of our brothers and sisters who may be agonizing over their kids, their marriages, the loss of their jobs, their illnesses, or their bereavements. But at other times, instead of feeling like swimming against the tide, prayer can be like going with the waterfall as we rejoice together. When together we bring our situations, needs, and triumphs before the throne of grace, that fellowship brings joy. That's how Paul felt about the Philippian believers. He prayed sorrowful and hopeful prayers alike with joy because of their shared partnership.

We can learn from Paul. He knew that fellowship with other believers could create thankful, prayerful, and joyful people. How are your prayers for those with whom God has brought you into gospel partnership going to reflect Paul's prayers for the gospel partners in his life?

PHILIPPIANS 1:1-11

JANUARY 29

GODLY LEADERSHIP

"Samuel said to all Israel, 'Behold, I have obeyed your voice in all that you have said to me and have made a king over you. And now, behold, the king walks before you, and I am old and gray; and behold, my sons are with you. I have walked before you from my youth until this day. Here I am; testify against me before the LORD and before his anointed. Whose ox have I taken? Or whose donkey have I taken? Or whom have I defrauded? Whom have I oppressed? Or from whose hand have I taken a bribe to blind my eyes with it? Testify against me and I will restore it to you.'" 1 SAMUEL 12:1-3

Leadership of any kind is very vulnerable. If you work at the front of a classroom, lead an industry, operate in politics, or serve in pastoral ministry, you're routinely in the spotlight and before people's scrutiny—and that can be a challenge.

As King Saul was coming to leadership, the role that Samuel had played as judge was about to change. Recognizing this pivotal moment of transition in Israel's history, Samuel used the opportunity to establish his legacy. He had enjoyed a privileged position, but he didn't focus on his skills and strategies as Israel's leader. Instead, he highlighted his character: that he had walked before the Lord from childhood, that he was upright before the people, and that, as a result, he had been able to enjoy and convey God's faithfulness and goodness through it all.

After recounting his track record, Samuel did something that so many leaders fear to do and fail to do: he put himself in the dock and asked the people to testify regarding the integrity of his leadership. He was willing to stand there while they determined whether his office had been marked by any bribery or self-promotion. That's a risky prospect! As the people considered Samuel's questions, they found nothing against him, either in his character or in the authority and influence that had been entrusted to him: "You have not defrauded us or oppressed us or taken anything from any man's hand" (1 Samuel 12:4). He had used his position neither to grow wealthy nor to dominate. Samuel's leadership was vindicated.

Because leadership comes with such focused attention, we must pray for leaders diligently and, if the Lord sees fit to place us in a leadership role ourselves, enter such roles thoughtfully, considering the purpose for which God has called us. James warns us not to take our leadership responsibilities, especially within the church, lightly or carelessly: "Not many of you should become teachers, my brothers, for you know that we who teach will be judged with greater strictness" (James 3:1).

Are you under the care of godly leaders? Then know that as they serve the Lord faithfully, they need your prayers, encouragement, and support! Be sure to pray for them regularly and seek to build them up frequently. Are you a leader yourself? Then follow Samuel's pattern: walk before the Lord as you lead, so that your leadership is marked by honesty and integrity and so that your example is truly worth following.

1 TIMOTHY 3:1-13

JANUARY 30

SEEING ALL OF CHRIST

"He said to them, 'O foolish ones, and slow of heart to believe all that the prophets have spoken! Was it not necessary that the Christ should suffer these things and enter into his glory?' And beginning with Moses and all the Prophets, he interpreted to them in all the Scriptures the things concerning himself."
LUKE 24:25-27

What are you expecting a life of following Jesus to be like?

Luke does not introduce to us a great variety of post-resurrection appearances by Jesus. He instead chooses to focus our attention on the interaction between the risen Christ and two individuals walking along the Emmaus road—individuals who were wavering between faith and fear as they tried to make sense of life in light of the crucifixion.

Jesus' death had confronted these early believers with a problem—namely, that their hope in Jesus as the Messiah had died with Him. Indeed, Luke records for us that they "*had* hoped that he was the one to redeem Israel" (Luke 24:21, emphasis added). These individuals had expected that when the Messiah came, He would bring victory, peace, and justice that would roll down like a vast and overwhelming river (Amos 5:24). But this hope had come to a crashing halt at the cross, where injustice seemed to have triumphed.

Yet something even better was about to happen: "While they were talking and discussing together, Jesus himself drew near and went with them" (Luke 24:15). Aware of their perplexity and hopelessness, Jesus, "beginning with Moses and all the Prophets … interpreted to them in all the Scriptures the things concerning himself."

It wasn't that these people were unbelievers. It wasn't that they didn't know certain things the prophets had said. But in their reading of the Old Testament and in their thinking about messiahship, they had failed to grasp the big picture. They had not been paying attention to *all* that the prophets had spoken. They had focused on only one side of the story. They had warmed to the idea of victory—but they had failed to see that glory and victory lay at the end of a path of suffering, even death.

We cannot embrace Jesus as Messiah apart from the cross. Jesus was very clear: victory surely awaits, but only for those who take His words in Luke 9:23 to heart: "If anyone would come after me, let him deny himself and take up his cross daily and follow me."

Are you willing to follow the path of suffering in order to enjoy a life with Christ in His glory? Are you at risk of turning away from God because He has not given you a victory in this life that He never promised? Be sure to see the whole story, so that setbacks and suffering do not defeat your faith or destroy the joy that comes from knowing that at the end of a hard path following a crucified King awaits the victory of seeing His face and living in His eternal kingdom. However hard or good the days of this life are, something better is always lying ahead.

2 TIMOTHY 4:6-8

JANUARY 31

NOTHING THWARTS GOD

"The kings of the earth set themselves, and the rulers take counsel together, against the LORD and against his Anointed, saying, 'Let us burst their bonds apart and cast away their cords from us.' He who sits in the heavens laughs; the LORD holds them in derision. Then he will speak to them in his wrath, and terrify them in his fury, saying, 'As for me, I have set my King on Zion, my holy hill.'" PSALM 2:1-6

As far back as 1939, the Dutch theologian Johan Herman Bavinck observed, "It looks more and more likely that our culture, based as it is on self-satisfaction, will at a certain moment collapse and then we as humanity will face a worldwide calamity that will occur without warning. It may yet take a while, but there's no doubt it will come."[10]

If Bavinck were here today, perhaps he would find our present circumstances to be something of a fulfillment of that prophetic word. For materialism, instant gratification, and individualistic autonomy were all sold to us as the path to satisfy ourselves—and, these things having failed, where do our societies turn?

We shouldn't misunderstand all the troubles of our world as being explicable in worldly terms alone. Mankind, the Bible tells us, is opposed to the gospel of Jesus Christ. As we consider our circumstances in light of the Scriptures, we recognize that this is what the psalmist meant when he wrote, "Why do the nations rage and the peoples plot in vain? The kings of the earth set themselves, and the rulers take counsel together, against the LORD and against his Anointed."

If we do not want to be buffeted and bowled over by opposition and persecution, we must remember that God is sovereign and that He cannot be defeated. The unfolding of His purposes from all of eternity is at the very heart of biblical Christianity. He is the Maker. He speaks, and He decides. Even the calamities of our world are all part of the plan God has predestined to take place. He has set His King to reign, and nothing can thwart His purpose. As His people, the church should therefore sound not retreat but reveille! We must remind ourselves and others of who the enemy is: our battle is primarily a spiritual one, waged not "against flesh and blood, but against the rulers, against the authorities, against the cosmic powers over this present darkness" (Ephesians 6:12). And we must remind ourselves and others of who the victor is and always shall be: the King God has appointed—His Son and our Savior.

As we consider the amazing juxtaposition between our sovereign God and this world full of rebellion, we ought to turn to Him in prayer. Indeed, Paul reminded his readers to pray "at all times in the Spirit, with all prayer and supplication" (Ephesians 6:18), encouraging them with the truth that "the weapons of our warfare are not of the flesh but have divine power to destroy strongholds" (2 Corinthians 10:4). We can pray boldly and live bravely because God stands sovereign. He is advancing His purpose—and nothing and no one can ultimately stand against His desire to glorify His King and bless His people.

EPHESIANS 6:10-20

10 *The Riddle of Life*, trans. Bert Hielema (Eerdmans, 2016), p 85.

FEBRUARY 1

GOD FINISHES WHAT HE STARTS

"I am sure of this, that he who began a good work in you will bring it to completion at the day of Jesus Christ." PHILIPPIANS 1:6

When God begins a work, He always completes it.

In Acts 16, we meet Lydia, a successful woman with her own business and a nice house in Philippi. She had an interest in religion—and then she was changed (Acts 16:14-15). What happened? God began a work. Later in the same chapter, we see a Philippian jailer come off his night shift also radically changed (v 30-34). What happened? Again, God began a work. We can imagine, then, that when Lydia or the jailer were tempted to give up, the word of God through Paul's letter to Philippi was there to remind them: "He who began a good work in you will bring it to completion at the day of Jesus Christ." In other words, *You didn't start the work within you, and you aren't going to finish it. If you feel that you can't keep going, you're right. You can't. But God did, and He can, and He will.*

God has a long-term plan for His people: that each of us will see and share in the glory of His Son. That is the end to which He is working (Romans 8:28-30). So we, like Lydia and the jailer, have both the need and ability to stay in the race of faith for the long haul.

While it always remains true that God gives all of us many gifts, our lives nonetheless can seem to be filled with disappointments. We continue to give in to sin. We struggle with doubts, and life's circumstances make it hard to keep going in faith. But we can and will continue on the journey, because Scripture promises us that our God "began a good work" and that He will finish it. As we stumble along the way and face difficulties, we're tempted to go back down to the bottom of the mountain, trade our hiking boots for slippers, and head back home. But there's a view at the top that's worth every ache and pain along the way! And so the word of God comes to us again and again, saying, *Come on, just a little farther. Don't be concerned about all of your tomorrows. God Himself is helping you. Keep walking the way today.*

God finishes what He starts. And if you are trusting Christ, then He has started something eternal in you. When you feel overwhelmed at the journey ahead of you, or when the route today looks too steep, find encouragement in these words:

My name from the palms of His hands
Eternity will not erase;
Impressed on His heart it remains,
In marks of indelible grace.
Yes, I to the end shall endure,
As sure as the earnest is giv'n;
More happy, but not more secure,
The glorified spirits in heav'n.[11]

PSALM 121

11 Augustus Toplady, "A Debtor to Mercy Alone" (1771).

FEBRUARY 2

LIVING BY FAITH

"Moses said to the people, 'Fear not, stand firm, and see the salvation of the LORD, which he will work for you today. For the Egyptians whom you see today, you shall never see again. The LORD will fight for you, and you have only to be silent.'" EXODUS 14:13-14

When we live by faith, we discover this great truth: God's promises are enough.

On their way out of Egypt, Moses and the Israelites were confronted by an insurmountable hurdle: the Red Sea. After striding out of Egypt "defiantly" (Exodus 14:8), God's people found themselves pursued and soon to be overtaken at the edge of the waters—and as "Pharaoh drew near, the people of Israel ... feared greatly." In their terror, they "cried out to the LORD" and began to berate and criticize Moses (v 10-11).

What would faith do in this situation? Exodus 14:13 presents us with Moses's response to the people: "Fear not, stand firm, and see the salvation of the LORD."

What a dramatic expression of faith on the part of Moses! He has little going for him at this point: the Egyptian chariots are at his back, the sea stretches out ahead, and he is surrounded by complaints and criticisms—and all he has is his staff and the command and promise of God.

But that was enough for Moses. All of his trust and confidence rested in his belief in God's promises. If God had said it, Moses believed it—and God had said that He would bring the people out of Egypt, to Mount Sinai on the opposite side of the sea, and on into the promised land (Exodus 3:7-12). It was not Moses' job to be concerned over the particulars. It was his job to trust and obey.

And the waters parted.

When the Egyptians tried to pursue the Israelites along the path through the sea, they were engulfed, never to be seen again (Exodus 14:27-28). Why? Because faith and presumption are two different things. The Egyptians were not living by faith in or in obedience to God. They had simply assumed that they could experience what the people of God experienced. They were wrong.

If God had said it, Moses believed it. And so can we, and so must we. We don't have to worry about whether or not God will part the sea, but we *do* have to take God at His word and act accordingly. Some of us have never known the joy of standing, as it were, on the edge of dangerous waters and seeing God's deliverance, because we're so worried about how God is going to handle every little detail. We retreat in anxiety and hold back in doubt rather than standing firm. God has promised to take you to the promised land of eternity with Him. What is insurmountable to you and me is nothing to Him. And so He says, *Don't worry about the route by which you get home. I'll take care of it. Just do what I told you, and trust in Me.* His promises are enough. It is your job today simply to trust and obey.

EXODUS 14:1-31

FEBRUARY 3

HARDENED BY SIN'S DECEIT

"When Herod saw Jesus, he was very glad, for he had long desired to see him, because he had heard about him, and he was hoping to see some sign done by him. So he questioned him at some length, but he made no answer." LUKE 23:8-9

Jesus' arrival at Herod's palace on the first Good Friday was an occasion of great delight for the intrigued king. As ruler over the districts where Jesus had conducted His public ministry, Herod would have routinely received news of Jesus' miracles, teaching, and influence. And so, following Jesus' arrest, Herod "questioned him at some length" and hoped "to see some sign done by him." But Jesus wouldn't speak. At the time when Herod was ready to do business with Jesus, the Son of God "made no answer."

Why didn't Jesus respond? Was He not missing an evangelistic opportunity? No—Jesus knew Herod's motives and his condition and that, in actual fact, Herod's heart was hardened and unrepentant. And so Jesus called Herod out by responding in silence, thus giving Herod the opportunity to display his true colors. And that's exactly what happened: the silence infuriated the king so much that he "treated him with contempt and mocked him. Then, arraying him in splendid clothing, he sent him back to Pilate" (Luke 23:11).

There had been a time in Herod's life when he hadn't already been hardened by sin's deceit. As he listened to John the Baptist preach, Herod "was greatly perplexed, and yet he heard him gladly" (Mark 6:20). John's preaching stirred Herod. But when the preacher's words began to confront Herod with his own sin—his adultery, his lustful heart—then, at that point, he didn't want to hear any more (Matthew 14:4-5).

What happened to Herod can happen to us. Herod was trapped by his sin, and when faced with his problem he refused to change. Rather than responding in humble repentance, he attempted to cover his sin, so much so that as time passed, he was less and less in a position to respond to the good news of the gospel. Ultimately, Herod's rejection of John's preaching resulted in a hardened heart that could only ridicule and mock the one of whom John had spoken. As Sinclair Ferguson writes, "Unless we silence sin, sin will silence our consciences. Unless we heed God's word, the day may come when we despise God's Son—and then God will have nothing more to say to us."[12] In the words of the hymn writer, Herod stands as a warning to:

Wait not till the shadows lengthen, till you older grow;
Rally now and sing for Jesus, ev'rywhere you go.[13]

Sin is deceitful, and it will harden you (Hebrews 3:13). So examine yourself. Are there areas of your life about which God's word has spoken clearly, but you are resisting rather than repenting? Resist no longer. Seek forgiveness and commit to change, and know that you need never fear the silence of Christ.

JAMES 4:4-10

12 *Let's Study Mark* (Banner of Truth, 1999), p 90.
13 John R. Colgan, "Mighty Army of the Young" (1891).

FEBRUARY 4

THE BONDS OF THE GOSPEL

"It is right for me to feel this way about you all, because I hold you in my heart, for you are all partakers with me of grace, both in my imprisonment and in the defense and confirmation of the gospel." PHILIPPIANS 1:7

Commitment to each other is a nonnegotiable in the Christian life.

We see this again and again in the life and writing of the apostle Paul. As he wrote to the church in Philippi, he was unashamed of sharing with them just how he felt about them, because he was so appreciative of the fellowship he enjoyed with them. Indeed, the word "partakers" in this verse actually comes from the Greek word *koinonia*, a word Paul frequently used to describe a sharing partnership.

Paul described the Philippian church as his "joy and crown" (Philippians 4:1). His heart was filled with love for all the churches who were under his care, but he regarded these brothers and sisters in a special way. They stood out, for they had stuck with Paul through thick and thin. Separated as the Philippians were from Paul when he wrote to them while under arrest in Rome, they could quite possibly have been swept away by other teachers with more impressive personalities, more striking characters, or more eloquent language. But they continued to stand with Paul. Their depth of fellowship was strengthened by their constancy, which filled the apostle with joy and stimulated his outburst of affection.

The example of this early church is a challenging call to contemporary Christianity, which, if we're honest, is all too often marked by fickleness. Many Christians tend to be uncommitted when times are good and unreliable when times are bad. We so easily treat the opportunities of fellowship, worship, and the hearing of God's word with an arm's-length approach. If a teacher or a book appeals to our sense of need, scratches where we itch, or tickles our fancy, then we engage with them for a while—but if things go awry, or if we find our way of life challenged, or if being alongside another Christian becomes costly rather than easy, then the temptation for many of us is to head for new pastures.

Paul shows us a better way—a more Christlike way. We are called to choose commitment to one another through the ups and downs of life. The binding element between Paul and the Philippians is the same element which can bind our hearts.

In seeing one another endure difficulties, in running to one another in the experience of loss, and in receiving from one another the enjoyment of restoration, we will discover that our hearts are actually being molded together in the bonds of the gospel. Through such constancy, we will find God strengthening our fellowship and increasing our joy with other believers.

So, does commitment describe your attitude to those the Lord has placed in fellowship around you? Do they know that you are there for them in the downs as well as the ups? To whom could you write an encouragement, and for whom will you say a prayer, right now?

PHILIPPIANS 1:21-26

FEBRUARY 5

HOW TO HAVE PEACE

"He shall be their peace." MICAH 5:5

You can find peace.

The context of the book of Micah was one of great humiliation for the people of God. Foreigners had besieged Jerusalem, and the city's people could barely lift a finger in their own defense. They longed for peace, but they found themselves in the midst of a war. They were a subjugated people, unable to gather troops together in order to fight back against the enemy. Theirs was a picture of absolute disgrace.

It must have been a very confusing time for God's people. They were supposed to be a chosen people, set apart for God, the carriers of His great promise to bless and restore the world, but now it appeared that all that was about to be destroyed. They likely would have thought to themselves, *Where are God's promises?*

It is in the midst of this perplexing scene that a light finally began to shine in the darkness. Though they were humiliated, the people of God received a glimmer of hope. The prophet Micah declared that the Messiah would come and stand in the place of authority, shepherd His flock in the strength of the Lord, and grant security to those who trust in Him (Micah 5:4). In Him, Micah said, they would finally find peace.

I have a little booklet in my house called *Five Minutes' Peace*.[14] It tells the story of a mother elephant who just wants five minutes of peace away from her children—but as soon as she attempts to get peace, only more chaos ensues. This is surely something that every mother can identify with! In the midst of chaos, we long for a few moments of respite. So did God's people—and during a time of great distress, the prophet Micah promised that the Messiah would come to finally bring them what they longed for.

While we all desire peace, it frequently seems unattainable. Look around you and you'll see that true peace appears to be virtually absent globally, nationally, locally, and personally. You may be thinking to yourself, "If only I could just find peace. All I want is five minutes!"

Is your life marked by fractured relationships, financial distress, personal loss, and other disappointments? If so, there is good news for you: in the Messiah, Jesus, you will find genuine, lasting peace—peace first and foremost with God Himself and then peace with ourselves and in our relationships and communities, as we learn to reflect the God of peace in the way we approach tensions, difficulties, and conflicts. The Messiah has come to bring this peace to all who trust in Him. After all, He *is* the Prince of Peace. Whatever else you face, you can enjoy the peace with your Creator that He died to win. Then, knowing you are at peace with the only one whose opinion matters eternally, you will be able to walk out into your world to seek, by His grace, to live at peace.

MICAH 5:1-9

14 Jill Murphy, *Five Minutes' Peace* (Walker, 1986).

FEBRUARY 6

AN EXPRESSION OF LOVE

"It is right for me to feel this way about you all, because I hold you in my heart ... For God is my witness, how I yearn for you all with the affection of Christ Jesus. And it is my prayer that your love may abound more and more, with knowledge and all discernment." PHILIPPIANS 1:7-9

One of the things my grandfather used to say as I bade him farewell was "I'll be *thinking away* about you." It always struck me as a strange thing to say. But by it he meant, "I care about how you are. I'm under the burden of what you're doing. I'm interested in where you're going."

Paul used similar phraseology when he wrote words like "feel," "heart," "yearn," and "affection" to the Philippian church. *Phronein*, which means "to think," is translated in the ESV as "to feel" because this verb is expressive not simply of a mental focus but also of a sympathetic interest and genuine concern. Paul was telling the Philippians that though he was physically separated from them, they were very dear to him and remained in his thoughts and prayers. He was "thinking away" about them.

Paul—that man who had once been consumed by a hatred for Jesus' followers—came to have this affection because Jesus gave it to him. He and his fellow believers were now bound together by God's amazing love toward them. The standard and source of his affection was none other than the Lord Jesus Himself. As Bishop Lightfoot wrote, Paul's "pulse beats with the pulse of Christ; his heart throbs with the heart of Christ."[15]

Because the Philippian believers were such an important part of Paul's life, his love for them moved him to prayer, for Paul understood that prayer is one of the key expressions of love. His love was not revealed in a cozy sentimentalism or in fine-sounding words. Instead, he prayed for his friends, and he did so daily.

When "God's love has been poured into our hearts through the Holy Spirit" (Romans 5:5), we will find ourselves immediately drawn to others who love in the same way. It is the love of family life, for we share the same Father—and one of the fundamental ways in which we will express that love is to pray.

Do you love your children? Pray for them. Do you love your church? Pray for them. As Christ's love expands your heart and flows through you, the affection you have for those you hold dear will move you to prayer. Be "thinking away" about those you love—and be "praying away" for them too!

1 THESSALONIANS 2b-13

15 Joseph Barber Lightfoot, *Saint Paul's Epistle to the Philippians* (Macmillan, 1898), p 85.

FEBRUARY 7

LIKE FATHER, LIKE CHILDREN

"If you then, who are evil, know how to give good gifts to your children, how much more will your Father who is in heaven give good things to those who ask him!" MATTHEW 7:11

When someone is born again, they begin a new life and are adopted into the family of God. This new child of God, in whom the Holy Spirit now dwells, begins increasingly to display characteristics of the Father. In other words, over time God's children should grow to resemble their heavenly Father.

One prominent feature of who God is—an aspect of His character displayed throughout Scripture—is His generosity. James says, "Every good gift and every perfect gift is from above, coming down from the Father" (James 1:17). Paul makes a similar point with a rhetorical question: "He who did not spare his own Son but gave him up for us all, how will he not also with him graciously give us all things?" (Romans 8:32). Our Father is generous, and it is the assumption of Scripture that God's people will be too. This applies to all of our lives—including, of course, our finances.

God-honoring generosity is displayed *in response to* God's grace. This is important, because so much talk of and thinking about finances goes awry at this very point. Any attempt to encourage ourselves to give to gospel work that doesn't begin with the grace of God is flawed from the start. It almost always results in the kind of giving in which God has no interest: the joyless type. If we give because we've been coaxed into it, we will be giving not with gladness but with a grudge. Begrudging giving says, "I have to." Dutiful giving says, "I need to." But thankful giving says, "I want to." That is the approach we should aim to take.

Growing in this kind of generosity requires growing in gratitude for God's grace. If you want to be more Christlike in your giving, you need to understand that you have absolutely nothing that you did not receive, from your physical existence to your faith in God and everything in between (1 Corinthians 4:7). It is all of grace. Knowing that, how could you and I respond with anything but joyful generosity?

This means that if we are stingy with our investment in gospel ministry, it may reflect a shallow grasp of God's character and goodness. The what, where, when, why, and how of our giving says something about our relationship with God and our commitment to Jesus Christ. Our banking records can speak volumes.

Ask yourself, then: What do my financial habits say about my commitment to Christ and my grasp of God's grace? What will change if my giving is an overflow of my gratitude to God for all He has given me? God is a giver, and He gives His children the calling and the joy of being like Him.

ROMANS 8:31-39

FEBRUARY 8

TRUE AFFECTION

"Then Samuel went to Ramah, and Saul went up to his house in Gibeah of Saul. And Samuel did not see Saul again until the day of his death, but Samuel grieved over Saul." 1 SAMUEL 15:34-35

Despite Saul's promising beginnings as Israel's first king, before long he floundered and failed. His problem was not a lack of ability but a lack of obedience. So Samuel confronted Saul about his rebellion against God's word and told him that God had rejected him as king (1 Samuel 15:23). Evidently, Samuel had some affection for Saul, which is why Saul's failure shook the prophet, causing him to grieve.

Though Samuel enjoyed a privileged and distinctive position as the one who brought the word of God to the people, he was not removed or distanced in his response to all that unfolded. Because the prophet loved those under his care, it was only fitting that he grieved over their sin and suffering. And this sadness also led him to prayer. At one point, dismayed by the people's actions, he declared, "Far be it from me that I should sin against the LORD by ceasing to pray for you" (1 Samuel 12:23). The prophet grieved for them and prayed for them because he cared for them.

Leadership brings with it particular privileges. But those privileges are partnered with perils. Effective leadership requires an emotional investment in those being led—and so the burdens of leadership are in large measure directly tied to those who are being led. Sometimes those people disappoint greatly and sometimes they suffer greatly, and both occurrences will weigh on a good leader. As we see with Samuel, it is not the shepherd's role to condemn when those in his care stumble and fall. Rather, the role of the shepherd is marked by grief. If it means anything for us to be united in heart, mind, and purpose, then it must mean something to us when those for whom we have affection stumble and fall.

Though this is particularly true of leadership, Samuel's example should cause all of us to stop and ask, "What makes me cry? What makes me smile? And what do I do when I cry and when I smile?" The answer to these questions is a real indication of where you are in your spiritual progress. Seek to make sure that your life is marked by true affection for those around you, and especially those the Lord has given you responsibility for in some way—a true affection that grieves over sin and suffering in the lives of those you care for. And then be sure to respond as Samuel did: with faithful prayer to the one who promises that, one day, as you stand in His presence, He will "wipe away every tear" (Revelation 21:4).

1 THESSALONIANS 3:6-13

FEBRUARY 9

A LIFE OF URGENCY

"I do not account my life of any value nor as precious to myself, if only I may finish my course and the ministry that I received from the Lord Jesus, to testify to the gospel of the grace of God." ACTS 20:24

As he took his leave of the Ephesian elders in Acts 20, the apostle Paul felt an urgent compulsion from the Spirit to go to Jerusalem. He had no idea what would happen to him when he got there, but he had a clear sense that hard times and imprisonment awaited him. Then he made this staggering statement: "I do not account my life of any value."

This was not masochism—some strange hatred of happiness, health, or physical life. So what, then, did Paul mean by declaring his life valueless? Simply this: that he did not regard his life as so precious a possession as to be held on to at all costs.

People often say, "Well, as long as you've got your health, that's all that matters!" But that is not all that matters! Our bodies are passing away. We're crumbling even as we live and breathe. We may have our health today, but a day will come when we do not. Unless we're able to say with Paul, "To live is Christ," we cannot legitimately affirm with him, "and to die is gain" (Philippians 1:21). The only way that death can be gain is if Christ is everything. And if Christ is everything, as Paul says He is, then we can declare with him, *My life is not ultimate. I don't need to protect it as the most precious thing I have. I want to spend it for the most precious person I know.*

What mattered most to Paul was that he finished his life trusting Christ and carried out to the best of his abilities the ministry Christ had given him. He felt a compelling resolve to complete the task of testifying to "the gospel of the grace of God" everywhere he could reach. *There's* a task! *There's* a purpose, significance, an agenda, a calling! And this is a task that has been entrusted to all of us—the commission to let everyone we meet know the good news of God's amazing grace.

How are you, like Paul, to live a life of urgency so that you might keep going until the end? You must run your race with all your might, with the finish line in view. Don't look for an opportunity to bow out or slow down before the final lap is over. Run with all your strength and run right through the tape, gripped by Christ's love, energized by God's Spirit, and guided by God's word.

PHILIPPIANS 1:27 –2:2

FEBRUARY 10

KNOWLEDGE AND DISCERNMENT

"It is my prayer that your love may abound more and more, with knowledge and all discernment, so that you may approve what is excellent, and so be pure and blameless for the day of Christ, filled with the fruit of righteousness that comes through Jesus Christ, to the glory and praise of God." PHILIPPIANS 1:9-11

Some of us can be far too content with a bumper-sticker mentality that defines our faith in a single, catchy phrase. While such slogans may provide glimpses of what it means to be a Christian, there's no way a few words can comprehensively sum up Christianity. On the other hand, a person can know all about the Bible's contents and have a great grasp of complex doctrinal points, and still lack an intimate knowledge of God Himself.

Paul understood that true Christian faith is much deeper than either of these approaches. He therefore prayed that his readers' love—their *agape*, the self-giving love of Christ—would develop in two ways: in knowledge and in discernment.

In these verses, the word for "knowledge" refers not merely to a knowledge of the head but also to a knowledge that is only possible as a result of God's self-disclosure: a cohesive intimacy with Him, similar to the intimacy that is built within the bonds of marriage. When we enjoy this kind of love, we enjoy the privilege of being able to say, "God, it says in the Bible that You will show Yourself to me. Please show Yourself to me!"

Yet Paul also prayed for discernment. He knew that love can go badly astray unless it is directed properly through perception and the ability to make a moral and correct decision. We can err greatly with the best of intentions. The insight we need comes from studying and knowing the Bible. As we cultivate and live in God's presence through His word, we become more like Him. Our thoughts and feelings conform to the way He thinks and feels. And so, in addition to loving God and therefore wanting to do what is right, we know in the various circumstances of our lives what doing right actually looks like. Are you, then, praying for the joy of this kind of intimate, wise love for God—and praying for it not just for yourself but for other believers too?

Each new day is an opportunity to commit yourself again to becoming fully mature in the Lord Jesus, allowing the clarity of God's love and the truth of His word to deepen your knowledge and sharpen your discernment. Each day is an invitation to go deeper into your faith and to grow more in love for your God. And, as your love flourishes, so will your life be full of the true goodness that brings glory and praise to Him.

2 CORINTHIANS 3:16-18

FEBRUARY 11

ENJOYING LIFE UNDER THE SUN

"There is a vanity that takes place on earth, that there are righteous people to whom it happens according to the deeds of the wicked, and there are wicked people to whom it happens according to the deeds of the righteous. I said that this also is vanity. And I commend joy, for man has nothing better under the sun but to eat and drink and be joyful, for this will go with him in his toil through the days of his life that God has given him under the sun." ECCLESIASTES 8:14-15

None of us, of course, are guaranteed to know the date of our death. But we know something just as certain: unless Christ returns first, that day *will* come. Until then, Scripture says, we will inhabit a creation that is subject to futility, with evil around us, sin within us, and chaos seeming to prevail more often than not. We will see the wicked prosper and the godly struggle. These truths are poignantly expressed in the words of the Preacher of Ecclesiastes: "There is a vanity that takes place on earth."

By itself, that observation could send us into a spiral of sorrow, sullenness, and despair. But the writer of Ecclesiastes does not leave us there. Instead, he makes a rather surprising recommendation: "I commend joy ... to eat and drink and be joyful." Observation: life is unmanageable. Recommendation: enjoy life's simple pleasures!

How can anyone know genuine enjoyment of such pleasures when life is futile and unjust and comes with an expiration date? This is something that is only possible for those who know the truth. We can freely and guiltlessly enjoy the pleasures God gives because we know God; indeed, it honors the Giver of such gifts to enjoy what He gives. The apostle Paul describes God as the one "who richly provides us with everything to enjoy" (1 Timothy 6:17). The fact that simple pleasures offer no *ultimate* satisfaction does not mean they offer *no* satisfaction. It is knowing that there is life *beyond* the sun that frees us to enjoy our life "under the sun." As the hymn writer puts it:

Heav'n above is softer blue,
Earth around is sweeter green;
Something lives in every hue
Christless eyes have never seen.[16]

When was the last time you asked someone, "Are you enjoying yourself?" When did you last ask *yourself* that question? It is a good, Christian thing to ask! We know both that the world is broken and that every good gift comes from God. So honor Him by enjoying your next cup of coffee, your next day with your spouse, your next day at work, the next thing that makes you smile, as a gift from Him. He's given these blessings to you for your God-honoring enjoyment, so that you can say with the psalmist, "This is the day that the Lord has made; let us rejoice and be glad in it" (Psalm 118:24).

1 TIMOTHY 6:6-10, 17-19

16 Wade Robinson, "I Am His, and He Is Mine" (1876).

FEBRUARY 12

STEALING GLORY

"He who brought the news answered and said, 'Israel has fled before the Philistines, and there has also been a great defeat among the people. Your two sons also, Hophni and Phinehas, are dead, and the ark of God has been captured.'" 1 SAMUEL 4:17

Is God *useful for* your life or *worthy of* your life?

At the start of 1 Samuel 4, the Israelite army had experienced a significant defeat after taking the ark of God to the battlefield, hoping to use it as a kind of magic box to ensure victory (1 Samuel 4:1-4). The high priest, Eli, had known better, but he'd agreed to the plan nevertheless.

At that time, the ark was God's dwelling place among His people. God wanted them to come to the ark to seek His presence, not use it as a talisman. Eli understood this—and so, as the army went out to battle, he sat trembling in Shiloh, waiting for news to come (1 Samuel 4:13). When a messenger finally arrived from the field, the message ended in a devastating punch line: "The ark of God has been captured." With this news, Eli's heart trembled, and he died (v 18), a 40-year career coming to a crashing end in a moment.

God's presence and glory, represented back then in the ark of God, is not to be taken lightly or used for our selfish purposes. What happened at Shiloh has been long remembered. The psalmist writes, "When God heard, he was full of wrath, and he utterly rejected Israel. He forsook his dwelling at Shiloh, the tent where he dwelt among mankind" (Psalm 78:59-60). Jeremiah, too, speaking at a time in the history of God's people when they were also tempted to "use" God, gave this word of warning: "Has this house, which is called by my name, become a den of robbers in your eyes? Behold, I myself have seen it, declares the LORD. Go now to my place that was in Shiloh, where I made my name dwell at first, and see what I did to it because of the evil of my people Israel" (Jeremiah 7:11-12). Shiloh was to serve as a reminder of the repercussions of attempting to use God as a good-luck charm instead of worshiping Him as the Lord.

Centuries later, as Jesus cleansed the temple in Jerusalem, He quoted part of Jeremiah's warning (Matthew 21:12-13). Once again, the people were using God for their purposes rather than honoring Him. But He came not only to expose sin but to deal with it. In allowing the forces of darkness to nail Him to a cross, the one who was all the glory of His Father (John 1:14) was taken far from the presence of His Father. Therefore, He is worthy of all authority and all honor (Revelation 5:9).

What about you? When you honestly consider your heart's inclination, do you say to God "You are useful" rather than "You are worthy"? Look with the eye of faith on Jesus cleansing the temple of sinners, and then cleansing sinners so they might live in the presence of God forever, and you will find yourself desiring to spend your days praising Him. "A day in [his] courts is better than a thousand elsewhere" (Psalm 84:10). As you believe this, your life will declare His worth, and you will look to worship Him, not to use Him.

PSALM 84

FEBRUARY 13

FOR THE SAKE OF THE GOSPEL

"I want you to know, brothers, that what has happened to me has really served to advance the gospel, so that it has become known throughout the whole imperial guard and to all the rest that my imprisonment is for Christ." PHILIPPIANS 1:12-13

Follow Paul through Acts and he leaves you breathless. He's constantly on the move, going from place to place. One moment he's stitching tents together, then he's bringing Eutychus back to life, and then he survives a snakebite and heals the sick on Malta. It's almost as if you can't imagine ever being able to keep up with him.

Surely the worst thing that could ever happen to someone like Paul is to be stuck in one house for two years. But at the conclusion of Acts, that's exactly how we find him (Acts 28:30-31).

You can just imagine the devil's response to Paul's imprisonment: *Now I've shut him down! That'll get rid of him. He won't be able to go anywhere for a long while. He'll just shrivel up and die a prisoner.* Not a chance! It was during Paul's imprisonment that he penned some of his most noteworthy letters under the inspiration of the Holy Spirit—letters that God is still using to transform lives 2,000 years later. And, remarkably, the gospel advanced not only despite Paul's chains but because of them.

Paul was likely very different from other prisoners. The soldiers who guarded him would have probably said to one another, *He is the most remarkable person we've ever had. We're used to people constantly cussing, screaming, agitating, and complaining. But this Paul has joy and purpose, and he just preaches!*

As a result of Paul's daily ministry among these soldiers, word began to spread throughout the entire palace guard: *The reason this guy is a prisoner is because of Jesus.* They got the point: *He's chained to us, he says, because he's chained to this man Jesus Christ.* And it appears that some of these guards not only heard the gospel but responded to it. As they were then redeployed throughout the Roman Empire, arriving at their new posts as new men, the gospel would advance to different places through them. And so Paul's imprisonment, which at first appeared to be diametrically opposed to the spread of the gospel, actually proved to be essential to it.

You do not need to be a prisoner, a missionary, or an apostle to be used by God in spreading the gospel, nor do you need to wait for all the circumstances in your life to line up just as you want them to before you talk about Jesus. Whether you are in prison, a hospital, an office, a field, or wherever, and whether you realize it or not, you are never far from someone who needs to hear the amazing story of God's grace. What are the situations you face that you naturally see as obstacles to sharing the gospel, and how might they in fact be opportunities? Who are the lost and longing people that God has placed in your life today? They need your God. And they might only meet Him through your loving boldness.

PHILIPPIANS 1:12-18a

FEBRUARY 14

IT'S JESUS, NOT ME

"I am the man who has seen affliction under the rod of his wrath."
LAMENTATIONS 3:1

In the popular series of British children's books *Where's Wally?* (or, as it's known in North America, *Where's Waldo?*), readers find themselves scurrying all over the page looking for a funny-looking fellow wearing red-and-white striped clothes who nonetheless is hard to spot in his suspiciously similarly-colored surroundings. In a similar manner, when we read our Bibles, we can find ourselves doing a comparable exercise, only instead of searching for a man in a red-and-white striped sweater and glasses, we ask ourselves, "Where am *I*?" We wonder which character we are like, or how a verse speaks directly of us and about us.

Yet the real question we should be asking is "Where's *Jesus*?"—for He is the primary focus of the Bible.

The truth is that if we really want to find ourselves in Scripture, we will discover that a large part of the story *is* about us. Yet that part is not very flattering. The Bible reveals us to be wretched sinners, who need a Savior. This is why we must train our eyes to look for that Savior when we read our Bibles. As has been said, in the Old Testament Jesus is expected, in the Gospels He's revealed, in Acts He's preached, in the Epistles He's explained, and in the book of Revelation He's anticipated.

When we read Lamentations 3 with Jesus as our focus, seeking Him rather than looking for ourselves, we will discover that He is clearly present. The chapter opens with the prophet Jeremiah declaring, "I am the man who has seen affliction under the rod of his wrath" (Lamentations 3:1). Who is more fit to utter those words than Jesus? On the cross, Jesus bore the wrath of God so that those of us who rightly deserved God's condemnation might be saved through the judgment that He endured in our place. That's the story of the gospel: another has done for us what we couldn't do for ourselves. In truth, then, as you read this verse, you do *not* see yourself here at all, even though you should—for you *do* see Christ here. He "redeemed us from the curse of the law by becoming a curse for us" (Galatians 3:13). Whatever trials you face as a Christian in this life and however inexplicable they feel, of one thing you can be sure: God is not punishing you in His wrath. All that was poured out upon another, on the cross.

As you read of God's persevering faithfulness to His downtrodden people in Lamentations 3, remember that "he who did not spare his own Son but gave him up for us all" is also the one who will "graciously give us all things" (Romans 8:32). And as you read of the man who saw affliction under the rod of God's wrath, rejoice that this verse speaks not of you but of Him.

JOHN 19:17-30

FEBRUARY 15

GROWING IN BOLDNESS

"I want you to know, brothers, that what has happened to me has really served to advance the gospel, so that it has become known throughout the whole imperial guard and to all the rest that my imprisonment is for Christ. And most of the brothers, having become confident in the Lord by my imprisonment, are much more bold to speak the word without fear." PHILIPPIANS 1:12-14

What must have looked like a tragedy turned out to be just the opposite.

When the Philippian church learned that Paul had been imprisoned in Rome, they were surely greatly concerned. Some may have even panicked, worrying that the gospel's influence would decline because its great teacher and apologist was shut away, unable to travel. It was a disaster for the gospel—wasn't it?

Paul himself had a radically different perspective on his imprisonment. Underpinning all that he wrote was an unshakable confidence in God's providence, for, as he wrote to the church in Rome, "If God is for us, who can be against us?" (Romans 8:31). Understanding that he had been placed in prison according to God's plan (Philippians 1:16), Paul was able to be an optimistic prisoner and a joyful servant, looking to the well-being of the church and not to his own predicament.

For Paul, it was imperative for the church to understand that his imprisonment was not hindering the gospel but furthering it. Being a prisoner was simply another opportunity to proclaim the good news of Jesus Christ. What had happened had "really served to advance the gospel." Roman soldiers were unlikely to seek out a converted Jew who was gathering crowds with his preaching—yet God wanted His good news to reach them. He therefore prepared a different method of ministry and sent Paul to them, albeit in chains. As a result, the good news spread among the entire guard and even went on to break into the very household of the Roman emperor himself. And the news of Paul's success in turn emboldened other believers. As they realized that God was able to provide for Paul in his circumstance, they grew in their trust that God could provide for them in their own circumstances. And so they became "much more bold to speak the word without fear."

Perhaps we, too, need the confidence that comes from remembering that God is in control. We tend to assume that circumstances have to be right if we're going to be effective Christians. But God's thinking is different from ours. He's not waiting for the circumstances to be right. He's committed to using His people for His glory, even when the circumstances appear less than ideal. And He's able to use those circumstances to further the cause of the gospel.

We would do well to spend less time trying to change our circumstances and more time growing in boldness and speaking the word without fear. We would do well to consider how we might be in danger of using our circumstances as an excuse not to speak rather than as an opportunity to do so. Perhaps then the good news of Jesus Christ will spread through us in some strange and wonderful way, just as it did through Paul.

ACTS 8:1b-8

Bible Through The Year: Isaiah 65–66; Mark 14:53-72

FEBRUARY 16

A CALL TO REMEMBER

"When your children ask in time to come, 'What do those stones mean to you?' then you shall tell them that the waters of the Jordan were cut off before the ark of the covenant of the Lord. When it passed over the Jordan, the waters of the Jordan were cut off. So these stones shall be to the people of Israel a memorial forever." JOSHUA 4:6-7

The Christian life is, in a sense, one big call to remember. Our Lord Jesus, speaking of the new-covenant meal of Communion, told us, "Do this *in remembrance* of me" (Luke 22:19, emphasis added). Every Lord's Supper, then, offers us the opportunity to remember together all that is pictured in the bread and wine.

Deuteronomy similarly envisions a scenario in which a son asks his father, "What is the meaning of the testimonies and statutes and the rules that the Lord our God has commanded you?" (Deuteronomy 6:20). The father responds by telling Israel's story of redemption, highlighting that what God instructs is "for our good always" (v 24). The book of Joshua, too, commends the same kind of commemoration when the Lord instructs the people to set up twelve memorial stones at the Jordan River, so that the stones would be "to the people of Israel a memorial forever." God wanted His people then—and wants His people today—to ever remember His faithfulness and to tell others what He has done.

Such remembrances and memorials have always been significant. But in a day with endless competing claims on our attention and affections, we perhaps need more reminders of God's faithfulness than ever before. It's notable that the examples above are concrete and interpersonal. We participate in the Lord's Supper together, and it offers us a multisensory experience to help us remember. The twelve stones at the Jordan River constituted a physical memorial. The instruction of Deuteronomy encourages us to have conversations about God's faithfulness and goodness in our homes.

For today's Christians, every Sunday presents us with the opportunity to gather and remember with God's people. But we are going to need more than a weekly touchpoint to sustain ourselves. Ask yourself: *What habits can I cultivate to remember God's goodness? How can I catalog His faithfulness to me and share that with others? What "memorials" can I set up so that I can remember how God delivered me?*

Opportunities to see and recall God's faithfulness abound. All we need to do is look and remember.

LUKE 22:14-20

FEBRUARY 17

DISPLAYS OF DIVINE PROVIDENCE

"The king's heart is a stream of water in the hand of the LORD; he turns it wherever he will." PROVERBS 21:1

Here is a picture of the doctrine of providence.

When men and women go about their business, God's hand is always involved. Question 2 of the New City Catechism includes a helpful summary of this doctrine: "Nothing happens except through him and by his will." The Bible is clear in its teaching that God is sovereign over every detail of every part of the universe. In creation, God exercised His divine energy to bring the world into being. In His perfect providence, He continues to exercise His divine energy to sustain the universe and bring all things to their appointed end—uniting all things in heaven and earth under Christ (Ephesians 1:9-10).

There is some mystery in how God directs the course of events without violating the nature of what or who is involved. Charles Bridges provides helpful insight on the way this unfolds: "In inert matter he acts by physical force; in brute animals, by instinct and appetite; in intelligent beings, by motives suited to their faculties; in his redeemed people, by the influence of grace."[17] In God's economy and purposes, the causality of natural events, circumstances, and free decisions is used by Him in order to achieve His glorious ends. Throughout Scripture this pattern is repeated, whether it's through Nebuchadnezzar, Pharaoh, Herod, Pilate, or other figures. Though earthly rulers set themselves against the Lord as they exercised their rebellious wills, they were at the same time part of God's foreordained plan of salvation (Psalm 2:1-2; Acts 4:25-26). He turns all plans, even the desires of the heart of the most powerful men and women, "wherever he will."

For those of us who belong to Jesus, God's providence brings security. When we become disheartened because it is obvious that the wicked flourish and that bad is called good, the Bible reminds us that God is sovereign over all affairs. These things neither surprise nor defeat Him; indeed, He has made use of the wicked often, sometimes to protect and shield His people and at other times to purify and refine them. After the event, we may sometimes discern His purpose; during the event, we are simply to trust His providence.

God is the heavenly Father who seeks to draw you to Himself and make you His own. It is likely that even now you are thinking of circumstances that seem contrary to God's will and that confuse you. Remember His sovereignty, rehearse His purpose, and sing:

I trust in God, I know He cares for me,
On mountain bleak or on the stormy sea;
Though billows roll, He keeps my soul,
My heav'nly Father watches over me.[18]

ACTS 4:24-31

17 *An Exposition of the Book of Proverbs*, 3rd ed. (London, 1850), 2:43.
18 William C. Martin, "My Father Watches Over Me" (1910).

FEBRUARY 18

MIXED MOTIVES

"Some indeed preach Christ from envy and rivalry, but others from good will. The latter do it out of love, knowing that I am put here for the defense of the gospel. The former proclaim Christ out of selfish ambition, not sincerely but thinking to afflict me in my imprisonment. What then? Only that in every way, whether in pretense or in truth, Christ is proclaimed, and in that I rejoice."

PHILIPPIANS 1:15-18

In his missionary letter to the Philippian church, Paul gets real. Though he shares encouraging news, the picture is not all rosy. The motivations some people had for sharing the gospel were downright bad—they were driven not by good will so much as by rivalry and a desire to stir up trouble for the apostle.

The wrong motives of other people didn't become the determining element in Paul's attitude, however. Their selfishly motivated preaching did not keep him awake at night or mar his commitment to seeing the kingdom advance. He passionately wanted the true gospel to be preached, so he wasn't primarily concerned about the reasons others had for preaching, as long as they were still preaching Christ. His concern was for the Lord's glory, not for his own stature or even for his safety.

Perhaps we find ourselves relating to Paul, surrounded by those who share their faith out of false motives. But if we allow these failings to determine our own attitude or actions, it will cripple us. We will spend too much of our time and energy either constantly questioning the intentions of others or continually refuting and rebutting what they're doing. That would be to give the devil a great gain, in that we would then be distracted from proclaiming the good news of Jesus Christ. It's a huge temptation! But Paul didn't fall into that trap.

Alternatively, you and I may wrestle with our own wrong motives for sharing the gospel. One of the most significant challenges we all face is the potential for dreadful self-centeredness and pride. Even in matters of our faith, we often wrongly want others to recognize us, and so we do the right thing but for the wrong reasons (or, more usually, a mix of right and wrong reasons). At the same time, we find that envy prevents us from rejoicing in the fruitfulness of another's life and ministry. But thanks be to God: He still uses broken vessels like us to carry forth the great gift of His message.

So, like Paul, fix your eyes on the goodness of Jesus and the advancement of His gospel, no matter the circumstances surrounding you or the flawed motives you suspect in others or see in yourself. Seek to set aside your own pride and ambition so that your greatest concern will be the Lord's glory—and as you do so, continue to share Him with those around you. What matters most is that Christ is preached, and in that we can all rejoice.

ISAIAH 52:7-10

FEBRUARY 19

PRIZE THE WORD

"Now the boy Samuel was ministering to the LORD in the presence of Eli. And the word of the LORD was rare in those days; there was no frequent vision … Then the LORD called Samuel." 1 SAMUEL 3:1, 4

The chaos at the end of Judges, when "everyone did what was right in his own eyes" (Judges 21:25) and there was an absence of effective leadership, indicated the spiritual darkness at that time among God's people. And what caused this darkness? Faithful proclamation of the word of God was becoming increasingly rare. Yet such silence is not reserved to that one era. Throughout the generations, the people of God have experienced periods of this silence and darkness.

But God is a God of clarity and of grace—and so He has never left people without His word. So it was that, despite the faithlessness of the people during the time of the judges, God was preparing to bring His words to them through "the boy Samuel."

God always ensures that, one way or another, His people can hear His word; and today in the West we can never claim that His word is "rare." It is our privilege to have easy access to God's word in the Scriptures. Only in the last few centuries has a minister been able to say to the congregation, "Please take your Bible and turn to…" because prior to the printing press, few people had a Bible to turn to, nor could they have read it themselves if they had had one. In the 18th century, when John Newton was addressing his congregation, he noted, "I account it my honour and happiness that I preach to a free people, who have the Bible in their hands."[19] And there are still many places in the world where Bibles are removed and destroyed and must be smuggled in. To receive even a portion of the Scriptures means a tremendous amount to many of our brothers and sisters in such countries.

Yet while many of us have the honor and privilege of owning a Bible, we nevertheless live in effective silence, allowing the word of God to become increasingly rare in our lives. Is the Bible truly present in your daily life and in your place of worship—that is, not only physically present but also audibly proclaimed and intently listened to? What matters is not simply owning a Bible, or even merely reading and knowing it, but living by it and loving the one to whom it points: the Lord Jesus.

Alec Motyer writes, "Have we got a Bible still in our hands? Let us prize it, read it and commit precious truths to heart and mind. It is not an inalienable possession; it may not be ours forever."[20] Let these words challenge you to seek out God's word and treasure it so that you may walk in the light of hearing from God, about His Son, by the work of His Spirit.

PSALM 119:17-24

---

19 "Of a Living and a Dead Faith," in *The Works of John Newton* (1820; reprinted Banner of Truth, 1985), 2:558.

20 *The Message of Amos: The Day of the Lion*, The Bible Speaks Today (InterVarsity, 1984), p 187.

FEBRUARY 20

CHOOSE YOUR REFUGE

"In the Lord I take refuge; how can you say to my soul, 'Flee like a bird to your mountain'?" PSALM 11:1

When it comes to crises in life, it is not a matter of *whether* they will come but *when*. And when they do, our response will be to flee to a refuge—somewhere or something or someone we trust will keep us safe and protect us from the storms. So the question then will not be *whether* we flee but *where* we flee.

Some of us will take the advice of David's friends in Psalm 11. These advisors urged him to "flee like a bird to your mountain." Difficulty had come for David, seemingly in the form of threats to his life, with wicked people preparing to aim their arrows at him (Psalm 11:2). The counsel he received was essentially to head for the hills, to get away, to go somewhere that removed him from adversity.

David did not heed this advice. But what about you? While you likely will not face armed foes threatening you with violence, crisis will come to you someday, in one form or another. It could be social pressure to compromise biblical convictions, an unwanted diagnosis, or intense relational strife. Where will you flee? Will you head for the hills, finding some form of escapism, be it numbing yourself with endless media consumption or abusing a substance, or throwing yourself into frenetic activity in another part of your life? Or will you be able to say with David, "In the Lord I take refuge"?

David had seen God deliver him from bears, lions, and a Philistine giant. The Lord had proven Himself to be a trustworthy refuge, and David took that to heart. David knew the Lord was a mighty refuge; that had been borne out again and again in his life. His trust in God was grounded in experience, making it sturdy enough to withstand life's darkness and the Evil One's darts.

Have your eyes been opened to God's trustworthiness? Have you trusted Him in response? If you are a Christian, remember that your new life began by taking refuge in the Lord Jesus Christ. You were facing the wrath of an eternal God, with no hope to be found. The only hope you had was to cast yourself on God's mercy and embrace the salvation offered in Christ. And so you fled to Him and found eternal refuge.

God desires for you to seek refuge in Him not only at the beginning of the journey but until Christ returns or calls you home, and not only for eternal salvation but in the storms of this life. Trouble will come—and when it does, you can either head for the hills or you can lift up your eyes beyond the hills and to the Lord "who made heaven and earth" (Psalm 121:2), facing the crisis with confidence and, yes, even joy.

PSALM 11

FEBRUARY 21

PRAYER AND GOD'S SOVEREIGNTY

"I know that through your prayers and the help of the Spirit of Jesus Christ this will turn out for my deliverance." PHILIPPIANS 1:19

Your prayers change things.

The apostle Paul understood this well. The book of Acts charts the rapid expansion of the church throughout the eastern Mediterranean world, fueled in large part by his three great missionary journeys. Yet it concludes with Paul living under house arrest at his own expense for two whole years (Acts 28:30). From a human perspective, it would seem that by this point his situation was hopeless. The Jews had been trying to kill him for years. He'd been in a series of trials because of trumped-up charges. He'd faced shipwreck, beatings, and hardships. And now he was chained to a Roman soldier, with no freedom to come and go as he pleased. His circumstances seemed to indicate that everything was against him and against what God might accomplish through him.

Yet in the midst of Paul's difficult circumstances, he was confident in the power of prayer. During his Roman imprisonment, Paul wrote to the Philippian church, "I know that *through your prayers* and the help of the Spirit of Jesus Christ this will turn out for my deliverance." He also wrote a letter to his friend Philemon that contained the following words: "Prepare a guest room for me, for I am hoping that *through your prayers* I will be graciously given to you" (Philemon 22, emphasis added).

Paul's letters indicate that he was confident that he would be released from prison, and he believed that his deliverance would come by means of the prayers of his believing friends. And though Acts never mentions Paul's release, we can be fairly confident, from reading his other letters and Acts side by side, that he was indeed allowed to leave.

Paul was convinced that God was sovereign and that He was working everything out according to the eternal counsel of His will (Ephesians 1:11). But at the same time, he was not a determinist—he did not believe that nothing we do matters because nothing we do changes anything. That is because he knew that very often God works His plans out through means—through people. So Paul didn't think that God's sovereignty made prayer irrelevant, because he understood that God had ordained not only the end to which he was moving but also the means that would bring him there—means that included the prayers of God's people.

God commands and expects you to pray. In a mysterious way that you cannot fully comprehend, your prayers are enfolded into the great outworking of His purposes. So when your life ceases to make sense and everything appears to be against you, don't assume that God's purposes for you have been thwarted. Direct your gaze to Him and ask others to join you in prayer. It may be that their prayers are the sovereign means that God will use to bring about your deliverance—for in His kindness, God has ordained that the prayers of His people really do change things.

LUKE 11:1-13

FEBRUARY 22

HEARING, BELIEVING, AND ACTING

"By faith the walls of Jericho fell down after they had been encircled for seven days." HEBREWS 11:30

If we desire to see fortresses fall, to see the gates of hell unhinged and laid in the dirt, to see pagan philosophies dismantled and the rampages of evil in our world torn down, we need to hear God's word, believe it, and act in obedience to it. In other words, we need to learn from Joshua and the Israelites at the walls of Jericho.

When God's people crossed into the promised land and reached the strategically vital city of Jericho, it was "shut up inside and outside because of the people of Israel. None went out, and none came in" (Joshua 6:1). Jericho was an impenetrable city. But the Lord came to Joshua and said, "See, I have given Jericho into your hand, with its king and mighty men of valor" (v 2). The means by which He would deliver the city to His people were detailed, and peculiar: they were to march round the city for six days and then seven times more on the seventh day, this time with the priests blowing their trumpets. In response to God's promise, Joshua called the priests and armed men of Israel before him and conveyed the Lord's word to the people, who then "went forward, blowing the trumpets, with the ark of the covenant of the LORD following them" as they marched around the city (v 8).

Why would anybody in their right mind do such a thing? The only plausible explanation is that the people had *heard* the word of the Lord spoken, *believed* that it was true, and *acted* in obedience. If this plan had been absent the word of God, it would have been nonsensical. If it had been heard by people who lacked real belief, they would never have carried it out. Because, and only because, Joshua and his men heard God's message and put their faith in Him, they responded in obedience.

God's way so often is to make a promise and then issue a command that makes no sense without that promise. He promised Noah that a flood was coming and commanded him to build the ark. He promised Abram that He would give him a family and land and commanded him to leave almost everything he had ever known. He promised Moses that He would rescue the people from Egypt and commanded him to make demands of the most powerful monarch in the world. Faith hears the promise, hears the command, believes both, and acts in obedience.

If we want to exercise faith on a daily basis in order that, like a muscle, it may grow to maturity, we have to abide in God's word. We have to read it and ask, "What am I being promised? What am I being commanded? What will obedience look like in my life today?" This kind of daily communion with the Lord through His word strengthens our faith and produces steadfast obedience so that as we live our Christian lives, as we persevere through trials, as we obey God simply and only because we believe His promises to us, God says, *I'll bring the walls down.*

JOSHUA 6:1-20

FEBRUARY 23

RELIGIOUS FORMALISM

"They brought to the Pharisees the man who had formerly been blind."
JOHN 9:13

The great tragedy of John 9 is not that a man had been blind for years until he met Jesus, but that a group of men were left spiritually blind despite having seen the work of Jesus.

The healing and transformation of the life of the man born blind caused a great stir in his community. Presumably he had been so much a part of people's surroundings that it was easy to disregard him. Yet suddenly their normal daily experience was disrupted. The man who was once blind could now see perfectly well, and he was no longer asking for money (John 9:8-10).

Unable to solve this mystery, they presented the formerly blind man to the religious leaders, the Pharisees, to see if they could shed some light on what had occurred. What followed was not a conversation between the man and the Pharisees so much as an interrogation. Instead of rejoicing in his story, they challenged his testimony.

The reason for the Pharisees' harsh reaction, at least on the surface, was that the man had been healed on the Sabbath (John 9:14-16). The religious leaders were unable to rejoice in the restoration of his sight because they were blinded by their religious formalism. The forms and structures of religion that they boasted in were the very things that proved to be a barrier to their faith in Jesus. They kept their lists of what was acceptable, and so they were unable to recognize the work of the God they claimed to worship, even when the evidence was quite literally (and miraculously) looking them in the face.

Religious formalism cannot face the dramatic impact that Jesus makes when He takes a person and turns him or her upside down—which is actually to turn them the right way up! Unwilling to acknowledge their own need for transformation—and the truth that only a radical internal transformation gives significance to the religious life—religious formalists hide behind maintaining appearances. Nothing challenges the religious formalist more than coming face-to-face with someone who has had their eyes opened to the salvation that is found in Jesus.

The Pharisees' reaction to the blind man's healing teaches us, then, to beware of the dangers of religious formalism. A blind commitment to religion has the potential to keep us from Jesus, just as it did with them.

Have your eyes been opened to the salvation found only in Jesus? Or has your focus on religious performance prevented you from rejoicing in the wonder of God's amazing grace? Are you weighed down by religion's burden or rejoicing in the awesome, often surprising work of the Lord Jesus? Look to Him alone for salvation and accept that He will not be constrained by your assumptions, for then you'll find a joy, a transformation, and an excitement in the gospel that no amount of rule-keeping could ever provide.

PHILIPPIANS 3:1-11

Bible Through The Year: Exodus 19–20; 1 Thessalonians 5

FEBRUARY 24

THE GIVER OF LAW AND LIBERTY

"God spoke all these words, saying, 'I am the LORD your God, who brought you out of the land of Egypt, out of the house of slavery.'" EXODUS 20:1-2

To faithfully read and respond to the Ten Commandments, we must first understand what they are and are not. We find clarity in the truth that lies at their head: "I am the LORD your God." This reminder of who God is precedes the instructions that follow. In other words, the *I am* of God's person grounds the *you shall* of His commands. He can command us because of who He is. The psalmist further expresses this: "Know that the LORD, he is God! It is he who made us, and we are his" (Psalm 100:3). God created us, and His being our Creator grants Him rights and authority over His creation. Regardless of the efforts of our world to reject the creational handiwork of God and thus His authority over our lives, His role as our Ruler remains unthreatened. He has made us; we are His.

When we remember who spoke the law, we are in a position to grasp the purpose of the Ten Commandments as well as to understand what they are *not.*

First, the commandments are not a formal list of dos and don'ts given to restrict our personal freedoms. God is not some cosmic killjoy. In fact, if you wanted to provide a heading for the Ten Commandments, you could call them "Guidelines to Freedom." They do not restrict our freedom but rather give us a blueprint for joy, showing us how life works best. Second, the commandments are not intended as a ladder up which we climb to attain acceptance with God. No such ladder has ever existed! God brought His people out of slavery—from Egypt in the exodus, and from sin and death at the cross—before He called us to obey Him. So we obey because we've been "brought out," not in order to persuade Him to do so. Rather than being rules that save us, the Ten Commandments serve as a mirror in which we see ourselves, revealing the depth of our sin and our need for a Savior—and they show how we can live to please our Savior. Third, the Ten Commandments have not been rendered obsolete by the coming of Christ. When Jesus said that the two greatest commandments were to love God and love our neighbor, He was summarizing the Ten Commandments (Mark 12:28-31). What does it mean to love God with our heart, soul, mind, and strength? The first four commandments tell us. What does it look like to love our neighbor as ourselves? The final six commandments flesh that out. Jesus, master teacher that He was, summed up the ten with the two.

When you see all this, you are ready to read the Ten Commandments and let them transform your life. You must see the sin that the commandments reveal and respond in repentance and faith in the one who fulfilled the law and offers Himself as your Savior. He, the Lord Jesus Christ, will ensure that this law is not merely etched into your conscience but also inscribed on your heart. Give yourself to the Lord and His ways, and you'll find everlasting joy and liberty.

EXODUS 20:1-17

FEBRUARY 25

NO OTHER GODS BEFORE ME

"I am the LORD your God, who brought you out of the land of Egypt, out of the house of slavery. You shall have no other gods before me." EXODUS 20:2-3

Perhaps the most basic truth about the God of Scripture is that He is the only one. There is no other. This truth ought to simplify things for us because it teaches us that there is only one who is the worthy object of our love, loyalty, and devotion. But the hearts of men and women are not so easily instructed. And so it is necessary for God to give us the first commandment: "You shall have no other gods before me." The danger is not that there are actual other gods for us to worship but that we have a proclivity for making them.

On first glance, this first command is straightforward. To live for a god other than the true God would be like taking a second spouse while your first spouse is still alive and still happy to be your spouse. Worse, it would be like taking a second spouse who is in truth a figment of your imagination. It would be a breach of an exclusive relationship.

We must not kid ourselves that we are immune from the possibility of breaking this commandment. Many of us read it and picture people bowing down before statues or going through elaborate rituals, and those mental images assure us that we're not in danger of violating it. Yet the commandments are not restricted to outward actions but also relate to the disposition of our minds and hearts. From this perspective, we may not be as far from those mental images as we assume. We may not have statues to which we bow down, but maybe we have segments of our lives that we keep away from God, preserving them under the authority of some other little "deity"—ourselves, perhaps.

Ask yourself: "Do I joyfully acknowledge God's comprehensive claim on my life? Is God in charge of my family, my work, my relationships, my money, my dating, my use of time?" Take a close and honest look to see if there are portions of life you try to keep from Him.

In addition to keeping things away from God, another form of danger is functionally replacing Him. When we put our family, our job, our hobbies, or anything else in the place that is God's alone, we violate the first commandment. To the degree that we allow anyone or anything besides obedience to God to direct our course day to day, we defy His law.

So we are not so safe from the possibility of breaking this commandment as we may think! While we must acknowledge the truth that there is one God, we must also beware our own ability to put things in His place. If we do not daily submit ourselves to Him and entrust the entirety of our lives to Him, something will take His place. We are made to worship. The question is, are you going to worship the living God or are you going to pretend there is another?

1 JOHN 1:8 – 2:3

FEBRUARY 26

NO IMAGE ENGRAVED OR IN MIND

"You shall not make for yourself a carved image, or any likeness of anything that is in heaven above, or that is in the earth beneath, or that is in the water under the earth." EXODUS 20:4

If the first commandment—"You shall have no other gods before me" (Exodus 20:3)—deals with the *object* of our worship, the second commandment deals with the *manner* of our worship. What the second commandment tells us is that it is not enough that we worship the correct God; we must also worship Him correctly.

The clear and immediate meaning of the command is that God is to be worshiped without any visual symbols of Him. Why the prohibition? Because God is spirit: infinite and unfathomably great. No physical representation could ever do justice to His glory and grandeur. The problem with statues, shrines, and pictures is not that they don't look good but that no matter how good they look, they will inevitably blur the truth about God's nature and character. Such images tend to distract men and women from worshiping the true and living God, instead leading them to worship whatever representation is before them.

Yet the second commandment takes us beyond mere images and idol-making and into our own thought life. Our hands may be innocent of making graven images, but our imaginations seldom are. Any conception of God in our minds and hearts that is not derived from Scripture runs foul of this command.

When God gave instructions for the building of the temple, He ordered that the ark of the covenant, on which His presence would dwell, should reside in the Most Holy Place (Exodus 26:34). What was inside the ark? Perhaps most significant is what was *not* in it: it contained no visible representation of God. Instead, there were the two tablets of the Ten Commandments. It was as if God was saying to His people, as He says to us, *Don't look for Me in shrines, paintings, or statues. I'm not there. Look for Me in My word.*

And so we take our cues from God. If we want to worship Him—if we want to meet with Him and know what He is like—we must conform our minds to His word. Our own attempts to conceive of God apart from divine revelation will invariably fail. He has published His truth in His word, and so we are to tether ourselves to what is revealed there.

What's at stake in this is the integrity not only of our worship but also of our lives—because when people go wrong in their worship, they end up wrong in their living. Anything and anyone that encourages us to worship the correct God incorrectly will prove to be a detriment to our spiritual growth. What a tragedy it would be to embrace an image and miss the person of Christ, to sit at a shrine and miss the Savior, to worship a misconception and fail to know Jesus. Instead, resist the urge to modify God in your mind or conform Him to your own image, and be sure to know Him as He has revealed Himself.

ISAIAH 40:12-25

FEBRUARY 27

DO NOT TAKE HIS NAME IN VAIN

"You shall not take the name of the L*ORD your God in vain, for the* L*ORD will not hold him guiltless who takes his name in vain."* EXODUS 20:7

If we were to take a poll asking people which of the Ten Commandments they regard as the least significant, I wonder if the "winner" would be the third. When compared to false gods and graven images, the third command doesn't seem like such a serious offense. But if the one who wrongly uses the name of God incurs guilt, then it must be important—and we need to understand why.

Scripture is clear that God's name is precious and powerful. One place where we see this is in the encounters between God and Moses. In Exodus 33, Moses asks God to reveal His glory. His request invites a death sentence because it is not possible to see God's glory and live. But God graciously grants the request in a way that prevents Moses' demise, for He demonstrates His glory not by a physical manifestation but by revealing His name: "The *LORD*, the *LORD*, a God merciful and gracious" (Exodus 34:6; emphasis added). His name reveals His character, which in turn reveals His glory.

Earlier, in Exodus 3, God had revealed Himself to Moses in the burning bush. Moses had been tasked with a weighty mission and wanted to know what to say when people asked who had sent him. God told Moses to say, "I AM has sent me to you" (Exodus 3:14). By using a form of the verb *to be* to name Himself, God declared that He is self-existent, self-sufficient, and sovereign, depending on no one and nothing. Who else can claim such a name?

In declaring and disclosing Himself, God does not merely identify Himself; He reveals the wonder of who He is. So to misuse God's name is to misunderstand His greatness and glory. Only when we grasp this can we understand why the third commandment is so significant.

In what ways, then, might we break this commandment? For one, we break it every time we use God's name to strengthen our vows and promises, bringing down the name of divinity in order to make ourselves sound more believable (James 5:12). We also blaspheme God when we use His name in anger, in arrogance, or in defiance of who He is. We misuse His name when we utter falsehoods and use it to back them up. Perhaps closer to home, in every worship service we attend where we worship God with our lips only and not from our heart, we break the third commandment.

Only when we see the glory of God's name and when we use it in praise, love, prayer, obedience, and gratitude do we understand why our Lord Jesus taught us to pray, "Our Father which art in heaven, *Hallowed* be thy name" (Matthew 6:9, KJV, emphasis added). His name is to be hallowed because it proclaims who He is, reveals His character, and is a strong refuge for all who call on it (Proverbs 18:10). And it is to be hallowed in the lives of His people—including in *your* life, as you bear the name of Christ and take it on your lips with reverence and love.

EXODUS 3:1-22

FEBRUARY 28

KEEP THE SABBATH, PART ONE

"Remember the Sabbath day, to keep it holy." EXODUS 20:8

Throughout history there have been well-meaning, earnest Christians who have, perhaps without knowing it, functionally believed that the Ten Commandments are really only the Nine Commandments. Somewhere along the way, some have decided that the fourth commandment is not like the rest of the commandments but rather is a relic that belongs in the past. In truth, though, the command to remember the Sabbath and keep it holy has abiding significance for us all, even today.

Why has this simple command fallen on such hard times? Some have claimed that its regulations and penalties were tied to the old covenant, so it must no longer be relevant. Yet we don't treat the other commandments this way. Others have said that the way Jesus spoke of being "lord of the Sabbath" (Matthew 12:8) diminished the commandment's significance and force. But what Jesus sought to overturn was not the Sabbath itself but the external rules of the Pharisees.

I suspect that what keeps most Christians from thinking of the fourth commandment as we ought to is simply that we don't like its implications. We don't like the way it intrudes into our lives, our leisure, and whatever else takes precedence in our hearts. And so we act as though this command is in a different category from the other nine.

If we want to grasp the significance of the Sabbath and respond to it in a God-honoring way, we must embrace, as a *conviction*, the truth that God has set aside the Sabbath day as distinct from the rest. This was the case in the week of creation, with God resting on the seventh day and declaring it sanctified. The church, in the age of the new covenant, then changed the day from the seventh of the week to the first to mark the resurrection of Christ. In both cases, we see that the distinction of the day is woven into God's work of creation and redemption.

With that conviction in place, we can see that the day is not simply a day set apart *from* other days, but it is a day set apart *to* the Lord. If we don't see it this way, we will be tempted to view our spiritual exercises on the Lord's Day as something to "get over with" in order to "get on with" our week. If this is our mentality, we stand condemned by the fourth commandment.

The Sabbath ought to be treasured for what it is: a gift of a day on which we enjoy, uninterrupted by leisure commitments or (if at all possible) by employment, the privilege of God's presence, the study of God's word, and the fellowship of God's people. Seen like that, this command becomes an invitation: not only something we *should* do but something we will *love* to do. If this is not how you have been viewing God's Sabbath, then ask yourself: What's preventing you from honoring the Lord's Day? Take stock of your habits and receive the gift of the Sabbath. From next Sunday, be sure that your priority is not to make the Lord's Day convenient but to keep it holy.

HEBREWS 4:1-11

MARCH 1

KEEP THE SABBATH, PART TWO

"Six days you shall labor, and do all your work, but the seventh day is a Sabbath to the LORD your God." EXODUS 20:9-10

Having established that the fourth commandment remains what it has always been—a commandment of the Lord—and as such is relevant to our lives, we can now think profitably about how to keep it. But we must be careful as we get specific about honoring the Sabbath. The Lord Jesus, after all, had some very strong words for the Pharisees regarding the way their moral specificity had become a means not of obedience but of self-righteousness (Mark 2:23 – 3:6).

With trembling and humility, then, let's consider how are we to remember the Sabbath and keep it holy. How do we prevent worldly concerns—those of leisure, recreation, and work—from infringing on our enjoyment and worship of God?

Let's think first of public worship. What kinds of conversations do you typically have prior to the worship service? Are they concerned at any point with the things of God, or only ever with sports, family, and every other thing? It takes an act of the will to give eternal matters priority in our minds and mouths. If you were to determine that in your preparation for worship you would set aside every priority which looms so large on other days, I guarantee your time at church would be changed.

The same goes for after the service. When the last song has been sung and the service is over, how long does it take for your mind and conversation to return to worldly matters? If we were instead to commit to spending time after the service speaking to one another about the greatness of God, the truth of His word, and the wonder of His dealings with us, and praying with one another about the week ahead and the trials we face, then we would begin to understand better the "one another" passages in the New Testament about encouraging one another (Hebrews 10:25), speaking the truth to one another (Ephesians 4:25), and building one another up (1 Thessalonians 5:11)—for we would be living them out.

Similarly, in our private affairs on the Lord's Day, spiritual improvement should still take priority. That may mean family worship, reading edifying books, prayer, discussion of what was preached that morning, and more—but whatever it means, we should make it our aim not to let the cares of the other six days push into our spiritual enjoyment of the first day of the week.

If you want to profit from keeping the Sabbath, and if you want to take the fourth commandment seriously, then your conviction must fuel your action, and aspiration must turn into practice. Avoid making rules that only foster self-righteousness, but consider whether anything needs to change. How will you keep the Sabbath holy the next time Sunday comes round?

ISAIAH 58:13 –59:2

MARCH 2

HONORING PARENTS, HONORING GOD

"Honor your father and your mother." EXODUS 20:12

The fifth commandment is simultaneously a simple instruction and an indispensable element of the well-being of entire societies. When the Lord gives the command "Honor your father and mother," He is laying down the blueprint for maintaining the stability of families, communities, and nations.

What does it mean to honor your parents? The word for "honor" carries the notion of weight and heaviness; children ought to *feel the weight* of respect for their parents. Parents are owed such regard because God has placed them in their roles, and the stewardship of such a role is worth its weight in honor. While children are in view here, the Bible also has much to say about parenting that honors God (see Ephesians 6:4; Colossians 3:21).

How does a child display this honor? In several ways. For one, a child ought to show practical respect to his or her parents. This can be as simple as speaking well of our parents, showing them courtesy, looking them in the eye, and addressing them with a due sense of deference. Second, it involves genuine love; there should be heartfelt expressions of affection between parents and their children. Third, unless it would involve disobeying God, a child ought to obey what his or her mom and dad say. This expectation is found all over Proverbs: for example, "Hear, my son, your father's instruction, and forsake not your mother's teaching" (Proverbs 1:8). Fourth, a child should submit to their parents' discipline. All good parents discipline their children (though it must not be done in anger nor vindictively or disproportionately), and children ought to trust that such discipline is for their good (Hebrews 12:5-11).

In ancient Israel, respect for parents was valued so highly that those who disregarded it flagrantly or persistently faced the death penalty (Deuteronomy 21:18-21). Why such a significant consequence? Because the home provides a vital training ground, the success of which affects how the child will relate to authorities of all kinds. We never outrun authority in our lives. There are political authorities we are called to obey (Romans 13:1-7), spiritual authorities we are to respect (Hebrews 13:17; 1 Thessalonians 5:12), and those of advanced years we are commanded to honor (Leviticus 19:32). Most significantly, when children learn to honor their parents, even despite their parents' many imperfections, they learn what it means to honor our perfect heavenly Father. Reverence for parents is an integral part of reverence for God. Because their authority is God-given, to honor them is to honor God Himself.

So if you are a parent with children at home, it is not loving (though it may be easier) to fail to insist that your children honor you. And if you are an adult with parents still living, it is a matter of obedience to God that you show them the honor they are due, not according to how well (or otherwise) you feel they raised you but according to the position the Lord gave them. As you honor them, you will be pleasing Him and showing those around you that God-given authority, when exercised in a godly way, is a blessing to all.

EPHESIANS 6:1-4

MARCH 3

LIFE IS SACRED

"You shall not murder." EXODUS 20:13

If you want to cut to the chase in learning how someone views the world, ask him or her why it's wrong to murder. The question gets at the issue of human life and its value—which is the issue addressed in the sixth commandment. It also gets past political differences and reveals what people think about life's meaning, purpose, and origin.

A vast number of people functionally think that life has no inherent value beyond someone's usefulness. So long as an individual contributes to society, his or her value remains intact. But this means that some deaths—abortion and euthanasia, for example—are deemed less tragic and perhaps even "good" because that person is unwanted or perceived as a drain on society and therefore, in the final analysis, of inferior worth.

This is not the way the Bible speaks. Scripture could not be clearer about the fact that men and women are valuable because they are made in God's image (Genesis 1:26; Psalm 8:5-6). Such value does not move along a spectrum but is fixed and immovable. Only when we see human life in this way, as God does, do we understand all that is implied in the simple command "You shall not murder."

Here are three ways unfortunately common ways we might violate the vision of life in the sixth commandment. First is *homicide*. God is the Giver of life, and He alone has the authority to take it. To wrongfully take someone's life is to make an assault on the divine image (Genesis 9:5-6). Second is *suicide*, the act of willfully causing one's own death. God says, "All souls are mine" (Ezekiel 18:4); we do not have the right to take our own life (though that is not to say that this cannot be forgiven). A third is *abortion*. From the moment of conception, the fetus in the womb is a human being (Psalm 139:13). The fact that for several months that child cannot survive outside the womb does not affect his or her right to the same protection given to other human beings (though again, there is forgiveness available for violating the sixth commandment in this way).

Perhaps you've made it this far and think you're doing fine. Not so fast! Jesus does not let us off that easily, for He says that the judgment the murderer deserves is also deserved by the one with unchecked anger (Matthew 5:21-22). All of us, if we're honest, have known murder in our hearts. We've harbored thoughts of contemptuous anger and its ugly bedfellows—animosity, malice, hostility, and gossip—whereby we kill people in our hearts all the time. Perhaps we are doing so right now. And so we stand condemned.

But here is the encouragement: if you are feeling the weight of guilt as you grasp the scope and gravity of this commandment, that is precisely the point! You will never conform perfectly to the perfect law of God—but He has still offered forgiveness that will wash away your sin and your guilt. Beyond that, He offers transformation—the kind that can take angry, murderous hearts and transform them into hearts of love and grace. Of what do you need to repent? For what do you need to be forgiven? In what way do you need the Spirit to change you?

MATTHEW 5:21-26

MARCH 4

THE FREEDOM OF PURITY

"You shall not commit adultery." EXODUS 20:14

Of all the lies proclaimed in the world around us, one of the most widely believed is that any limits imposed on personal freedom amount to oppression. This is perhaps most clear in the realm of sexual morality, where the only thing off limits seems to be the setting of limits itself. The tragic irony is that this so-called freedom is in truth bondage to sinful desires, and it results not in wholeness but in broken bodies and broken hearts.

What God's word tells us when it comes to sexual morality is straightforward: we are to practice chastity outside marriage and fidelity within it. This is the path not to oppression but to true liberty and blessing (James 1:25). That is why the seventh commandment is what it is: "You shall not commit adultery." In marriage, two people enter into a covenant, becoming one. And this comprehensive union, in which husband and wife become interwoven emotionally, physically, spiritually, and in every other dimension, serves as a parable of the relationship between Christ and His bride, the church (Ephesians 5:22-33). The sacred union is not, then, to be intruded upon or broken (Matthew 19:6).

When a husband or wife commits adultery, it sets off a chain reaction of tragedies: there is sin against God, against the body, against the spouse, against the partner in adultery, and against the partner's spouse. In other words, disaster ensues. Sex is intended for the marriage bond alone, so when you remove it from that context, it becomes monstrous, consuming, and devastating.

Yet we ought not to think that adultery is limited to just the physical act. We learn from the Lord Jesus that adultery starts internally: "I say to you that everyone who looks at a woman with lustful intent has already committed adultery with her in his heart" (Matthew 5:28). We know, of course, that the consequences of physical adultery far outpace those of lust, but the deserved judgment and our guilt before God are equal no matter the sin.

What can Christian men and women do to guard themselves and one another against adulterous acts and thoughts? For starters, we can practice the presence of God, communing with Him and remembering that we have no secrets before Him. We can memorize the word of God, filling our hearts with it that we might not sin against Him (Psalm 119:11). And we can stick with the people of God, pursuing fellowship in worship and accountability, all to the end of being stirred up to love and good deeds (Hebrews 10:24-25).

Nevertheless, we all stand guilty before the seventh commandment. We are in no position to look down on others or see ourselves as spotless. Our lives, our hands, and our thoughts do not pass the test of purity. And yet you are never out of the reach of God's grace in Christ, no matter how much baggage you carry. If you truly and earnestly repent of your sins, if you truly and earnestly cast yourself upon God's mercy and grace, you will be forgiven, pardoned, cleansed, and set free—free for the Spirit of God to work in your life, enabling you to think and live in a way that pleases Him.

1 THESSALONIANS 4:1-8

MARCH 5

GUILTY THIEVES

"You shall not steal." EXODUS 20:15

This eighth commandment is, on its face, a simple instruction. But like all of Scripture, the commandments reward prayerful reflection. And when we approach this command carefully, we find that it reaches further into our lives than we first imagined.

To understand the true offense of stealing, we need to see the two biblical principles that undergird the eighth commandment. One is the right to private property; the other is the sovereign ownership of God over all He has made. In other words, God owns all things, and He grants temporary stewardship to us. So to steal something from someone is an offense against God as the ultimate owner and against the person who is stewarding it.

We will not, however, fully understand this commandment until we grasp the various ways it extends into our lives. Stealing can take many forms. There are the more obvious ones:

- blatant theft
- borrowing something we fail to return
- keeping dishonest records
- misusing our employer's time
- paying unjust wages, withholding wages, or delaying wages

But there are other, less obvious ways to steal, which this commandment also speaks to:

- slandering others, thereby stealing their reputation
- sinning sexually with another, thereby stealing their moral purity
- plagiarizing, thereby stealing someone else's work
- cheating in the classroom
- failing to give God what we owe Him (Malachi 3:8)

The eighth commandment leaves no stone of our lives unturned, and, if we are honest, we all find ourselves guilty of breaking it in one way or another. Yet in His grace and wisdom God not only tells us what *not* to do; He also tells us what to *pursue*: "Let the thief no longer steal, but rather let him labor, doing honest work with his own hands, so that he may have something to share with anyone in need" (Ephesians 4:28). The right response to the eighth commandment is not merely not to steal but to commit ourselves to lives of honesty, integrity, hard work, and generosity.

This is what we see in the life of Zacchaeus. He was a tax collector and guilty of stealing, yet when he encountered the Lord Jesus, he repented of his sin and restored what he had stolen, committing himself to making things right (Luke 19:7-8). This is what repentance and obedience look like when it comes to this command. So consider first: How have I been guilty of stealing? Of what am I being called to repent? And then ask yourself: How will I now commit myself to giving and sharing where once I was stealing?

2 THESSALONIANS 3:6-13

MARCH 6

TELL THE TRUTH

"You shall not bear false witness against your neighbor." EXODUS 20:16

Every command of Scripture serves not only as an instruction for our lives but also as a reflection of who God is. The command against adultery is rooted in His faithfulness. The forbidding of murder flows from the life-giving Lord. So it is with the ninth commandment against bearing false witness, which comes from the promise-keeping God of all truth, who does not and cannot lie (Numbers 23:19).

What does the Lord have in view when He instructs us not to bear false witness? It is surely safe to assume that this commandment concerns any form of speech that is less than truthful. There are many ways we fall short. We do it by outright deceit, when we provide false information or withhold the truth in some way. We do it when we participate in rumors, spreading gossip about others. We do it by slandering and flattering others. We do it when we exaggerate the truth, give false impressions, and are careless with the facts. All of this falls short of the divine standard.

A vital component of fighting against the temptation to lie is to understand why we lie in the first place. The source of lies is none other than Satan himself, about whom Jesus says, "When he lies, he speaks out of his own character, for he is a liar and the father of lies" (John 8:44). Deceit was his strategy in the Garden of Eden, when he approached Eve with a lying tongue. Tragically, we are often driven by the same motives as the Evil One when we lie: pride, hatred, and fear. We lie out of pride when we want others to think highly of us. We deceive out of hatred because we want to tear down someone else. We speak untruth out of a fear of the consequences that we think would result from the truth being known. In all of this, we lie because in those moments we love ourselves more than we love God and our neighbors.

The reality is that God hates deception (Proverbs 6:16-19). In order for us to walk in the truth, we must crucify our pride and be more concerned with what God thinks of us than with what someone else thinks of us. We must put away malice and pursue love for others, committing to never speaking slanderously or spreading gossip. And we must fight an ungodly fear of man, replacing it with the fear of God, who came in flesh and declared Himself to be "the way, and the truth, and the life" (John 14:6).

The Lord Jesus has given His people His Spirit of truth (John 15:26), who empowers us to walk in the truth and put away falsehood. Only by His power are we increasingly conformed into the image of Christ and ever more reflecting the character of the God who gave the ninth commandment. Consider now in which situations and in what ways you are most often tempted to bear false witness. How will the truth about Jesus, His saving gospel, and His indwelling Spirit motivate you to speak differently from now on—to speak the truth, as a follower of *the* truth?

PROVERBS 6:16-19

MARCH 7

NOT CONTENT TO COVET

"You shall not covet your neighbor's house; you shall not covet your neighbor's wife, or his male servant, or his female servant, or his ox, or his donkey, or anything that is your neighbor's." EXODUS 20:17

The Ten Commandments do not go easy on us as they come to their close. Each of the four commands prior to the tenth deal primarily (though not exclusively) with our actions. This one takes a different approach, taking aim at our desires and our attitudes.

When God forbids coveting, He confronts us with a seemingly universal problem—the desire to have for ourselves what God has chosen to give to another. The object of our envy may take any number of forms—prestige, positions, and possessions, to name just a few. The apostle John knew how easily our hearts fall into coveting when he warned us, "Do not love the world or the things in the world … All that is in the world—the desires of the flesh and the desires of the eyes and pride of life—is not from the Father but is from the world" (1 John 2:15-17).

In addition to understanding what and how easily we are tempted to covet, it's important to acknowledge the ruinous effects coveting has on us. It spoils relationships and lies behind many of our disagreements; it is impossible to love someone while we covet something they have. It makes us selfish. And it causes us to fixate on material things.

All of these effects are touched on by one of Jesus' warnings related to coveting. When a man approached Him with concerns about his inheritance, Jesus bypassed the question to get to the heart of the problem—and the warning is precisely what our covetous hearts need to hear: "Take care, and be on your guard against all covetousness, for one's life does not consist in the abundance of his possessions" (Luke 12:15). How easily we forget this very truth, believing instead that true and lasting joy would be ours if we could only have a little more money, a little more fame, a little more free time, or a little more of whatever else we see others enjoying and covet for ourselves.

So how do we combat this dangerous sin? If coveting is a disordering of our desires, then we must actively cultivate *right* desires. Through Bible reading and prayer, through worship and fellowship, we can increase our appetite for godly things, all the while purposefully shrinking our appetite for worldly things. These kinds of habits will lead us into lives of contentment, so that we can say with the psalmist, "Whom have I in heaven but you? And there is nothing on earth that I desire besides you. My flesh and my heart may fail, but God is the strength of my heart and my portion forever" (Psalm 73:25-26).

Do you long for your heart to be content? Do you want to guard against coveting? Then seek and find satisfaction in God alone. Next time you find you are sad for yourself rather than happy for another because they have a blessing that you do not, ask God to enable you to say to yourself, and to mean, "There is nothing on earth as great as knowing God. There is no earthly blessing that can endure to eternity. Therefore, I shall be satisfied in Him, and Him alone."

PHILIPPIANS 4:8-13

MARCH 8

A PATH OF PEACE

"When he drew near and saw the city, he wept over it, saying, 'Would that you, even you, had known on this day the things that make for peace! But now they are hidden from your eyes.'" LUKE 19:41-42

Here is an opportunity to look, in the words of some past theologians, into "the human face of God."

As the Son of God entered the city of God, Jerusalem, He wept. Why? He was shedding tears of compassion for its people, on account of the judgment that awaited them. Jesus loved the city, and He knew that the people who greeted Him did not understand the kind of peace He would bring—the peace that comes with *knowing* Him—and that many would reject Him and the offer of peace that He brought.

It wasn't that the Jews were disinterested in peace. Indeed, they longed for it. But they thought it would come militarily or politically—that Jesus' arrival would bring them triumph over the Roman authorities. They thought the peace they needed most was a horizontal peace. They didn't know that in their desire for that peace they were in fact rejecting the message Jesus was bringing and the offer of a great peace He was making. On account of their ignorance and their blindness, then, Jesus wept.

In many ways, we are no different from the Jews who witnessed that first Holy Week. By nature, we experience the same blindness because of our sin. We tend to think of sin in terms of what we shouldn't have done but have, or what we've failed to do even though we know we should. But in actual fact sin is a condition before it is an action. It blinds us to any awareness that we are at enmity with God. We cannot see our need for peace with God. We cannot see that all the other ways in which we lack peace horizontally stem ultimately from our lack of that vertical peace with our Maker. We cannot see the provision that has been made for peace through Jesus.

This lack of peace pervades individual hearts as well as families, communities, and nations. Only a relationship with the Prince of Peace can show us that He who once came to conquer sin and will come again to rule and reign as King also came as a prophet to speak into our ignorance and blindness.

The Bible says that it is first in knowing peace *with* God that we discover the peace *of* God—and that peace has been granted in the person and work of Jesus. So, meditate on the peace that you enjoy with your Creator because of the death and resurrection of His Son. Give thanks that His Spirit has opened your eyes to that which was hidden by sin from the city of Jerusalem. And pray that your heart would be as compassionate as His was, so that you weep over those who are seeking peace everywhere except where it may truly be found, and so that your tears cause you to hold out the offer of the peace that Jesus came to give and died to make.

COLOSSIANS 1:15-23

MARCH 9

BOASTING IN WEAKNESS

"'Let the one who boasts, boast in the Lord.' For it is not the one who commends himself who is approved, but the one whom the Lord commends." 2 CORINTHIANS 10:17-18

The world has always been quick to encourage people to believe in and boast in themselves. In Paul's day, as now, the more you were able to say about yourself, what you'd done, and what you were planning to do, the greater the possibility that you'd advance your career, be well-liked, and prove yourself a "success." And this thinking, if we are not careful, pervades our perspective on our lives, including our personal ministries. We ask ourselves, "Have I done 'great' things? Am I well-liked? Have I been a success?" But according to Paul, "What you say about yourself means nothing in God's work. It's what God says about you that makes the difference" (2 Corinthians 10:18, MSG).

Paul's second letter to the Corinthian church is part of a very personal correspondence. Part of this letter involves a lengthy defense of his ministry in the face of strong criticism. While Paul isn't concerned for his own reputation, he *is* concerned for the members of the body of Christ under his shepherding care. And out of that care emerge significant truths concerning boasting and humility, which we must take to heart.

Paul could easily have matched his critics in their own boasting (2 Corinthians 11:21b-23a), but instead he took a different approach (v 23b-29). Instead of bragging about his status and his service to God, he ran through an extensive list of his sufferings and weaknesses. He shared these failures, these weaknesses, because he viewed them as assets, as the key to knowing and experiencing God's power and the ways in which God had weakened him before working through him. The principle here is often lost. We want everybody to know that we have it together, that we're successful, that we don't have any problems. But what are we doing? We're making much of our accomplishments instead of making much of Christ! We're giving the impression of our strength rather than relying on God's. We put a fake shine on our old clay pots (2 Corinthians 4:7), forgetting that the beauty and usefulness come from what the pot holds: Christ's power, which fills and flows over and through our cracks, our weaknesses.

We cannot boast in what God is doing as though we deserve it or boast in what God is doing through us as though we did it all ourselves. There is nothing uglier than spiritual pride—a boasting in something not our own, a boasting in something God-given. Where there is spiritual pride, there is no view of the cross. Make sure that in your successes and in your failings your song remains the same:

Naught have I gotten but what I received;
Grace hath bestowed it when I have believed;
Boasting excluded, pride I abase;
I'm only a sinner, saved by grace![21]

2 CORINTHIANS 11:21b-33

21 James Martin Gray, "Only a Sinner" (1905).

MARCH 10

RIGHTEOUSNESS IN ACTION

"At one time you were darkness, but now you are light in the Lord. Walk as children of light (for the fruit of light is found in all that is good and right and true), and try to discern what is pleasing to the Lord." EPHESIANS 5:8-10

Being made righteous should lead to us living righteously.

We trust Christ alone for our righteousness and never our good works. We must never lose sight of that. But we must also realize that the righteousness Christ gives us inevitably manifests itself in righteous deeds. Paul puts it this way: as believers, we are to "walk as children of light." And why? Because "the *fruit of light* is found in all that is good and right and true." In short, the Lord has made us righteous; therefore, we are to act righteously.

We cannot be the beneficiaries of the objective righteousness of Christ without the evidence presenting itself in our righteous living. Sinclair Ferguson puts it wonderfully when he says that "we are now the recipients of an irrevocable justification (or righteousness) in Christ, which in turn leads to a growth in righteousness in ourselves."[22] Similarly, John Calvin wrote that "the Son of God though spotlessly pure took upon himself the ignominy and shame of our sin and in return clothed us with his purity."[23] Christ bears our sin for us, grants us His unblemished record, and then empowers us, by His Spirit, to "walk in a manner worthy of the Lord, fully pleasing to him" (Colossians 1:10).

The Puritans used to speak in terms of a righteousness that was *imputed* and then a righteousness that was *imparted.* They were seeking to distinguish between the objective righteousness that Christ affords us and the subjective righteousness that we enact in our lives in the power of the Spirit. As believers, we are the grateful possessors of both.

Whatever your preferred terminology, this much is always true: the gospel of our Lord Jesus Christ isn't simply a free pass that excuses us to do as we please. No, the gospel calls us and empowers us to do what pleases the Lord. The key is that the gospel always turns us back to Jesus. As you look to Christ for your righteousness, He will enable you to "lay aside every weight, and sin which clings so closely" and strengthen you to run the unique race God has set out for you (Hebrews 12:1-2). So today, be sure not to trust in your righteous living to earn you salvation or blessing from the Lord. But equally, be sure not to make the mistake of allowing your salvation to tempt you to be half-hearted in your pursuit of righteous living. You have been made righteous; now go and live righteously.

EPHESIANS 5:8-15

---

22 *Let's Study Ephesians* (Banner of Truth, 2015), p 181.

23 *Institutes of the Christian Religion* 2.16.6, quoted in Bruce Milne, *Know the Truth: A Handbook of Christian Belief,* 3rd ed. (InterVarsity, 2009), p 212.

MARCH 11

QUIT YOUR HURRYING

"This God—his way is perfect; the word of the LORD proves true." PSALM 18:30

God is never in a hurry. He's never late. His timing is always perfect. Yet so many of us spend so much of our lives hurrying from place to place, anxious to make things happen when we think they should happen.

Consider Esther 6 as an example. There's a lot of hurry-up in this one chapter. It's not the hurry-up of God, though, but the hurry-up of humanity.

Haman woke up and hurried off to see the king about hanging Mordecai (Esther 6:4). When King Ahasuerus requested that he hurry with the king's robes to exalt the person the king delighted to honor (v 10), it was no problem for Haman to do so, assuming that the honor was intended for himself. Later we see Haman hurrying once more—but this time it is to his house in shame (v 12), embarrassed at being ordered to honor his most hated enemy, Mordecai. He didn't want anyone to see him. He covered his head, like an arrested criminal trying to shield himself from the gaze of the TV cameras. He was a picture of disappointment and pain.

Mordecai, however, was not in a hurry. He had been overlooked. His warning of an assassination plot had been significant, yet apparently nobody cared about it, not least the very king who was the beneficiary of what he had done. Four or five years had passed without any honor or recognition (Esther 6:3), and still Mordecai patiently and faithfully continued to do what was right. He trusted in God and His timing. He knew that "this God—his way is perfect."

Derek Kidner writes that "'all God's delays are maturings, either of the time ... or of the man."[24] The psalmist says, "Before I was afflicted I went astray, but now I keep your word" (Psalm 119:67). Like the psalmist, our default is to just do our own thing and wander any way we want. But when God in His providence makes us wait longer than we might like or even brings disappointment, pain, and heartache into our lives, we are given the opportunity to pay attention to His words and to trust that His plan is unfolding perfectly.

We are called to believe that God's way is perfect and His word is true—not just when His favor is evident but when the wheels are falling off and the good that we've done, which is deserving of honor and acclaim, is largely ignored. Do you believe that? Remember that even God's ultimate plan of salvation did not require hurry: "For while we were still weak, *at the right time* Christ died for the ungodly" (Romans 5:6, emphasis added). God's ways are perfect and His timing impeccable. Set aside your hurry, then, and give up your anxiety, learning instead to trust God to do His work at the right time.

PROVERBS 3:5-12

---

24 *Psalms 1–72: An Introduction and Commentary on Books I and II of the Psalms*, Tyndale Old Testament Commentaries, ed. D. J. Wiseman (InterVarsity, 1973), p 61.

MARCH 12

IN HEAVEN HE STANDS

"He holds his priesthood permanently, because he continues forever. Consequently, he is able to save to the uttermost those who draw near to God through him, since he always lives to make intercession for them." HEBREWS 7:24-25

Jesus' sacrificial work as our High Priest is a finished work, a once-and-for-all accomplishment with regard to sin. There is no need for repetition and no possibility of addition. But why is it, exactly, that He is able to "save to the uttermost those who draw near to God through him"?

Because, first, Christ's role as our Great High Priest is the solution to our rebellion. Deep down inside, each of us knows that we have rejected our dependence upon God, instead making a bid for independence. In trying to live our lives independently, we reveal that our stubborn hearts are curved into themselves. We pridefully think, "I don't need an advocate. I don't need anybody to do anything on my behalf. I can handle this myself."

But despite the fact that we have rebelled against God, amazingly, He seeks us out and saves us. Jesus brings about reconciliation by dealing with our alienation from God, which is two-sided: we are alienated on our side by our sin and on God's side by His wrath. Jesus has paid the penalty for our sins; He has satisfied God's wrath by offering Himself as an unblemished sacrifice.

Second, Jesus saves "to the uttermost" because He has destroyed the leverage that the Evil One uses to fill us with fear. In Hebrews 2, the writer explains, "Since therefore the children share in flesh and blood, he himself likewise partook of the same things, that through death he might destroy the one who has the power of death, that is, the devil, and deliver all those who through fear of death were subject to lifelong slavery" (v 14-15). Through His own death, Jesus has set us free from Satan's grip, liberating us from what ought to be our greatest fear: death itself. When Satan seeks to accuse us before the Father, Jesus is, as it were, able to point out that his words are empty—that he has nothing to say against us. And Jesus' priestly work still continues in His continual intercession on our behalf. In Jesus we have a Priest who sheds His grace on our lives day by day through His heavenly mediation. As Jesus enjoys being in His Father's presence today, right now, He is not offering a sacrifice, but rather speaking as our advocate before the Father. We may picture Him standing by His Father, saying, *That one is mine. I died for her. She is covered by my blood and is clothed in my righteousness.*

So, "When Satan tempts me to despair, and tells me of my guilt within / Upward I look and see Him there, who made an end of all my sin." Therefore, "I know that while in heaven He stands, no power can bid me thence depart."[25] Jesus, your Priest forever, stands in His Father's presence today, speaking of you and for you. There is nothing to fear.

HEBREWS 7:23 – 8:6

25 Charitie Lees Bancroft, "Before the Throne of God Above" (1863).

MARCH 13

RESPECTING THE TEMPLE

"He entered the temple and began to drive out those who sold, saying to them, 'It is written, "My house shall be a house of prayer," but you have made it a den of robbers.' And he was teaching daily in the temple. The chief priests and the scribes and the principal men of the people were seeking to destroy him, but they did not find anything they could do, for all the people were hanging on his words." LUKE 19:45-48

From the beginning of His life, the Jerusalem Temple was significant to Jesus. When He was a baby, the elderly Simeon had taken Him in his arms and declared Him in the temple courts to be the wonder of God's salvation (Luke 2:25-35). As a twelve-year-old boy, Jesus had sought out His Father's house and engaged in conversation with the religious leaders (v 46-49). Jesus' comfort in and love of His Father's house was palpable—and therefore so was His grief when He discovered irreverent behavior in that holy place.

The temple in Jerusalem was the place where God met His people. So when Jesus encountered an irreligious marketplace set up in its courts, He was justifiably grieved and angry. The individuals responsible for the disrespect in the temple were the same who had jeered at His triumphal entry into Jerusalem. They didn't bat an eye at exchanging money on the temple floor for an inordinate profit and deeming people's offerings of creatures "unacceptable" in order to sell them "acceptable" offerings at unfair prices. The way the temple courts were being used was so far removed from His Father's intentions that Jesus, as the Great High Priest, inevitably needed to come set it right. Jesus' knowledge of Old Testament prophecy allowed Him to speak with ultimate authority and remind the people of the temple's holy purpose, referencing Scripture that they knew and could not contest: "My house shall be a house of prayer" (Isaiah 56:7; see also Jeremiah 7:11).

Jesus' next action—using a whip made out of cords to drive out the livestock and stop the bazaar in its tracks (John 2:15)—was certainly justified. Zeal for His Father's reputation consumed Him (v 17). And yet we know that these were people over whom Jesus had wept (Luke 19:41-44). That whip was held by a Savior who had tears in His eyes.

Jesus is the perfect Son, who cares more than anything about bringing glory to His Father and who is angered more than anything by lies, greed, and pursuit of power that comes between His Father and sinners in need of grace. He looks at those who reject God and weeps, because He knows how far they have fallen. He looks at those who place barriers in the way of others meeting God and is angry, because He longs for His Father to receive the praise He is due and for people to be saved. We, too, would do well to weep over the lost and be angry over those who twist truth for their own ends. We would do well to pray for the same zeal for God's glory, even as we give thanks that Jesus came not only to reveal His zeal for His Father but to be the means by which we can dwell in His house forever.

ISAIAH 56:1-8

MARCH 14

CHRIST IS VICTORIOUS

"Whoever practices righteousness is righteous, as he is righteous. Whoever makes a practice of sinning is of the devil, for the devil has been sinning from the beginning. The reason the Son of God appeared was to destroy the works of the devil." 1 JOHN 3:7-8

Just as the bright light of the coming Messiah is anticipated in the pages of the Old Testament, so the devil is a shadowy figure throughout it. When we reach the New Testament, we discover that Christ's coming drew Satan out from the shadows and into the open.

In the Bible, the devil is revealed as the instigator of sin and sorrow. In fact, the word *devil* comes from a Greek root word which means "to throw," as in the sense of throwing out slanderous statements. The devil, we learn, twists the truth about Christ and the character of God. The word *Satan*, meanwhile, can be translated as "adversary" and can convey the sense of someone lying in ambush. Our irrational fears, doubts, and evil thoughts can be traced back to this Evil One. He is the deceiver, the accuser, the liar, and the hinderer. He blinds the minds of unbelievers and seeks to cloud the believer's mind with reminders of guilt and failure.

Satan is a powerful foe—but he is also a defeated one. The very real power of the Evil One should only ever be considered in light of the victory of the Lord Jesus. The devil has been chained by the cross of Christ. On that chain he may snarl and roar and grab for us, but nevertheless, his works will be destroyed by Christ. The apostle John assures us, "Everyone who has been born of God does not keep on sinning, but he who was born of God protects him, and the evil one does not touch him" (1 John 5:18).

In our homes, most of us have a process for the disposal of garbage: it goes from under the sink to outside the back door to the end of the driveway, and then the garbage truck comes and takes it to its final destination. In a very real sense, that is the experience of the Evil One: he has been put out the back door, awaiting final destruction on the day of Christ's revelation (Revelation 20:10). He is not yet destroyed, but he is dethroned and defeated.

In the conflicts we encounter, some of us are keenly aware that "we do not wrestle against flesh and blood, but against ... the spiritual forces of evil in the heavenly places" (Ephesians 6:12). And those of us who are not aware of this probably should be. All of us need to remind ourselves that there is a real struggle going on and that we are part of it; and all of us need also to remember in the midst of that struggle that "the reason the Son of God appeared was to destroy the works of the devil." Take courage from the fact that Satan does not have the final say. He is beaten, and Jesus has prayed for you that you would be kept safe (John 17:15). Let that knowledge cause you to stand firm against the devil's wiles and run to Christ for forgiveness when you give in to the devil's lies. This is how we live in light of Christ's victory!

LUKE 4:1-13

MARCH 15

THE NEED FOR SPIRITUAL LEADERSHIP

"Now from Miletus he sent to Ephesus and called the elders of the church to come to him." ACTS 20:17

In the middle of the 20th century, the Church of England commissioned a report entitled *Towards the Conversion of England.* The goal was to discover what was taking place within the parishes of the Anglican Communion. In that report, the writers came very quickly to the topic of leadership, on which they observed, "A spiritual leader can often make an astonishing difference."[26] The adjective "spiritual" is crucial. If the church is going to flourish in the world, it must have spiritual men in the position of leadership. Although we are distanced from that report by many years, and although a lot has changed since then, the strategic necessity for spiritually mature leaders, in whatever country or denomination we are in, has not changed. No church of Jesus Christ progresses beyond the spiritual progress of its leaders.

Every sports team has a captain or equivalent. Each member of the team may be equally valuable, but someone has to lead. Without a captain, a team loses direction and will often lack the discipline needed to win. The same is true in an orchestra: without a conductor, it risks losing coordination and any meaningful sense of harmony.

The necessary role of leadership is true in every area of life—and it's no different with God's people. Jesus was the leader of a group of twelve disciples. When He ascended to heaven, Peter and James appear to have become the leaders of the apostles and the church in Jerusalem. The apostles then established leadership in the local churches. When Paul wrote to Titus, he was very concerned that the right kinds of men were appointed to positions of leadership within the church (Titus 1:5-9). If an error was made in who was appointed, then the resulting damage would not be easily undone. And when he had limited time near Ephesus, it was "the elders of the church" who Paul summoned to Miletus in order to encourage and exhort.

Without good leadership, chaos easily follows. Many of the unsolved problems in the life of local churches can be traced back to defective leadership. Conversely, the resolution of problems almost always can be traced back to *effective* leadership.

If success depends upon the quality of leadership, then Christians should care deeply about leaders within their local church. Christ purchased the church with His own blood, and it is through the church that God intends to display His glory in the world and to the spiritual realms (Ephesians 3:10). Take time, then, to pray for your leaders. Consider how you can actively encourage them to faithfulness and in their labors. Be someone whom to lead is an occasion for joy and not groaning (Hebrews 13:17)—for your leaders' sake, and for yours.

ACTS 20:17-35

26 *Towards the Conversion of England* (J. M. Dent, 1946), p 3.

MARCH 16

I HAVE CHOSEN YOU

"You whom I took from the ends of the earth, and called from its farthest corners, saying to you, 'You are my servant, I have chosen you and not cast you off'; fear not, for I am with you; be not dismayed, for I am your God."

ISAIAH 41:9-10

It is tempting to think that our significance is determined by what we've achieved, where we've been, or where we are going in this life. Yet each of these is irrelevant when considering our lasting significance, which is grounded only in our relationship with God. This relationship is not based upon our wishful thinking or elevated opinions of ourselves. No, it's based on the surety of these words: "I have chosen you and not cast you off."

Have we not given God grounds to reject us? If God's covenant with us and acceptance of us were based upon our daily performance, then none of us would remain in relationship with Him for more than 24 hours. But the wonder of His covenant with us is that it is founded upon *His* choice. He has chosen us, He has called us from the farthest corners of the world, and He will not cast us off.

Before we can obey and experience God's grace, we must *understand* it. Grace is the antidote to all fear and anxiety. We will never be able to overcome worry by simply repeating self-help mantras, nor will we gain victory over fear only by the exhortations of others to obey what Scripture calls for. Such an approach will result in discouragement and doubt, even in despair.

When dreadful thoughts arise—*I am afraid and overwhelmed, and I don't know what to do* or *I am weak and insignificant, and I don't know how to go on*—we must remind ourselves of God's grace, which says to us, *I called you. I chose you. I love you. I have not rejected you.* Only the grace of God can help us to overcome our fears and give us this confidence. His promises put all else in perspective, teaching us to fix our minds on the hope of eternity and live in light of its reality.

Do you have any rivers that you think are uncrossable? Are there any mountains that you can't tunnel through? Are you afraid of a new task that is awaiting you? Are you faced with continual difficulties? Remember that God's truth doesn't change. His purposes don't change. His Son doesn't change. This unchanging God is the one who is with you and for you. Listen to Him now: "I have chosen you and not cast you off; fear not, for I am with you; be not dismayed, for I am your God."

1 JOHN 3:1-3

MARCH 17

THE LIMITS AND BENEFITS OF SUFFERING

"In this you rejoice, though now for a little while, if necessary, you have been grieved by various trials, so that the tested genuineness of your faith—more precious than gold that perishes though it is tested by fire—may be found to result in praise and glory and honor at the revelation of Jesus Christ." 1 PETER 1:6-7

Suffering is a reality we all must face. Our union with Christ does not remove us from the pain that is part and parcel of life this side of eternity. And since "for a little while" we are to be "grieved by various trials," we need to have a biblical perspective on suffering.

In his first letter, Peter addressed early believers who had been exiled for the sake of Christ. Their suffering had caused them great grief, which Peter noted empathetically—but he also commanded them to rejoice in the midst of their trials. He reminded the early church, as he reminds us, that suffering is inevitably limited in its timeframe: it will only last "for a little while."

Our pain often does not feel temporary. If it is a chronic physical ailment or an unresolved relational break, it does not feel as though it is lasting "a little while." Indeed, there are many whose whole earthly pilgrimage is marked by great suffering. Yet it is for this very reason that the Bible says so much about heaven: to remind us that our lives are incredibly brief compared with eternity. "We do not lose heart," says Paul. "For this light momentary affliction is preparing for us an eternal weight of glory beyond all comparison ... The things that are seen are transient, but the things that are unseen are eternal" (2 Corinthians 4:16-18).

Not only this, but as we walk through trials clinging to Christ, our pain is telling us something about our faith. It isn't difficult to be a Christian when the band is playing and everyone's marching along, doing just fine. But when difficulties arise, when we have unanswered questions, when we awake in the night and weep uncontrollably, when sometimes all we are able to say is "Father, help," and yet we do say that... that is when our faith is tested, and that is when it is proved genuine.

Furthermore, we can rejoice in the reality that no matter what we're going through, God sees, He hears, He cares, and He acts to guard our faith and bring us to our glorious inheritance, in a world where nothing perishes or fades (1 Peter 1:4-5). The road through the valley may be a long one, but He will bring us through it.

God promises to use suffering in the lives of His children to display His glory. None of us will become all that God intends for us to be if we choose always to run in the sunshine of ease and comfort. But when we trust that He will use life's trials to refine us, we will surely be filled with the hope of eternity and live in a manner that is increasingly like that of our Savior. How does it comfort you to consider the riches and the duration of eternity with Him today? How could you use that prospect to encourage someone else?

1 PETER 1:1-9

MARCH 18

TOTAL SATISFACTION

"He answered them, 'You give them something to eat' ... And they all ate and were satisfied." MARK 6:37, 42

When Jesus directed the disciples to feed a crowd of 5,000 men, plus women and children, with nothing but a young boy's five loaves of bread and two fish, they faced a seemingly impossible situation. As Andrew questioned, "What are they for so many?" (John 6:9). But the Twelve did as Jesus directed them: they sat the people down, separated them into groups, and then divided the loaves and fish. And divided. And divided. And before they knew it, a miracle had unfolded.

The five loaves and two fish managed to feed thousands—and not just with the tiniest servings of food but with such an abundance that "they all ate and were satisfied." In fact, in a rather humorous turn of events, there were even leftovers. Just as God had done centuries earlier with the manna in the wilderness (Exodus 16), here the Shepherd of Israel proved His identity and provided for His people's needs, both literally and symbolically.

It should be impossible for us to consider this story and not recognize that God takes unmanageable situations and unbelievably limited resources and multiplies them for the well-being of others and the glory of His name. And He can do this with our lives as well.

Perhaps, if you are the only Christian in your family, in your class, or at your job, you may wonder, like Andrew, "What am I among so many? What can I say? What can I do?" But here is the real question to ask: "Have I truly offered up my resources to God—my time, talents, energy, gifts, and finances?" They may not be much. But He can multiply them!

The missionary Gladys Aylward lived in London with no education and no savings. What she had, though, was a passionate longing to go to China to share the gospel. This small-statured lady, who had long, straight, black hair, thus began a journey by train and then by ocean liner, and eventually ended up in Shanghai. As she stood on the deck, looking out on the city, she saw all the small-statured Chinese people with their straight, black hair, and she suddenly realized that God had had a plan and purpose for her all along. He'd even established her DNA in such a way that she would be perfectly suited to become the "Little Woman" who would reach countless tiny children with the gospel—all because she offered up her life to God and He multiplied it for His glory.

As you look out on your day and your week, offer yourself to God. Your inability is His opportunity. Your weaknesses and your sense of dependence form the very basis upon which He shows Himself to be strong. With nothing but mere loaves and fish, He satisfied thousands. Be in no doubt that He can use you to do great things of eternal worth, if you will only ask Him.

MARK 6:30-44

MARCH 19

LEARNING IN THE FAMILY OF FAITH

"Let brotherly love continue. Do not neglect to show hospitality to strangers, for thereby some have entertained angels unawares. Remember those who are in prison, as though in prison with them, and those who are mistreated, since you also are in the body. Let marriage be held in honor among all, and let the marriage bed be undefiled, for God will judge the sexually immoral and adulterous." HEBREWS 13:1-4

There's all the difference in the world between describing what it means to ride a bicycle and actually helping somebody get on the seat and pedal away. Making a cake seems to be fairly straightforward when I look at the recipe books, but I haven't had much success in making one that actually tastes right! What I need is hands-on guidance: somebody to do it in front of me and then allow me to try my hand at it too.

The moral instruction provided for us in Hebrews 13 is to be trained and formed in our lives not by learning to apply abstract principles but as a result of seeing these principles worked out in the family of faith. We can read, for example, about what it means to love one another, but it is far better to observe such love in the lives of loving people. We can understand that we're supposed to care for strangers, but we can experience it firsthand if we're brought up in a home where such care is faithfully practiced. We can read the principles and demands for sexual purity, but we will do far better if we are raised in a flourishing home where they're modeled or are able to sit in such homes as we visit other families in our church. The list goes on and on.

Establishing these ethical norms is demanding. It takes time, patience, and involvement. They cannot be achieved by watching a video or reading an article. If information was enough to bring about transformation, then all we would need to do is write it down or say it. But you can't learn love, honor, and faithfulness from the content on a screen. No, if you are to be content, pure, loving, and hospitable, then that is going to have to be discovered and worked out in the family of faith.

Look, then, to your brothers and sisters who exemplify Christlikeness in these ways. Read Hebrews 13:1-4 again, praise God for those you know who live these verses out, and then be sure to learn from them so that in these ways you become like them. Make it your aim to so follow their example that you, like Paul, might humbly be able to say to others, "Be imitators of me, as I am of Christ" (1 Corinthians 11:1). What will that look like this week?

HEBREWS 13:1-8, 16-17

MARCH 20

SPIRITUAL PERCEPTION

"Now Samuel did not yet know the LORD, and the word of the LORD had not yet been revealed to him. And the LORD called Samuel again the third time. And he arose and went to Eli and said, 'Here I am, for you called me.' Then Eli perceived that the LORD was calling the boy. Therefore Eli said to Samuel, 'Go, lie down, and if he calls you, you shall say, "Speak, LORD, for your servant hears."' So Samuel went and lay down in his place. And the LORD came and stood, calling as at other times, 'Samuel! Samuel!' And Samuel said, 'Speak, for your servant hears.'" 1 SAMUEL 3:7-10

When we struggle to understand a new model or theory, we are not helped by a teacher who leaves us on our own if we don't grasp the concept the first time. Instead, we need a teacher who patiently, encouragingly explains the idea again and again until we get it.

When He called Samuel to be His prophet, God dealt graciously with His servant who didn't get it—in fact, with *two* of His servants who didn't get it!

Samuel was involved at the temple, ministering and engaged. But there was a personal dimension of faith which he had not yet experienced. God's word hadn't been revealed to him—and so God took the initiative and was gracious enough to persist by calling to Samuel repeatedly. In this quadruple call of God, we have a reminder of His tenderness and His kindness.

Yet while Samuel is the focus of this passage, Eli also needed God's patient interactions. Even as a priest, he did not think in the first or second instance that the Lord was speaking to Samuel. Then, suddenly "Eli perceived..." And when there is perception, it is an indication of the work of God.

This gradual perception was true of Jesus' disciples as well. He told them He still had many things to say to them, but they weren't ready to understand yet (John 16:12). He didn't give up on them, though. Instead, He patiently explained again and again.

Some of us may be able to relate to Samuel: perhaps you have read books and listened to sermons many times without experiencing any true impact. Or you may be like the disciples: you've begun to understand, but you still find so many matters of faith confusing. No matter how many years we follow Christ and read God's word, there will always be more to understand and enjoy. Sometimes we may even feel we have gone backwards! But we can be confident that in God we have a gracious teacher to guide us. So, join the psalmist in praying, "Open my eyes, that I may behold wondrous things out of your law" (Psalm 119:18). And then work hard to understand God's word and perceive its meaning for your life, prayerfully confident that as you find yourself grasping more and more of what it says, God is at work in you.

ROMANS 12:1-3

MARCH 21

THE FREEDOM OF HIS RULE

"Pilate said to him, 'So you are a king?' Jesus answered, 'You say that I am a king. For this purpose I was born and for this purpose I have come into the world—to bear witness to the truth. Everyone who is of the truth listens to my voice.'" JOHN 18:37

By nature, we believe we have the right to rule our own lives. We think that nobody has the authority to tell us what to do or to rule over us. We will decide for ourselves, define who we are, and mold our own future. Yet this is a dreadful path, and it leads only to despair. For when we look within, however much we have been told to think positively and to believe in ourselves, we are still confronted by our need, our failure, our frailty, and our inadequacy. And when we look without, we see a divided culture and flawed institutions. To what, then, should we look?

The Old Testament records Israel's repeated rebellion against God's rule. In an attempt to look just like the nations around them, the Israelites demanded an earthly king (1 Samuel 8:5). Tragically, all of Israel's kings eventually crumbled to dust: the mighty Saul, the great David, and the wise Solomon all failed politically, morally, and religiously. Surely, the people in the streets were making the same complaints that we hear today: "This is not what we were led to expect when this person became our leader! There must be someone better than this!"

Indeed, there *is* someone better. Jesus, Son of Man and Son of God, is the Creator, Sustainer, and King of the universe: "For by him all things were created .... He is before all things, and in him all things hold together" (Colossians 1:16-17). He is the King who will perfectly fulfill the demands of the role: "In his days ... the righteous flourish, and peace abound[s]" (Psalm 72:7); He will deliver the needy, the poor, and the helpless (v 12-13); all nations will serve Him, and "the whole earth" will "be filled with his glory!" (v 19).

As question 26 of the Westminster Shorter Catechism explains, Jesus carries out His kingly office "in subduing us to himself, in ruling and defending us, and in restraining and conquering all his and our enemies." He comes to reign over us in such a way that we find real freedom in giving up our autonomy and real rest in quitting from our efforts to make our own future. "Come to me," He says. "Take my yoke upon you, and learn from me ... and you will find rest for your souls" (Matthew 11:28-29).

Jesus is the resurrected and ascended King. His claim on us is total, and our response is all or it is nothing. We must decide whether Christ's right to rule and reign over the universe will extend to every facet of our lives as well. Only then will we find Him to be "our shield and defender."[27] It is as you bow the knee to Him in those areas of life where you find it hardest, trusting that His rule is better than yours, that you give Him the place that He deserves and find the freedom and the future that you long for.

PSALM 72

27 Robert Grant, "O Worship the King" (1833).

MARCH 22

PATTERNS FOR OUR GIVING

"Now concerning the collection for the saints: as I directed the churches of Galatia, so you also are to do. On the first day of every week, each of you is to put something aside and store it up, as he may prosper, so that there will be no collecting when I come." 1 CORINTHIANS 16:1-2

In 1 Corinthians 15, Paul spends most of his time soaring among the glories of the resurrection and then ends with the wonderful reminder that our labor in the Lord is not in vain. What would you expect to come next? What would you predict would be a practical application of the resurrection's life-changing reality?

I imagine your answers would *not* include "financial stewardship." And yet this is precisely where Paul takes his readers: "Now concerning the collection for the saints…" Our financial stewardship is not, it turns out, an "unspiritual" part of life, disconnected from things that really matter. Rather, stewardship is an aspect of the work we do in the name of our risen Lord on this side of our own resurrection.

While Paul's instructions here were given specifically for a collection for the believers in Jerusalem, they are instructive for us in our own contexts. There are three principles that he lays out, and each should shape our own giving.

First, Paul wants giving to be regular and deliberate: "On the first day of every week, each of you is to put something aside and store it up, as he may prosper." This was to take place on the first day of every week. For many of us, regular giving keeps us disciplined and prevents us from waiting until we "feel like" giving. Whether it's weekly, monthly, or at other set times, regular giving is Paul's wise instruction.

Second, giving should be proportionate. Funds were to be set aside by each person "as he may prosper"—or, as the NIV puts it, "in keeping with your income." That leaves the details very much with the individual. God is the one with whom we need to deal, because He's the one who searches our hearts, and He knows whether our giving is in keeping with what He has given into our care.

Third, we are to give to our family of faith first and foremost. The collection to which Paul refers is being made in churches and for churches. Where we are spiritually fed is where we contribute first (1 Timothy 5:17-18). The local church and then the wider church are not necessarily the only places that should receive our giving, but they are the primary places.

Your task now is to consider whether your own giving patterns need to be changed according to these principles. Ultimately, this is a personal matter, but it is also a profoundly spiritual matter, flowing out of our love and devotion to our Lord Jesus Christ, who has risen, is reigning, and shall return. Be assured, therefore, that as you strive for faithfulness in your giving, that striving will not be in vain.

PHILIPPIANS 4:10-19

MARCH 23

DEATH IS BUT A DOORWAY

"A good name is better than precious ointment, and the day of death than the day of birth. It is better to go to the house of mourning than to go to the house of feasting, for this is the end of all mankind, and the living will lay it to heart."
ECCLESIASTES 7:1-2

Death confuses most of us. We fear it, and though we know it is inevitable, we would much rather not have to deal with it. We seek to isolate ourselves from its reality, turning the music up to drown out the ominous silence that accompanies it. Our denial is understandable; death is the hardest fact of life to face. Yet in our more sober moments, we realize that our lives are as precarious as a child's sandcastle on the seashore: that sooner or later, the tide will come in and wash it all away.

As with all the issues it addresses, the Bible aims to reorient our perspective on death. Solomon, writing with the all-surpassing wisdom that God had granted him (see 1 Kings 3:5-12), said that death "is the end of all mankind, and *the living will lay it to heart.*" Likewise, Moses tells us that "a heart of wisdom" comes from our contemplating our limited number of days on earth, which "end like a sigh" (Psalm 90:9, 12). This is why we learn more about reality at a funeral in a "house of mourning" than at a party in a "house of feasting."

While it may be tempting to try to shy away from death, then, wisdom looks like accepting that we must face it head on. In fact, the key to learning how to live is to be found in learning how to die. We will never know the reason for our earthly pilgrimage until we've come face to face with the fact of death, for it is death that lies at the end of every path. Without considering our death, we'll end up like the one whose tombstone reads, "Here lies a man who went out of the world without knowing why he came into it." Such is the lot of so many who spend day after day after day separated from Christ, "having no hope and without God in the world" (Ephesians 2:12).

But if by faith God has made you alive together with Christ (Ephesians 2:5), then you have already passed from the domain of death to the land of the living. You can say with Paul, "Thanks be to God, who gives us the victory through our Lord Jesus Christ" (1 Corinthians 15:57). For you, death is no longer an end that you must dread but the doorway to "fullness of joy" (Psalm 16:11). And with that perspective on your final day, you will be ready to make the most of this day, endeavoring in all that you do to glorify the Lord, who has Himself triumphed over death and who will lead you through it (1 Corinthians 10:31).

ECCLESIASTES 7:1-7

MARCH 24

HOW TO DEAL WITH FALSE TEACHERS

"They must be silenced ... Rebuke them sharply, that they may be sound in the faith." TITUS 1:11, 13

When a building is on fire, what is needed is not only an alarm that alerts everyone to the danger but a means of dousing the flames.

In his letter to Titus, Paul didn't only raise the alarm about those who could harm the members of the congregation with dangerous teaching; he also provided his protégé with instructions for how to put the fire out.

Paul's instructions are not mild-mannered. First he says, "They must be silenced." The word "silenced" can also be translated "muzzled." If a dog barks and bites people all of the time, there's a clear solution. That is what Paul is instructing Titus to do with these teachers, in no uncertain terms: *Muzzle them!* He also tells Titus to "rebuke them sharply." He is not pulling his punches!

When we hear this passage with the ears of an outsider, we can understand why someone might say, "Well, I don't know much about Paul, but he *sounds* like a mean guy. There's a level of intolerance here that I don't really like. He sounds very judgmental." Indeed, some may hear Paul's teaching and reject the truth of the gospel on the strength of its offensiveness—unless we translate Paul's meaning for them.

For it is the seriousness of the situation that explains the directness of his speech. Paul's intolerance is similar to the cancer specialist's intolerance of the cancer that he or she seeks to eradicate from a patient's body. The problem must be dealt with vigorously so that health might be restored. There's nothing remotely unkind about this kind of focused, principled opposition. Paul is saying, *We can't allow this disease to spread through the congregation, for it can be spiritually fatal.*

God looks for those who will fall down at the feet of His Son and say, "All that I could ever do is love You in response to the majestic nature of Your love for me, which has been revealed in Your cross." The people in Crete were in danger of losing that appreciation. Whether it is in Crete, Cape Town, or Cleveland, false teaching must be responded to graciously, firmly, immediately, and compassionately so that God's people will be protected from error. Churches must not give a platform to teaching which denies the gospel, and Christians must not give their ear to it.

In the Bible, even those commands that appear harsh and intolerant are motivated by God's love for His children and His desire to protect us from harm. He wants us to continue to live in wonder at His love—and as we do so, He wants us to be sure to guard our hearts and our churches.

2 PETER 2:1-10a

MARCH 25

HIS GLORY, OUR CONCERN

"She bowed and gave birth, for her pains came upon her. And about the time of her death ... she named the child Ichabod, saying, 'The glory has departed from Israel!' because the ark of God had been captured and because of her father-in-law and her husband." 1 SAMUEL 4:19-21

Do you ever see somebody in passing, perhaps on a bus or in a store, and find yourself struck by the thought that there's a whole life wrapped up in that person—hopes, dreams, sadnesses, regrets? Phinehas's wife—we don't even know her name—is someone who may cause us to wonder, "What had her life been?"

Presumably, there would have been great joy and celebration at this woman's wedding. After all, she was marrying a priest! As time went by, however, she likely became aware of her husband's double standards: he fulfilled his priestly duties, but he also abused his role to sleep with other women, which was a matter of public knowledge (1 Samuel 2:22).

Now, heavily pregnant with his child, "she heard the news" (1 Samuel 4:19) that the Philistines had slain her husband and captured the ark of the Lord (v 11). Typically, you would think that the death of a spouse would head the list of concerns, with every other consideration in the world receding in comparison. But this was not the case for Phinehas's wife. For this woman, the spiritual implications of the ark of God being captured far outweighed even the most distressing temporal concerns. Even the news that she had borne a son did not rally her. And so she named her child Ichabod, which simply means "no glory" or "Where is the glory?"

In all her pain, disappointment, and loss, somehow, deep inside, Phinehas's wife had laid hold of something that even those closest to her had not grasped. She knew that God's glory mattered more than Eli's name, mattered more than Shiloh, and mattered more than victory in battle. As Dale Ralph Davis writes, "She taught more theology in her death than Phinehas had done in his whole life."[28]

This woman must have lived in the presence of God. When her husband let her down and she was aware of the discrepancy between his public profession and his private reality, she must have run to the Lord, her "very present help in trouble" (Psalm 46:1). Otherwise, concern over His glory would not have been her response.

What about you? Is God's glory and presence your greatest concern? Does the advance of His cause and honor of His name matter more to you than anything? This way lies real freedom, for it means you always look forward to life in the very presence of God—that city where there is no temple, "for its temple is the Lord God the Almighty and the Lamb. And the city has no need of sun or moon to shine on it, for the glory of God gives it light" (Revelation 21:22-23). In the details of your day, in the trials of life, and at the moment of your death, turn to God as your refuge and strong tower (Proverbs 18:10). Only then will you discover or remember that God's glory truly is our greatest hope and joy.

PSALM 18

28 *1 Samuel: Looking on the Heart* (Christian Focus, 2000), p 57.

MARCH 26

A TEMPLE WITH FOUNDATIONS

"The Lord is in his holy temple; the Lord's throne is in heaven; his eyes see, his eyelids test the children of man. The Lord tests the righteous." PSALM 11:4-5

It's possible for all of us to read certain passages or verses of Scripture many times yet miss goldmines of truth. Sometimes we pass by because we're overly familiar with what we've read, and other times it's because we don't take the time to meditate and savor the wealth before us.

So let's take the opportunity to dwell on the truth that "the Lord is in his holy temple." This simple truth offers both comfort and chastening. Its reality is affirmed in many places in the Old Testament (for example Habakkuk 2:20; Psalm 18:6; Micah 1:2), but David provides some additional angles from which to consider it here in Psalm 11.

The first is that "the Lord's throne is in heaven," making Him the *exalted* Lord. He reigns not as a mortal with limited perspective and control but as the all-powerful, immortal, all-knowing God of heaven. He outlasts all rulers, and all nations are as nothing before Him.

Second, God is the *observing* Lord: "His eyes see." From the exalted position of His heavenly throne, nothing is hidden from God's sight. No good thing done in His name goes unobserved, and no impure motive or thought is secret to Him. What a comfort to know that every day of our lives, going back to when we were merely "unformed substance," is visible to God (Psalm 139:15-16)! And what a sobering reality to realize that every word, thought, and deed is laid bare before Him!

Third, God is the *examining* Lord: "The Lord tests the righteous." His tests are not always or often easy, but they are always precisely what we need. None of us will reach heaven without tests and trials along the way. This may be an unpleasant reality to consider, but it should be precious to us, for it means we will not panic when God, in His sometimes inscrutable wisdom, routes our path through a valley. God's tests are never without a purpose; they are always for the sake of preparing us for the day when we shall see Him in His holy temple.

Keep the truth of this verse in mind the next time you feel as though "the foundations are destroyed" (Psalm 11:3). The instability we sometimes feel is meant to remind us that worldly stability is only an illusion and that true security is found in God alone. He alone is exalted, He alone sees all, and He alone directs our lives and tests us for our good. When the foundations tremble, we can remember that this world is not our home and that our sovereign God is leading us to one day inhabit a city with foundations that will not shake (Hebrews 11:10; 12:28). You can know that He is in His holy temple—and He has promised to bring you to that very place.

HEBREWS 12:22-29

MARCH 27

A NEW KIND OF PEACE

"Jesus came and stood among them and said to them, 'Peace be with you.' When he had said this, he showed them his hands and his side. Then the disciples were glad." JOHN 20:19-20

Many of us who have lost someone dear can recall evenings in the aftermath of loss when it felt difficult even to breathe. We sat there with others, grieving in a silence punctuated every so often by reflection.

On the Sunday evening following Jesus' death, we can imagine His disciples going through a similar experience. Maybe one said, *Do you remember how excited and hopeful we were when He walked on water?* Perhaps another added, *I remember Him weeping at the tomb of Lazarus. I won't ever forget it.* In all their reminiscence, they doubtless felt a stabbing awareness that they would never again on earth see Jesus' face. Of that they were convinced. They were fearful of the future. They had just witnessed Christ's execution, and they had locked the door behind them (John 20:19), worried that they would be the next targets.

Jesus knew this. Therefore, when He appeared quietly among them that night, the first word to come out of His mouth was "Peace," or *Shalom*. This was a customary Semitic greeting that came with warmth and without rebuke, blame, or disappointment. Then He showed them His hands and His side. *It was Him.* The Jesus whom they were convinced they would never see again was actually standing among them!

"Peace be with you" gave the disciples an indication not simply that their gladness should be prompted by the awareness that He was no longer dead but of something far greater: that by His resurrection, Jesus had now come to bestow a new kind of peace as a result of His blood shed upon the cross. And the peace with which He greeted them is the same peace that He gives to every pardoned sinner.

Shalom takes on a whole new meaning for those who discover this peace. In our weary world, bowing under the weight of all that is difficult and broken, tainted by indifference toward or denial of Almighty God in all His majesty, we know that He still seeks us out. Just as He came up behind Mary Magdalene at the open tomb (John 20:11-18) and the two disciples on the road to Emmaus (Luke 24:13-35), so He pursues you and me in love, bidding us find peace in Him, the one at whose birth the angels sang, "Peace on earth" (Luke 2:14, CSB).

In the face of fear, our world aches for peace. But longing for it and singing about it will not create it. Peace can only be found in Jesus' words: "In *me* you may have peace" (John 16:33; emphasis added). The resurrection doesn't simply mean there is a Christ. It means that Christ is alive forever and that He gives us peace with the Father and peace in ourselves, today and forever. Whatever storms are raging around you or inside you, make sure you hear the voice of your risen Savior today, saying, "Peace be with you."

JOHN 20:11-23

MARCH 28

THE GOD OF BROKEN PIECES

"The angel of the Lord *also said to [Hagar], 'I will surely multiply your offspring so that they cannot be numbered for multitude' ... And God said to [Abram], 'Behold, my covenant is with you, and you shall be the father of a multitude of nations.'"* GENESIS 16:10; 17:3-4

Have you ever watched children play with a Lego set, building a little house or spacecraft but completely ignoring the plans for its construction? Eventually, with pieces strewn across the floor, they end up with a monstrosity—pieces every which way, doors that open to nowhere—and they come to you, bemoaning the fact that it just doesn't look right. And so you take the child, the pieces, and the mess, you sit down together, and you say, "Let's take the plans and this brokenness, and let's do it right this time."

When Abraham and Sarah grew weary and restless as they waited for God to fulfill His promise of an heir, they took matters into their own hands. Trying to piece together life on their own, they agreed that Abraham would sleep with Hagar, Sarah's servant, in order to have a child (Genesis 16:1-4). Their decision sowed discord, chaos, contempt, and unhappiness: after Hagar "saw that she had conceived" (v 4), she became proud and "looked with contempt on her mistress." Sarah then blamed Abraham for her misfortune, and he responded by wiping his hands clean of the whole mess: "Your servant is in your power; do to her as you please" (v 6). Their lives had become a disheveled mess.

But God overruled their wrong decisions and intervened with mercy and grace. First, an angel of the Lord met Hagar in her need, assured her of God's presence, and told her God's promise: "I will surely multiply your offspring so that they cannot be numbered for multitude." Likewise, Abraham and Sarah's blunder couldn't derail God's covenant purposes and steadfast love. God promised that Sarah would bear a son, whom they were to call Isaac, and promised Abraham, "I will establish my covenant with him as an everlasting covenant" (Genesis 17:19).

In many ways, God treats us similarly. Like a parent with a dismayed child, He comes and picks up the scattered parts of our lives. He comes to us in our brokenness, with the scraps of our self-effort strewn around us and His plans tucked somewhere off to the side, and He replaces the pieces, points us back to His plans, and restores us to the right path.

How many times has God overruled your blundering? How many times has God come to you in your error and rebellion, in your emptiness and brokenness, and brought about, to His glory, events that are unimaginable? Praise God today for His steadfast love and faithfulness. The words of Moses to Joshua still ring true today: "It is the Lord who goes before you. He will be with you; he will not leave you or forsake you" (Deuteronomy 31:8).

PSALM 40

HOW TO APPROACH GOD IN PRAYER

"But let him ask in faith, with no doubting, for the one who doubts is like a wave of the sea that is driven and tossed by the wind. For that person must not suppose that he will receive anything from the Lord; he is a double-minded man, unstable in all his ways." JAMES 1:6-8

There is a kind of prayer that receives nothing from God.

It is the prayer of the doubter, the one who does not "ask in faith." When James says we are to make our requests to God "with no doubting," he's not saying we must never have any uncertainty or confusion in our minds, ever. To doubt in the sense that James uses the term here is more than simply saying, "I am struggling to be certain about this" or "I know this to be true but sometimes I wonder"; it is a refusal to entrust ourselves to our Father's care. It is to make a back-up plan that relies on our efforts even as we ask God for His intervention, or to ask for something that deep down we do not really want.

J.B. Phillips paraphrases this verse in a helpful way: "He must ask in sincere faith without secret doubts as to whether he really wants God's help or not." James is addressing the issue of divided loyalty, describing the doubter as one whose prayers and desires are clearly at odds with each other. This person comes before God and asks for things that he or she has no intention of doing, much as the great 5th-century theologian Augustine famously prayed prior to his conversion: "Lord, make me pure, but not yet."[29]

God knows when we are simply playing the game, using the language, and singing the song without any desire to match our lives to our words. He knows whether we really want His help or are reserving the right to do what we feel like doing if His wisdom doesn't lead us in the direction we naturally desire. Faith says no to this kind of hypocrisy, which prays for wisdom but acts in foolishness. The faith James describes is therefore more than comprehension; it is an expression of trust and devotion.

Honesty lies at the heart of any genuine appeal, whether to an earthly father or our heavenly Father. When you come before God, you must "draw near with a true heart in full assurance of faith" (Hebrews 10:22). With this kind of sincerity, you will make it clear in your own soul and to God that you are trusting Him to be faithful to His promises and that you are serious about acting on whatever wisdom He provides. In what area of your life are you particularly aware that you need God's wisdom? Entrust yourself to your heavenly Father and be ready to follow His guidance, so that you will walk steady in your faith and joy, and not be tossed about by the wind.

1 PETER 5:5-7

29 *Confessions*, 8.7.17.

MARCH 30

THE KINGDOM AND THE CROSS

"My kingdom is not of this world. If my kingdom were of this world, my servants would have been fighting, that I might not be delivered over to the Jews. But my kingdom is not from the world." JOHN 18:36

When Jesus arrived in Jerusalem on the first Palm Sunday, He was a king on a donkey, a king without a palace, a king without a throne—a king with no apparent kingdom. It rapidly became abundantly and controversially clear that Christ had come as the suffering king whom the Scriptures had foretold, not as the triumphant king whom people wanted.

Many who admired Jesus on that day in Jerusalem eventually discarded Him. They said, *I don't want any suffering. I only want victory. I only want power. I only want rule.* Not much is different today. We often ignore what we don't like in Jesus' ministry and content ourselves with Jesus the great example, Jesus the problem-fixer, Jesus the guru, or Jesus the political reformer.

But God's kingdom centers on the cross: "I decided to know nothing among you," says Paul, "except Jesus Christ and *him crucified*" (1 Corinthians 2:2, emphasis added). In other words, we will never understand Jesus—never truly know Him, never really love Him, never actually be in His kingdom—until we understand that the entrance to and the heart of Christ's kingdom is His death and resurrection. It is the means by which we come into it and the pattern by which we live in it.

A renewed culture comes about not because we transform institutions and policies but because that cross-centered kingdom transforms human hearts. Never in history has a revival been sparked by political activity; it has always resulted from Christians praying, preaching, pleading, and living as Christ calls us to live. The world will only ever be changed when we ourselves are changed.

God's kingdom is a cause great enough to live for and great enough to die for. Do you want to give up your small ambitions and give yourself to God? Then give up championing a political cause as a means of safeguarding the health of the church or your society or of making revival happen. Instead, go somewhere where nobody knows Jesus and tell them. Maybe it's your office. Maybe it's your neighborhood. Or maybe it's Tehran, Jakarta, or Algiers. It could be anywhere, for God is everywhere and is needed by everyone. Give up living by the maxims of the systems of this world and follow the King who tasted death before He entered His glory (Luke 24:26).

Believers have the immense privilege and the incredible challenge of offering the good news of God's kingdom to a society that fears death and knows little of true life. That is no easy commission, and heeding it may very well cost you dearly in this life. But no one who gives much for Jesus has cause to regret it, now or through all eternity.

LUKE 9:18-26

MARCH 31

AWAKENED TO NEW LIFE

"God, being rich in mercy, because of the great love with which he loved us, even when we were dead in our trespasses, made us alive together with Christ."
EPHESIANS 2:4-5

Some claim that mankind's problem is not that we're sinful but that we're sick. If only we could provide for ourselves the right kind of care, medicine, or technology, then our lives would be transformed and we'd be ok, for surely man is essentially good, not innately sinful. At least, so goes the thinking.

According to the Bible, however, the only adequate explanation for the predicament we face is that man is spiritually lifeless. It's not even that we are spiritually sick; outside of Christ we are "*dead* in [our] trespasses and sins" (Ephesians 2:1, emphasis added). And how much can a dead person do to make themselves alive? Nothing.

So you and I quite literally have a grave problem—unless, that is, there is one who is able to speak into the deadness of our experience and, by His very words, bring us to life. And that, of course, is Christianity's great message: "As in Adam all die, so also in Christ shall all be made alive" (1 Corinthians 15:22).

The best physical picture of this spiritual reality is the story of Jesus raising Lazarus from the dead. Imagine the scene. Lazarus was gone, and everyone knew it. He had been buried for four days. And yet Jesus walked up to the tomb and addressed the dead man: he "cried out with a loud voice, 'Lazarus, come out.'" (John 11:43). *And Lazarus came out.*

How was it that Lazarus came to life? It was a result of the voice of Jesus, who alone can speak so that the spiritually dead hear. Just as Jesus brought life to lifeless Lazarus, so He breathes life into the deadness of men's and women's spiritual condition. Spiritually, we are corpses—just as dead and decaying as Lazarus in his tomb. But when God chooses, He utters His word and awakens us to life. As the hymn writer puts it:

He speaks, and, listening to His voice,
New life the dead receive.
The mournful, broken hearts rejoice;
The humble poor believe.[30]

We are not to think too much of ourselves. Left to our own devices and efforts, we are dead. We can never think too much of Jesus. He and He alone is the reason we have life. And we must never think too little of the call to share His gospel with those around us; for we have been given the inestimable privilege of being the means by which Jesus calls dead people to come out of their spiritual grave and discover eternal life with Him. To whom is He prompting you to speak of Him today?

EZEKIEL 37

---

30 Charles Wesley, "O for a Thousand Tongues to Sing" (1739).

APRIL 1

GOING BACK TO GOD

"Return to me, says the LORD of hosts, and I will return to you, says the LORD of hosts." ZECHARIAH 1:3

Marriage can be tough. We surely need not look much further than divorce statistics to know that. Even before the advent of no-fault divorce and a culture in which the dissolution of marriage is no big deal, husbands and wives struggled. Relational strife inevitably comes with the territory of bringing two sinners together in a close covenant.

We like to talk about the three special words, *I love you*, which can sustain spouses. But three other words might be even more important during times of distress: *I am sorry.* Of course, they are meaningless if uttered in a flippant, trite, or angry way; but sincere apology and earnest, tenderhearted forgiveness (Ephesians 4:32) can really sustain a marriage: *I am sorry. I messed up. Would you please forgive me? Let's try this again. I love you. Let's go forward together.* A marriage necessarily involves a constant series of new beginnings, of reparations, of restorations. And when a marriage fails, it's often because the husband or the wife has refused to make the return to the other. (Sometimes, of course, for justifiable reasons, the Lord permitted the end of a marriage, as in the case of adultery, and 1 Corinthians 7 speaks the departure of an unbelieving spouse.)

This need for return applies not only to our relationship with our spouse but also to our relationship with God too. We often fail Him and make mistakes that bring dishonor to His name. We turn from Him in rebellion, disobey His word, and seek to chart our own destiny. And so, as in marriage, we must commit to returning to Him—though, in this case, we are always and ever the ones who stray.

James instructs us very directly to "draw near to God" (James 4:8). This was the Lord's call through Zechariah too: "Return to me, says the LORD of hosts." In both passages, the result is essentially the same, and it is wonderful: "He will draw near to you"; "I will return to you." If we hope to enjoy the presence of our great God and to know His blessing, then we must make sure that we are repenting of sin and returning to the Lord, constantly going back to Him, telling Him that we are sorry and we need His forgiveness, and recommitting to going forward together with Him.

In our failures, we may think that God wants nothing to do with us—that He's disgusted and angry. But the truth is that He is just waiting for us to come to Him, that He might once again draw close to us. God never refuses to allow us to return. So today, in which areas of your life do you need to return to God and say, *I am sorry.* Know that as you do that, He is delighted to receive you and to assure you once more, *I love you.*

HOSEA 14:1-9

APRIL 2

THE HUMBLE KING

"He sent two of the disciples, saying, 'Go into the village in front of you, where on entering you will find a colt tied, on which no one has ever yet sat. Untie it and bring it here' ... And they brought it to Jesus, and throwing their cloaks on the colt, they set Jesus on it." LUKE 19:29-30, 35

What we now call Palm Sunday was a crucial day in the most momentous week in the history of the entire world. Jesus' triumphal entry into Jerusalem prior to His crucifixion appears in all four Gospels, each of which approaches it from a slightly different vantage point. A closer look at the various iterations of this story would show us the complexity of the social dynamics that may not be apparent in reading Luke's account alone. Indeed, John's Gospel tells us that even Jesus' disciples didn't understand the impact of His entry into Jerusalem until after the resurrection (John 12:16).

We see in Jesus' triumphal entry a deliberate statement regarding His identity as He set His face steadfastly toward Jerusalem. He knew that He was fulfilling Old Testament prophecy from hundreds of years earlier: "Shout aloud, O daughter of Jerusalem! Behold, your king is coming to you; righteous and having salvation is he, humble and mounted on a donkey" (Zechariah 9:9). John tells us that the crowds swelled as they watched Jesus ride through the city gates because they had recently seen Him raise Lazarus from the grave (John 12:17-18). There was doubtlessly tremendous interest not only in Lazarus himself but also in the one who had performed that great miracle. When they sang "Blessed is the King who comes in the name of the Lord" (Luke 19:38), they therefore sang with great expectation that their Savior was in their midst. Few would have thought that their praise would soon turn to jeers.

Even as He proclaims His messiahship in this grand entrance, we ought to notice that Jesus is also presenting Himself as the ruler who is "gentle and lowly in heart" (Matthew 11:29)—the King on a donkey. Nowhere else in Scripture do we see Jesus riding any beast of burden, and certainly not a colt. To be the rider of an unbroken colt would be uncomfortable at the least. Yet our all-powerful King demonstrated His perfect humility by doing exactly that.

Pause to ask yourself: What kind of king arrives on a donkey and then proceeds to wear a crown of thorns? What sort of humility does that require, and what sort of love would do that? Many in the crowd expected the Messiah to be a conquering, nationalist hero. That was why their enthusiasm for Jesus lasted only as long as He met their expectations. We need to be careful that we do not decide what sort of king Jesus should be for us and to us and then fling accusations at Him when He does not meet our demands. Instead, we must see Him as He is: the King who came to carry a cross, who calls you and me to do the same as we follow Him, and who promises us not a comfortable life now but an eternal one to come. Here is a better, gentler, humbler, more loving King than any our own imaginations could ever conceive of.

LUKE 19:28-40

APRIL 3

THE PROMISE OF PARADISE

"He said, 'Jesus, remember me when you come into your kingdom.' And he said to him, 'Truly, I say to you, today you will be with me in paradise.'"
LUKE 23:42-43

Jesus was crucified between two convicted criminals—and those criminals both heard the words of Christ, yet they responded very differently. The first dying man regarded the cross as a contradiction. He concluded that because Jesus was on the cross, He was no Savior. So he ridiculed the man on the middle cross: "Are you not the Christ? Save yourself and us!" (Luke 23:39). But the second man saw the cross as confirmation. He recognized that because Jesus was on the cross, He must be the Savior.

This once hard-bitten criminal had seen and heard enough of Jesus in His final hours to conclude that He was innocent of any crime. And the Holy Spirit had opened his eyes to realize that his predicament was far greater and different from what he had formerly thought. Not only was he being punished justly, receiving the condemnation his sins deserved, but his punishment would extend into eternity if he lacked the forgiveness of which Jesus spoke.

Following this realization, the condemned man made a humble request to Jesus for what he knew he didn't deserve: "Jesus, remember me when you come into your kingdom." Presumably, he had processed the evidence, concluding, *If this man is the Messiah, then He's the long-promised King. If He's that King, then He's going to have a kingdom—the eternal kingdom of God. And when He reaches His kingdom, then perhaps He will remember me when He arrives there.*

Jesus' reply is wonderful: "Truly, I say to you, today you will be with me in paradise." Not only did Jesus promise that this man—even *this* man—would go to heaven; He also emphasized the immediate nature of that reality for this dying man: "today"! We may imagine them finishing their conversation not hanging on crosses at Calvary but sitting in the kingdom of God.

This criminal offered nothing and asked the King for everything. *And He said yes.* This should never fail to strike us and reassure us, for you and I are in the same position as that criminal. We have nothing to bring to Jesus, as though our deeds might be the key that opens the way into His kingdom. All we bring is all that the criminal brought: our sin. But that is why Jesus hung on the cross: so that we might bring our sin to Him and that He might take it and bear it. That is why Jesus' promise to the criminal is also His promise to every believer who dies: "Today you will be with me in paradise." Let that knowledge be your joy and fuel for your praise today. One day, you—even you—will be with your King in paradise.

REVELATION 21:1-7

APRIL 4

A TOTAL BLACKOUT

"It was now about the sixth hour, and there was darkness over the whole land until the ninth hour, while the sun's light failed." LUKE 23:44-45

Following Jesus' crucifixion, right around midday, the land was swallowed up in darkness. Imagine how unsettling that must have been! All of a sudden, people surely felt more vulnerable, more on edge. There may have been some who had been present at the arrest of Jesus and remembered that He had warned, "This is your hour, and the power of darkness" (Luke 22:53). But the majority probably said to one another, *I wonder what this darkness is about? I wonder why this is taking place?*

In one sense, they should have known the answer to that question. Jesus' death occurred during the celebration of the Passover in Jerusalem—a celebration that had taken place annually for hundreds of years. During this time, the Jews would recall that the final plague God sent over Egypt before the arrival of the angel of death and the death of the firstborn sons was that of darkness over all the land. They would recall that after the darkness came death: that on that occasion, only those who were protected by the blood of the Passover lamb awakened in the morning to find their firstborn still with them. And now, here, in the greater exodus previewed by that first one, darkness preceded the death of Christ, who was and is the perfect Passover Lamb.

It is as Sin-Bearer—as the perfect, spotless Lamb—that Jesus entered into the presence of the sinless God. What's more, He carried with Him no substitutionary sacrifice aside from Himself. Prior to this moment in history, to enter the holy place of God's presence in the temple in Jerusalem, the high priest had to make a sacrifice for his own sin, and *then* make sacrifice for the sins of those whom he represented. But this High Priest entered the heavenly presence of the holy God carrying nothing. Why? Because He Himself needed no sacrifice, for He was perfect, sinless; and yet *He Himself* was the sacrifice. Jesus was the Lamb. There was nothing else He *could* carry, and nothing else He *should* carry. As Peter explains, "He himself bore our sins in his body on the tree" (1 Peter 2:24).

And so the darkness of God's judgment did not have the last word. Because Jesus became sin, incurring the full fury of God's wrath, we can be transferred into God's kingdom, "into his marvelous light" (1 Peter 2:9). There is nothing else in all the world that demonstrates how real God's love is for sinners and how real our sin is to God.

Well might the sun in darkness hide
And shut his glories in
When Christ the mighty Maker died
For man the creature's sin.[31]

AMOS 8:1-14

31 Isaac Watts, "Alas, and Did My Savior Bleed" (1707).

APRIL 5

DIVINE VANDALISM

"It was now about the sixth hour, and there was darkness over the whole land until the ninth hour, while the sun's light failed. And the curtain of the temple was torn in two." LUKE 23:44-45

As Jesus' ministry progressed, one of the great concerns of the Jewish religious establishment was that He had, it appeared, claimed that He would destroy the temple and raise it again in three days (John 2:19). Indeed, this was one of the main charges brought against Him (Mark 14:58). When Jesus was on the cross, then, passersby mocked and ridiculed Him, shouting, "You who would destroy the temple and rebuild it in three days, save yourself!" (Matthew 27:40). But there He remained, hanging on the cross, in the darkness.

And then, in the midst of the darkness and the upheaval of the crucifixion, all of a sudden something mysterious and utterly unexpected happened: God Himself desecrated the temple.

"The curtain of the temple was torn in two," Luke tells us. This was the very curtain that hung in the temple to symbolically bar the way into God's presence. It was the great sign that imperfect people could not be in the same space as the holy God. All through the Old Testament, anyone who had presumed to come into God's presence without observing the ceremonial cleansing rituals and making the necessary sacrifices had died (for instance, Numbers 3:2-4). But now, suddenly, as Jesus was on the very verge of death, this symbol of restrictive exclusivity was destroyed. By destroying it, God declared that the old priestly ritual for entrance into His presence had been abolished and the barrier of sin dividing humanity from their Maker had been obliterated. There is no longer any need to keep our distance from God. Instead, "we have confidence to enter the holy places by the blood of Jesus, by the new and living way that he opened for us through the curtain" (Hebrews 10:19-20).

Our access to God isn't restricted to a temple or a church or any other building, nor must it be through a merely human priest or a guru. No, 2,000 years ago God broke into history to establish direct access to Himself through Jesus. Now there is "one mediator between God and men, the man Christ Jesus, who gave himself as a ransom for all" (1 Timothy 2:5-6). The temple curtain being torn in two was divine vandalism on your behalf! You don't have to be sidetracked by priests and rituals anymore. They can be nothing but pointless. Instead, you can come to God, just as you are, confident of welcome and mercy and help, all because of Jesus.

HEBREWS 10:19-25

APRIL 6

HE BREATHED HIS LAST

"Jesus, calling out with a loud voice, said, 'Father, into your hands I commit my spirit!' And having said this he breathed his last." LUKE 23:46

The simplicity of these words point us to truths that lie too deep for tears.

Luke, with his eye for detail, gives us an "orderly account" of Jesus' crucifixion—an account which, he explains at the start of his Gospel, is the result of careful investigation and has been written in order that his readers "may have certainty concerning the things you have been taught" (Luke 1:3-4). He doesn't seek to bathe his writing in pathos. Instead, he writes in order that we may understand truth. And so Jesus' dying breath is recounted for us in a simple phrase: "He breathed his last."

What Luke does want us to linger on is Jesus' control over His final breath. He chose to commit His spirit into His Father's loving hands. He knew that His work was done. Sin was paid for, the curtain was torn, and His people could come into His Father's presence eternally. Coupled with everything Jesus said prior to His crucifixion, His final words refute the notion that His death was simply that of a helpless victim being overwhelmed by cruel circumstances. He had told His disciples months before that He was going up to Jerusalem and that "the Son of Man must suffer many things and be ... killed" (Luke 9:22). John tells us that He had explained to them, "I lay down my life that I may take it up again. No one takes it from me, but I lay it down of my own accord. I have authority to lay it down, and I have authority to take it up again" (John 10:17-18).

Jesus went to the cross not helplessly but willingly. In accord with the Father's purpose, He chose the exact moment that He would lay down his life for His sheep (John 10:11). Here, then, we see the very Author of life willingly taking His final breaths and reminding us of His absolute authority as well as His inexhaustible love. "He breathed his last" so that you might breathe in the fresh, purified air that was made available to you the moment you were born again. "He breathed his last" so that one day you will stand in a restored creation and breathe air into lungs that will never decay or perish. He who is sovereign over the air you breathe sovereignly breathed His last. He is worthy of nothing less than your praise and adoration.

REVELATION 5:1-14

APRIL 7

THE CROSS OPENS OUR EYES

"When the centurion saw what had taken place, he praised God, saying, 'Certainly this man was innocent!'" LUKE 23:47

We have not understood the cross unless it has changed us personally.

After Jesus "breathed his last" (Luke 23:46), Luke records for us the reactions of those who witnessed the crucifixion. "All the crowds that had assembled for this spectacle, when they saw what had taken place, returned home beating their breasts" (v 48). Yes, there was sadness, but once the spectacle was over, they left to get on with their lives. Verse 49 then informs us that "all his acquaintances ... stood at a distance watching"—and we can only imagine what was running through their minds. But the most striking and the most personal reaction that Luke captures is that of the Roman centurion, who, seeing what had happened, "praised God, saying, 'Certainly this man was innocent!'"—or, as the NIV renders it, "Surely this was a righteous man."

Here, amid the darkness of hypocritical religious leaders, cynical rulers, and callous passersby, is a glimmer of light. Perhaps the last person we would expect to see the truth—a man with no previous connection to Jesus, no background in Old Testament studies, and no predisposition to the things of God—not only grasped what he was looking at but responded personally to it. He saw "what had taken place"—the words of Jesus, the darkness overhead, the manner of His death—and realized, *Here is no ordinary man. Here is a man who is different from every other man. Here is a man who is entirely innocent, wholly righteous.* Indeed, Mark adds that the centurion confessed that the man on the cross was "the Son of God" (Mark 15:39).

With his eye for detail, Luke places a clear emphasis on seeing what took place on the cross. He probably hoped that some readers would remember that when Jesus had read from the scroll of Isaiah earlier in His ministry, He had said, "The Spirit of the Lord ... has anointed me to proclaim good news to the poor ... to proclaim liberty to the captives and recovering of sight to the blind" (Luke 4:18). Indeed, a great theme found throughout the Gospel of Luke is that of darkness being invaded by light—the confusion and hardness of people's hearts and minds being invaded by the liberating power of God's truth.

Any attempt to articulate Christianity that denies the centrality of the cross can never lead to saving faith. And while we do not always understand how the Spirit moves in leading men and women to be born again, our message must always and ever be the same: "Christ crucified" (1 Corinthians 1:23). It is beholding the cross that brings life for anyone who responds to the man who hung there by confessing who He is and praising God for His saving work. Unless and until the cross is personal to us, it is useless for us. So, when was the last time you simply looked at your Savior on the cross and praised God?

1 CORINTHIANS 1:18-31

APRIL 8

OUT OF THE SHADOWS

"There was a man named Joseph, from the Jewish town of Arimathea. He was a member of the council, a good and righteous man, who had not consented to their decision and action; and he was looking for the kingdom of God. This man went to Pilate and asked for the body of Jesus." LUKE 23:50-52

Jesus' burial was by no means a foregone conclusion, for two main reasons. First, the crucifixion of criminals was often not the end of their humiliation; they were often barred from the honor of a proper burial. Second, the release of a corpse depended solely on a relative or friend requesting permission to bury the body—and who was left to bury Jesus? The disciples had fled, the crowd had dispersed, and the women were unprepared to make such a request.

It is into this moment of history that an individual emerges suddenly and silently—an individual who "was a disciple of Jesus, but secretly for fear of the Jews" (John 19:38).

Fear had silenced Joseph of Arimathea up to this point. Jesus' life and teaching had attracted him and brought him to saving faith, but his faith remained clandestine. He went about his spiritual business in a secretive way—that is, until the cross brought him out into the open. And so, after too long hanging back in the shadows, Joseph "went to Pilate and asked for the body of Jesus."

The Gospel narrative describes Joseph's careful handling of Jesus' body as he "took it down" from the cross, "wrapped it in a linen shroud and laid him in a tomb cut in stone, where no one had ever yet been laid" (Luke 23:53). We read likewise of Nicodemus, "who earlier had come to Jesus by night ... bringing a mixture of myrrh and aloes" to assist Joseph in the burial process (John 19:39).

Joseph's brief and singular appearance is also a clear reminder to us of God's providence at work at all times and in all places. God prepared Joseph for this very moment. Joseph was fearful and secretive, but God used him for good, just as He does us. Joseph had presumably missed many opportunities to stand up for his King; he had presumably kept quiet so many times when he should have spoken out. Yet it was this man whom God ensured would be present on this day for this important task. And Joseph rose to it, risking everything—his status, his reputation, his safety—to honor Jesus by ensuring that He had a proper burial.

You may find yourself identifying with Joseph: you have been living as a secret disciple, believing but afraid to let anyone in your neighborhood or workplace know about your faith. If so, then today, ask the Lord Jesus Christ to forgive your fearfulness and enable you, like Joseph, in the light of the cross, to take your stand boldly for Him in the love of Christ. You may have missed moments in the past when you had the chance to stand for your King; but God is always ready to give you the task of honoring His Son, and you need not pass up the next opportunity.

ACTS 4:1-22

APRIL 9

THE STONE WAS ROLLED AWAY

"Why do you seek the living among the dead? He is not here, but has risen."
LUKE 24:5-6

When we consider Jesus as Messiah, most of us think immediately in personal terms: *Jesus is my Messiah. He forgives my sins. He lives in me.* All of which, of course, is true. But 1st-century Jewish expectations concerning the messiahship of Jesus were far broader than that. If we had talked with a 1st-century Jew about his or her messianic expectations, we would have discovered hopes that were, in a sense, far grander in scope.

The Jews anticipated that their long-awaited Messiah would come to defeat the pagans who held sway over them, to rebuild the temple, and to establish God's just rule upon the earth. Theirs was a nationalistic hope—a hope that the Messiah would come and vindicate the nation of Israel. Jesus' arrival, together with the miracles He performed, the stories He told, and the prophecies He fulfilled, built to a great crescendo of expectation among His followers. But just when they began to think that He really would be the one to politically redeem the people of Israel, at Calvary they saw all their messianic hopes hanging up on a Roman gibbet. And when Jesus cried out, "It is finished" (John 19:30), many of them must have agreed.

How, then, did this group of believers, whose messianic hopes had been buried in a Palestinian tomb, not only continue to believe that Jesus was the Messiah but stand in the streets near where He had been executed and make an unashamed declaration of His messiahship? The answer which comes reverberating through the pages of the New Testament is found in the bodily resurrection of Jesus. The angelic announcement to the women who had brought spices to embalm a corpse provoked a radical reassessment of what the believers had witnessed on the Friday and a complete change in their view of their lives and futures. When the Messiah reappeared among them, as alive as ever, these previously sad, sorrowful, defeated, and brokenhearted disciples were transformed into bold, joyful witnesses. They now bore testimony to the reality of Christ resurrected with a body that could be seen, handled, and touched, and yet possessing capacities to do what His pre-resurrection body had not done. His work of salvation was finished; His life and His reign were most certainly not!

Only in the disciples' recognition of His risen presence did Christ's messiahship finally make sense. Indeed, what the early Jewish believers discovered when they "found the stone rolled away from the tomb" (Luke 24:2) and saw that "Jesus himself stood among them" (v 36) was that an eternal hope, joy, and power ignited within their hearts. And these remain available to all who put their trust in Jesus, the resurrected Messiah. It is the resurrection, and only the resurrection, that changes sadness, sorrow, and defeat into hope, joy, and power. It is the resurrection, and only the resurrection, that declares that our Messiah will defeat His enemies, will restore His people, and will rule from sea to sea. The resurrection of Jesus will change everything about how you go about your day today.

LUKE 24:1-12

APRIL 10

OVERCOME WITH KINDNESS

"Be kind to one another, tenderhearted, forgiving one another, as God in Christ forgave you." EPHESIANS 4:32

Polarization is common in our world—and always has been. Perhaps the vitriol that's spewed back and forth from the different sides of hot-button issues is more explicit and obvious in our media-saturated context. But the reality is that sin is the ultimate polarizer and has always pitted people against one another—and tragically, this has been true even among the people of God.

So how can we pursue peace in a polarized world? There is no easy solution, but there is a simple one: kindness. Through the apostle Paul, God commands us to "be kind to one another." 1 Thessalonians 5:15 contains a similar cue: "Seek to do good to one another and to everyone."

Perhaps commands like these sound a touch trite, even naive, given all the angst and hostility around (and which we so easily, and sometimes without even noticing, contribute to ourselves). But what if your life were characterized by kind words, emerging from kind thoughts and manifesting themselves in kind deeds? What sort of difference do you think that would make? If you think in concentric circles beginning with your family, and then neighbors, coworkers, and so on, what would your relationships look like if they were truly saturated with kindness?

Of course, it is one thing to imagine ourselves being kind; it is quite another altogether to actually demonstrate kindness to those around us—especially in disagreeable circumstances. In those moments when kindness seems like a pipe dream, don't forget the rest of Ephesians 4:32: we can only demonstrate kindness, tenderheartedness, and forgiveness *because God Himself has lavished every single one of those on us through Jesus Christ.*

Ephesians 2:14 puts it this way: "He himself is our peace." When Jesus Christ is your peace and you find steadfast hope in Him, and when you have a clear view on how in Him God forgave you, then you are ready to overflow with kindness to others. You'll encounter plenty of obstacles, to be sure, including from your own heart. But you simply cannot go wrong when you endeavor to shower others with kindness "by the strength that God supplies" (1 Peter 4:11).

EPHESIANS 4:32 – 5:2

APRIL 11

THE MIRROR OF GOD'S WORD

"For if anyone is a hearer of the word and not a doer, he is like a man who looks intently at his natural face in a mirror. For he looks at himself and goes away and at once forgets what he was like." JAMES 1:23-24

It's possible to be charmed by God's word without being changed by it.

The Bible gives us several accounts of those who listened carefully to the good news yet who remained unchanged (see, for example, Acts 19:9; Mark 6:20). How do we ensure that we avoid such a response when we open up the Bible and read its words?

We need to be clear that reading God's word is in and of itself not sufficient. To merely hear what God says is, James says, to be like a man who looks in a mirror and then does nothing about what he has seen. Seemingly, there are two ways that we forget what we have seen in the mirror of Scripture. One is by taking a *superficial* glance—looking in the mirror and immediately forgetting because we have not thoroughly considered what we have seen. When listening becomes its own end, then any benefit that may be gained is inevitably imperfect and short-lived. Casual observance does not lead to careful obedience, and lasting change cannot occur when we fool ourselves into thinking otherwise.

There is also *purposeful* forgetting—trying to deny or distract ourselves from the implications of the truth. One New Testament commentator writes that if a man "does see glimpses on his countenance of the ravages being wrought by sin, sickness, anxiety, or the inevitable passage of time, his instinct is to banish such a vision quickly from his memory. He turns at once to other things."[32] We gain a clear indication of what is going on in our hearts and minds when we desire to immediately forget—through use of excuse, caveat, or in simply refusing to think—what we have seen in the Bible because it has confronted us, challenged us, and called us to change.

There is great danger when we listen to the word superficially or with purposeful forgetfulness. The more we sit under the instruction of the Bible without being changed by it, the less likely the possibility of such change becomes. We grow hardened to the truth and more and more impervious to its transforming power.

The next time you sit under the tutelage of the Bible, then, consciously and prayerfully set aside any tendency toward casual observance or distraction. Instead, allow a holy awe to settle over you as you consider the significance of what you have heard and seen in God's word. Take a minute or two to contemplate it so that you do not forget what you have experienced, and then allow yourself, by God's enabling, to be transformed by the truth, doing what it says.

PSALM 119:25-32

32 R.V.G. Tasker, *The General Epistle of James: An Introduction and Commentary* (1956; repr., Eerdmans, 1971), p 52.

APRIL 12

WHAT TRUE FRIENDS LOOK LIKE

"A friend loves at all times, and a brother is born for adversity." PROVERBS 17:17

In the days before the internet, ham-radio operation was very popular. Individuals skilled with these radios placed giant antennae in their backyards or attached them to their sheds, and if you rode by on a bicycle in the evening, you could hear them shouting into the night, "Hello? Is anyone out there?" At times they'd be awake deep into the night, hoping that someone in the hemisphere would respond—hoping that eventually they might hear, "Hello, I'm in Anchorage, and I'm reading you loud and clear."

Our conversations today, whether in person, via texts, or through social media, really aren't that different. They all demonstrate a great yearning for friendship. We are all wired by God to look for others with whom we may be joined in intimacy and affection. So what are some of the characteristics of true friendship?

First, a true friend is always *loyal*. Friendship is not built on superficial or fleeting commonalities that might pass away. A loyal friend is prepared to be faithful through thick or thin, whether you are successful or unsuccessful, whether you enjoy the same movies or not, and irrespective of whether you have offended them or not. Even when you've made a real mess of things, they will be there to remind you that there's still a reason for hope.

Second, a true friend is always *honest*. It is impossible to enjoy or even to establish friendship where there is dishonesty. "Faithful are the wounds of a friend; profuse are the kisses of an enemy" (Proverbs 27:6). When a friend wounds your pride by being honest about your sin, you know that you can trust them—their willingness to risk your disapproval in order to tell you the truth reveals that they are worthy of your trust. The honest friend looks out for your well-being because they long for your best.

Third, a true friend is *sensitive*. They choose their words carefully, unlike "the man who deceives his neighbor and says, 'I am only joking'" (Proverbs 26:19). They refrain from gossip, because gossip always separates friends (16:28). A sensitive heart will cover an offense (17:9) because such a heart understands that "love covers a multitude of sins" (1 Peter 4:8). It's not that such friends don't call sin what it is, but that where matters of illegality or injustice are not at stake, they cast a veil of silence over our transgressions, much in the same way that our heavenly Father chooses to remember our sins no more (Hebrews 8:12).

Who is a friend such as this? Only one truly is this friend who "loves at all times"—your friend Jesus. Yet we are called not only to enjoy His friendship but also to imitate it—and with Jesus as our role model, we can learn to be true friends to those He places in our care. Whom has the Lord given you to be a friend to? What will it look like for you to show them loyalty, speak to them honestly, and treat them sensitively? What a glorious realization it would be for them to see that, in you, they have a friend who truly seeks to love them at all times.

PHILIPPIANS 2:19-30

APRIL 13

GOD'S PLAN ALL ALONG

"By a single offering he has perfected for all time those who are being sanctified."
HEBREWS 10:14

It's hard to fathom Christ's final, agonizing hours upon a Roman cross. The floggings, torture, and humiliation He endured were reserved for the worst of criminals. It is no wonder, then, that with His last breath, Jesus cried out in a loud voice, *Tetelestai!*—"It is finished" (John 19:30).

But what was this cry? Was Jesus simply announcing His own death? Was it an acknowledgment that the cruelty and pain were now finished? Was it even something of a cry of defeat?

On this point, the Bible is clear: Jesus' final word was actually a shout of victory, of triumphant recognition (Colossians 2:15; Hebrews 10:12-14; 1 Peter 3:18). He had fully accomplished the work He had come to earth to do. In the realm of eternity, in perfect fellowship and harmony with one another, the Father had planned, and the Son along with the Spirit had willingly agreed, that this would be the way—and now their purpose was being accomplished.

So we must always remember that Christ's sacrificial death was according to the Father's plan. Christ was chosen to bear the penalty of mankind's sins "before the foundation of the world" (1 Peter 1:20). Likewise, Isaiah prophesied concerning the Suffering Servant who was to come, saying, "It was the will of the LORD to crush him" (Isaiah 53:10). From all of eternity, the Father chose the Son to be the one who would provide an atoning sacrifice for the sins of many.

The Father's plan is paralleled by the Son's sacrifice. When Jesus walked onto the stage of human history, He was clear concerning His role and mission: "I have come down from heaven, not to do my own will but the will of him who sent me" (John 6:38). The sacrifice of the Lord Jesus was not coerced. Rather, He laid down His life in full awareness of and voluntary submission to the Father's plan.

The truth and reality of this covenant plan of redemption is applied to our lives by the Spirit's testimony. The Spirit of God testifies through God's word, reminding us of the wonder of what God has accomplished for us through Christ's finished work on the cross (Hebrews 10:15). Christ's offering means you stand perfected in God's sight. Your sin has been removed by His Son, and you are clothed in the righteousness of His Son.

The death and resurrection of the Lord Jesus Christ was never Plan B. Nothing could be further from the truth! In eternity past, the triune God determined that the road to Calvary would be the way of salvation. Bow today under the beauty and wisdom of God's redemption plan, asking the Holy Spirit to help you understand more fully and appreciate more deeply what it meant for the Son of God to bear and take away your sin.

ISAIAH 52:13 – 53:12

APRIL 14

GRACE FOR EVERY FAILURE

"They found the eleven and those who were with them gathered together, saying, 'The Lord has risen indeed, and has appeared to Simon!' Then they told what had happened on the road, and how he was known to them in the breaking of the bread." LUKE 24:33-35

The New Testament mentions twice that the risen Christ appeared to Peter: once in this passage and again in 1 Corinthians 15:5. Why would Peter, of all people, receive such special treatment?

After all, not long before this event, Peter had failed his Master in His darkest hour. Just before Jesus was arrested, He told Peter that a trial lay ahead: "Simon, Simon, behold, Satan demanded to have you, that he might sift you like wheat, but I have prayed for you that your faith may not fail." Peter responded, rather audaciously, "Lord, I am ready to go with you both to prison and to death." But Jesus knew Peter's heart: "I tell you, Peter, the rooster will not crow this day, until you deny three times that you know me" (Luke 22:31-34).

As it turned out, Peter wasn't as ready to face prison and death as he had imagined. We all know now, as did Jesus that very day, that Peter did indeed go on to deny his Lord three times. And afterward, when Peter recalled what Jesus had predicted and realized what he had done, he was reduced to tears (Matthew 26:75; Luke 22:62).

So why does the New Testament emphasize that the risen Lord Jesus appeared to Peter? Certainly not because Peter *deserved* it more than anybody else. But it's fair to wonder if Jesus appeared to Peter because he *needed* it more than anybody else. Peter knew that he had blown it completely—and yet while Peter had denied Jesus, Jesus didn't deny Peter. What mercy, what goodness, what kindness, what grace, what compassion, that Jesus still chose to go to the cross for His flawed disciple and then chose to make a special appearance to him!

We have stumbled. We have been deniers, deserters, staggerers. We know that we do not deserve for God to come to us. And yet as we go to God's word and as we open our lives to its truth, it's almost as though Jesus comes, sits right down beside us, and says, *I'm here. I want to speak to you. I want to assure you. I want to forgive you. I want to send you out in My power.*

Peter didn't deserve the compassion he received from Jesus—and honestly, neither do we. Our failures show us time and time again that we are far from being worthy of God's grace. But in His mercy, He is pleased to give it anyway—and then give some more. He's just that kind of God. And you, like Peter, get to be His beloved disciple.

JOHN 21:15-24

APRIL 15

A GOD-GIVEN BURDEN

"He has made everything beautiful in its time. Also, he has put eternity into man's heart, yet so that he cannot find out what God has done from the beginning to the end." ECCLESIASTES 3:11

Ultimately, there are no true atheists. Those who claim atheism may be unwilling to acknowledge this about themselves, but God has given to every person a heavy burden. In the deep recesses of their being, they know that God *is*—and it is the very "is-ness" of God which creates a dilemma in men's and women's hearts and minds.

God created the world, and He made it beautiful in all of its perfection. God also made mankind to know Him, to commune with Him, to walk with Him in the garden, and to enjoy all the benefits of His companionship. But man turned his back on the Designer, and as a result the perception of eternity that has been implanted within us now largely tyrannizes and tests us.

People naturally seek to repress a knowledge of God (Romans 1:18-19), but a knowledge of God is inescapable. God has created us for a divine purpose—to know and worship Him—and unless we discover and fulfill that purpose, we will never be fully satisfied with anything else offered along life's journey. No relationship with a child, parent, spouse, lover, or friend can fulfill this great longing, nor can any experience, any possession, or any achievement. This is the burden that God has laid on humanity: we will be forever dissatisfied until we come to know the only thing that can bear the weight of our eternity—namely, to know Him and live in fellowship with Him.

You and I, who are creatures of time, were made for eternity. We were made for God's presence. It should therefore be no surprise to us that when we turn away from Him, our lives are marked by frustration and confusion. When we choose to live in the dark, we lose our sight. The day that we finally acknowledge this is a great day. The burden of being without God will weigh you down until you realize there has to be an answer somewhere, in someone else. And, of course, there is.

There are many things in this life that are beautiful, and we are free to enjoy them in accordance with the way God designed us to. But there is nothing in this life that is ultimate, and we will not be free until we not only acknowledge this intellectually but live it out in our experience. Is there something that you are determined to have, or to get, in your life because you think it will make you truly alive and fulfilled? What is it that you feel you could not live, or could not be happy, without? Be careful not to allow something good to become your god. Instead, place your ultimate hopes on the shoulders of the only one who is strong enough to bear them: the Eternal One.

MATTHEW 6:25-34

APRIL 16

GOD'S POWER IN TIMES OF PAIN

"We were so utterly burdened beyond our strength that we despaired of life itself. Indeed, we felt that we had received the sentence of death. But that was to make us rely not on ourselves but on God who raises the dead. He delivered us from such a deadly peril, and he will deliver us. On him we have set our hope that he will deliver us again." 2 CORINTHIANS 1:8-10

Christians do not have to pretend that life feels great all the time.

The apostle Paul certainly didn't mind admitting to hardship. In fact, Paul's trials led him to say of his troubles in Asia, "We despaired of life itself. Indeed, we felt that we had received the sentence of death." Trials and troubles will inevitably come—and, like Paul, we don't have to act as though everything is always fine.

As we are honest with ourselves and others about our trials, we must also remind ourselves that God has a purpose in our pain. Paul says of his burden that "this was to make us rely not on ourselves." Isn't it true that when life is going great, when everything seems rosy, we tend to just cruise along? Then trouble hits, and suddenly we're forced back to reliance on God. He purposes affliction—illness, loss, difficulty in the workplace, a wayward child—that we might not rely on ourselves but on Him alone.

And what kind of God does Paul say we rely on in our trouble? One "who raises the dead." In every death—both in the deaths of dreams, hopes, and health in life and then in death itself at the end of life—we can cling to the God who has triumphed over death and will lead us to fullness of life in eternity. It is through the resurrection of Jesus Christ that God delivers us from sin now and frees us to hope in a final deliverance from all suffering and death. As we await our full experience of resurrection hope, God uses our trials and weaknesses to keep us close to Him.

In Jesus' own life, resurrection power came *after* crucifixion pain. The same pattern holds for us. It is in dying that we live. It is in weakness that we are strong. It is in emptiness that we are full. It is in self-forgetfulness that we find true security and confidence in God.

When God sovereignly allows affliction to shake up your life, remember that He has designed that very trial for you to draw closer to Him and rely more fully on Him. And as you learn to rely on Him more and more, His strength will shine through your weakness, and you will know true spiritual power, even through the pain.

2 CORINTHIANS 1:3-11

APRIL 17

THE HOPE OF THE RIGHTEOUS

"The hope of the righteous brings joy, but the expectation of the wicked will perish." PROVERBS 10:28

There's a prevailing notion in contemporary Western culture that death is the great equalizer—that no matter what you've believed or what you've done or haven't done, it will all be evened out when we die. The Bible says that this is not the case—that it is the righteous alone who can look forward to discovering that in God's "presence there is fullness of joy" and that at His "right hand are pleasures forevermore" (Psalm 16:11).

In the book of Esther, we can see the contrast between the hope of the righteous and the expectation of the wicked. Following counsel from his wife and friends, Haman decided to build a gallows that could hang the man who annoyed him most, Mordecai (Esther 5:14). The next day, however, Haman went back to his wife and that same group of friends and told them how the king had made him lead Mordecai through the streets to honor him. His confidants quickly went from coming up with an idea that pleased Haman to offering these sobering words: "If Mordecai, before whom you have begun to fall, is of the Jewish people, you will not overcome him but will surely fall before him" (6:13). While Haman had expected to be exalted and to see his enemy defeated, his friends seemed to recognize that his wicked plans were failing and that God's purposes would be fulfilled for His people.

In the night between these conversations, Mordecai was presumably asleep. The threat of death was hanging over his head—but he was blissfully ignorant of his probable doom. Yet even if he had known what Haman had planned for him, Mordecai still had no means of intervening to save himself. His only hope was the providence of God—and that hope alone would have been enough to bring him peace.

It turned out that, in the event, Haman had to unwillingly declare Mordecai's honor. He wasn't happy about it. Similarly, the Bible says that on the day of Christ's return, when every knee will bow before Jesus Christ and declare Him to be Lord (Philippians 2:10-11), some will bow unwillingly while others will bow rejoicing. In other words, as with Haman, "the expectation of the wicked will perish," but "the hope of the righteous" will carry on for all eternity.

If you have trusted in Christ and received His righteousness as your own, you can bow before Him with great joy as your Savior and friend, as well as your Lord. With this hope, you have every reason to rest peacefully, for you can joyfully look forward—even through tears, pain, disappointment, and regret—to being in God's presence forevermore.

LUKE 23:32-43

APRIL 18

AN INVITATION TO WISDOM

"If any of you lacks wisdom, let him ask God, who gives generously to all without reproach, and it will be given him." JAMES 1:5

"Wisdom" has fallen rather out of fashion. Did you encounter the word with any frequency over the past week or so? Most likely, you didn't read it in any articles or hear about it from schoolteachers. *Wisdom* has become almost an old-fashioned word, neglected in favor of terms like *insight*, *information*, and *intelligence*. But none of these words, individually or combined, still do not add up to wisdom.

Wisdom is not mental; it is moral. It is knowing how to live God's way in God's world and acting on that. Jesus memorably talked about wisdom in terms of the wise and the foolish builders (Luke 6:46-49). The wise man built his house upon the rock, and the waves came tumbling round, and the house stood firm. The foolish man built his house upon the sand, and it collapsed. The difference between the two types of people this story represents is that while both hear Jesus' words, only the wise put them into practice, building their lives upon them, allowing their decisions to be directed and their desires to be shaped by what He says.

By nature, we lack such wisdom. But the invitation to wisdom in this verse from James is gracious and inclusive. To accept it, we first must recognize our need of wisdom; humility is always wisdom's precursor (Proverbs 1:7). Once we acknowledge that need, James then encourages us to simply ask God, who abides in faithfulness and provides "every good gift and every perfect gift" (James 1:17). Jesus has likewise told us, "Ask, and it will be given to you; seek, and you will find; knock, and it will be opened to you. For everyone who asks receives, and the one who seeks finds, and to the one who knocks it will be opened" (Matthew 7:7-8).

If we come to God sincerely, He promises to give His wisdom generously without making us feel guilty or foolish. We often repeat our requests and concerns because the trials are real and the hills are steep, but God is not annoyed or dismissive. He is eager to help!

James understood that through life's joys and sorrows we may be tempted to think differently than from God's perspective. With wisdom, though, we are able to act in the light of God's revelation of Himself, walking through life with sure footsteps as we seek to obey His commands and trust that He will be guiding our steps. Through His wisdom, you can act simply and properly, with thankfulness that God is so generous and gracious. All you need do is to accept that you need it and to ask for it—and then get on with your day, secure in the knowledge that, once you've asked, "it will be given" to you.

PROVERBS 1:1-8

Bible Through The Year: Daniel 1-2; Revelation 5

APRIL 19

OUR RESURRECTED BODIES

"As they were talking about these things, Jesus himself stood among them, and said to them, 'Peace to you!'" LUKE 24:36

The resurrection of Jesus shows us not only that we have an eternal future but what kind of eternal future it is.

Jesus' death left His disciples in a state of shock and defeat. Death had won. Then, when conflicting reports arose concerning His post-resurrection appearances, confusion reigned, and it became obvious that only one thing would settle the matter: if Jesus would appear and reveal Himself. And that is exactly what took place!

It was while the disciples "were talking about these things"—about Jesus' death and resurrection—that "Jesus himself stood among them." You can imagine the disciples in full flow, debating with one another as to the whereabouts of their Master. Then, in the middle of their discussion, suddenly Jesus was part of the discussion! His appearance was so dramatic, in fact, that the disciples "were startled and frightened and thought they saw a spirit" (Luke 24:37).

Jesus' appearance provided His disciples with more than just the physical proof of His bodily resurrection. It also testified to what awaits all believers in eternity—namely, a glorified body. He rose from the dead with a transformed body that would never die again—indeed, which cannot die again. Over His body, death is now impotent—and as Paul later wrote, "So is it with the resurrection of the dead" (1 Corinthians 15:42). When we die in Christ, we will never die again, "for as in Adam all die, so also in Christ shall all be made alive. But each in his own order: Christ the firstfruits, then at his coming those who belong to Christ" (v 22-23). Our bodies, which are perishable now, will be raised imperishable (v 42). No longer will we be subject to disease, decay, and death. Furthermore, our present physical bodies, which are "sown in dishonor" and "weakness," will be "raised in glory" and "power" (v 43). We will be free from every selfish, passionate desire of the flesh and will no longer be subject to its weaknesses and limitations.

The resurrected Lord Jesus didn't only conquer sin and death in His own body; He conquered the power of sin and death in our bodies too. One day we shall look in the mirror and see nothing to make us feel sad, or sorry, or scared. So today, no matter how frail your body or sinful your flesh, press on, fixing your eyes on what lies ahead, for "our citizenship is in heaven, and from it we await a Savior, the Lord Jesus Christ, who will transform our lowly body to be like his glorious body, by the power that enables him even to subject all things to himself" (Philippians 3:20-21). What a hope! What an inheritance!

1 CORINTHIANS 15:35-49

APRIL 20

JOYFUL REST IN A FRANTIC WORLD

"There are many who say, 'Who will show us some good? Lift up the light of your face upon us, O Lord!' You have put more joy in my heart than they have when their grain and wine abound. In peace I will both lie down and sleep; for you alone, O Lord, make me dwell in safety." PSALM 4:6-8

The great majority of humans are striving after wind. We chase all sorts of things to satisfy our souls but keep ending up empty-handed. We wonder, "Who will show us some good?" Put differently, "Where can I find joy, meaning, and hope in the frenetic pace and frustrating pursuits of this life?"

Thankfully, the psalmist does not leave us to wonder about what we need most: "Lift up the light of your face upon us, O Lord." The great need of David's day—and our day, thousands of years later—is to embrace and be embraced by the living God. So David points out just how the greatest pleasures pale in comparison to finding the one true, living God. Abounding in life's good gifts, be they grain or wine or anything else, is certainly no bad thing. But knowing God is infinitely, gloriously better.

How many people today live in the hope that the experience of tomorrow will bring the joy they seem to lack today? "Just a little more money; then I can be happy. Just a little more of this or that, and then I will be satisfied." But it's not the promise of a nicer car, a bigger house, a perfect spouse, or a better job that truly gives us lasting peace and rest. There is only one way to be able to lie down and sleep in peace, content and secure. What makes such rest possible? "You alone, O Lord, make me dwell in safety." Only when we find all we need in knowing the Lord and know that He is smiling at us will we be able to lie down without anxiety or regret.

As you lie on your bed at night and reflect on the day, or as all of tomorrow's to-dos race through your mind, how will you hold it together? What will give you the stability and security that every human being in the world longs for? In the end, it won't be the money in your account. It won't be the home-security system. It won't be enjoying admiration from your community. It is the Lord alone who leads His beloved children to true peace, rest, and security. In the arms of the Good Shepherd, you can dwell in safety and rest in peace. Be sure, when you lie down tonight or when worries rear their heads today, to remember that the Lord loves you and is looking after you. That is where rest and peace are truly and eternally to be found.

PHILIPPIANS 4:4-9

APRIL 21

LIVING WATER

"Jesus said to her, 'Everyone who drinks of this water will be thirsty again, but whoever drinks of the water that I will give him will never be thirsty again. The water that I will give him will become in him a spring of water welling up to eternal life.'" JOHN 4:13-14

When Jesus met the Samaritan woman at the well and asked her for a drink, she assumed that she would be providing what He needed: a literal drink of water. Instead, she discovered that actually she needed what only this stranger was able to provide: a spiritual drink of living water.

Jesus helped her to see this need with one simple command: "Go, call your husband, and come here" (John 4:16). He asked her to do what she couldn't do, because although she had been married five times she was now living with a man who was not her husband. He helped her see how her ongoing search for satisfaction had left her wanting. Famed mathematician and philosopher Blaise Pascal wrote that we have within each of us a God-shaped void.[33] She was no exception.

Every one of us digs figurative wells all over the place that will never truly satisfy (Jeremiah 2:13)—our careers, our marriages, our friendships, our families, our wealth, our next vacation, or whatever experiences give us a high. But they all leave us thirsty for more. We will keep digging and drinking until we are confronted by our *real* need: that our sin needs to be cleansed and forgiven, our desires need to be transformed, and our hearts need to be filled with Jesus. He is the only one able to hold the weight of all our hopes and longings.

This woman arrived at the well empty, searching, and desperate. In Christ she met God—the same God who created our inmost being, who knows the words we've yet to speak, who can tell us everything we've ever done (John 4:19; see also Psalm 139: 4, 13). She brought her empty life to this wonderful source of living water: Christ Himself. She brought her sinful past to the cleansing supply that only Jesus provides. She brought her hopes for the future to the one who knew everything about her and loved her still, enough to quench her thirst forever.

On what are you tempted to hang your hopes, other than God? Where do you look for satisfaction, other than to Jesus? He has offered you the drink that will quench your thirst forever and become a spring that can never run dry. He has taken what He doesn't deserve—the punishment for your sin—so that He can give you what you don't deserve: salvation, forgiveness, freedom, hope. Draw from this saving well moment by moment, today and every day, and thirst no more.

JOHN 4:1-26

33 *Pensées*, 7.425.

APRIL 22

TURN TO THE SCRIPTURES

"The word of God is living and active, sharper than any two-edged sword, piercing to the division of soul and of spirit, of joints and of marrow, and discerning the thoughts and intentions of the heart." HEBREWS 4:12

For the first readers of the book of Hebrews, the metaphor in this verse would have drawn to mind the *gladius*, the Roman short sword. These swords had y-shaped tips that looked almost like steel tongues. It is to this that the writer to the Hebrews compares the word of God. In Revelation, too, Jesus refers to His authoritative word as the "sword of my mouth" (Revelation 2:16). Whether pricking the conscience, cutting away our camouflages, piercing through Satan's lies, or offering us encouragement, the sword of God's word is sharp enough for all our needs.

Jesus understood the sufficiency of Scripture in every situation and modeled for us a complete dependence upon it. In the face of temptation, He turned to the Bible to answer the Evil One, warding off his attacks (Matthew 4:1-11; Luke 4:1-12). After His resurrection, in order to revitalize the despondent duo on the road to Emmaus, He turned them to God's word and "beginning with Moses and all the Prophets, he interpreted to them in all the Scriptures the things concerning himself" (24:27). Why did He not simply show them His nail-pierced hands? Because He knew that while the opportunity to see His wounds would be limited to a moment and a few observers, there would be many generations who followed them who could not walk along the road with Him—but they would still have the Scriptures and would be able to read them to see "the things concerning himself." The unerring truth of God's word would be sufficient for God's people in all times and in all places.

We live in an environment in which long-held convictions have been shaken. Confidence in Scripture has significantly eroded. Few truly trust in its authority and its sufficiency to accomplish the purposes for which God has ordained it. It may not become fully apparent in one generation, but as time passes the declension, the rot, the misgivings, the disinterest, and the wrongful preoccupations will yield bitter fruit.

Beware anything that encourages you to waver on your convictions concerning the singular authority and absolute sufficiency of Scripture. Beware moments when your own heart seeks to blunt God's word, either by not reading it or not applying it. Instead, open your Bible and ask the Spirit of God to go to work with His sword, piercing your thoughts and intentions, showing you Jesus, and reminding you time and time again of His love and of the power of His word.

MATTHEW 4:1-11

APRIL 23

LIVING THE RISEN LIFE

"If then you have been raised with Christ, seek the things that are above, where Christ is, seated at the right hand of God." COLOSSIANS 3:1

In the miracle of conversion, a number of things happen. Our sins are forgiven, we're adopted into God's family, and we're given the status of sons and daughters. Not only that, but we're also given a new location with Christ in the heavenly places. There is for the Christian a radical change in our spiritual environment as a result of our union with the risen Christ—and it is our place in Christ that establishes our priorities. It is because we have been "raised with Christ" that we are to "seek the things that are above."

This reality was important for the Colossian church to grasp. As Paul was writing to them, they were being influenced by deceptive doctrine. False teachers were imposing man-made rules upon them, saying, "Do not handle, Do not taste, Do not touch" (Colossians 2:21). Yet these external rules, which were intended to improve moral behavior, ironically were "of no value in stopping the indulgence of the flesh" (v 23). The same remains true for us: even when we attempt to remove ourselves from sin, we won't be able to stop our own propensity towards that which is impure, unholy, and untrue.

This form of external religion was a bad virus that was threatening to embed itself within the Colossian church, combining doctrinal confusion with moral carelessness. (The two go hand in hand.) So Paul addressed the issue by reminding his Colossian readers that the way to get to grips with our behavior is by understanding who we are—what we have become in the Lord Jesus Christ.

As Christians, our lives are wrapped up in Jesus. We are in Him, and He is in us. We have been raised with Christ, and our lives are hidden in Him. This fact alone is the only sure basis of our security—our confidence in the face of our own propensity to do wrong things.

Are you trying to live the Christian life by your own efforts and fight sin in your own strength? Are you seeking to be a better Christian and wondering why it is proving elusive—or, worse, are you beginning to wonder whether you are a Christian at all or whether it is worth the effort? As you live in this world, don't dwell upon your failures or look to your own performance as the basis of your security. You have been raised with Christ. He alone is your hope. Make His glory, and not your own goodness, the focus of your days and you will find that your behavior will bear testimony to His life-transforming power.

GALATIANS 5:16-25

APRIL 24

THINKING DEEPLY FOR GOD'S SAKE

"Think over what I say, for the Lord will give you understanding in everything."
2 TIMOTHY 2:7

It is not unusual—in fact, it's quite common—for Christian faith to be regarded as a kind of illogical belief in improbable events. For some, faith is seen as a crutch to prop up less rational people as they navigate life's challenges. Such critics may be surprised to learn that in reality, Christianity calls its followers not to *neglect* their minds but to *critically engage* them.

When we read the Bible, we discover that it never invites us simply to feel things; it never attempts merely to sweep us up in an emotional surge. God never once asks for or endorses the disengagement of our thinking processes. Instead, God's word repeatedly shows us that Christianity is actually a call to think rightly and deeply about God, His world, and our place in it.

When the apostle Paul addressed the Ephesians, we read that he was "reasoning daily in the hall of Tyrannus," which was likely a school for philosophy or rhetoric (Acts 19:9). Paul wasn't just singing songs or attempting to stir up some emotional experience. No, he essentially said, *Citizens of Ephesus, I want you to think and reason with me today.* In Thessalonica, too, Acts tells us that Paul "reasoned" with the people, "explaining and proving that it was necessary for the Christ to suffer and to rise from the dead" (17:2-3). The book of Isaiah begins with a similar call to think earnestly: "Come now, let us reason together, says the LORD" (Isaiah 1:18).

This exhortation to think and reason isn't just for proclaiming the gospel but for growth in Christian maturity too. Writing to the Corinthians, Paul said, "Brothers, do not be children in your thinking" (1 Corinthians 14:20). He wanted the church to think intently and intensely about the issues they were facing. Paul was even more direct when he wrote to Timothy: "Think over what I say, for the Lord will give you understanding in everything." We do need God's Spirit to be at work in order to think rightly (Luke 24:45; 1 Corinthians 12:3), for our intellects are as affected by sin as every other part of ourselves (Ephesians 4:17). But it is as we expend mental energy to consider the wisdom of the Scriptures that God will give us greater and greater understanding.

To follow Christ, then, is not to take a step of blind faith into the darkness but to have your eyes opened to the light of rigorous truth. It will take a lifetime—and more!—to unearth the riches of the truth you encounter in God's word about His Son, but one thing is sure: today, as every day, God wants you to love Him and honor Him with all your mind.

PSALM 1

APRIL 25

THE WAY TO HAVE HOPE

"This I call to mind, and therefore I have hope: The steadfast love of the LORD never ceases; his mercies never come to an end." LAMENTATIONS 3:21-22

Where, ultimately, do you find your hope?

The exile in Babylon left the people of Israel without any hope. Everything that had been theirs—all that had brought them joy—had vanished, left far behind in Judah. Jeremiah expressed their common sentiment: "My endurance has perished; so has my hope from the LORD" (Lamentations 3:18). Yet just a few verses letter, his tone completely changes: "This I call to mind, and therefore I have hope" (v 21). The circumstances hadn't improved. Nothing had changed. So why the sudden positivity?

The answer is simple: because of faith.

Christianity is about history. It's about reality. It's about real people in real time having real encounters with a real God. It's not fiction. And so it makes a real difference.

No one's experience of this life is marked only by great seasons of joy and triumph. Difficulties confront us with our finitude. Our loved ones die, marriages disintegrate even when we've done our best to sustain them, our health proves frail, and our failures from the past arise like demons in the night.

So what do we need to do when we encounter life's difficulties? We need to do what Jeremiah does! He starts with his faith—with what he believes about God—and he thinks. He brings his mind to bear upon his feelings—and so must we. In our trials, we must remember who God is and then bring our honest petitions before Him. You can pray, "Gracious God, You made me. You love me in Jesus. You've promised that You'll hold me fast. I'm not feeling very secure right now, Lord, but I also know what Your word says: that Your steadfast love never ceases and Your mercies never come to an end."

In the midst of triumphs and trials alike, here is what can give you stability: that God's steadfast love and mercies toward you will never expire. Rest secure in this, then: that though all hell may be let loose against you, the Lord God omnipotent reigns, and He does so perfectly, with love and mercy. He will accomplish His purposes. Nothing can stand in His way. Call to mind these truths in the day of trouble and you can live with an unassailable hope in your heart and remain firm in your faith to the end.

LAMENTATIONS 3:16-33

APRIL 26

SEEING JESUS ONE MORE TIME

"He presented himself alive to them after his suffering by many proofs, appearing to them during forty days and speaking about the kingdom of God." ACTS 1:3

Jesus could have simply risen from the dead and gone directly to heaven. After all, the work of redemption was complete. He had made full atonement in His death, and He had triumphed over death. Why not just return directly to the Father? Because Jesus did not intend to leave His followers with their final memories of Him bloodied and beaten, hanging on a cross. Rather, their last memories were to be of a *resurrected* Christ.

It is a mark of His grace and kindness that after His resurrection Jesus "presented himself alive" to His disciples. He answered their questions. He banished their fears. He "opened their minds" to better understand the Old Testament Scriptures (Luke 24:45). He prepared them for the coming of the Holy Spirit. And then, and only then, did He leave.

How glad doubting Thomas must have been that Jesus did not leave immediately! Had Jesus done so, Thomas would have been unable to meet his Savior and to have his questions answered and his fears dispelled (John 20:24-29). Surely Peter, too, in all of his discouragement and in his disgrace, was equally glad of the opportunity to spend time with the risen Jesus. He had denied Christ repeatedly at the crucial hour. But then Jesus came and met him on the shore, made him breakfast, and gave him the opportunity to be reinstated as he gave a threefold affirmation of his love for Christ (21:15-19). And don't you think the mother of Jesus was also glad for these 40 days? She who had laid Him in the manger had witnessed the brutality that was meted out upon her son, her boy, on the cross. But Mary's final vision of Jesus was of Him resurrected and ascending—a vision that prompted her and those with her to worship Him and return to Jerusalem "with great joy" (Luke 24:52).

This final vision of Jesus as the resurrected, all-powerful, ascended King is the answer for those of us who have been looking in other places to find an antidote to doubt, shame, fear, or grief. The cross is empty, as is the tomb. King Jesus is in His heavenly dwelling place, and He is coming back. Until then, lift up your head, know that your Savior lives and His kingdom is open, and encourage your soul as you praise your King:

Jesus, hail! enthroned in glory,
There forever to abide;
All the heavenly hosts adore Thee,
Seated at Thy Father's side.
There for sinners Thou art pleading;
There Thou dost our place prepare;
Thou for saints art interceding
Till in glory they appear.[34]

LUKE 24:36-43

34 John Bakewell, "Hail, Thou Once Despisèd Jesus!" (1757).

APRIL 27

GOD WORKS THROUGH EVERY GIFT

"As each has received a gift, use it to serve one another, as good stewards of God's varied grace." 1 PETER 4:10

Good parents give gifts to all their children, excluding none. Thoughtful parents select appropriate gifts for each child to match their stage, aptitudes, and character. If we care for our children and love them without favoritism, we will give to each one what is fitting at any given time to meet his or her unique needs and desires. And often the best gifts are ones that can, while owned by one child, then be enjoyed by the whole family.

Our heavenly Father operates in the same way. He gives gifts to all His people—generously, lavishly, and purposefully.

Three verses in 1 Corinthians 12 confirm to us God's generosity to all His children:

- "It is the same God who empowers" all kinds of gifts and service and activities "in *everyone*" (v 6, emphasis added).
- "*To each* is given the manifestation of the Spirit for the common good" (v 7, emphasis added).
- Every spiritual gift is "empowered by one and the same Spirit, who apportions *to each* individually as he wills" (v 11, emphasis added).

Like a good parent, God gives gifts to all His children, all for the good of Christ's body, the church family.

Sometimes, though, untaught by our Bibles and unguided by the Spirit, we take the view that the people who really count are those who possess certain gifts—whatever those gifts might be, in whatever given context. This elitism leads to defeatism: those without the "privileged" gifts feel they have no meaningful contribution to make.

We must therefore be very clear on the basics of spiritual gifts. Who gives them? *God.* Who gets them? *All believers.* Spiritual gifts are not reserved for a chosen few; they are the privilege of the whole Christian family. Our gifts differ, but we all have them, and every gift is good, necessary, and integral to the life of the body. Each one is given for the "common good," as 1 Corinthians 12:7 puts it.

Instead of wondering about what we haven't received, being jealous of what someone else has been given, or wishing we could exchange our gift, God wants us to enjoy and make use of what He *has* kindly provided to us. "As each has received a gift," says Peter, "use it to serve one another, as good stewards of God's varied grace." As God's child, you are a recipient of God's grace. He has given you abilities and opportunities. He calls you, in the strength He supplies, to steward that grace for the fame of Christ's name and the good of His family. So consider: What are the gifts He has given you? Have you thanked Him? And how might you use those gifts to serve your church? Remember, God-given gifts are most enjoyed when they are used for the good of the family.

1 CORINTHIANS 12:4-13

APRIL 28

THE COMFORT OF GOD'S WAYS

"Blessed be the God and Father of our Lord Jesus Christ, the Father of mercies and God of all comfort, who comforts us in all our affliction, so that we may be able to comfort those who are in any affliction, with the comfort with which we ourselves are comforted by God." 2 CORINTHIANS 1:3-4

The suffering that God brings into our lives enables and equips us to comfort others in their trials. Yet this enabling is only possible because of the great comfort we receive from God in the midst of our own affliction. Indeed, in tenderness and mercy, God ministers to us specifically "so that we may be able to comfort those who are in any affliction."

If we are to bestow compassion on those who are suffering, we must first battle the tendency to grow bitter and inward-focused as a result of our own troubles. In the Old Testament, we read the story of a young Israelite girl who was captured in a Syrian raid, taken far from her family, and forced into servitude. Her life held great potential for bitterness, anger, and vengefulness. But when she learned that the master of her household had contracted leprosy, she encouraged him to seek the Lord's healing, even directing him to someone who could help (2 Kings 5:1-3). How was she able to have such compassion that she was willing to point him towards such comfort? At least in part, it must have been that when she witnessed all her master's turmoil and heartache, her own experience had already so softened her heart as to make her empathetic to his concerns.

In addition, we must avoid offering merely intellectual or pat answers, which often hurt rather than heal. In-depth philosophical discussions on the nature of suffering might stimulate the mind, but nothing but the gospel can settle the heart. And we do well to remind ourselves that God's ways are beyond our understanding. We do not have to have all the answers. We must not forget the eloquence of empathetic silence. Arguably, one of the most helpful ways in which Job's companions entered into his suffering and offered comfort was when they simply "sat with him on the ground seven days and seven nights, and no one spoke a word to him" (Job 2:13). In fact, they were being good friends to him until they decided to open their mouths!

The greatest comfort we can extend to others in their suffering is, gently and with tears over their trials, to point them to Christ Himself, because only Christ can fully enter into our pain. As our ascended King and Great High Priest, He is able to "sympathize with our weaknesses" as "one who in every respect has been tempted as we are" (Hebrews 4:15).

Are there wounds in your life that you have never allowed to surface—deep sorrows that you have never given over to God? Today, ask the Lord to help you cast your burdens afresh on Him. Ask for His divine enabling to view your suffering through the prism of Christ's cross so that you may be overwhelmed by His amazing compassion—and, in turn, be a blessing to others.

2 KINGS 5:1-5, 9-14

APRIL 29

THE SECOND REACTION

"But the thing displeased Samuel when they said, 'Give us a king to judge us.' And Samuel prayed to the LORD." 1 SAMUEL 8:6

How do you react when something displeases you?

It is understandable that when the people of Israel asked for a king, the prophet Samuel was displeased. After all, there was a personal slight in the request. Samuel had judged the people well, demonstrating leadership at its finest. He had preached repentance, and the people had repented. He had prayed for them, and the Philistine forces had been vanquished without any weapons being lifted in defense or to attack (1 Samuel 7:5-10). Finally, a stone of remembrance had been set up to signify God's goodness to Israel for time immemorial (v 12-13). Samuel had done his best—and his best had been good.

But the years had passed since those victories. Samuel had grown old, and the leaders of Israel had decided it was time for a change. They were ready to push Samuel out and move on.

Samuel's immediate and understandable reaction was to be unhappy and angry. But he didn't dwell there. Instead, his second reaction was to pray. Samuel's disapproval led him to talk to God about all that was happening and to seek His counsel and His intervention.

We see a similar first and second reaction in the book of Nehemiah. When Nehemiah heard the news that had come out of Jerusalem concerning the destruction and chaos that was taking place there, he sat down and wept. But then, for many days, he prayed to God and fasted (Nehemiah 1:1-4). His first reaction was to weep; his second reaction was to pray.

The actions of Samuel and Nehemiah set us a challenging example. When something displeases you and your first reaction to a situation is anger, sorrow, or disappointment, what's your *second* reaction? Perhaps you tend to tell everybody how let down you have been, or you brood in self-pity or lash out. But here's the challenge: while it is understandable to weep or to feel displeased, we are not to stay like that, and we are to make sure that our second reaction is to pray. Like Samuel, when something has caused you displeasure, let your second reaction be to talk to God about all that is happening, seeking His perspective and His help in the situations before you.

NEHEMIAH 1:1-11

APRIL 30

ON KINGDOM BUSINESS

"Let the lowly brother boast in his exaltation, and the rich in his humiliation, because like a flower of the grass he will pass away. For the sun rises with its scorching heat and withers the grass; its flower falls, and its beauty perishes. So also will the rich man fade away in the midst of his pursuits." JAMES 1:9-11

The most famous work of the Scottish economist Adam Smith, *The Wealth of Nations*, was first published in 1776, the same year that the Thirteen American Colonies declared their independence from Great Britain. In the years that followed, the new nation (along with most of what became the Western world) embraced this book and its argument, becoming one of the finest examples of economic prosperity that the world has ever witnessed—and, along the way, reinforcing for its population the unfortunate idea that human existence is largely about financial success.

James does not say that there is anything wrong with wealth. Through him, though, the Holy Spirit does remind the affluent that life in God's world is not about the accumulation of riches. Rather, we are to remember that we are as frail as a summer flower and that riches are fleeting. James calls us to use godly wisdom, which enables us to view our possessions and circumstances from a perspective that is both right and radical—right because it is a view based on the reality of eternity; and radical because it will lead us to hold loosely to what we have, being far quicker to give it away than to grasp it tightly.

There is nothing wrong with wealth, but there is danger in having it. Jesus gave his own warning: "Be on your guard against all covetousness, for one's life does not consist in the abundance of his possessions" (Luke 12:15). He spoke of a rich fool who didn't apply this wisdom, instead building bigger barns in which to store all his crops and relying on his wealth to enjoy his life—yet that very night God demanded that life from him (v 16-20). This man relied on foolish wisdom rather than God's, and Jesus said we, too, are foolish if we lay up treasure for ourselves and yet are not rich toward God (v 21).

True riches can never be found or placed in earthly banks, vaults, or portfolios. We might be tempted to use these as a basis for significance or security, but the wisdom of God shows their hollowness. So, instead of pursuing that which will fade, do as James instructs: focus on using your possessions wisely, generously, and for kingdom business—no matter how great or small they might be.

MATTHEW 6:19-34

MAY 1

GLORIFYING GOD WITH EVERY GIFT

"Whether you eat or drink, or whatever you do, do all to the glory of God."
1 CORINTHIANS 10:31

Dramatic displays tend to draw our attention. Think about a hole in one on the golf course or the buzzer-beater on the basketball court. The steady putts and consistent lay-ups or free throws get overshadowed by the sensational moments.

The same thing that happens on the green or between the hoops can happen inside the church with spiritual gifts: we can end up focusing all our attention on the more visible, obvious gifts—perhaps like teaching or leadership—and neglect to see gifts that can be a little harder to glimpse, like helping or administrating. But what we must understand is that spiritual gifts are not valuable just because they are dramatic. The body of Christ needs every part, from head to toe, and every gift of each member (1 Corinthians 12:14-20). Every gift is important. Every gift matters.

Our external expressions of spirituality do not prove that we are pleasing God, nor do they guarantee our salvation. That's a sobering thought! It is easy to focus on what we do as the evidence of what we are. As we teach, help, give, speak, sing, create, or heal, we can be tempted to look to those deeds as the only necessary evidence of our spiritual life. But according to Jesus, even great performances of seemingly good works do not necessarily indicate that we truly know Him or that He truly knows us (Matthew 7:21-23).

So is there anything we can look to as evidence for faith? The apostle Paul offers us a simple yet profound criterion in 1 Corinthians 6:19-20: "You are not your own, for you were bought with a price. So glorify God in your body." As you serve God and exercise your gifts, what is your aim? What is your intention? We can't expect to have perfectly pure motives on this side of heaven, but as we recall the great purchase God has made, we can make it our goal to glorify Him in all that we do. And this is reliable evidence of real faith: for a Christian is someone who knows they have been bought from sin and death at the price of Christ's blood and who now seeks to serve God with all that they are—to "do all to the glory of God."

This applies as much to the outgoing, well-known leader as it does to the quiet, unnoticed laborer. Whatever your gifts, whatever your role, whatever your situation, make it your goal to glorify God in all that you do. When that is your aim, you'll not only serve Him better, but you'll find yourself experiencing the great, counterintuitive truth that "it is more blessed to give than to receive" (Acts 20:35). Make it your goal today to ask yourself at every moment: "What would it look like, here and now, to do all for the glory of the God who loves me and gave Himself for me?"

MICAH 6:6-8

MAY 2

THE SEEING AND SAVING LORD

"The LORD is king forever and ever … you will incline your ear to do justice to the fatherless and the oppressed." PSALM 10:16-18

The pages of the Psalms express most, if not all, emotions known to the human heart. These divinely inspired songs show full awareness that life this side of the fall will involve not only joy and exaltation but also pain, disappointment, and confusion. We can all relate to the psalmist and find comfort when we encounter questions of God like "Why do you hide yourself in times of trouble?" (Psalm 10:1) and "How long, O LORD? Will you forget me forever?" (Psalm 13:1). We are clearly not the first people to face hardship!

The Scriptures respond to these realities with neither abject hopelessness nor optimistic platitudes. Rather, hope is offered and found in the character and promises of God Himself.

This hope can come from different angles. From one, there is the wonderful truth that God sees the distress of His people, as when the Israelites were in Egypt and the Lord assured them, "I have surely seen the affliction of my people" (Exodus 3:7). If you are in the midst of trouble and grief, know that God sees, knows, and is able and willing to save—even if it's not exactly the sort of salvation you have in mind.

Those who are victims of mistreatment of any kind, meanwhile, are met with the promise that God will settle all accounts. Sometimes justice comes in this life, fully or in part; but some matters will have to wait to be settled until this life is over. We can rest assured, though, that they *will* be settled. God "has a day" when every wrong will be made right and every tear wiped dry (Isaiah 2:12; 25:8).

Yet another way to find hope in God is to consider that "the LORD is king forever and ever." He lifts up nations and brings them down. He exalts rulers and humbles them. Indeed, the power of life and death belongs to Him.

Why is this a comfort? Because we know who is in charge. Who would you rather have in charge? Who else is infinite in power and might, with an equal measure of love and wisdom? Who else knows the end from the beginning and the thoughts of all? Only our God, and it is He alone who reigns.

Whatever circumstances you find yourself in right now, the Psalms invite you prayerfully to soak your soul in them and fill your heart with a vision of God's grace and grandeur. Doing so may not make your particular difficulties disappear—but it *will* put them into proper perspective. Casting the eyes of our hearts on the God of glory reminds us that He is the greatest reality in our lives, greater even than the struggles we face. He sees, He will make things right, and He reigns. Look to Him and, when facing difficult days and confusing and conflicting emotions, resolve to do as the psalmist does: "Hope in God; for I shall again praise him, my salvation and my God" (Psalm 42:11).

HABAKKUK 3:17-19

MAY 3

GOD CAN HANDLE OUR DOUBTS

"He appeared to Cephas, then to the twelve. Then he appeared to more than five hundred brothers at one time, most of whom are still alive, though some have fallen asleep. Then he appeared to James, then to all the apostles. Last of all, as to one untimely born, he appeared also to me." 1 CORINTHIANS 15:5-8

Have you ever felt a little shaky in your faith? Maybe while saying your prayers at night you've experienced the unwanted and unwelcome thought that you're merely talking into the darkness. Or perhaps you get an uncomfortable feeling in the pit of your stomach as you wonder if the only reason why you are professing faith at all is because you're just following the crowd on a Sunday.

1 Corinthians 15:5-8 was written to address these sorts of concerns and feelings. The apostle Paul refers us to the witnesses of Jesus' real, physical appearances following His resurrection. Cephas (Peter), James, Paul, the apostles, and 500 others physically saw the risen Lord Jesus with their very own eyes. Paul points us to these eyewitnesses to help us see that their faith, and ours, rests on facts.

What facts? The fact of the empty tomb, for one; there has to be an explanation for it. There also has to be a reason for why the disciples changed from hiding in a house in Jerusalem for fear of the Jews (John 20:19) to standing on the streets of the same city and boldly proclaiming the resurrection of Jesus (Acts 2:14-40). And there has to be something that accounts for the existence of the church. The Scriptures are clear: the explanation is the resurrection of Jesus Christ from the dead. Through history, attempts to explain these realities on any basis other than the fact of the resurrected Christ have fallen flat.

The resurrection of the Son of God is the pivotal event of world history and the foundation stone of our faith, and Paul recognized that we need a reasonable basis to believe it. He names eyewitnesses so that when we examine the record of Scripture, even 2,000 years removed from the events it describes, we find that it was not, as skeptics claim, faith that concocted evidence for the resurrection, but rather it was the evidence of the resurrection that created faith.

So when you are feeling shaky in your faith, when you're feeling a little unsettled, remember: there is a reasonable, historical basis to Christianity. God has poured out His Spirit and revealed His Word for your assurance. Pray that God will meet all your doubts with the gift of faith, and look to the resurrection, for there you will find your faith bolstered by fact and your confidence founded on reality.

1 CORINTHIANS 15:14-28

MAY 4

FEARLESS FAITH

"'If this man were not from God, he could do nothing.' They answered him, 'You were born in utter sin, and would you teach us?' And they cast him out."
JOHN 9:33-34

When the blind beggar in John 9 encountered Jesus, not only did he receive physical sight, but his spiritual eyes also were opened so that he came to believe in Him as Lord. Unfortunately, though, his troubles weren't over. When he encountered the religious leaders, he discovered that, unwilling as they were to accept this man's physical transformation and newfound faith, they were determined to discredit him by challenging both the miraculous sign and his personal testimony.

The Pharisees were such an intimidating presence that when questioned, the man's parents refused to answer for fear that they would be put out of the synagogue. Instead, they redirected the Pharisees to their son, saying, "He is of age; ask him" (John 9:23). But when the man was duly summoned for his second round of questioning and intimidation at the hands of the religious leaders, he did not waver. In the face of their opposition, his newfound faith made him fearless.

The Pharisees repeatedly asked the same questions and made the same accusations because there was nothing left for them to say. They were confronted with irrefutable evidence. And what did they have by way of response? Nothing. So they began to do what people usually do when the weakness of their argument becomes evident: they resorted to insults. "You were born in utter sin," they said to the man, "and would you teach us?" In other words, *You are a miserable sinner and we are righteous people. How dare you lecture us?! Don't you realize that we've gone to school for this? And you, some upstart beggar from the streets, think you can come in and confront us!* The Pharisees were challenged and, because it did not fit with their own assumptions nor their own view of themselves, they couldn't handle it. So they cast out the man who could have led them to the truth.

As fellow followers of Jesus in a world that is hostile to God and His ways, we ought not to be surprised when our friends and neighbors want to throw us out too. Frankly, we should probably get thrown out a lot more than we do! The reason many of us are under no such threat may be that we are more like the fearful parents than their faithful son, keeping quiet rather than speaking up.

Your faith in Christ does not guarantee that you will have an easy path in life. In fact, faith in Christ will almost certainly lead you to be opposed by others. Are you afraid of how others may respond to your faith? Does fear cause you to keep quiet instead of telling others, "I once was lost, but now am found, was blind, but now I see"?[35] Has your faith led you to be bold in the face of opposition like this blind man? And if not, will you pray right now that God will grant you that kind of faith so that you would speak these kinds of words?

JOHN 9:18-38

35 John Newton, "Amazing Grace" (1779).

MAY 5

A DOSE OF REALITY

"Vanity of vanities, says the Preacher, vanity of vanities! All is vanity."
ECCLESIASTES 1:2

Once when I was visiting a small village in England, I stumbled upon a graveyard. As I walked among the tombstones, I observed a variety of ages chiseled into their surfaces. Some people had lived to be 91 and others 84, while some did not make it past 20. Yet when all these ages were taken together, the average life span was around 70 to 80 years—just as the Bible says: "The years of our life are seventy, or even by reason of strength eighty" (Psalm 90:10). And more time than that had gone by since most of these people had passed.

This sobering reminder of life's brevity returned me to a question that all of us ask at one point or another: *Is this life all there is?*

The book of Ecclesiastes addresses this deep question by giving us a solid dose of reality. Truthfully, most of us don't do well with reality; we prefer fantasy, mirage, and distraction. Yet the author of Ecclesiastes, Solomon, begins his discourse by encouraging us to reflect upon the absolute meaninglessness of life, stating bluntly, "Vanity of vanities! All is vanity."

Solomon seeks to prove his thesis by showing us that life is marked by drudgery: "What does man gain by all the toil at which he toils under the sun? A generation goes, and a generation comes, but the earth remains forever" (Ecclesiastes 1:3-4). Life, in other words, is just a perpetual series of clockings in and clockings out until you die. No matter who you are—whether you are an executive, a schoolteacher, or a stay-at-home mom—life "under the sun" contains much toil, and then it ends.

Does this leave you thoroughly depressed? It should—*if* you rule out the existence of God. When God is taken out of the equation, life truly has no meaning. There is a reason why some people desire to escape reality through a drug-induced stupor or through mindless indulgence in pleasure and entertainment. What may seem like strange behavior to us may actually be the response of one who has gotten a heavy, albeit incomplete, dose of reality.

The book of Ecclesiastes forces us to consider the meaning of life in view of death. But read the rest of the Bible and you will discover that you may receive eternal life by trusting in Him who said, "I am the way, and the truth, and the life. No one comes to the Father except through me" (John 14:6). Only through Jesus will you discover life's true meaning and find the reason why all is *not* vanity. Only if you remember there is life beyond the grave will you be able to live with joy, and meet with the ups and downs of life with a healthy perspective, on this side of the grave.

ECCLESIASTES 1:1-11

MAY 6

ABOUNDING IN THE LORD'S WORK

"Whatever you do, work heartily, as for the Lord and not for men, knowing that from the Lord you will receive the inheritance as your reward. You are serving the Lord Christ." COLOSSIANS 3:23-24

What's the most important part of your job? Whether you punch in at a factory, report to an office, labor in a field, or work at making a home, what's most significant about your work? If you're a Christian, then the answer is this: that you "work heartily, as for the Lord and not for men."

Work is an inevitable part of life. It is something we were created to do (Genesis 1:28; 2:15). But our view of our work is transformed, rescuing us both from idleness in it and idolatry of it, when we understand this truth: that we don't ultimately work for our bosses or bank accounts; we work for Jesus. It is Him we aim to honor above all else. When we understand this, then our every occupation is instilled with dignity, and we can abound in the work of the Lord in whatever we do (1 Corinthians 15:58). Raising children is the Lord's work. Selling paint is the Lord's work. Managing staff is the Lord's work. Realizing that we work for the Lord Jesus first and foremost can make a big difference every morning as we rise to our labors and every evening as we rest from them.

Of course, it's easy to be discouraged in our work and frustrated by our work. The thorns, thistles, and cursed ground of Genesis 3 are all too apparent some days. But 1 Corinthians holds out the hope to us that when we labor for the Lord, our work is never in vain (1 Corinthians 15:58). No work done for Him is ever wasted. God weaves all that we do in His sight, and for His glory, into the great story of what He is doing in His world.

Paul reminds us, though, that evidence of success in the Lord's work may never be fully apparent in this life. In fact, the things that we think indicate success may just be hoodwinking us! We can *see* an annual bonus given, a promotion secured, or a sales target hit; we cannot see the eternal reward to be given when we reach our inheritance, nor all that God is doing through us. So we must live by faith, trusting that He is watching all our labors and is pleased when we serve Him, and that He is at work in all our labors and is using what we do to further His purposes.

In whatever vocation God has called you to at present, then, make it your highest aim to honor Jesus in how you do your job. Aim to please your boss and your clients, certainly—but when each new workday begins, don't forget who is really to be honored by your effort. Labor "by the strength that God supplies—in order that in everything God may be glorified through Jesus Christ" (1 Peter 4:11). For, whatever it is that you will be doing today, you can be serving the Lord Christ as you do it—and that is where real job satisfaction is to be found.

EPHESIANS 6:5-9

MAY 7

NEW LIFE, NEW LIFESTYLE

"Therefore let us be grateful for receiving a kingdom that cannot be shaken, and thus let us offer to God acceptable worship, with reverence and awe."
HEBREWS 12:28

This verse introduces us to the Christian goals of being grateful and worshiping God acceptably. But how exactly can we show that such aims have become a reality in our lives? The answer is provided in part in the following chapter: we are to love one another, show hospitality to strangers, remember those who are in prison, and maintain sexual purity within marriage (Hebrews 13:1-4).

These attitudes of gratitude and worship are founded upon and a response to all of the previous twelve chapters in the book of Hebrews. The writer has made it clear that he is writing to those who have already come to hold firmly to Christ. In other words, they have acknowledged their sin, they have embraced Christ as their Savior, and they have been included in the family of faith. They have been given a place in "a kingdom that cannot be shaken"—a perfect, eternal realm that will encompass the whole renewed world when its King returns.

So worship does not precede kingdom membership; it reveals it. It is because we are members of that kingdom that we live lives of gratitude and worship. God's commands are not a list of regulations that allow individuals to make themselves acceptable to God and to one another. Our *lifestyle* is an evidence of our *life*. These godly behaviors do not create the life. They simply reveal it.

God will never exhort you to do something without providing you with the resources to be able to fulfill it. When He says He wants you to love others, care for the stranger, and remember the prisoner, He also provides the grace that enables you to do it. You are called to genuinely care for people because He, the Lord Jesus, looked on people and saw them as sheep without a shepherd (Matthew 9:36; Mark 6:34). You are called to a life of purity because you were bought with "the precious blood of Christ, like that of a lamb without blemish or spot" (1 Peter 1:19).

What, then, are your actions saying to your friends, to your neighbors, to your family, and to your entire sphere of influence—no matter how big or small? Be known for your gratitude. Be known for your worship. But do not finish reading this and simply determine to be more grateful, more worshipful, and more obedient. Finish it rejoicing that you have been given "a kingdom that cannot be shaken," ruled by a gentle King who cannot be defeated. It is as you look at Him, and not at yourself, that you will find yourself filling with gratitude and desiring to worship Him throughout all of your life.

2 PETER 1:3-10

MAY 8

OUR ONLY BOAST

"Thus says the LORD: 'Let not the wise man boast in his wisdom, let not the mighty man boast in his might, let not the rich man boast in his riches, but let him who boasts boast in this, that he understands and knows me, that I am the LORD who practices steadfast love, justice, and righteousness in the earth. For in these things I delight, declares the LORD.'" JEREMIAH 9:23-24

We live in a culture of self-promotion which encourages us to trust in ourselves instead of our Creator. Aware of our need to battle against self-reliance, God speaks to us through His word, encouraging us to boast—to find our confidence—in Him alone.

In an attempt to find wisdom apart from God, some pursue instead education and knowledge. Some are prone to rely primarily on physical strength or beauty, ignoring the reality that our bodies will decay and eventually fail us. Still others are enticed to look to money and riches rather than God as their ultimate provider.

It's a delusion, though, says Jeremiah, to think even for a nanosecond that we can boast in an agile mind, a healthy body, or a fat portfolio. Where, then, are we to place our confidence? The prophet's answer is clear: we are to place our trust in God Himself.

We can trust God because He is a God of justice. He rules in equity, He deals in truth, and He is not arbitrary in what He does. We can have full assurance that His actions are always in keeping with His character.

We can trust God because He is characterized by His steadfast covenant love for His people—a love made known to us in the person and work of the Lord Jesus Christ. And because of the depth of the Father's love for us, we are "called children of God" (1 John 3:1)! Therefore, we are to take refuge in His righteousness, not our own. Our confidence rests in Jesus, who fulfilled the Father's will so that we may know Him and love Him as our Creator and Sustainer, as our Savior and King.

A biblical worldview does not denigrate people's aspirations in the pursuit of wisdom, the exercise of physical prowess, or the ability to earn. But it does stand against the idea that our identity, satisfaction, or salvation can successfully be based on any of these things. There is still a glory that outshines these lesser lights. Our lives should proclaim purposefully, graciously, and straightforwardly that God created us to give Him glory by our walking humbly before Him and enjoying Him into eternity. Where is your confidence for today, for tomorrow, and forever? What do you look to to get you through difficult days? Let it be the loving, just, righteous Lord of all, and know that as you trust Him, He delights in you.

GALATIANS 6:12-16

MAY 9

YOU HAVE A SHEPHERD

"They went away in the boat to a desolate place by themselves. Now many saw them going and recognized them, and they ran there on foot ... When he went ashore he saw a great crowd, and he had compassion on them, because they were like sheep without a shepherd. And he began to teach them many things." MARK 6:32-34

Christian, you have a Shepherd.

Jesus had a pattern of slipping away from time to time to rest, refresh himself, and talk with His heavenly Father. He also encouraged His disciples to take up this same practice in Mark 6, after they had labored in ministry, telling them, "Come away by yourselves to a desolate place and rest a while" (Mark 6:31). Yet on this occasion, just as Jesus and the disciples arrived at their destination to rest, a great crowd formed. If this crowd was not necessarily unwanted, it was certainly unsought. There would be no possibility of rest. But Jesus did not lash out in frustration, seeing these people as an intrusion. Instead, He "had compassion on them." Literally, as the Greek puts it, His bowels churned. We might say our stomach lurched.

Jesus was stirred to the very core of His being by this crowd. Why? "Because they were like sheep without a shepherd." Indeed, they may literally have looked like sheep: thousands of people in their light-colored Middle Eastern clothing, scattered against the landscape. But, more importantly, they were in need of a shepherd for their souls. They needed help navigating safely through life and securely through death. Jesus had come to be that Shepherd, looking for the lost sheep—looking for you and for me.

Jesus went on to feed the crowd, physically and spiritually, proving Himself to be the Shepherd who makes us lie down in green pastures, leads us beside still waters, and restores our souls (Psalm 23:1-3). Here is the King inviting people into His kingdom, the Shepherd inviting sheep into His fold. Where the disciples said, *Send them away*, Jesus said, *Sit them down* (Mark 6:36, 39). This is what Jesus does for us: He sees us, hungry and thirsty, straying and lost, and He welcomes us, even at the cost of His own life. Where else can we find a love so true?

Souls of men, why will ye scatter
Like a crowd of frightened sheep?
Foolish hearts, why will ye wander
From a love so true and deep?[36]

Today, see the leading of your Shepherd not as an imposition on your life but as an act of grace toward you. If you are confused about your way forward, trust Him to guide you through, in this life and to the next. When you struggle to love others, ask Him to give you His heart of compassion for fellow lost sheep in need of a heavenly Shepherd. Christian, you have a Shepherd.

PSALM 23

36 Frederick William Faber, "Souls of Men, Why Will Ye Scatter" (1854).

MAY 10

A MARK OF TRUE GODLINESS

"Clothe yourselves, all of you, with humility toward one another, for 'God opposes the proud but gives grace to the humble.'" 1 PETER 5:5

True godliness grows in the soil of humility. We may have great giftings, wonderful abilities, great aspirations, tremendous passion, and the utmost diligence, and we may even apparently be successful and useful—but all of that amounts to nothing if we lack humility.

So, what *is* humility? Genuine humility reveals itself in keeping short accounts in regard to sin: coming continually to God with a repentant heart and recognizing ourselves to be in desperate need of God's help every day and for every occasion. It lies in understanding that our need of Jesus and His transforming power in our lives is not partial; it's total. As Jesus Himself told us, "Apart from me you can do nothing" (John 15:5). Humility recognizes that the very breath we breathe, all that we possess, and all that we are result from God's grace and goodness to us.

Humility means serving rather than being served. It means giving rather than taking. It means responding to the leadership of others rather than always insisting upon our own. It means fitting into others' arrangements rather than demanding that everyone fit into ours.

Yet the humility of those who serve Christ is not merely an absence of pride or an awareness of our limitations. The opposite of self-love is not self-denigration but love for God. The answer to our being puffed up is not to hate ourselves or to deny the gifts God has given us; it is to steel our focus on the Lord Himself, recognizing, as the psalmist says, that God has exalted above all things His name and His word (Psalm 138:2).

The only people whom God will ultimately lift up are humble people—those who have recognized who they are, what they are, and how great their need of God is. Through the prophet Isaiah God declared, "I dwell in the high and holy place, *and also* with him who is of a contrite and lowly spirit" (Isaiah 57:15, emphasis added). Later, He added, "This is the one to whom I will look: he who is humble and contrite in spirit and trembles at my word" (Isaiah 66:2).

Keep your eyes on the Lord Jesus, and He will look to you. You did not make yourself. You did not save yourself. You did not gift yourself. You are utterly dependent upon God's grace. Look to Him, and He will lift you up. And when you know yourself to be lifted up in His loving sight, then you are ready to serve His people with all that He has given you.

LUKE 1:46-55

MAY 11

BOUND TO THE BOOK

"The law of the LORD is perfect, reviving the soul; the testimony of the LORD is sure, making wise the simple; the precepts of the LORD are right, rejoicing the heart; the commandment of the LORD is pure, enlightening the eyes."
PSALM 19:7-8

The Bible is often regarded as a useless relic from a bygone age. As the horse and buggy were superseded by the internal combustion engine, and as the internal combustion engine itself will soon be replaced, so it is, some would contend, with the Bible. There may be a measure of historical or literary value in it, they say, but ultimately it is of no relevance to the needs of 21st-century people—and, indeed, may stand opposed to our progress.

In *The Bondage of the Will*, Martin Luther makes a staggering statement that cuts right to the heart of such flippant attitudes toward the Bible: "Nobody who has not the Spirit of God sees a jot of what is in the Scriptures. All men have their hearts darkened, so that, even when they can discuss and quote all that is in Scripture, they do not understand or really know any of it."[37]

We could never hope to understand God—or His word, for that matter—on our own terms. Man does not know God by investigation but by revelation, by God's self-disclosure, by His very words. *General* revelation—what we see in God's world—indeed points us toward Him, but, according to Romans 1:20-23, that revelation is only enough to condemn, for by nature we all suppress the truth we see there, preferring to worship ourselves and our idols than the Creator of all things. We need *special* revelation—God's word—to enlighten our understanding and enable us to properly interpret what we see and experience in the world.

God has authored, and preserved, a book—*His* book—so that we might know Him. And in that book we have recorded for us a written record of God's inestimable love for those who have turned their backs on Him. If that written record is the voice of God, if it is from the mouth of God, where else can you go to substantiate its truth? There is no higher authority.

Ultimately, we need new eyes to see Scripture's beauty and authority. Once God grants us faith, we see His word entirely differently. The world may regard the words of the Bible as irrelevant or worse; but one look at the state of the world will remind us that it does not have all the answers, or indeed any of the answers that matter. Do not neglect your Bible. Ask God to work in you as you open it up to revive your soul, to make you wise, to bring you joy, and to light your path.

PSALM 19

37 *Martin Luther: Selections from His Writings*, ed. John Dillenberger (Anchor, 1962), p 174.

MAY 12

THE JOY OF INADEQUACY

"Not that we are sufficient in ourselves to claim anything as coming from us, but our sufficiency is from God, who has made us sufficient to be ministers of a new covenant." 2 CORINTHIANS 3:5-6

God's purpose for His people in every age is that we will depend upon Him entirely. This dependence does not come naturally to us because one of the great idols of every age is that of power. Its allure is strong, its ability to corrupt even stronger. And what's true now has always been so: those who obtain power are those bold enough to pursue it, and they tend to be marked by characteristics like charisma and strong personalities. This is how many measure strength and usefulness. Tragically, even within the church, leaders have often been given authority and influence because of their magnetism rather than their character and because of their ambition rather than their humility.

Paul was well acquainted with such miscalculations. In fact, he even spent portions of two letters instructing the Corinthian church not to evaluate spiritual leaders by worldly standards. On some occasions, the Corinthians were tempted to align themselves with their favorite orators and to cherish worldly wisdom. On others, Paul had to combat the influence of so-called "super-apostles" whose strength, gifting, and power were observable in a way which the Corinthians found appealing (2 Corinthians 11:5; 12:11).

By contrast, Paul said, "When I am weak, then I am strong" (2 Corinthians 12:10). He knew that the power of Christ was put on display in his weakness, and he readily confessed that he was not adequate for the work entrusted to him: "Who is sufficient for these things?" (2:16).

We may not be "super-apostles," but we can relate to the temptation of worldly thinking. We are all prone to rely on ourselves—on our personalities or on our gifts. What we must learn is that spiritual usefulness isn't found in such things. Instead, it is discovered when we humble ourselves before God, when we acknowledge that we are wholly inadequate. Paul's confession must be ours: weakness is actually strength. The very nature of the "new covenant," made by Jesus in His blood and to which we bring nothing but our sin, should be all we need to remind us that we do not have what we need but that He does. God is at work to bring us to that point—to convince us that He alone is adequate. Do we want to grow in boldness? Then we must embrace our weakness before God, and He will lead us to faith-filled boldness before others. Do we want to grow in usefulness? Then we must embrace our inadequacy in private, and God will prove His sufficiency through us.

Have you considered the possibility that one of the greatest barriers to your usefulness in serving God may actually be your own sense of personal adequacy? Be sure to commit time to prayer and ask God to show you whether the delusion of self-sufficiency has seeped into your thinking in one way or another. Ask Him to take it from you, that you may serve in the freedom and joy of inadequacy—and watch Him do the work!

JUDGES 7:1-8, 16-32

MAY 13

THE GIFT OF GODLY FRIENDS

"Embarking in a ship of Adramyttium, which was about to sail to the ports along the coast of Asia, we put to sea, accompanied by Aristarchus, a Macedonian from Thessalonica. The next day we put in at Sidon. And Julius treated Paul kindly and gave him leave to go to his friends and be cared for."
ACTS 27:2-3

The day had dawned, and Paul's great longing to go to Rome was nearing its realization. He was one of a number of prisoners whose destination was the city at the center of the known world. But at the outset of their journey, Luke provides us with details that appear at first glance to be extraneous and irrelevant. He and Paul, he tells us, were "accompanied by Aristarchus, a Macedonian from Thessalonica."

Aristarchus is not a well-known Bible character. From the few places where he's mentioned, we know that he was a good man to have around at any time, but especially during difficult times. He first appears in Acts 19:29, where he ends up in harm's way when Paul and his companions are set upon by a mob. He is also mentioned at the end of Colossians (Colossians 4:10) and of Philemon (Philemon 24). If these two epistles were written from Rome, as is likely, then Aristarchus evidently remained with Paul throughout his entire journey to Rome and his subsequent imprisonment.

The mention of Aristarchus's presence with Paul reminds us that even this great apostle to the Gentiles was not beyond the need of friendship. Paul is such a significant figure that we may be tempted almost to deify him, assuming that he was above and beyond such "worldly necessities." But in actual fact, he cherished friendship. When he wrote his second letter to Timothy at the end of his life, he finished the epistle by asking not only for scrolls and his cloak (2 Timothy 4:13) but also the quick arrival of Timothy (v 9). The scrolls would stimulate his mind. His cloak would deal with the cold. But he needed Timothy because, to Paul, friendship really mattered.

Paul's need for friendship is revealed again when Luke tells us that, upon reaching Sidon on the way to Rome, Paul was allowed by the centurion overseeing the prisoners "to go to his friends and be cared for." Was it out of place for the mighty apostle to be cared for by others? Not at all! Paul embraced his weakness and dependence on others because he knew that Christ's "power is made perfect in weakness" (2 Corinthians 12:9).

The sooner we discover how weak we really are, the sooner we learn the value of friendship. No matter how strong or gifted you may be, you are not Superman. If this mighty apostle needed companions in his life, then you do as well. Friendship is a wonderful gift that God has given so that you might be encouraged and supported as you journey through this life. Today, then, consider the godly friends that the Lord has placed around you. Offer thanks for their love and support. And above all, pray for their endurance and encouragement in the faith, knowing that just as you need them to point you to Christ, so they need you.

PROVERBS 27:5-10

MAY 14

HOW TO START YOUR DAY

"O Lord, in the morning you hear my voice." PSALM 5:3

Every day begins with a routine. Even if we think we don't have a routine, we all in fact have some habits and patterns that take up and shape the first few minutes or hours of each new morning. Psalm 5 encourages us to make our morning routine a godly one. Here we discover that David begins his day with God and demonstrates for us five postures for approaching Him: directly, humbly, personally, consistently, and expectantly.

Verse 1 shows us that David takes God's name upon his lips and comes to Him *directly*: "Give ear to my words, O Lord." We can approach the triune God in this way because of our Lord Jesus. "For … there is one mediator between God and men, the man Christ Jesus" (1 Timothy 2:5), and this mediator grants us the ability to "draw near to the throne of grace" (Hebrews 4:16).

Though we can approach God confidently, we must still come to Him *humbly*. In Psalm 5:2, David cries out to God for help and addresses Him as "my King and my God." David is himself a king, yet he bows before the one who is sovereign over all. He puts himself in the right place. One of the great challenges at the beginning of every day is to put ourselves in a proper perspective before our almighty yet benevolent God.

We also draw near to the Lord *personally*. He hears the sound of our cries (Psalm 5:2) and listens to our voice (v 3). What a wonder it is that the God who created the universe would be mindful of us, giving ear to everyone who calls upon Him!

With these first three postures in mind, we will approach God *consistently*. David mentions the morning twice in Psalm 5:3, implying that for him, beginning the day with God is a priority. Psalm 145:2 states the principle clearly: "*Every day* I will bless you and praise your name forever and ever" (emphasis added). We miss out on the richness of God's fellowship if we call out to Him only haphazardly.

Finally, David comes to God *expectantly*: "In the morning I prepare a sacrifice for you and watch" (Psalm 5:3). As David worships, he watches. He waits for his Lord and expects Him to respond.

However precisely or flexibly you handle the opening moments of your day, and whatever else your routine includes, don't miss out on the privilege of casting your cares on your good God. When you come to Him consistently and directly, in humble expectation with your personal requests, He will not withhold His blessing. Tomorrow morning, whatever else you must do, will the Lord God hear your voice?

COLOSSIANS 1:9-14

MAY 15

A SACRIFICE OF NOBLER NAME

"I will be merciful toward their iniquities, and I will remember their sins no more." HEBREWS 8:12

When we feel estranged from God, others, and even ourselves, we can often trace this sense of angst to a guilty conscience. Despite the passage of time and despite all of our endeavors, somehow or another we find ourselves unable to relieve ourselves of this heavy burden, this deepening sense of unworthiness. The Bible teaches that we are created with an innate sense of right and wrong—that we are moral beings and that so we understand when we've violated God's moral demands. We may sear our consciences, but we cannot erase them. The word of God, then, comes to our troubled consciences not to dishearten us but to direct us to the Savior who can cleanse us from our sin and guilt.

The Old Testament sacrificial system, while divinely prescribed by God, was meant only as a shadow and copy of the reality to come. Even with all the various ceremonies, washings, and external regulations, access to God was still restricted, cleansing was only partial and temporary, and pardon was limited. Those sacrifices could only do so much. They could not take away the real barrier between God and humanity: our sinful hearts, which need to be cleansed before we can enter the presence of a holy God.

Here, though, is the good news of the gospel! Since no amount of external work can save, forgive, or cleanse a guilty conscience completely, God's promise to "be merciful toward [our] inequities and … remember [our] sins no more" through Jesus' atoning death is an absolutely mind-blowing, life-altering reality. It wasn't just the death of a man that paid for our sins; it was the death of the incarnate God. And so there is hope for the individual who is haunted by remorse, who is driven by failure, who longs for a cleansing from sin that is full and complete. As the hymn writer puts it:

Not all the blood of beasts
On Jewish altars slain
Could give the guilty conscience peace
Or wash away the stain.
But Christ, the heav'nly Lamb,
Takes all our sins away,
A sacrifice of nobler name
And richer blood than they.[38]

When you are prepared to admit that you have unrelieved, unmitigated guilt for which all of your best endeavors can provide no satisfaction, true peace awaits. There is a way to have your sins forgiven—the sins of yesterday, the sins of today, and all the sins of tomorrow. Is there something you need to bring to the cross and confess and ask forgiveness for? Do so now, and know with joy that He remembers your sins no more.

PSALM 51

38 Isaac Watts, "Not All the Blood of Beasts" (1709).

MAY 16

A LIVING HOPE

"Blessed be the God and Father of our Lord Jesus Christ! According to his great mercy, he has caused us to be born again to a living hope through the resurrection of Jesus Christ from the dead, to an inheritance that is imperishable, undefiled, and unfading, kept in heaven for you, who by God's power are being guarded through faith for a salvation ready to be revealed in the last time."

1 PETER 1:3-5

Without encountering God in the Lord Jesus Christ, life can be extraordinarily bleak—an empty, hopeless existence. There are not enough things to do that will fill the emptiness. There are not enough occasions to look forward to. It is impossible to amass enough material possessions or take enough vacations to be able to fill up the human soul.

But the child of God has been delivered from this realm of hopelessness. When we place our trust in Christ, we are removed from bondage to "the domain of darkness" (Colossians 1:13) and are "born again to a living hope." The believer's hope is alive and it is fulfilling because it is rooted firmly in our risen, ascended, and reigning Savior. Our hope no longer hinges on ourselves or our circumstances; rather, "the resurrection of Jesus Christ from the dead" is the guarantee that our hope is secure.

Our hope is also eternal. God promises believers a future inheritance that is absolutely certain. Peter describes for us the unique nature of this inheritance; it is untouched by death, unstained by evil, and unimpaired by time. There is no possibility of it diminishing or disappointing because it can't perish, it can't spoil, and it can't fade—and it's kept in heaven with our name on it.

Not only is our hope living and eternal, but it is also shielded by the power of God Himself. Indeed, Peter describes believers as those "who by God's power are being guarded." When we become aware of the rigors of sin or we are buffeted by the brokenness of this fallen world in our life and we're tempted to despair, here's the wonderful truth: God has garrisoned us and shielded us. We will not be lost. And in this promise the beleaguered believer finds strength and renewed hope.

What is it that puts a spring in our step, no matter how steep the path? What is it that lifts our chins off our chests and keeps us looking forward with joy? What can truly fill your soul and bring you through whatever hard situations you are facing as you read these words? It is this truth: that, because of God's great mercy, you have been born again to a living hope—a hope which nothing can ever spoil and that no one can ever take from you (John 10:28).

ROMANS 8:18-30

MAY 17

A CALL TO LISTEN

"Know this, my beloved brothers: let every person be quick to hear, slow to speak, slow to anger; for the anger of man does not produce the righteousness of God."
JAMES 1:19-20

These verses issue a challenging statement that makes many of us squirm under the impact of its truth. Whether it's around the dining-room table with friends who came over to eat but not really to listen to us talk nonstop, or at the coffee shop where we can't wait to share tidbits from the latest newspaper or book we've been reading, the truth is that many of us do far too much talking.

If we ever find ourselves doing all the talking, we can be sure of one thing: we're not listening. While this is true in terms of interpersonal relationships, it is true in relation to the Bible and theology as well. One 19th-century pastor wrote about this correlation: "There are some people who are always talking … and by their incessant talking they disable themselves from thinking. They lose the power of grasping the real meaning of anything serious that is said to them … And further, this habit prevents them from listening even to God's word and from thinking about it."[39]

What we most need to listen to is "the word of truth" (James 1:18). We should, James says, "receive" this word and then "be doers" of it (v 21-22). It seems that he has in mind the peculiar danger of being quick to proclaim the truth to others before really paying proper attention to it ourselves.

If being too quick to speak with our tongues makes us too slow to listen to God and to others, so also does being quick to anger in our hearts. And in many cases, a fast flow of words is the sign of a quick temper. The individual who talks a lot is often greatly opinionated and grows angry when other people don't share their strength of feeling. Heat and passion are not necessarily expressions of fidelity and godliness. They may be the opposite, and our forcefulness may be a cause of stumbling rather than of helpfulness.

Anger "does not produce the righteousness of God" in our lives. Our intensity, focus, and emphasis, if driven by self-centered annoyance or anger, do not ultimately work God's righteous purposes. Otherwise, Jesus would have operated in a different way than He did; but He was gentle, meek, humble, and persuasive. That is why the cleansing of the temple was so striking in the life of Jesus—because it was an unusual, though legitimate, expression of His righteous anger.

It is God's word that not only gives you life (James 1:18) but also transforms your life. Aspire to be someone transformed: to listen well to God's word and to those around you by being slower to speak and slower to grow cross, so that you will grow in and help others grow in the kind of life that God desires.

JAMES 1:17-25

39 R.W. Dale, *The Epistle of James: And Other Discourses* (Hodder and Stoughton, 1895), p 38.

MAY 18

CONTINUAL WORSHIP

"While he blessed them, he parted from them and was carried up into heaven. And they worshiped him and returned to Jerusalem with great joy, and were continually in the temple blessing God." LUKE 24:51-53

When Jesus ascended, those who witnessed Him being "carried up into heaven" responded with worship. They knew, as we know, that worship is due to God alone. In this final moment of departure, the pieces of the jigsaw puzzle must have all come together as they beheld Christ in His glorified body, ascending to the Father, leading them to rejoice. Perhaps their reaction calls to mind that of the leper in Luke 17:11-18, who, when he had been healed, returned to Jesus, fell at His feet, and gave thanks.

But the response of these believers wasn't limited to worship in the moment. They also "returned to Jerusalem with great joy," where they continued thanking God for what He had done and adoring Him for the wonder of Jesus. They were marked, then, by worship and joy—and by obedience. Jesus had told them, "Behold, I am sending the promise of my Father upon you. But stay in the city until you are clothed with power from on high" (Luke 24:49). And that's exactly what they did.

Christ is the object of all our worship. He is the source of all our joy. He is the one who deserves all our obedience. He is the focus of all our praise. And we are accepted in Him. These early disciples understood that. Do we? Our worship, joy, obedience, and praise are pleasing to God not because of anything we have done but in light of His gracious work within us. It is only by His enabling that we can ask for unwavering faith in the ascended Son of God—faith that moves us to worship Him and to follow His example in all we think, in all we say, and in all we do. If you are finding it hard to worship, to know joy, or to obey the Lord today, ask Him to fix your eyes of faith on your risen, ascended, reigning Savior. It is as you see the same Jesus those first disciples knew that you will be moved to worshipful joy and that your obedience will cease to be mere duty and become your delight.

PSALM 146

MAY 19

THE NEW YOU

"Put off your old self, which belongs to your former manner of life and is corrupt through deceitful desires, and ... be renewed in the spirit of your minds, and ... put on the new self, created after the likeness of God in true righteousness and holiness." EPHESIANS 4:22-24

God doesn't save us just so that we can escape hell and go to heaven. Wonderful as our rescue is, His plan for us and the world is much grander than that! In Christ, God is working to "reconcile to himself all things, whether on earth or in heaven, making peace by the blood of his cross" (Colossians 1:19-20).

One element of that reconciliation is the righteous and holy living that God calls His people to put on. But as we "put on the new self," we must also "put off [the] old self." What does that look like from a practical standpoint? Paul doesn't leave us searching for answers. He says we are to "put away falsehood" and "speak the truth," because we all belong to each other and are united to each other (Ephesians 4:25), and when we lie, we short-circuit the nervous system of Christ's body. If we're prone to anger, we must not let it drive us to sin; rather, we put our anger to bed before we let ourselves rest, lest we give the devil a foothold in our lives (v 26-27). If we've taken what is not ours, we must instead begin earning our own keep and sharing instead of taking (v 28). We do not allow our tongues to utter anything that tears others down but only what graciously builds them up (v 29).

Startlingly, when we behave in line with our former way of life, we distress the Holy Spirit (Ephesians 4:30). To avoid grieving Him, we must put away bitterness, rage, anger, quarreling, slander, and malice (v 31). Just as God is with us in Christ, we are to be kind and tenderhearted, pushing ourselves to forgive, however difficult that is, because God in Christ forgave us (v 32).

The apostle Paul reminds us in 2 Corinthians 5:17 that anyone who is in Christ "is a new creation. The old has passed away; behold, the new has come." Still, putting on the new person requires hard work. But as we work, we do so knowing that God Himself works in us, enabling us and empowering us to look more like Christ (Philippians 2:13).

If you are in Christ, God has already begun His restorative work in you, and He will complete it (Philippians 1:6). What better assurance could there be? What better motivation to put on the new self while forsaking the old? What will that look like for you today?

EPHESIANS 4:20-32

MAY 20

ONE GRAND STORY

"The L*ORD will be king over all the earth. On that day the* L*ORD will be one and his name one."* ZECHARIAH 14:9

God's people are a waiting people.

From Genesis to Revelation, the Bible tells one grand story: both the Old Testament and the New reveal to us the redemptive plan of our God through the Lord Jesus Christ.

Sometimes we get the impression that the Scriptures are just an amalgamation of stories from all over the place. Yet while it is true that the Bible's timeline spans from eternity past to eternity future, and that the Bible's territory covers quite a bit of space, what we have in its pages is one word from the one God concerning the one salvation that is found in the one King of kings and Lord of lords, Jesus Christ. Yes, we should devote ourselves to knowing and understanding all the different contours of the story—but we must not miss the big picture.

When the prophet Zechariah had a vision of the comprehensive rule and reign of the Lord, he was living in a day when the restoration of God's people felt incomplete. The people had returned to Jerusalem after being exiled due to their ongoing sin, and they had rebuilt the walls of the city and the temple at its heart. Yet life hardly felt like the gladsome, joyous, sorrowless experience that Isaiah had prophesied it would be (Isaiah 51:11). Had the Lord not kept His promise? Had Isaiah been mistaken? No, said Zechariah. This was never meant to be it! Zechariah was looking past the restoration of the Jerusalem temple to where that small victory pointed: the global reign of the Lord's Anointed, Jesus Christ. God's people would not be waiting forever.

In our day, He has come. We are not only witnesses but partakers in the building of His true temple: His body, the church. Still, though more and more people turn to Him across the globe each day, we still await the day when every knee should bow and "every tongue confess that Jesus Christ is Lord" (Philippians 2:10-11). But as we wait, we can look back across the Scriptures and see just how faithful God has always been. We can see with our own eyes how He has orchestrated "a plan for the fullness of time, to unite all things in [Christ], things in heaven and things on earth" (Ephesians 1:10).

As the narrative of this grand story continues to unfold, and as each of our lives contributes little portions to the plot, we can press on in hope. If you are feeling that life is not the gladsome, joyous, sorrowless experience that the Scriptures promise, remember this: this is not meant to be it. There is better ahead, and one day soon "the LORD will be king over all the earth." For now we must wait, and serve, and hope—for we will not be waiting forever.

PSALM 130

MAY 21

GOD'S SCANDALOUS GRACE

"All have sinned and fall short of the glory of God, and are justified by his grace as a gift, through the redemption that is in Christ Jesus." ROMANS 3:23-24

When an accused person is brought before a judge in a court of law, they are either justified or condemned. The accused is not made righteous or unrighteous but is declared either righteous or unrighteous; the defendant is either acquitted and set free or is found guilty and punished.

Romans 3:23-24 explains to us that the sinner, who deserves condemnation, is justified through faith alone in Christ alone—not as a result of some quality inherent to them but as a result of God's grace. At Calvary, Christ took the sinner's place, and now, because of His finished work, God bestows upon us a declaration of righteousness.

How else could someone like the thief on the cross receive salvation? Here was a man who was in the process of "receiving the due reward of [his] deeds" (Luke 23:41). He had absolutely zero chance of making up for whatever evil he had committed which had led to his crucifixion. And yet, when he asked the Lord to remember him, Jesus was able to say in all sincerity, "Truly, I say to you, today you will be with me in paradise" (v 43).

The thief didn't deserve such scandalous grace—and neither do we. But that is precisely the point: God justifies us "by his grace as a gift." He doesn't save us because we're great or good, or even because we're making progress. He saves those who confess and believe in Jesus Christ (Romans 10:9) because of the immensity of His own great love (5:8).

Such scandalous grace can be a stumbling block. We want to *do something* about our sorry condition. We want to bring something to the table and contribute to our salvation. Before we become Christians, we want to offer our sense of moral goodness. And after we have been Christians for a while, we often want to offer our Christian obedience. But the truth of the matter is that we all come before the cross empty-handed. We couldn't hope to add even a single ounce to our worth before God. There is no reason to pat yourself on the back and every reason to praise the Lord Jesus. For it is when you realize you have nothing that you are in just the right position for Christ to be your everything:

Nothing in my hand I bring
Simply to Thy cross I cling.[40]

So, when your days in this life have drawn to a close and you reach the gates of glory, what will you say? Be sure that there is not an ounce of you that would offer your own goodness as your reason for gaining entry. Be sure that you are ready to say what we can imagine the thief on the cross said after his earthly life had ebbed away on that first Good Friday: *The man on the middle cross said I could come in.*

EPHESIANS 2:1-10

40 Augustus Toplady, "Rock of Ages" (1776).

MAY 22

PUT ON LOVE

"And above all these put on love, which binds everything together in perfect harmony." COLOSSIANS 3:14

For quite some time now, Western culture has been enamored with the idea that love will solve all our problems. "All you need is love," we sing.[41] "Love conquers all," we say.[42] Now, there is some truth to that. God's love could indeed fix quite literally everything if we all submitted ourselves to Him on His terms. But the problem is that by nature we do not submit to Him in this way; and, moreover, society at large tends to have a notion of what love is that bears little resemblance to real love as seen in and defined by its source—God Himself.

Often, what binds people together in "love" is shared interests or natural instincts. People who are like us or to whom we are attracted are those we instinctively are drawn toward and care for. In the church, however, our mutual love and affection is anchored in something *outside* of ourselves—namely, Jesus Christ. Ultimately, we are not bound together by some inherent characteristic or shared interest or even mutual attraction but by God, who has acted through Jesus Christ to tear down "the dividing wall of hostility" (Ephesians 2:14)—any barrier between people, such as race, class, gender, language, or nationality.

Despite what our culture desires, so long as we base our idea of love subjectively on whatever we choose and however we feel, a society defined by *true* love will remain an impossibility. Only an objective, unchanging love—the love of God for us in Christ—can bind "everything together in perfect harmony" (Colossians 3:14). Only the steadfast love of God for us, through His Son and by His Spirit, can fill us enough so that we actually love one another in the way He has intended us to from the beginning.

Without God's love as their soil, the seeds of love we plant in this life can never grow and flourish to their fullest eternal potential. So, as you seek God and His truth today, ask Him to fill you with mercy, kindness, compassion, grace—and, yes, love! And make sure that what matters most to your heart is not how others feel about you, or how you feel about others, but how your Father feels about you because, by faith, you are united with His Son, the Lord Jesus. Knowing that "*this* is love … that *he loved us* and sent his Son to be the propitiation for our sins" (1 John 4:10, NIV, emphasis added)—knowing that you could not be more loved by God than you already are—is what both shows you how to love others and frees you from needing anything from them so that you are able simply to give to them. So, "put on love"; for your loving Father in heaven will be more than pleased to sustain you as you seek to love Him and others more and more.

COLOSSIANS 3:5-14

---

41 John Lennon, "All You Need Is Love" (1967).

42 Virgil, *Eclogues* X.69.

MAY 23

THE DOWNWARD SPIRAL OF SIN

"It happened, late one afternoon, when David arose from his couch and was walking on the roof of the king's house, that he saw from the roof a woman bathing; and the woman was very beautiful. And David sent and inquired about the woman. And one said, 'Is not this Bathsheba, the daughter of Eliam, the wife of Uriah the Hittite?'" 2 SAMUEL 11:2-3

How did David go from godly king to abusive adulterer? It happened by degrees, as sin tends to.

First, David was all alone. This may appear to be a minor detail, but 2 Samuel 11:1 reveals how it was "the time when kings go out to battle"—yet David, instead of leading his men, had sent Joab to do the fighting in his stead. And so, instead of fulfilling his role as king, David was all alone on the roof of his house.

From the roof, David *saw* a very beautiful woman bathing. He might have seen Bathsheba accidentally, but he could have prevented himself from staring at her. The problem wasn't that he unintentionally caught a glimpse; the problem was that he started to gaze. The eye was the point of entry through which temptation came to David, as it so often is.

But David not only saw; he also *sent*. After seeing Bathsheba, he began to think about her. He could have put that thought away and ended his descent into sin right there. But having failed at this point, his thoughts led to action, and he sent for information about the woman. He learned that she was Bathsheba, the wife of one of his greatest warriors. The realization that Bathsheba was married to Uriah should have ended the matter for David. He knew the commandment of God: "You shall not commit adultery" (Exodus 20:14). Yet even this did not stop him! When lust grips, conscience fades, and reason is obliterated. And so "David sent messengers and took her, and she came to him, and he lay with her" (2 Samuel 11:4). There is no sense that she was given a choice in the matter.

This narrative should serve as a great warning to all of us. Paul warned the Corinthians, "Let anyone who thinks that he stands take heed lest he fall" (1 Corinthians 10:12). If David, a man who was greatly loved by God, could fall in this way, then we must never think that we are incapable of such a fall. Complacency is often the mother of sin. If David had taken heed, he would have led his men to war. He would have looked away. He would have stopped his thoughts. He would not have misused his power to sleep with Bathsheba. God has promised that "with the temptation he will also provide the way of escape, that you may be able to endure it" (1 Corinthians 10:13). And he provided David with many opportunities to stop. The tragedy is that David took none of them.

Like David, you *will* be tempted in this life—but God has promised that there will always be a way out. With which temptations are you particularly struggling at the moment? Thank God for His faithfulness. Pray that He will give you strength to endure temptation and so avoid sin's downward spiral. Take heed.

1 CORINTHIANS 10:12-14

MAY 24

A SINNER, BUT FORGIVEN

"David sent messengers and took her, and she came to him, and he lay with her."
2 SAMUEL 11:4

David's affair with Bathsheba is one of the most awful moments of Old Testament history. It is an account of unhindered lust, adultery, treachery, and murder. Perhaps we would rather not think about it—yet the Bible does not cast a veil of silence over it. We are actually provided with far more than we would ever want to know about David—and far more than we want to face about ourselves.

David was the great king of Israel. For most of his life, he was a man of exemplary character. He had built a magnificent reputation by triumphing over God's enemies, showing kindness to those who did not deserve it, and ruling with justice. By 2 Samuel 11, David was at the pinnacle of his power. He was able to command and to control everyone and everything, it would seem—everyone and everything, that is, except himself. And so he used—in fact, abused—his power to compel a woman to break her marriage vow, as well as breaking his own, and then to cause a man to lose his life (v 14-15).

And yet, even with this great failure, David remained chosen of God. The prophet Samuel had been sent by God with the instructions, "I will send you to Jesse the Bethlehemite, for I have provided for myself a king among his sons" (1 Samuel 16:1). David was God's designated king—and remained so. The promises of God had been given to him, and through him the purposes of God for His people were being set forward. David's heinous sin did not alter that.

Is it really possible that God's purpose in history could have been accomplished through this man? Yes. The Lord Jesus, the one man in history who exercised perfect self-control, who always protected women, and who came to bring life, was the descendant of great, flawed, repentant David. And so the story of David teaches us that God's grace triumphs even over the greatest failures. God doesn't only use those who are morally spotless—for, apart from His own Son, no human matches that description. In fact, God uses very sinful people like David; He uses very sinful people like me and like you.

Maybe you, like David eventually was, are very aware of your sins, and you are wondering if you are too filthy for God to forgive or to use. Be reassured and be encouraged. Though your sins have real consequences, they are utterly incapable of putting you beyond the reach of God's grace. Nothing can. There is no one who does not need His forgiveness and there is no one who is beyond the reach of His forgiveness. The blood of Christ cleanses even the deepest stains, so long as you humble yourself and repent. And, cleansed by that blood, as a repentant sinner you are in that place where God is delighted to work in and through you—not for your glory but for His.

1 TIMOTHY 1:12-17

MAY 25

TWO PRIDEFUL RESPONSES TO THE GOSPEL

"Let the one who boasts, boast in the Lord." 1 CORINTHIANS 1:31

There are two ways to respond wrongly to the good news of the gospel: the self-righteous response that refuses to see a need for Christ and the self-deprecating response that refuses to see Christ's ability to forgive. Both issue from the common root of pride.

The self-righteous response says, "I'm actually a pretty good person. I'm not sure I need forgiveness. Maybe it's good for some other people, but to be honest I don't need it." People who respond this way perhaps sense slight deficiencies in themselves and try to make up for them with good behavior. Maybe they even go to church to get some more "frequent attender miles" so that they'll get better seats in heaven. But still, their place in eternity will be, they think, secured by themselves—their goodness, their efforts. The pride at the heart of this response is obvious: it is to think we are *too good* to need the gospel. Christ's sacrifice is a nice example of love to us but unnecessary for us as a way to be saved.

The self-deprecating response says, "I'm such a mess that I don't think there's any hope for me. I am too terrible to deserve forgiveness. It must be great to know you're forgiven, but to be honest I know I could never have that." People who respond this way simply cannot bring themselves to believe that Jesus could ever love and forgive them. The pride in this response is subtler than in the first, but just as real: we believe we are *too dreadful* for the gospel, that our actions have taken us too far away for Jesus to reach us. Christ's sacrifice is great for those who are better than us, but it could never be enough for us.

Whenever someone feels too good or too bad for the gospel (and Christians are not immune from this temptation), it is pride that is restraining them from coming to Christ. Their confidence—their boasting—lies in what they have done, for good or for ill. What pride misses, however, is that we can be neither good enough nor too far gone. The self-righteous among us need to hear that even our best days are filled with more flaws than we know. The self-deprecating among us need to hear that even our worst days are never beyond the reach of God's grace.

Both responses miss the core gospel truth that Christ's cross simultaneously knocks down your self-worth and lifts you from your worthlessness. When you're tempted to boast about your worth, then, remember that what you most need—salvation—comes from Christ alone. And when you're tempted to despair in worthlessness, remember that what you most need—salvation—was only ever yours because of Christ alone. No matter what, Christ is your confidence, your boast—and you can never brag about Him too much!

MARK 2:13-17

MAY 26

FREED FROM DEATH'S GRIP

"When Jesus had stepped out of the boat, immediately there met him out of the tombs a man with an unclean spirit ... Night and day among the tombs and on the mountains he was always crying out and cutting himself with stones. And when he saw Jesus from afar, he ran and fell down before him." MARK 5:2, 5-6

The man possessed by demons in Mark 5 was utterly alone. He was alienated from his community and, in a very real sense, alienated from himself. He defined isolation. He was greatly in need of help.

We may think we are nothing like this man. After all, we go about clothed. We are able to reason. No one has tied us up. We are not possessed by demons. Yet this man serves as a sobering illustration of our spiritual condition. The Bible says that, by nature, we are all ruled by dark and sinister forces and are dead in our trespasses (Ephesians 2:1-3). Outside of Christ, we may as well be living among the tombs. Outside of Christ, we are the living dead.

This reality is what makes an encounter with Christ so dramatic. For each of us, salvation is an encounter between life and death, light and dark, the power of Christ and the power of evil. The gospel does not just give purpose to life. The gospel *is life itself.*

This reality is also what makes our transformation in Christ so painful. We should not pretend that surrendering to Christ is easy. When this man possessed by demons encountered Jesus, he seemed to know that Christ was the one who could set him free—but at the same time, he was afraid of what that change would mean. Sinclair Ferguson says, "No man yields to Jesus easily by nature. Tragically, like [this man], men often hold on to their bondage in evil rather than yield to the pain of transformation by Christ's power and grace."[43] It is painful to give up our little gods, painful to leave our dark captivity and emerge blinking into the light. But Jesus will allow no other gods before Him, for He will not allow any of His people to remain enslaved.

Only Jesus can cast out evil permanently. That is what this man experienced (Mark 5:15, 18-20), and that is what our lost friends and neighbors ultimately want. They don't just need a religion or system to make them better people. When they're honest, they know the problem lies primarily within them, not around them. Then they wonder, "Is there a power strong enough to conquer the evil within me?" There certainly is, and His name is Jesus—the one who went through His death in order to rescue us from ours!

Today, let God remind you of what you are apart from Christ: alienated, lonely, lost. And then ask Him to assure you of what you are in Christ: an ever-living recipient of His eternal mercy. By nature you are a sinner, and in Christ you are saved. The more you grasp this, the more humble and joyful you will be.

MARK 5:1-20

43 *Let's Study Mark* (Banner of Truth, 1999), p 64-65.

MAY 27

FINDING HAPPINESS

"But the one who looks into the perfect law, the law of liberty, and perseveres, being no hearer who forgets but a doer who acts, he will be blessed in his doing."
JAMES 1:25

Genuine happiness is to be found in following the pathway of obedience.

This is not the way the world sees it. In 21st-century Western culture, personal happiness and obedience to an authority are held to be mutually incompatible. But the Bible is clear: it is by obeying that we find ourselves "blessed."

So how do we take this path?

The first step is simple: look intently into God's word. The word James uses for "look," *parakupsas*, is the same word used elsewhere to describe a looking that is not mere glance but rather a careful, considered focus (for example, 1 Peter 1:12; John 20:5, 11). To benefit from the Bible, we need to have a genuine desire to miss nothing of its truth and a genuine willingness to consider carefully what we are reading.

Second, make your study of the Bible one of steady perseverance rather than a burst of enthusiasm followed by chronic inertia. We are called to meditate on the law day and night (Psalm 1:2) and to keep returning to God's word as our source of insight and understanding (Proverbs 2:1-5). As we do this we will notice, over time, that we are living more and more in line with God's word and are more and more able to discern how God's word applies in the situations we find ourselves in.

Third, act on what you read. If the word of God calls us to action but we give no expression to that, then it should be no surprise when we find ourselves disappointed and disheartened. Blessing is found not merely in reading God's word but in living it. Ultimately, we are to respond obediently by doing what we have heard God say.

The formula that James gives is straightforward: *Hearing plus doing equals blessing.* We see this principle throughout the Bible, including in the very words of Christ Himself. After He had washed the disciples' feet, Jesus turned to them and said, "If you know these things, blessed are you if you do them" (John 13:17). Knowledge, in other words, should lead to action, and the blessing is directly related to Spirit-empowered doing.

To help you look intently at what the Bible says, ask simple questions: What does this passage teach me about God the Father, God the Son, and God the Holy Spirit? What does this passage teach me about myself and what sin to avoid, what promise to accept, or what command to obey? As you continue along the pathway of obedience through God's enabling grace, the truth of His word will find a resting place in your heart and mind, and you will discover the freedom and blessing of a life lived God's way in His world.

JOHN 13:1-17

MAY 28

MAKE THE BOOK LIVE TO ME

"Then he said to them, 'These are my words that I spoke to you while I was still with you, that everything written about me in the Law of Moses and the Prophets and the Psalms must be fulfilled.' Then he opened their minds to understand the Scriptures." LUKE 24:44-45

Over the years, several films have sought to portray the sheer brutality surrounding Jesus' crucifixion—the unrelenting, unmitigated torture that transformed Christ into little more than a barely conscious mass of blood and flesh by the time He reached Golgotha. After viewing such a horrific scene, we may respond with tears and feelings of pity and remorse, or with confusion, wondering, *Why did this have to take place? What actually happened here?*

But however moved we may be, witnessing Jesus' crucifixion—whether in person, as the disciples did, or through an artist's rendering—is not enough in and of itself to bring an individual to saving faith. Rather, we meet Jesus savingly and definitively primarily through God's word. The apostle Paul exhorted fellow believers along these lines: "How then will they call on him in whom they have not believed? And how are they to believe in him of whom they have never heard? And how are they to hear without someone preaching? And how are they to preach unless they are sent?" (Romans 10:14-15). The great need of every age is the proclamation of God's word.

This was the purpose of Jesus' interaction with the disciples in Jerusalem on the first Easter Sunday. They were confused and despairing following Jesus' crucifixion. Then, as they cowered in a locked room, their Savior appeared, frightening them (Luke 24:37). And how did He still their souls? He assured them of His physical resurrection; but He also pointed them back to God's word, which He'd spoken to them before His resurrection and which they would still have after He had ascended back to heaven. He gave them information and then He gifted them with illumination: He "opened their minds to understand."

What these disciples needed is what we need: to meet Jesus in the pages of Scripture. We may not be able to see Jesus physically, but we can read all that they read: all that is written about Him in the Old Testament and in the apostolic teaching of the New. We can see Him there as He opens our minds to do so. We need more than intellectual ability (though that is necessary); we need His supernatural activity. We need to ask the Spirit of God to show us the Lord Jesus, our Savior, as we read. May this humble prayer therefore be the cry of your heart today: "Lord, make the book live to me."[44]

LUKE 24:44-52

44 R. Hudson Pope, "Make the Book Live to Me" (1943).

BE CAREFUL WHAT YOU ASK FOR

"The Lord said to Samuel, 'Obey the voice of the people in all that they say to you, for they have not rejected you, but they have rejected me from being king over them. According to all the deeds that they have done, from the day I brought them up out of Egypt even to this day, forsaking me and serving other gods, so they are also doing to you. Now then, obey their voice; only you shall solemnly warn them and show them the ways of the king who shall reign over them.'" 1 SAMUEL 8:7-9

Have you ever wanted something, worked for it and secured it, and then realized that you were worse off than before? Sooner or later, most of us discover that all that glitters is not gold—and so we should be careful what we aim for, work for, and wish for.

The people of Israel were, by the eighth chapter of 1 Samuel, very sure of what they needed. And so they asked for and insisted on "a king to judge us like all the nations" (1 Samuel 8:5). But in doing so, the people of Israel had essentially rejected God as King. They no longer wanted to be known as a holy people and a distinctive nation. Instead, they wanted to be free of God's perfect rule and absorbed into the surrounding culture.

To this entreaty God gave a solemn warning: *Be careful what you ask for!* He would give the people what they wanted—but His willingness to grant them a king would turn out to be an act of judgment for their foolish, faithless request. A king would take their children as soldiers and servants (1 Samuel 8:11-14). He would take their best possessions (v 15). Worse of all, He said, "You shall be his slaves" (v 17).

In the book of Romans, Paul recounts the folly of humanity that courses from the Garden of Eden through the whole history of the world: though we recognize there is a God, we don't honor Him and instead exchange His glory for idols we deem to be better (Romans 1:21-23). "And since [we] did not see fit to acknowledge God, God gave [us] up" to live according to our passions and desires—and to suffer the natural outcome of our choices (v 28-31). God's present judgment is seen not in withholding from humanity what we want but in letting us have it. Sin is its own punishment.

How easy it is to declare, whether with our lips or by our decisions and our deeds, that we no longer want to live under God's kingship—that we want to be free to be our own person and make our own decisions about who we are, what we have, and what we believe. But God's kindness is seen in not giving us what we think we need. Having shown them in King Saul the insecurity and disappointment that the king they wanted would bring, God brought Israel the kind of king they had not asked for but truly needed—David. And He offers us today the Savior and Lord who we would never have asked for but who we desperately need. So, as you consider what you want in life, remember this: God has already given you what you most need in giving us His Son. And His kindness is seen not just in what He gives but what He withholds, for He knows better than you do what you truly need in your life.

ROMANS 1:18-32

MAY 30

SOLID GROUND TO STAND ON

"Therefore take up the whole armor of God, that you may be able to withstand in the evil day, and having done all, to stand firm. Stand therefore, having fastened on the belt of truth." EPHESIANS 6:13-14

Western culture is confused about many things—but it's *certainly* confused about truth. We often trade in vague platitudes that sound great at first but which crumble under closer examination. "Just be a good person," we hear. "It doesn't really matter what you believe, just as long as you lead a good life and do your best." That all sounds quite pleasant, and we ought to thank God for the common grace that prevents our world from tearing itself apart. But it's not enough—because the obvious question is this: Who gets to define *good*? What does it really mean to live a good life or to be a good person? When we have competing visions for what exactly *good* means and can't agree on the fundamentals, we find ourselves in all sorts of trouble—not unlike the present state of affairs in much of the West.

We all feel the pressure to cave in to our society's relativization of truth, in which "you decide your truth and I'll decide mine." The Bible, however, calls us to find a firm foothold on God's truth—a truth that is objective and is not up for debate. Paul instructs us, "Stand … having fastened on the belt of truth" (Ephesians 6:14). When we embrace our culture's confusion about truth, we are left to be "tossed to and fro by the waves and carried about by every wind of doctrine, by human cunning, by craftiness in deceitful schemes" (4:14). We simply have no solid ground to stand on. But when we plant ourselves in God's truth, we can firmly hold our ground and be ready to face whatever comes our way (Luke 12:35; 1 Peter 1:13).

Standing for truth won't prove easy. People might consider us hopelessly old-fashioned, dogmatic, or worse. But in reality, to stand on and advocate for truth is one of the most loving things we can do—for it is to call people to live in line with reality, and to call them away from building on falsehoods that, sooner or later, will crumble beneath them. As Paul writes elsewhere, love "does not rejoice at wrongdoing, but rejoices with the truth" (1 Corinthians 13:6). What might it take for you to rejoice with the truth today in your own thinking and in your conversations with others? However high the cost may seem, you can stand and speak with confidence, knowing that Christ has sent His Spirit to "guide you into all the truth" (John 16:13).

JOHN 8:31-36

MAY 31

STAND ON THE GOSPEL

"Stand therefore, having fastened on the belt of truth, and having put on the breastplate of righteousness, and, as shoes for your feet, having put on the readiness given by the gospel of peace." EPHESIANS 6:14-15

When we picture soldiers on the frontlines of battle, we often imagine firearms, artillery, and other tactical equipment. But there's a piece of gear we often overlook, without which a soldier would be utterly ineffective: *his boots.* Without appropriate footwear, no soldier, and therefore no army, can hope to defend a position.

The apostle Paul calls believers to stand firm in our *gospel shoes,* so to speak—to be at the ready with appropriate footwear. When in his first letter to the Corinthian church he writes his great chapter on the resurrection, he begins, "Now I would remind you, brothers, of the gospel I preached to you, which you received, *in which you stand*" (1 Corinthians 15:1, emphasis added). The gospel provides us with firm footing. Even when everything else around us is shaking, we always have a place to stand. Even when temptation is fierce, we never need to retreat.

What was it that empowered Martin Luther to stand against the tide, nail his theses to the church door at Wittenberg, and then proclaim before an emperor, "Here I stand; I can do no other"? Gospel shoes. What was it that enabled the English Protestants Hugh Latimer and Nicholas Ridley to face with courage the horror of being burnt at the stake for their faith? Gospel shoes. What is it that sees our brothers and sisters in so many places around the world joyfully proclaim their faith in Christ even as they are threatened with death? Gospel shoes.

When you go to your workplace, to your school, to your unbelieving family and friends, or into your local community, what will give you the power to stand for Jesus? Only the gospel shoes that Christ provides. If you try to stand on your own strength, you will inevitably stumble and fall. But when you enter each new day with your feet rooted in the hope, peace, forgiveness, and assurance of the gospel, then you will find yourself able to stand firm, even through the fiercest opposition from the world and temptation from the devil. So before you go and get on with your day, rehearse the gospel to yourself. Enjoy its truths. Praise your Savior. Or, to put it a different way: put your shoes on.

1 CORINTHIANS 15:1-8

JUNE 1

SHIELDED BY FAITH

"In all circumstances take up the shield of faith, with which you can extinguish all the flaming darts of the evil one." EPHESIANS 6:16

You are under attack.

We might not feel as though this is the case, but in reality we face a spiritual onslaught in which the Evil One daily employs any tactic in his arsenal to undermine our identity and our unity in Jesus Christ. His fiery arrows are constantly being loosed against the people of God. What is a Christian to do in the face of such assaults?

When warfare reaches us—and it will—we must reach for our shields. We are to "take up the shield of faith." The shield Paul's readers would have imagined when they heard these words was no small shield, for in Roman times a soldier's shield was four feet long by two and a half feet wide. Wielding one would have been like walking around with a door. It was not a Frisbee-like toy but a formidable piece of armor.

The key to understanding the proper use of our shields is that when we come to trust in Christ, He grants to us gospel armor. Having died in our place, He clothes us with His righteousness. So when we take up the shield of faith, we are actively trusting the gospel to shield us from Satan's lies. The only way we can deal with the hostilities of ongoing spiritual warfare is to find our strength—our spiritual weapons and armor—in the Lord Jesus.

John Newton, in a seldom-sung hymn, pictures an encounter with the devil like this:

When Satan appears to stop up our path
And fills us with fears, we triumph by faith;
He cannot take from us, though oft he has tried,
The heart-cheering promise, "The Lord will provide."[45]

Christ has already triumphed and, by faith, He invites us to share in His spoils. This victory is what led one of the Westminster Divines, William Gouge, to pen in his diary, "When I look upon myself, I see nothing but emptiness and weakness; but when I look upon Christ, I see nothing but fullness and sufficiency."[46] The Evil One is a defeated foe, though still a powerful one. When we seek to fight him in our own strength, we will find ourselves defeated. But God has provided all the armor we need. Our faith is our shield, for our faith tells us that we are forgiven children of the living God, empowered by His Spirit to obey Him and enjoying the certain hope of eternal life with Him.

You will come under attack today. Where in your life might the battle rage? Be sure to look to your faith in those moments, for it will shield you against temptation, and you will stand in victory against the devil's darts.

1 PETER 5:6-11

---

45 John Newton, "The Lord Will Provide" (1775).

46 Quoted in James Reid, *Memoirs of the Lives and Writings of Those Eminent Divines, Who Convened in the Famous Assembly at Westminster, in the Seventeenth Century* (Stephen and Andrew Young, 1811), p 357.

JUNE 2

TAKE UP YOUR SWORD

Take the … sword of the Spirit, which is the word of God." EPHESIANS 6:17

The devil knows the Bible. He knows what it says, and he can quote it with ease—better than most of us, undoubtedly. Satan quoted Scripture to Jesus when He was fasting in the wilderness (Matthew 4:1-11)—though notice that Satan also twisted what the Bible says for his own deceitful schemes. This shouldn't surprise us, since the best lies usually have at least a bit of truth in them.

In that encounter, when Satan took Jesus to the pinnacle of the temple, he enticed Him with an appeal to a spectacular, angelic rescue. But the devil misused Psalm 91 by taking it out of context (Matthew 4:5-6), and Jesus rebuked him by quoting Deuteronomy 6:16: "You shall not put the Lord your God to the test." The Son of God repeatedly quoted Scripture to Satan, and he eventually fled (Matthew 4:11).

Our best defense against Satan, then, is Scripture rightly understood and rightly applied. This is why Paul tells us that in order to stand firm against "all the flaming darts of the evil one," we must "take up … the sword of the Spirit, which is the word of God" (Ephesians 6:16). There is no better tool to resist temptation and devilish ploys than the Bible. God's word is what we use to resist the devil, and the overwhelming spiritual power of that word is precisely why he flees (James 4:7).

Psalm 119:11 encourages God's people to store up God's word in their hearts in order that we might not sin against Him. This might sound like a nice, gentle invitation at first—but while it may prove true that the Bible can be consumed and meditated upon in the comfortable company of a warm beverage and a cozy chair, the call to memorize Scripture is in fact a call to arms. Every soldier needs a weapon. Every Christian needs the word of God. Think about the temptations to sin that you regularly face (and, perhaps, give in to). What verses of Scripture do you need to deliberately memorize and then deploy against the devil's half-truths and lies? Think about the times when the Evil One suggests that you are not really a child of God, not really forgiven. What parts of Scripture will you fling back at him in those moments? The word of God is your sword against Satan. Take it up today, and make him flee.

PSALM 119:9-16

JUNE 3

PRAYING IN THE SPIRIT

"Take the helmet of salvation, and the sword of the Spirit, which is the word of God, praying at all times in the Spirit, with all prayer and supplication."
EPHESIANS 6:17-18

What does it mean to pray "in the Spirit"?

One answer is to tie this text to 1 Corinthians 12 and speaking in tongues, but that was probably not Paul's intention. Paul certainly did not speak in tongues "at all times" as he prayed. Instead of thinking of this as one way to pray among many, then, we should recognize that praying "in the Spirit" is the *only* way to pray.

Jesus' exchange with the Samaritan woman at the well in John 4 is instructive for us on this point. During their dialogue, the woman raises the issue of Gerizim and Jerusalem as potential places of public worship, over which there was disagreement between Samaritans and Jews. In response, Jesus says, "The hour is coming, and is now here, when the true worshipers will worship the Father in spirit and truth" (John 4:23).

People sometimes suggest that what Jesus is saying here is that *anyone* can worship *anywhere*, as long as they're sincere. But He's not actually saying that! Instead, He's revealing that only those who receive the Holy Spirit can worship God at all. It is only in the Spirit, by the Spirit, and through the Spirit that worship—and, by extension, prayer—that is pleasing to God can even take place.

Paul also illuminates what he means for us in Romans 8:15-16: "You did not receive the spirit of slavery to fall back into fear, but you have received the Spirit of adoption as sons, by whom we cry, 'Abba! Father!' The Spirit himself bears witness with our spirit that we are children of God." God has given us His Spirit, and it is by His Spirit in us that we cry out to Him, even—perhaps *especially*—in our weakness (v 26).

This is why "no one can say 'Jesus is Lord' except in the Holy Spirit" (1 Corinthians 12:3). Sure, someone might say the words "Jesus is Lord," but no one can really mean them apart from the work of the Spirit in his or her life. So it is with prayer: our adoption into the family of God, including our receiving of the Holy Spirit, is the foundation of our prayer life.

When you come to God in prayer today, then—perhaps even as you finish this reading—and call God "Father," you will be "praying in the Spirit." Depend on the Spirit, who by faith lives in you. He will help you. He will prompt you. He will guide you. And He will remind you of what a wonderful, undeserved joy it is to be able to speak to the Creator and Sustainer of the universe and address Him as your Abba, Father.

ROMANS 8:9-17

JUNE 4

THE MYSTERY OF PRAYER

"... Praying at all times in the Spirit, with all prayer and supplication."
EPHESIANS 6:18

If God has already determined what He is going to do, why bother to pray? What possible difference can prayer make? Can we change God's mind in our prayers? Nearly all of us will have voiced or at least given thought to questions like these. We think like finite creatures, and we naturally project our own perception of reality onto God. Even the Bible regularly personifies God in human categories. But though the Bible itself sometimes portrays God in ways that represent Him with human characteristics—as if He were changeable, for instance (1 Samuel 15:10-11, 35)—the full testimony of Scripture causes us to conclude that *God does not change His mind.*

James puts it plainly for us: in God "there is no variation or shadow due to change" (James 1:17). And the Old Testament agrees with the New: "God is not man, that he should lie, or a son of man, that he should change his mind. Has he said, and will he not do it? Or has he spoken, and will he not fulfill it?" (Numbers 23:19). When it appears that God changes His mind, then, it is in actual fact circumstances or human behavior that has changed, and God is responding differently than He had done but still entirely consistently with His character. So, if God never changes His mind and yet He repeatedly calls His people to pray, then we are led to this conclusion: in His sovereignty, God has ordained both the ends and the means to those ends, and we will not reach God's intended ends without His foreordained means. (If that sounds like a mystery, that's because it is!)

Think of God's eternal ends as found in Revelation 7:9-10: "After this I looked, and behold, a great multitude that no one could number, from every nation, from all tribes and peoples and languages, standing before the throne and before the Lamb, clothed in white robes, with palm branches in their hands, and crying out with a loud voice, 'Salvation belongs to our God who sits on the throne, and to the Lamb!'" Now, is God simply going to bring that innumerable company before His throne, irrespective of anything anyone says or does? No! Otherwise, why would Jesus have said to His followers, "Pray earnestly to the Lord of the harvest to send out laborers into his harvest" (Matthew 9:38)? In God's plans, the prayers of His people are the means by which He raises up servants who herald His word. And men and women receiving the word of God from those heralds (Romans 10:17) are the God-appointed means for fulfilling His purpose from all eternity: *to have a people that are His very own.*

Ultimately, how the sovereign God uses the prayers of His people in His plans remains a mystery. We won't have all the answers to all our questions about prayer, at least not for now. And that's ok, because we can be confident that God ordains means such as prayer for His eternal purposes. And knowing that is enough to bring us to our knees so that we might enjoy the privilege of knowing in all eternity that our prayers were used as part of His sovereign purposes to save His people.

COLOSSIANS 4:2-6

JUNE 5

OUR GREATEST MOTIVATION TO PRAY

"... Praying at all times in the Spirit, with all prayer and supplication."
EPHESIANS 6:18

The Bible is replete with commands like this, urging us to pray without pause. This might sound like an overwhelming expectation, and we may wonder whether we could ever meet it, or even desire to. But perhaps if we see our need more clearly, we will be motivated to pray more consistently.

Our need for prayer becomes most obvious when we understand that our Lord Jesus Christ Himself believed in the absolute necessity of prayer. At the beginning of Mark's Gospel, we have this account of Jesus: "Rising very early in the morning, while it was still dark, he departed and went out to a desolate place, and there he prayed" (Mark 1:35). Even for the Son of God, prayer was important enough business to attend to early and not to allow the demands of the day to intrude upon.

Jesus knew that "he must go to Jerusalem and suffer many things from the elders and chief priests and scribes, and be killed" (Matthew 16:21). Even so, in the Garden of Gethsemane we overhear Him praying for the cup of God's wrath to pass from Him if it is His Father's will (Matthew 26:39; Mark 14:36; Luke 22:42). The Son of God clearly knew that He needed to go before His Father. The writer to the Hebrews summarizes it perfectly for us: "In the days of his flesh, Jesus offered up prayers and supplications, with loud cries and tears, to him who was able to save him from death, and he was heard because of his reverence" (Hebrews 5:7).

Surely it cannot be that prayer was a necessity for Jesus and yet is simply optional for us. If anything, it must be the very reverse! If the Son of God Himself needed to spend time concentrated on prayer to His Father, then how much more does the one who follows after Christ! Prayer is simply too great a privilege for any Christian to ignore and too great a necessity for any of us to neglect. So, ask His Spirit to show you the wonder of prayer and to help you enter into it. When you recognize that there is no end to God's capacity to help or His willingness to do so, and that there is no moment in which you do not need His help, you will find yourself "praying at all times."

EPHESIANS 3:14-21

JUNE 6

PRAYER OF ALL KINDS

"... Praying at all times in the Spirit, with all prayer and supplication."
EPHESIANS 6:18

Prayer should never become a routine experience any more than it should be a rare occurrence. There is never a circumstance in which we are not called to pray. Scripture shows us that sometimes we cry out to God from the darkness (for instance, Psalm 88); at other times we pour out to God our joyful praise over the resplendent majesty of Christ (for instance, Revelation 5:12-14)—and oftentimes we find ourselves somewhere in between.

In Ephesians 6:18, Paul encourages us to come to God (as the NIV puts it) "with all kinds of prayers and requests." We do not always need to say everything, but it is wise not always to say the same thing. So, what might it look like in practice to speak to our Father about "all kinds" of things? The acronym ACTS serves as a simple and useful memory aid for remembering different kinds of prayer:

A — *Adoration:* We can come to God and just revel in His greatness. "Magnify the LORD with me, and let us exalt his name together!" (Psalm 34:3). There are an infinite number of reasons to praise God, not only or primarily for what He has done but also for who He is. God is perfect in every way, and so God is worthy of our adoration.

C — *Confession:* We should recognize in prayer that, as Martin Luther said, repentance is not something that should only be triggered by particular instances of sin but rather should be a daily experience: "When our Lord and Master Jesus Christ said, 'Repent,' he willed the entire life of believers to be one of repentance."[47] "I am a man [or woman] of unclean lips," we might confess with Isaiah, "and I dwell in the midst of a people of unclean lips" (Isaiah 6:5). God is worthy of our honest confession.

T — *Thanksgiving:* The real test for our hearts is what we say and pray when there doesn't appear to be much to be thankful for. Paul exhorts us, "Give thanks in *all* circumstances" (1 Thessalonians 5:18, emphasis added)—including those we would never have chosen. We are not called to thank Him for all things, but we are to remember that there are always reasons to thank Him, even in the hardest of times.

S — *Supplication:* It is right to express our needs to our heavenly Father, from whom "every good gift and every perfect gift" comes (James 1:17) and who knows exactly what His children need (Matthew 6:8). We ask, seek, and knock (7:7)—sometimes for big things, sometimes for small ones. Whatever we ask for, God is worthy of our supplication.

Scripture encourages us and guides us to pray in all manner of ways. And when, among all these options, we can't seem to find the right words, we have no cause for despair. Whatever kinds of prayers and requests we can muster—or can't—the Spirit of our Lord Jesus always "intercedes for us with groanings too deep for words" (Romans 8:26). God is eager to hear you. So pray!

PSALM 30

47 The Ninety-Five Theses, number 1.

JUNE 7

PRAYING WITH PERSEVERANCE

"Keep alert with all perseverance, making supplication for all the saints."
EPHESIANS 6:18

Almost every Christian finds prayer hard at some time (or most of the time). Why is that?

One of the reasons why we're tempted to give up on prayer is that we don't always receive an immediate response from God. In a world that so highly exalts instant gratification, this is a real difficulty. It's the same issue as in trying to maintain a proper exercise regimen or diet: we want to see results now, today. If our new approach does not quickly show its benefits, most of us are unlikely to persevere.

Our tendency to lack endurance is one reason that Jesus told the parable about the persistent widow, who was relentless in seeking out justice from the judge. Luke makes the editorial comment that Jesus was encouraging his listeners to understand that they "ought always to pray and not lose heart" (Luke 18:1). In other words, Jesus wants us to pray—and then to keep on praying.

When Paul tells us to "keep alert" and to pray "with all perseverance," he is echoing Jesus' words to His disciples in the Garden of Gethsemane on the night before He died: "Watch and pray that you may not enter into temptation" (Matthew 26:41). Paul spoke similarly to the Ephesian elders, telling them to "be alert" (Acts 20:31). In a world embroiled in a cosmic spiritual battle, the stakes are too high to give up on prayer.

As we keep coming to God with prayer and supplication, we will all have to learn to be content with trusting that God will answer us in His good timing, and we will all need to remember that Satan would love to persuade us that prayer makes no difference and that God does not listen or act. You may not see an answer to a desperate prayer on this side of eternity. Sometimes persistence may appear to be met with silence. But in due time, God will show you that "the Lord is not slow to fulfill his promises" (2 Peter 3:9). He answers all your prayers exactly when He knows it is right to and in precisely the manner that is always best for you. God is always doing far more than we can ask or even imagined. Sometimes we can glimpse some of His purposes, but sometimes we are asked to live by faith, not by sight.

Are there people or situations that you have given up praying for because you have had no clear and positive response? Remember, you have not had such a response *yet*. One day, you will see what God was doing in directing matters differently than how you would have chosen. Until that day, you can persevere in prayer, because it is what He commands and because He has promised to work for the good of His people. Why not begin today to pray with perseverance for something you have quit speaking to God about?

EPHESIANS 1:15-23

JUNE 8

A WORD TO PLANNERS

"Come now, you who say, 'Today or tomorrow we will go into such and such a town and spend a year there and trade and make a profit'—yet you do not know what tomorrow will bring." JAMES 4:13-14

In and of itself, there's nothing wrong with planning ahead. John Wesley, the great evangelist, even used to plan out his day in twenty-minute segments, ensuring that a third of an hour wouldn't pass without him addressing himself to matters of God's kingdom. But in these verses, James offers a word to men and women in every generation who are addicted to their calendars, who clutch at their phones, and who live with the impression deep down that the world will stop turning if they get off track.

At the heart of the matter is this rock-solid fact: to us, the future is unknown. Will it be sunny tomorrow? Will your flight be on time? Will the traffic be busier than usual and interrupt your schedule? We can plan as best as we're able to, but ultimately all our best plans may fall into tatters. Indeed, they do so routinely. To presume upon the future is foolish when our ignorance of that future is an indisputable fact.

Facing this fact ought to have two effects. First, it ought to humble us. James has already reminded his readers that "God opposes the proud but gives grace to the humble" (James 4:6), and issued the challenging call: "Humble yourselves before the Lord, and he will exalt you" (v 10). Now he reminds us that we ought not to take for ourselves the seat that belongs to God alone—we are not in control. It is our response to disruption and disappointment that reveals whether we have truly grasped this.

Secondly, tomorrow being unknown to us ought to help us, for the future is hidden from us for our good and for God's glory. If we knew of some success that awaited us, we might become unbearable, preening our feathers and basking in our own sense of self-importance. By the same token, we should be thankful that we don't live in the constant awareness of our future stumblings and struggles, fears and failures, bereavements and heartaches—for what advantage would that give us? God knows. That is enough.

So remember this: God the Creator established you, made you, and gave you all your abilities, your looks, your opportunities. He has ordered your life right up until today, and will continue to do so until He welcomes you home. Because of this, you can actually rejoice in what you do not know. There is beauty in the mystery. There is great wonder in knowing that God is ordering all things and will accomplish His purposes in and for you, whatever tomorrow brings. It is this perspective that will enable you to look at your plans for today, tomorrow, and further on down the path of your life, and say with a humble peace in your heart, "*If the Lord wills*, we will live and do this or that" (James 4:15, emphasis added).

JOB 39

◇ Bible Through The Year: Jeremiah 9–11; Matthew 22:1-22

JUNE 9

WITHOUT GOD IN THE WORLD

"Man in his pomp yet without understanding is like the beasts that perish."
PSALM 49:20

For centuries, Western society has benefited from the widespread influence of the Christian faith. While the history of the West is filled with examples of human depravity, where there has been a consistent Christian presence it has, in many ways and at many times, stayed the hand of evil. Most of us have not had to experience what a society looks like when it completely rejects and forgets God.

The Scriptures, however, do give us a grim picture of what happens when people have convinced themselves that there is no God. It is a picture of a rejection of humility, where "the wicked boasts of the desires of his soul" and rejects God in pride (Psalm 10:3-4). Humility is where the knowledge of God begins; therefore, those who reject God reject humility too.

Not only do such proud people *reject* God; they also *revile* Him, cursing and renouncing Him (Psalm 10:3). It is often prosperity that leads people to curse God. Their lives are going so well that they believe nothing can touch them and they will give no account to their Maker. Their prosperity gives them a false sense of security. They think they can live as they like, that "God has forgotten, he has hidden his face, he will never see it" (v 11), and that there will be no repercussions for their behavior. With no accountability for how people live, there is no need for the powerful to serve or the strong to be gentle: we can treat others however we please, and so the godless man "sits in ambush … he murders the innocent … he lurks that he may seize the poor" (v 8-9).

It is with good reason, then, that the psalmist says, "Man in his pomp yet without understanding is like the beasts that perish." When we reject and revile God, we foolishly think we are secure, which convinces us that it's acceptable for us to mistreat others.

It is tempting to think that passages like this one only describe other people. But we should not be too quick to look away from ourselves. Are there ways we have rejected humility, believing ourselves to be sufficient without God? Have *we* let our prosperity numb us to our neediness and accountability before God? Has *our* treatment of those around us been marked by self-interest and arrogance instead of love and service? We may confess to have faith in God, but perhaps there are areas of our lives that require repentance.

The picture of man "in his pomp yet without understanding" is indeed a bleak one—both in this life and at its end. So praise God that this is not the whole picture. If you understand that we have a Creator to whom we are valuable and accountable, and that that Creator has ransomed your soul and will receive you into eternal life (Psalm 49:15), then the pomp of this world will assume its proper place, and in Jesus Christ you will enjoy purpose, hope, forgiveness, and pleasures forevermore.

PSALM 49

JUNE 10

THE GENUINE ARTICLE

"In this you rejoice, though now for a little while, if necessary, you have been grieved by various trials, so that the tested genuineness of your faith—more precious than gold that perishes though it is tested by fire—may be found to result in praise and glory and honor at the revelation of Jesus Christ." 1 PETER 1:6-7

Some things can only be tested by time.

If you have ever attempted to buy a dresser or cabinet at a reasonable price, perhaps you've considered whether to buy a secondhand piece or, for nearly the same price, a new piece from a discount store. The drawback is that such pieces may prove, when they're opened and closed, to have doors and drawers that won't go back into place. The item of furniture quickly becomes a real mess. It may look good on the outside on first inspection, but the real issue is with its day-by-day use and what the test of time will show, which will prove whether you have the genuine article or not.

How do we know whether our faith is the real thing? The answer, at least in part, is that genuine faith is to be discovered in the day-by-day "opening and closing"—in facing up to the challenges and trials that come our way.

Some suggest that victorious Christian living means the absence of trials—that if we are really men and women of faith, then trials will be an uncommon experience. Peter says the exact opposite is true: the experience of trials and difficulties is not uncommon, unusual, or unproductive in a Christian's life, but is purposeful in God's plan.

We prove to ourselves and those who may be watching that our faith is genuine when we face challenges and refuse to run away, instead holding on to our trust in Christ's goodness no matter how difficult the path that He is leading us along. When trials come and everything goes askew, we find out whether our testimonies and the professions we've made about God's grace, peace, and securing providence are genuine.

Charles Spurgeon wrote in *Morning and Evening*, "The one who would glorify his God must be prepared to meet with many trials. No one can be illustrious before the Lord unless his conflicts are many. If, then, yours is a much-tried path"—that is, a path of many trials—"rejoice in it, because you will be better able to display the all-sufficient grace of God. As for His failing you, never dream of it—hate the thought. The God who has been sufficient until now should be trusted to the end."[48]

Will your faith prove genuine through life's greatest challenges? It is not only possible to hold on by God's grace, but it is also profitable on account of God's grace. As you trust in His grace, you will discover that you can rejoice, because your happiness ultimately is not tied to circumstances but found in persevering in your faith—in knowing the sufficiency of Christ in circumstances you would never have chosen and in looking forward to the day when your Savior is revealed.

JAMES 5:7-11

48 *Morning and Evening*, revised and updated by Alistair Begg (Crossway, 2003), March 4 morning reading.

JUNE 11

RETURN TO THE LORD

"Return, O Israel, to the L*ORD your God, for you have stumbled because of your iniquity."* HOSEA 14:1

From the beginning, men and women have shown a great ability for avoiding responsibility. When the Lord called to Adam in Eden to hold him accountable for the first sin, Adam's response was not to accept responsibility but to blame the "woman whom you gave to be with me" (Genesis 3:12). Eve responded similarly: "The serpent deceived me" (v 13). And so the trend continues to this day. We recognize that we have problems and do not walk with God the way we are designed to. But our instinct is to find reasons to explain away our error.

Is your spouse difficult? Is your church unexciting? Is your job or home life too stressful? No matter what the excuse might be, we're often slow to recognize that when we feel out of touch with God, the cause primarily lies within and that there is no legitimate excuse for our sin.

This is the point the prophet Hosea made to the people of Israel. They found themselves far from God, and the reason should not have been difficult to discern: "You have stumbled because of your iniquity." It was their sin that was causing them to stumble—nothing and no one else.

God's people had been called to live in a way that was noticeably distinct from the surrounding nations, but they had not lived up to their calling. Instead, it could be said that "Ephraim [God's people] mixes himself with the peoples" around them (Hosea 7:8). The holiness of God's people was partial. The Lord described them in that same verse as "a cake not turned"—their holiness was like a cake with an entire side uncooked—one that looked good but was inedible. Why were they so half-hearted? Because their love for God was not faithful but superficial, "like a morning cloud, like the dew that goes early away" (6:4).

Do you see yourself in these descriptions? Is your life indistinct from the unbelieving world? Do you like to keep areas of your life to yourself rather than give all your life to God? Do you regularly resolve to love and obey God, but never turn resolution into reality? If you do, what is the road to recovery? It can only be the road of return. The Lord God extended His compassionate hand to these wayward people and invited them back: "Return, O Israel, to the LORD your God." If they would just turn from their sins and come back to Him, they would experience spiritual and relational restoration.

If you have been walking waywardly, estranged from God, perhaps you can identify with the prodigal son from Luke 15. What did he do when he realized how badly wrong things had gone? He came to his senses, he accepted full responsibility, and he returned to his father. And the response of that father is the response of God to any of His wandering children if we return, without excuses and asking for forgiveness: an eager reunion, abundant blessing, and restored fellowship with the God whose love never evaporates.

LUKE 15:11-32

JUNE 12

THE SAME OLD ROUTINE

"For everything there is a season, and a time for every matter under heaven."
ECCLESIASTES 3:1

The first eight verses of Ecclesiastes 3 give us a description of the cycle of life, and it has been said, rather cynically, that these verses contain 28 statements—14 pluses and 14 minuses—that add up to nothing at all. Such a perspective represents the struggle that many have in trying to make sense of the cyclical nature of life in this world without giving in to pessimism.

We know that there is a time to be born and a time to die. We weren't in control of our arrival, and we're not in control of our departure—and that's part of the problem, because we like to be in control. Between these two fixed points, we can sow, we can gather, and we can rake leaves, but even in these activities we have no complete control over *when* we do them. Plants grow in springtime, the summer sustains them, and in autumn we gather the sheaves and watch the leaves fall. There is a cycle that's out of our hands.

And so the ultimate problem for us is that we live in an unending cycle that continues throughout our lives and will continue long after we are gone. When this reality dawns on us, we are confronted with our finitude, and we become aware that our lives are tremendously insignificant in the grand scheme of things. How do we respond? One way is to fill our days with noise and activity. We don't want to face the tyranny of the cycle of life or to confront its end. We want distraction.

Here is the godly, and much more fulfilling, response: to live knowing that the God who made you knows exactly where you are, what you're thinking, how you're feeling, and how you are trying to make sense of life as it is presented to you. Your life is an open book to God, and it's His grace alone that yields in you the realization that you are not in charge, but also that you do not need to be, for He is.

Your significance and security do not come from your ability to control your life: whatever you do, the seasons will pass, and one day so will you. Rather, whatever season you are in, you find true peace by knowing and loving Him who rules over all of history. In whatever remains of today, allow yourself to enjoy all that God in His sovereignty brings into your life, seek to obey Him in those things, and rest easy in Him who orders every season for your good and His glory.

PSALM 90

JUNE 13

DEALING WITH INDWELLING SIN

"When Christ who is your life appears, then you also will appear with him in glory. Put to death therefore what is earthly in you: sexual immorality, impurity, passion, evil desire, and covetousness, which is idolatry." COLOSSIANS 3:4-5

If becoming a Christian meant we no longer sinned, Paul would have been wasting ink when he wrote, "Put to death therefore what is earthly in you." It is possible to embrace a form of externalism that makes us look really good to people on the outside when really we know that what the Bible says is true: that while we are saved children of God, we are also sinners.

How is it, then, that sin continues to wreak havoc? It is because while we are indeed in Christ, who liberates us from the bondage of sin, we are also in our flesh. That's the problem: we experience "the desires of the flesh that "are against the Spirit ... for these are opposed to each other, to keep you from doing the things you want to do" (Galatians 5:17). We are justified in Christ; all of the guilt that attaches to our lives is dealt with in Jesus. We have died to sin in Christ so that it no longer has a tyrannical rule in our lives. But although sin no longer reigns, it still remains and rages. It no longer defines us, but it still clings to us.

We therefore need to learn not to underestimate the seriousness of sin; instead, we must watch out for its subtleties and insinuations. To fight against sin, we must come to understand its addictive and enslaving power. As the saying goes, "Sow a thought, reap an action. Sow an action, reap a habit. Sow a habit, reap a character. Sow a character, reap a destiny." Sin, then, must be attacked at the point of entry before it takes root within our hearts.

The only way to tackle sin is to recognize that we need to kill it, without compromise, so as to prevent all future damage, seen or unseen. We will only be able to overcome sin when we are motivated to take strong measures against it.

Yet we make a serious mistake if we think that we are the ones who can overcome sin's indwelling power. Since Christ "is your life," your battle against sin is not faced in your own strength but in God's mighty power; and since Christ "is your life," your battle against sin is not a battle for salvation, for He has already secured that for you. So now you need to commit to putting your sin to death, and you need to ask the Holy Spirit to overwhelm you with His wonderful love and fullness so as to create within you the desire to do that which God's word calls you to do: to seek out, find, and kill off all that "is earthly in you." As you read this list of earthly things which you are called to "put to death," which are you being called to fight, in His strength, today?

ROMANS 7:21 – 8:11

JUNE 14

THE WEIGHT OF GRIEF

"She was deeply distressed and prayed to the LORD and wept bitterly. And she vowed a vow and said, 'O LORD of hosts, if you will indeed look on the affliction of your servant and remember me and not forget your servant, but will give to your servant a son, then I will give him to the LORD all the days of his life, and no razor shall touch his head' ... Then the woman went her way and ate, and her face was no longer sad." 1 SAMUEL 1:10-11, 18

When we cannot see the way forward in life, we must look up to our God.

This is what Hannah did. Her childlessness meant she bore a weight of grief, which was compounded by being provoked by Peninnah, her husband's second wife, who had given birth to many children (1 Samuel 1:4, 6), and by her husband's insensitive and thoughtless questions (v 8). When we are facing trial or grief, Hannah serves as our example first in what she did *not* do. She did not become resentful toward God, nor did she seek vengeance against her rival, Peninnah. Instead, she removed herself from the environment that provoked her sense of disappointment and placed herself in the presence of the one who holds the answers. She brought her tears, her sighs, her longings—all expressions of her sad heart—before God.

As Hannah prayed, she was not attempting to induce God's favor with a promise. Hannah recognized God as majestic and sovereign and herself as His servant. She simply asked God to do for her what He had done for His people in the past.

After Hannah brought her grief to the Lord, but *before* her prayer was answered, her appetite returned and her countenance changed. In other words, the resolution for Hannah was not in her pregnancy or the subsequent arrival of a child but in the fact that she had cast her anxieties on the Lord. That was what settled her spirit and lightened her step.

Psalm 73 recounts the difficulties the psalmist faced which caused him nearly to lose his faith. He knew God was good and looked after His people—but his experience seemed to differ. That all changed, though, when he came before God in his desperation: "When I thought how to understand this, it seemed to me a wearisome task, until I went into the sanctuary of God" (Psalm 73:16-17). For both Hannah and the psalmist, peace and understanding came as they brought their griefs and troubles into the sanctuary—into the very presence of God Himself.

When you encounter difficult circumstances that provoke you and test your belief in God's goodness, where do you go? Do you submerge yourself beneath your troubles? Or do you enter the sanctuary of God's presence in prayer? When you face distress, cry out to God, in whose presence you stand because of the finished work of Christ. As you remember that He is sovereign and good and acts on behalf of His people, you can pray with confidence and boldness and experience the peace that comes only from above—even before you see how He will answer your prayer.

1 SAMUEL 1:1-20

JUNE 15

COURAGE AND COMPASSION

"Jesus said to them, 'My food is to do the will of him who sent me and to accomplish his work. Do you not say, "There are yet four months, then comes the harvest"? Look, I tell you, lift up your eyes, and see that the fields are white for harvest. Already the one who reaps is receiving wages and gathering fruit for eternal life, so that sower and reaper may rejoice together.'" JOHN 4:34-36

Although God has His pulpit in heaven, He has His servants on earth.

It's clear from Scripture that in the mystery and kindness of His purposes, God has determined to use our feeble voices to enable others to hear His voice. By the power of the Holy Spirit, our words about His word further His plans and change people's lives and futures.

The question, then, is this: Are we stepping forward into this privilege, or are we holding back from it? Following His encounter with the woman at the well, Jesus encouraged His disciples to open their eyes and "see that the fields are white for harvest." If we, like the disciples, look up to see the harvest before us, then we too must proclaim the word of Christ, declaring with urgency and joy that "there is salvation in no one else, for there is no other name under heaven given among men by which we must be saved" (Acts 4:12).

Saying this takes courage and confidence. The gospel message runs completely counter to the prevailing worldviews. It is the prime enemy of much contemporary thought. Claims for final truth in Jesus are not simply ignored; they are opposed. Our confidence, however, rests in the fact that the gospel message was given to us by God. We did not invent it and we must not modify it. Instead, "all authority in heaven and on earth" is Christ's, and He has commanded us to "go ... and make disciples of all nations" (Matthew 28:18-19).

Yet while we need confidence in our message, we also need compassion in our tone. Jesus came as a humble servant. He rode into town on a lowly donkey and spoke with gentleness and humility. When He saw the crowds, He was moved with compassion, because He saw them as sheep without a shepherd (Matthew 9:36). And by the enabling power of His Holy Spirit, we can demonstrate the same care as we recall that we too were once "foolish, disobedient," and "led astray" before Christ sought us out and transformed us (Titus 3:3).

Difficult days have perhaps created an increased willingness in the hearts of those around you to talk about what weighs them down, what concerns them about the brokenness in our world. Uncertain times must move you and me to be ready to seize the opportunity to proclaim to our family and friends "Jesus Christ and him crucified" (1 Corinthians 2:2), confident that the Spirit of God can use our efforts for eternal gain. Be bold. Be loving. Be active. Be prayerful. For only in Jesus can darkness be turned to light. Only in Jesus is there a fresh start and a whole new future.

1 PETER 3:14-17

JUNE 16

YOUR KEY TO USEFULNESS

"Consider your calling, brothers: not many of you were wise according to worldly standards, not many were powerful, not many were of noble birth."
1 CORINTHIANS 1:26

The British sitcom *Dad's Army* depicted a ragtag group of characters, exempt from conscription because of age and other factors, assembled on the home front during World War II. This unlikely group was preparing to repel a German invasion armed with some old rifles and a variety of broomsticks and bits and pieces. Somehow, this was supposed to give a sense of confidence to their community.

Like the characters in *Dad's Army*, the believers in Corinth, Smyrna, and Philadelphia looked a lot like ragtag groups. If these early Christians were known for anything by those around them, it was for their poverty, for their weakness, and for their suffering at the hands of the authorities (Revelation 2:9; 3:8).

We might tend to think that people or places like this have little prospect of doing anything significant for God. Certainly, that's what the Corinthian church was tempted to think as they sought worldly wisdom and power. But that's because we often think far too little of God. He is not looking for the strong, powerful, and mighty, as if He needs them on His side in order to set forward His purposes in the world. No, the reverse is the case: He is looking for the weak ones, so that through them He may demonstrate His strength.

As in Smyrna, Philadelphia, and Corinth, and throughout the world, God has chosen deliberately "what is foolish in the world to shame the wise" and "what is weak in the world to shame the strong" (1 Corinthians 1:27). And He has given us a message which seems to be total foolishness (v 18), so that when people are gripped and changed by it, their faith will rest not on the persuasive arguments or inspiring eloquence of a man or woman but on the very power of God.

We're often tempted to try to make out that we're better than we really are, thinking that if we could just present a good front, then people would be impressed and drawn to listen to the message we carry. But what we should seek more than anything is for people to be drawn to Christ—and nothing exalts and magnifies Christ quite like our testimony that God's grace is sufficient and His "power is made perfect in weakness" (2 Corinthians 12:9).

If you are all too aware of your flaws, shortcomings, or weaknesses, then you are ready to rejoice with the apostle Paul, who wrote, "Therefore I will boast all the more gladly of my weaknesses, so that the power of Christ may rest upon me. For the sake of Christ, then, I am content with weaknesses, insults, hardships, persecutions, and calamities. For when I am weak, then I am strong" (2 Corinthians 12:9-10). Have you considered the possibility that your personal weaknesses may be the very key to your usefulness in God's hand? He does not need your strength, and He can work with your weakness.

ACTS 18:1-11

◇ Bible Through The Year: Jeremiah 30–31; Matthew 26:1-25

JUNE 17

THE GREAT TRANSFER

"Believe in the Lord Jesus, and you will be saved." ACTS 16:31

When the Bible uses the term "believe," it doesn't refer merely to intellectual assent. To believe is not simply to agree with certain propositions, ideas, or doctrines. To believe in a biblical sense involves *a transfer of trust from ourselves to Christ*. It's as if we had all our assets stored at the Central Bank of Self, withdrew everything, and deposited it all into the Royal Bank of Christ.

Too often we hear (or perhaps even think to ourselves) sentiments like this: "I have lived a pretty good life. I'm sure that God will be gracious to me and make up for any deficit. I'll be fine." We are all tempted to think in one way that if we *do* certain things and *abstain* from certain others, then God will do His part. But these notions portray a sense of self-reliance, be it dressed in religious garb or not, that is unbiblical to its core.

Biblically speaking, true belief knows only reliance on and trust in Christ. This is how the apostle Paul spoke of faith time and time again. He wanted to "be found in him, not having a righteousness of my own ... but that which comes through faith in Christ, the righteousness from God that depends on faith" (Philippians 3:9).

When the great Reformer Martin Luther finally came to understand faith as trusting in Christ alone for righteousness, he exclaimed, "Here I felt that I was altogether born again and had entered paradise itself through open gates."[49] Those gates open only to those who have transferred their trust to Jesus Christ. As Revelation puts it, "Blessed are those who wash their robes ... that they may enter the city by the gates" (Revelation 22:14). These blessed ones haven't cleansed themselves; they have "washed their robes and made them white *in the blood of the Lamb*" (7:14, emphasis added).

God accepts into His eternal paradise those who have entrusted the entirety of their lives to the Lord Jesus Christ. If you are trusting Christ today, then you, too, have received "redemption through His blood, the forgiveness of our trespasses" (Ephesians 1:7). If you have deposited all your faith and hope with Christ—in short, if you have truly *believed*—then the eternal dividends of everlasting life and joy await. Be sure to bank on Him, and on nothing and no one else.

ROMANS 3:21-31

49 "Preface to the Complete Edition of Luther's Latin Writings," in *Martin Luther: Selections from His Writings*, ed. John Dillenberger (Anchor, 1962), p 11.

JUNE 18

LOOKING BACK, LOOKING FORWARD

"I will make for you a great name, like the name of the great ones of the earth. And I will appoint a place for my people Israel and will plant them, so that they may dwell in their own place and be disturbed no more. And violent men shall afflict them no more, as formerly, from the time that I appointed judges over my people Israel. And I will give you rest from all your enemies." 2 SAMUEL 7:9-11

As God made His covenant with David, He was prompting David to look both back to the past and forward to the future.

God's promise to make David's name like "the great ones of the earth" was an echo of His covenant with David's ancestor Abraham, centuries before (Genesis 12:1-3). Up to this point in biblical history, there had been no name greater than that of Abraham, and the Lord now announced that He would fulfill His promise to make Abraham's name great by making David's name great. This promise, however, not only looked back but also forward—to the Lord Jesus Christ, at whose name "every knee should bow" (Philippians 2:10).

The promise that God's people would have a place in which to dwell also was an echo of the past, in this case of the exodus from Egypt. (See, for instance, Exodus 15:17.) Yet by the time David was ruling, the people had been living in the promised land for centuries, so God's promise of them being planted and secure surely hinted at something greater. The place called Israel, while significant, was merely a shadow of the reality that was yet to come. It pointed forward to another place—the *ultimate* place, the new Jerusalem, which would later be called "a new heaven and a new earth" (Revelation 21:1-2).

With the promise of a place also came the promise of peace, security, and rest. Again, here was a reminder that the goal was not yet reached. True, by this point in David's reign, the people had been enjoying rest (2 Samuel 7:1)—but it was not the ultimate rest of the people of God to which the covenant pointed (Hebrews 4:9-10).

When God's revelation later culminated in the coming of David's descendant Jesus, the ultimate Christ, the people were able to say, "Oh, *that's* what God's promises meant!" The covenant that was first made to Abraham and took on a new dimension as it was made to David was completely fulfilled in the Lord Jesus Christ, the King of all kings; and it will be finally and fully realized when Christ returns.

So what does God's promise to David mean for us? The apostle Paul declares, "If you are Christ's, then you are Abraham's offspring, heirs according to promise" (Galatians 3:29). The church consists of those who are privileged to be heirs and partakers of the promise that is in Christ Jesus through the gospel. Stand amazed at this, and rejoice that you have been included in the blessings of this great covenant. Look back to God working through your spiritual ancestors Abraham, David, and, supremely, Jesus—and look forward with hope to the final fulfillment of all that God has promised!

2 SAMUEL 7:1-17

JUNE 19

LEANING IN TO GOD'S WORD

"Therefore put away all filthiness and rampant wickedness and receive with meekness the implanted word, which is able to save your souls." JAMES 1:21

Every so often someone might ask, "What have you been leaning against?" As I look at my clothes, it becomes clear by the residue left behind that I have in fact been leaning against something—something that has left a mark. And I resolve at that moment to be far more careful in the future about what I choose to lean on.

Spiritually, we must also be careful about what we're leaning against. Just as we may become inadvertently dirty by leaning against a chalkboard, we are also prone to becoming morally polluted by "leaning against" sin. We should not be unaware of the evil that is so prevalent around us—and in us. It is all too easy to sin with our eyes and minds, realizing only when it is too late that the sin has left its mark.

Our attitude toward sin in the week will affect how we listen to God's word preached to us on a Sunday. Moral filth is a barrier to listening to and profiting from the Bible. The way in which we come to the preaching of the word is so vitally important. Some of us come to God's word covered in the clay of compromise with the world's wickedness and filth, or marked with the stains of willful disobedience. We simply cannot act with such instability and still expect that we will receive anything from the Lord (James 1:7-8). When the word is preached Sunday after Sunday and some people in the congregation grow and mature while others do not, it speaks to the soil, not the seed.

Notice that James doesn't tell us merely to pray about this filthiness but to get rid of it. How? By the enabling power of God by His Spirit through the word. As the psalmist wrote, "How can a young man keep his way pure? By guarding it according to your word" (Psalm 119:9). The Bible acts as a purifying instrument. Day after day, committed to walking away from sin that we have all too often been leaning upon, we are to "receive with meekness the implanted word." We may not understand everything, but we humbly accept and act upon what we do understand.

As you meekly receive God's word, you are saved—today, tomorrow, for all eternity. His word saves you from the silent spiritual killer of hypocrisy. His word reminds you that He has saved you from sin's penalty through the death of His Son. His word assures you that you are being saved from sin's power and can choose righteousness instead.

What are you leaning against? Are there sins that the world around you accepts and promotes but which you need to walk away from? Come before God's word today. Lean on His Spirit to be restored and revived. Receive His word, and rejoice that it has the power to cleanse!

MARK 9:42-50

JUNE 20

WHAT WILL YOU DO WITH JESUS?

"A third time he said to them, 'Why? What evil has he done? I have found in him no guilt deserving death. I will therefore punish and release him.' But they were urgent, demanding with loud cries that he should be crucified. And their voices prevailed." LUKE 23:22-23

As governor over Judea, Pontius Pilate was responsible for maintaining order and quelling civil disruption within his jurisdiction. He was accustomed to using his power and influence to determine the outcome for those awaiting their sentence. But Jesus' arrival in his courtroom confronted Pilate with the greatest dilemma of his life.

Accompanied by a large crowd of religious officials, Jesus was brought before Pilate. When Pilate pressed the mob and asked them explicitly, "What evil has he done?" all they seemed able to do was to raise their voices louder. (A raised voice is often indicative of a weak argument.) Pilate knew that Jesus was innocent, and so he essentially declared to those assembled, *I find no guilt in this man.* But the cries of the crowd grew more demanding and more insistent, and Pilate must have started asking himself, *What can I do with this Jesus of Nazareth?*

Pilate wanted to release Jesus. He knew that he *should* release Jesus. But Pilate capitulated to his desire to placate the crowd and to maintain favor with the religious leaders, and the voices of the frenzied throng prevailed.

Pilate's dilemma is not unfamiliar. In fact, it is *the* great dilemma that confronts men and women: what to do with Jesus of Nazareth. Pilate came face-to-face with the Son of God and heard His testimony from His own lips—and still he chose the world and all of its noise over bending his knee to the King of kings.

In Jesus' sentencing, God's eternal plan of salvation unfolded in a moment in time. Jesus was not accused and condemned for His own sin. He was not dying for Himself. He was dying for *us*. He who was totally innocent became totally guilty in order that we who are totally guilty might be declared completely innocent.

All of Pilate's attempts to dismiss Jesus, to turn Him over for other officials to pass judgment, to wipe his hands clean of the matter, didn't work. Neither will ours. Our only hope in life and death is to respond in our hearts to the glory of what happened on the cross. Like Pilate, we face a choice: either we bow our knee to Christ and His lordship or we capitulate to the pressures of the surrounding culture. And while that is a decision we make in the privacy of our hearts, it is one that reveals itself, as it did with Pilate, in what we say when those around us are urging us to deny the rule or goodness of Christ. However loud those voices become, if you are His, then be ready to stand for Him.

2 TIMOTHY 4:9-18

JUNE 21

TO THE TEACHING!

"To the teaching and to the testimony! If they will not speak according to this word, it is because they have no dawn." ISAIAH 8:20

We live in an age that is unique in many ways. We have technology at our fingertips that gives us access to information that would have remained out of reach decades ago. We can stay in touch with friends across the world, we can share our thoughts online at a whim, and we don't need to wait until tomorrow to catch up on the headlines.

But we would be off base to assume that *everything* about our lives is historically unique. The Israelites to whom Isaiah prophesied over two and a half millennia ago may not have had 24/7 news and social media, but they were just as tempted as we are to be distracted by noisy and unhelpful voices. Isaiah reports that some Israelites wanted to "inquire of the mediums and the necromancers who chirp and mutter," and others wanted to "inquire of the dead on behalf of the living" (Isaiah 8:19).

We have this in common with the Israelites. We may not be consulting with fortune-tellers and the dead (though such things remain popular even in our so-called rational scientific age), but we are by no means starved of sources of "truth" around us. The basic problem now, as then, is not the absence of good information and wise counsel. The problem is that we turn our ears and hearts to listen to lies.

Isaiah's response to his original audience, then, is his response to us too: "To the teaching and to the testimony!" God has spoken, and it is His word that should be the dominant voice in our lives—the primary influence on how we think and act. If we give ourselves to unrelenting information and news, we should not be surprised when we face increased anxiety. If we spend loads of time scrolling online, we should not be surprised to find ourselves feeling more isolated than ever. If we look to the sages of our age for guidance, we should not be surprised to find ourselves going off track.

Do you give priority to God's voice? Do you let His word hold pride of place among the voices you listen to? Or do you give Him an hour on Sunday and assume that will be enough to hold you over for a week? The Almighty God calls His people to allow their minds to be renewed, transformed by exposure to and meditation upon His holy word (Romans 12:2). The blessed person is not the one who knows the ins and outs of every news story or cultural crisis but the one whose "delight is in the law of the Lord, and on his law he meditates day and night" (Psalm 1:2).

What are you reading most, hearing most, and dwelling on most? Perhaps now is a time to recommit yourself "to the teaching"—to reading, meditating upon, and memorizing it—for the good and stability of your soul.

LUKE 9:28-35

JUNE 22

GUARDED BY GOD'S POWER

"How much worse punishment, do you think, will be deserved by the one who has trampled underfoot the Son of God, and has profaned the blood of the covenant by which he was sanctified, and has outraged the Spirit of grace?"
HEBREWS 10:29

If we're honest, we all can recall times when we've failed, faltered, or temporarily lost interest in the things of Christ. These experiences can unsettle the faith of even the most seasoned believer. What, then, are we to make of our stumblings?

The Bible is clear that once we are in Jesus' hand, we are not coming out. Jesus said, "My sheep hear my voice, and I know them, and they follow me ... No one will snatch them out of my hand" (John 10:27-28). Indeed, our failures serve as a daily reminder to cling to God's promises all the more and not to our own merit. For those hidden in Christ, "all the promises of God find their Yes in him" (2 Corinthians 1:20). When God promises that *nothing* will separate us from the love of Christ (Romans 8:38-39), that includes our stumbling and sinning.

When we have been redeemed by Christ, when we have been brought into His orbit of grace, He promises to complete the good work He began in us (Philippians 1:6). We must conclude, then, that a genuine believer *cannot* be lost. It is not possible! According to God's mercy, we are brought into His family and guarded by His power until the day of salvation (1 Peter 1:5).

The Bible is equally clear, however, that there are those who for a time are marked by some dedication to God but who then turn in opposition to Jesus and His word, never to return to Him again. Their repudiation of what they once professed reveals that they never genuinely belonged to Jesus at all. Such individuals, notes the author of Hebrews, receive the knowledge of truth and perhaps even suggest to others around them that their faith is sincere, but in reality, they are trampling the Son of God underfoot. They engage in the reverse of what Paul describes in Philippians 3:8: "I count everything as loss because of the surpassing worth of knowing Christ Jesus my Lord." Paul counted everything in life as rubbish compared to knowing Jesus. But these men and women taste the goodness of the Lord yet count Him as rubbish when offered earthly pleasures.

The aim of the writer to the Hebrews is to warn against complacency, which leads to dangerous drifting (Hebrews 2:1). He is urging his readers to run to the cross in their weakness and failures, for the wonder of the cross is that there is no sinful believer that cannot be forgiven, and the glory of the Spirit is that there is no weak believer He cannot preserve. When you stumble, then, stumble toward the cross. And when you awake each day, ask the one who died in your place for a fresh outpouring of His grace in order that you may persevere in your faith.

HEBREWS 2:1-9

JUNE 23

GOD IS AT WORK IN YOU

"The grace of God has appeared, bringing salvation for all people, training us to renounce ungodliness and worldly passions." TITUS 2:11-12

The main problem with our lives is not that we're unhappy or have made a couple of minor missteps. Our diagnosis isn't merely that we have some existential gaps that just need to be filled by a new hobby or an outlet for charitable service. It's not that we're lost and just need a little bit of direction or that we have low self-esteem and need to think more positively. Biblically speaking, our problem is actually this: we are by nature "foolish, disobedient, led astray, slaves to various passions and pleasures, passing our days in malice and envy, hated by others and hating one another" (Titus 3:3).

That's quite a condition to find ourselves in. The problem goes far deeper and spreads much wider than we like to think. Whether we are three or eighty-three years old when the Lord Jesus Christ breaks into our lives and saves us, our state before God until then is one of utter hopelessness. In His grace, however, God washes us and renews us through the Holy Spirit and causes us to become "heirs according to the hope of eternal life" (Titus 3:4-7). God's grace is far greater than we tend to imagine!

But once we are "justified by his grace" (Titus 3:7), what then? God goes to work, progressively and incrementally, to rid us of our foolishness and disobedience. God's grace comes to us as we are, but it does not leave us as we are, for it teaches us "to renounce ungodliness and worldly passions, and to live self-controlled, upright, and godly lives" (Titus 2:12).

Imagine a new brother in Christ named George. He's been a Christian for two days. Last week, George was deceived, he was destructive, he was filled with hate, he was lost in idolatry, and he was committed to sensuality. Suddenly, George met Christ. The Spirit of God regenerated him, and now George finds himself in the church. George is saved but he is not yet the finished article. No, he is a work in progress. Of course he still has some messes that need to be cleaned up. Of course he has some confusion in his mind about what following Christ means for his life.

All of us are like George to one degree or another. No matter how many years we've believed in Jesus, we are all works in progress. We need the Bible to guide us. We need other members of Christ's body to help us along. We need to trust that God will do what He has promised and finish the good work He began in us (Philippians 1:6).

Progress might seem slow at times, but with His Spirit at work, you will make it all the way home. Until then, reflect on your condition apart from Christ, for it will humble you. Remember what God's grace did in saving you, for it will encourage you. See the ways in which the Spirit has grown you in godliness, for it will reassure you. And ask the Lord, in His grace, to keep on changing you, bit by bit, as you wait for the appearing of your Savior and the day when you are perfected in glory (Titus 2:13-14).

TITUS 3:3-8

Bible Through The Year: Jeremiah 48–49; Philippians 1

JUNE 24

SAVE, O LORD

"Save, O Lord, *for the godly one is gone; for the faithful have vanished from among the children of man."* PSALM 12:1

God's people in every age have learned that being a child of God does not make us immune to life's difficulties. One reason why the Psalms are such a treasure is that they give us a record of God's people enduring "trials of various kinds" (James 1:2). And what the Psalms then provide is not a blueprint for how to fix our problems but a model for a faithful response to our problems.

David's life was full of difficulties. He faced attempts to take his life by the likes of Goliath and Saul (1 Samuel 17; 19). He was the target of a coup perpetrated by his own son (2 Samuel 14 – 15). He confronted difficulties and tragedies that resulted from his own sin and folly (2 Samuel 11 – 12). Psalm 12, though, describes another sort of struggle: that of living in the midst of wicked people.

The evil surrounding David came in the form of double-talk: "Everyone utters lies to his neighbor; with flattering lips and a double heart they speak" (Psalm 12:2). It came in the form of defiant tongues: "those who say, 'With our tongue we will prevail, our lips are with us; who is master over us?'" (v 4). It came from degraded values, seen in the way that "vileness is exalted among the children of man" (v 8). It's not hard to imagine how difficult it would be to live in such an environment.

Imagine the ways David could have responded. He could have recorded his grumbling for us, written down his rage, or told us the way he took matters into his own hands. (And there is certainly a place for wise and righteous action!) But what is his first response? It's in the opening words of the psalm: "Save, O Lord." David's response to the wretchedness around him is to humbly and urgently plead with God for help.

Some of us can look around and see much in common with what David describes in Psalm 12. We hear double-talk, we see defiance, and we watch as evil is celebrated as good. We know how David felt, and we share his struggle. But do we share his response? Paul tells us that if we want to be "children of God without blemish in the midst of a crooked and twisted generation," then we must "do all things without grumbling or disputing" (Philippians 2:14-15). Further, he tells us not to be anxious about anything but instead to pray for everything (4:6).

When confronted by ungodliness, it is easy to grow angry or proud or despairing. It is easy to give up and go with the flow. It is harder, but always better, to follow David's example: pray, trust, and obey. A commitment to prayer is a powerful way of declaring your allegiance to Jesus Christ alone. Next time you are struck by an aspect of your community or culture that is wicked, pray; ask Him to save, help, and deliver you from evil. "He who calls you is faithful; he will surely do it" (1 Thessalonians 5:24).

PHILIPPIANS 2:12-16

JUNE 25

INVEST IN ETERNITY

"We want you to know, brothers, about the grace of God that has been given among the churches of Macedonia, for in a severe test of affliction, their abundance of joy and their extreme poverty have overflowed in a wealth of generosity."
2 CORINTHIANS 8:1-2

Affliction is a significant means by which God forms our character, but it is also a means by which He *reveals* our character. While Scripture gives us many examples of affliction exposing weak moral fiber, there are numerous examples of affliction highlighting virtue, too. One such example is that of the Macedonian church. Paul said that these early believers were "in a severe test of affliction" and in "extreme poverty." What did this affliction reveal? An "abundance of joy" and "a wealth of generosity."

The Macedonian model is worth pondering. That's precisely why Paul mentioned them: he wanted the Corinthian church to learn from them—to "excel in this act of grace" (2 Corinthians 8:7). Consider what made the Macedonians worth emulating:

1. "They gave themselves first to the Lord" (2 Corinthians 8:5). Their generosity was simply an expression of their devotion to Christ. As Lord of all things, He ruled their finances.
2. They gave in response to God's grace, which had been "given among the churches of Macedonia."
3. They gave "beyond their means" (v 3). They were willing to forgo some legitimate wants in order that they might supply others' real needs.
4. They gave "of their own accord" (v 3), not in response to external prodding.
5. They were "begging … earnestly for the favor" of giving to others (v 4)—generous giving was something they *wanted* to do, not what they felt they *ought* to do.

Paul wants us to compare ourselves with the Macedonians, so that we are prompted to ask ourselves questions such as these:

1. Am I giving myself first to the Lord?
2. Am I giving in response to God's grace? Is that what directs the extent of my giving?
3. Am I giving beyond my comfort zone?
4. Am I giving without external compulsion, without being prodded and prompted?
5. Am I clamoring for the privilege of serving the saints?

We don't know how the Corinthians responded. We can be sure, though, that God wants us to respond with faithful, joyful investment in eternal things. Eventually, we will all stand before Him, and none of that which offers earthly security—savings accounts, stock portfolios, real-estate investments, pension provisions—will mean a thing. On that day, all we will have is the treasure that we have laid up in heaven through our support for the gospel (Matthew 6:19-21). What does your giving reveal about your character?

2 CORINTHIANS 8:1-7

JUNE 26

SEARCHING FOR LOST SHEEP

"Jesus heard that they had cast him out, and having found him he said, 'Do you believe in the Son of Man?'" JOHN 9:35

Jesus' encounter with the blind man in John 9 is part of the great panorama of God's redemptive purpose from all of eternity. This apparently inconsequential stop in the middle of the day was part of the fulfillment of God's promise to Abraham that "in your offspring shall all the nations of the earth be blessed" (Genesis 22:18). It's part of the great, ongoing, unfolding purpose of God to put together a company of people that no one can count from every tribe, nation, language, and tongue (Revelation 7:9).

The healing of this man, as well as what follows from it, is remarkable. It raises questions: How did Jesus find this man? And how did Jesus change this man? In the answers, we gain a better understanding of how Jesus finds men and women in their lostness and then changes them into sheep that have been found.

This story is not only an illustration of saving faith but also, as C.H. Spurgeon says, "an example of what you may do in endeavoring to lead [souls] to exercise faith in Jesus." If you want to follow Christ's example in reaching people, the first thing you must do, says Spurgeon, is "*seek out the oppressed* ... seek out the sick, the sad, the weary, the poor, the broken-down ones, and especially such as have been put out of the synagogues."[50]

The people that no one wants and no one will have, Jesus wants and Jesus will have. Jesus has every right to anticipate that His followers will do the same. It's only in knowing that you were once lost that you understand what it means to be found. Jesus has sought you and found you—and if He did that for you, He can do it for anyone! Our tendency is to spend time with those who are like us. But the Son of God did not do that—otherwise He would never have been born as a man, to seek and to save sinners like us. Who are the "broken-down ones" the Lord is calling you to reach out to with the gospel of the Son of Man? With God's help, go out and tell them that Jesus is alive and that He seeks and saves those who are lost.

LUKE 15:1-7

50 "A Pressed Man Yielding to Christ," *The Metropolitan Tabernacle Pulpit* 46, no. 2667, p 142.

JUNE 27

THE KING WHO DOES NOT TAKE

"These will be the ways of the king who will reign over you: he will take your sons and appoint them to his chariots and to be his horsemen and to run before his chariots ... He will take your daughters to be perfumers and cooks and bakers. He will take the best of your fields and vineyards and olive orchards ... He will take the tenth of your grain ... He will take your male servants and female servants ... He will take the tenth of your flocks, and you shall be his slaves." 1 SAMUEL 8:11, 13-17

All leaders always take: all except one.

When in Samuel's time the Israelites requested a king so that they would be like the other nations, God granted their request. But He also told Samuel to solemnly warn the people about what to expect of a king's ways (1 Samuel 8:7-9). The picture Samuel painted was of a king who would line his own pocket at the people's expense and lead them back into a kind of slavery. It was a dismal prospect!

And it was one that, over the next few centuries, became a reality. Some kings had ups as well as downs, but the majority were corrupt; none of them were completely good. All the Israelites' leaders always, in one way or another, took from them what the people had, instead of giving them what they had hoped.

Yet God would ultimately provide a King that was different from the rest. The New Testament begins with this King. "The time is fulfilled," said Jesus, "and the kingdom of God is at hand" (Mark 1:15). By establishing God's kingdom, He was declaring Himself to be King. Afterward, Jesus entered Jerusalem riding on the foal of a donkey, fulfilling the prophet's words announcing that the King of God's people would arrive in this manner (Zechariah 9:9). What kind of king comes on a donkey rather than in a chariot or on a war horse? The same King that would be crowned with thorns a few days later. Here was a King unlike any other king.

There is a great and prevalent lie that goes something like this: "If you trust Jesus, He'll take away all the good stuff, and you won't have a good time. If you want a good time, go with another leader. If you go with Jesus, it'll be boring, restrictive, life-sapping." But actually, the reverse is true! Unlike the kings of Israel, who would take from the people, Jesus was and is the King who gives—and He does so lavishly. He is the King who came to "give his life as a ransom for many" (Mark 10:45), who gives His sheep "eternal life, and they will never perish" (John 10:28), and who takes burdens and gives rest to those who accept His light yoke (Matthew 11:28-30).

Is Jesus your King? Many other voices will be attractive and persuasive—but if you let them rule you, you will be disappointed in the end. The Lord Jesus Christ will never disappoint you. He is the King who always gives all that you need, and the only thing He takes from you is your sin. Today, recognize and give thanks for the abundant goodness and generosity you have in your great King!

MARK 10:32-45

JUNE 28

RECKONING WITH REPENTANCE

"What shall we say then? Are we to continue in sin that grace may abound? By no means! How can we who died to sin still live in it?" ROMANS 6:1-2

In Christ we find ultimate happiness. Peter tells us that our belief in Jesus can lead us to "joy that is inexpressible and filled with glory" (1 Peter 1:8). But it's not possible to be happy in Jesus while living in sin. To borrow the image of Psalm 24, how often do we attempt to ascend the hill of the Lord, in corporate or private worship, with dirty hands and hearts, wondering why the word of God doesn't delight us in the midst of our sin? It's spiritual insanity to think that we can rejoice in the Lord while seeking out pleasure in some hidden transgression.

As fallen creatures, we often develop patterns that trick us into thinking that we can make peace with our fallenness and can indulge some sin. Perhaps we have become accustomed to minimizing it or justifying it, so that we hardly even notice it. Yet Scripture knows no such pattern of thinking. David, for example, knew he was dirty and grimy before God, thoroughly permeated with sin: "I was brought forth in iniquity, and in sin did my mother conceive me" (Psalm 51:5). Elsewhere he asks the Lord, "Declare me innocent from hidden faults" (19:12). He knew he needed forgiveness from sins he didn't even know about! But mercifully, David's awareness of his own shortcomings led him to God, to whom he pleaded, "Create in me a clean heart, O God, and renew a right spirit within me" (51:10).

We need to recover this same disposition for our daily walk with Christ. Repentance isn't a one-time event. We must continually battle sin. We must repeatedly turn away from temptation and look to Christ. We must press on to know Him better, so that He is ever more and more attractive to us than fleeting pleasures and sordid desires.

If you are a Christian, you have already died to sin. God has already granted that you "walk in newness of life" (Romans 6:4). Now, "by the Spirit," you are called to "put to death the deeds of the body" (8:13)—that is, to take hold of the new life God has given you and slay the sins that still beset you. You have "died to sin." Do not give in to the temptation of still living in it.

If you trust Christ, you are always acceptable to God. But when you give yourself fully to the cause of rooting out whatever weeds of sin keep creeping up, then you'll reap a joy that is inexpressibly better than whatever false promises sin and temptation may make. Is there a sinful pattern you have grown used to? Is there something of which you need to repent, asking God to forgive you and change your heart? Joy will be found not in ignoring that prompting of the Spirit but in responding to it.

PSALM 32

JUNE 29

A RIGHTEOUS AND MERCIFUL GOD

"The Lord is righteous; he loves righteous deeds; the upright shall behold his face." PSALM 11:7

A righteous God will not accept unrighteous requests. We cannot expect that God, who always does the right thing, will do the expedient thing just for our sake. In our prayers and decision-making processes, then, we ought not to ask ourselves, "What is the easy thing? What is the thing that will get me out of this difficulty the quickest?" Rather, we need to ask, "What is the *right* thing for me to do?" This is not to say that we will always know precisely what is right. But in our prayers and in our lives, we must remember that we call upon and walk before the face of a supremely holy and righteous God.

Thankfully, God is not only righteous but also merciful. David cries in Psalm 4:1, "Answer me when I call, O God of my righteousness!" Just as it is unimaginable that a mother would forget the cry of a child that she nurtured at her own breast, so it is unthinkable that God would not hear the pleas of His children (Isaiah 49:15). Such mercy is an astounding truth. We live in a world that operates on the principle that we get what we "deserve," that we get out what we put in: *This is what you've earned, and what you've earned is what you're going to get—whether good or bad*. But when we come to God, we come to the one who is by His very nature rich in mercy, who gives us what we do not deserve. From Him, we get what we have not earned.

Perhaps your heart has been fractured or your life is buffeted by serious trouble. Still you can cry out to your righteous God: "I need Your unmerited kindness today. I've nothing with which to commend myself. Lord, be merciful to me and hear my prayer."

When that is our approach to God, then we will find fostered within us an attitude of seeking to do what is right, not what is easy. The path to seeking to do "righteous deeds" is to know that the Lord is merciful to His children.

This does not mean that as we come to Him for mercy and seek to live righteously, God will give immediate deliverance. Nowhere has He promised His people immediate relief. He answers us out of the righteousness of His sovereign plan—and sometimes, in His providence, He allows the thorn to continue to pain us (2 Corinthians 12:7-10). Yet when the thorn remains, "though the fig tree should not blossom," still you can "rejoice in the Lord" and "take joy in the God of [your] salvation" (Habakkuk 3:17-18). Because He is righteous, His mercy is never wrong. What may taste bitter for a time God will sweeten soon enough. And one day you will "behold his face," not just by faith but by sight as you stand with the saints around His throne. With that day in mind, come to Him now for the mercy and strength you need to live righteously today.

ISAIAH 49:13-23

JUNE 30

MERCIFUL INTERVENTION

"In those days there will be such tribulation as has not been from the beginning of the creation that God created until now, and never will be. And if the Lord had not cut short the days, no human being would be saved. But for the sake of the elect, whom he chose, he shortened the days." MARK 13:19-20

At the very heart of the greatest drama in history is the amazing encounter that's first hinted at in Genesis chapter 3: Christ is the one who has come, and will come, to vanquish the Evil One. Through His death on the cross, Jesus bruised the head of the serpent (Genesis 3:15) and secured eternal victory for His people. But for us the battle is not yet over. Behind every act of hatred, every broken marriage, every act of injustice—all that represents chaos and carnage and wickedness—the Evil One still engages in his skirmishes, seeking to destroy until he himself is destroyed.

The Christian lives in light of this tension, this reality: there will be trials and tribulations for the totality of our earthly pilgrimage, yet we never need to lose heart or hope. We can stand firm in our faith because Christ is the great Conqueror. Though His victory is not yet fully realized or expressed, it is no less complete, for the cross has disarmed Satan and his followers (Colossians 2:13-15).

Jesus warned us that tribulation would take place—and increasingly so until His return. He commands us to "be on guard" (Mark 13:23, 33) that we might not be led astray. In other words, Jesus forewarned us so that we might be forearmed for suffering. When it confronts us, we should not be taken by surprise, because our Captain has readied us.

We are not to be alarmed by "wars and rumors of wars," by nation rising against nation, or by an increase in devastating natural calamities (Mark 13:7-8). The Lord tells us that some believers will even "be beaten" (v 9), "deliver[ed] ... over to death" (v 12), and, above all, "hated by all for [Christ's] name's sake" (v 13). In addition, "false christs and false prophets will arise and perform signs and wonders, to lead astray, if possible, the elect" (v 22).

In the middle of all the chaos, however, we can remember where God's focus lies: on His people, His elect. As Jesus Himself said, "for the sake of the elect, whom he chose, he shortened the days." God intervenes on behalf of His own and protects His children from succumbing to perils within and without. He will not let us be pushed beyond that for which He has given us faith to remain faithful through.

Jesus' warnings resound with an unequivocal declaration of His kingship: no matter what happens—no matter who's elected, no matter whether your civic freedoms stay or go, no matter if you're imprisoned, tormented, or even killed for your faith—you can be absolutely sure that our God reigns and our Savior has won. That is firm ground on which to stand, however your life may be shaken.

REVELATION 12:1-12

JULY 1

WE NEED YOU

"To each is given the manifestation of the Spirit for the common good."
1 CORINTHIANS 12:7

If you disappeared one day from your local church, who would notice? If you were absent for an extended period of time, what would your church miss?

God has given every believer at least one gift to use for the good of His body. And while none of us should be irreplaceable in the sense that the church couldn't go on without us, we *should* be missed if we were absent, because God has gifted us in a specific way at a precise point in time to be uniquely useful in a particular group of people.

But how often do we sit on the sidelines, waiting for others to minister to us when the thrust of Scripture is that God ministers *through* us? Yes, every single one of us must be ready to receive ministry from others as they use the gifts God has given them for our good. But our default setting should be to give, not only or primarily to receive. The church really doesn't have much space for spectators. Even the youngest among us, be it in faith or in age, has something to contribute.

When we exercise our gifts, we manifest the Spirit's work and power for the common good. Most immediately, that includes the edification of our brothers and sisters in our local assembly, but it also includes witnessing to our friends and neighbors beyond the church walls. While they might be confused and bemused by the very idea of "spiritual gifts," they will understand a compassionate heart. They will respond to hospitality. They will be open to a word of concern or encouragement.

You have something to contribute, uniquely. Yet our ability to participate in God's work should never puff us up, for it is a gift given by the Spirit of God, and it is the Gift-Giver who deserves the praise as we use it to serve His people and His world.

So, assured that to *each* is given a gift, by God's Spirit, for the common good, be encouraged to pour yourself out rather than holding yourself back. Your church needs what you, through God's Spirit, have to offer. As an old children's song puts it, "There's a work for Jesus none but you can do."[51] What is He asking of you?

1 CORINTHIANS 12:12-31

51 Elsie Duncan Yale, "There's a Work for Jesus" (1912).

JULY 2

MARKED BY NEWNESS

"But the people refused to obey the voice of Samuel. And they said, 'No! But there shall be a king over us, that we also may be like all the nations, and that our king may judge us and go out before us and fight our battles.'"
1 SAMUEL 8:19-20

It wasn't wrong for Israel to desire a king. The request they made to Samuel to give them such a ruler was not in itself sinful. In fact, centuries before, Moses had anticipated this day, and God had prescribed the exact way in which this kingly rule should be put in place (Deuteronomy 17:14-20). The issue was not the request but the people's motivation: they wished to "be like all the nations" around them. And that was a problem because they were not like those nations: they were God's people, His "treasured possession among all peoples ... a kingdom of priests and a holy nation" (Exodus 19:5-6). By refusing to be different from those around them, they were essentially refusing to be God's people.

There are many points of overlap between Israel's request for a king in order to be like the surrounding nations and the warnings that Paul gave in his epistle to the church at Rome. Paul wrote concerning the danger of being swallowed up by the surrounding culture: "Do not be conformed to this world, but be transformed by the renewal of your mind" (Romans 12:2). The Living Bible translates this verse afresh: "Don't copy the behavior and customs of this world, but be a new and different person with a fresh newness in all you do and think."

Paul cautioned the church in this way because he understood the pressure for the believers in 1st-century Rome to accommodate themselves to the lifestyle and the values of the pagan world around them. We face the same challenge in our day. Therefore, we ought not to be surprised when back to the 11th century BC we find the Israelites struggling with the same temptation—and we hear the same kind of warning being sounded.

What about us? Do we live with an evident newness of life? Do we expect to be different from the world around us in how we think and what we say and the way we live, or are we busy trying to fit in with our neighbors? Are our churches copying the cultural customs, expectations, and behaviors of those around us, or are they filled with a marked vibrancy that only comes as a result of the Holy Spirit's work and inspiration?

Where are you most tempted to be indistinguishable from those around you? That is the place where you have the opportunity to resist the pressure to adapt to the world and compromise your distinctiveness. That is the place where you have the opportunity to allow yourself to be molded by God alone and to live in a way that is different—pleasing to Him and intriguing to others.

1 PETER 2:9-17

JULY 3

WHEN DOUBTS AND FEARS ASSAIL

"I am sure that neither death nor life, nor angels nor rulers, nor things present nor things to come, nor powers, nor height nor depth, nor anything else in all creation, will be able to separate us from the love of God in Christ Jesus our Lord." ROMANS 8:38-39

For almost every Christian, there comes a moment when we're tempted to despair over whether we will make it to heaven, whether we will be able to keep trusting Christ for another day, and whether we can continue in faith amid our own waywardness and sinfulness. And when that moment comes, we must take hold of this promise: it is God who perseveres, God who keeps us, and God who guards His people.

When we talk about the great Reformation doctrine of the "perseverance of the saints" we are, strictly speaking, talking about the perseverance of God Himself. In Romans 8:31-36, Paul poses a series of rhetorical questions that are intended to underscore the reality that nothing can separate God's children from Christ's love and to reinforce the truth that once we are laid hold of by the Good Shepherd, who "lays down his life for the sheep" (John 10:11), we remain in His fold forever. And Paul ends with these glorious words: nothing that he (or you) can possibly conceive of "will be able to separate us from the love of God in Christ Jesus our Lord." If you are in Christ, you can never be lost.

So what are we to do about the doubts and fears that assail us? We must fix our gaze on the Lord Jesus Himself. When we look at ourselves, we have good reason for discouragement and trepidation. It is by looking to Jesus that we are enabled to run the race set before us. He endured the cross, scorned its shame, and sat down at the right hand of the throne of God (Hebrews 12:2), that we might be forgiven and continue through our days.

Our faith will not fail, because God sustains it. Those who have already run the race, breasted the tape, and entered into the joy of the Lord are today *happier* but no more *secure* than the stumbling, struggling, trusting, growing, persevering believer. There is no power or plot that can separate those who trust in Christ from the love of God. You could not be more loved than you are. You could not be more secure than you are.

The work which His goodness began
The arm of His strength will complete;
His promise is Yea and Amen
And never was forfeited yet.
Things future, nor things that are now,
Nor all things below or above,
Can make Him His purpose forgo
Or sever my soul from His love.[52]

PHILIPPIANS 1:1-6

52 Augustus M. Toplady, "A Debtor to Mercy Alone" (1771).

JULY 4

STAY WITH US

"They drew near to the village to which they were going. He acted as if he were going farther, but they urged him strongly, saying, 'Stay with us, for it is toward evening and the day is now far spent.' So he went in to stay with them."

LUKE 24:28-29

Jesus' encounter with the individuals on the Emmaus road started strangely, to say the least. He appeared suddenly. He kept His identity from them. He asked questions. He told them that they were "foolish … and slow of heart" (Luke 24:25)! Yet, as He'd gone through the Old Testament "interpret[ing] to them in all the Scriptures the things concerning himself" (v 27), their hearts had been stirred and set on fire (v 32).

It's quite possible that the reason Jesus stopped this impromptu Bible study was that His fellow travelers had arrived at their destination. Darkness was coming, but He made as if to continue His journey. But these two disciples did not want to part from Him; they longed for this man to stay with them.

And so they gave Jesus an invitation. Indeed, they "urged him strongly" to remain with them. Without this invitation, Jesus would have kept going. And if Jesus had kept going, then these disciples would have missed the wonderful privilege of realizing that their teacher on the road, who to this point they had not recognized, was none other than the risen Lord Himself (Luke 24:31).

How often do we encounter Jesus along life's journey and neglect to invite Him in? How often do we seek to do day-to-day life on our own, relying on our own efforts and ingenuity and sleepless anxiety to get us through? When was the last time you extended an invitation to Jesus, who knows all about your troubles, your pains, and your difficulties—the things that other people can't know and can't fix? The risen Christ comes and stands at the door and knocks (Revelation 3:20). Will you invite Him to come in and stay? Will you say, "Jesus, stay with me. I can't do this on my own"? Doing so may well be the way that you get a fresh, heart-stirring glimpse of Jesus and His love for you.

LUKE 24:25-35

JULY 5

BEFORE THE SILVER CORD IS SNAPPED

"Remember also your Creator ... before the silver cord is snapped, or the golden bowl is broken, or the pitcher is shattered at the fountain, or the wheel broken at the cistern." ECCLESIASTES 12:1, 6

Life is extremely fragile—and the poetry written here by the author of Ecclesiastes is intended to demonstrate just how fragile it is. It's like a hanging lamp that is shattered as a result of just one little piece of the cord breaking. Our lives here are held by a very, very slender thread.

In the poetic world of the Preacher, it would take only the slightest movement for a cord to sever, a bowl to shatter, a pitcher to fall into the spring, or a wheel that has been used to bring the bucket up from the well to find itself out of commission. This list reminds us that one day, and very possibly without warning, our time will be up as well.

Perhaps you work in the world of investments, engineering, technology, or scientific research, or you know someone who does. In these fields of employment, all sorts of calculations are required—oftentimes vitally important ones. Every single one of us, however, is called to calculate something even more crucial: our life. And if we are ever going to number our days rightly or figure out life's meaning and purpose, it will only be through divine grace.

The book of Ecclesiastes frequently reminds us that the end of our lives is coming. We are told that "the dust returns to the earth as it was, and the spirit returns to God who gave it" (Ecclesiastes 12:7). But we are not at the conclusion of our lives—yet. So today is a day of opportunity.

What is the opportunity that we are being called to take? God, by His word, isn't asking you to do something particularly difficult. He isn't asking you to start a charity organization, to climb the height of Kilimanjaro, or to run around the block 47 times saying various prayers. He's simply asking you to remember Him and commit all of your life to Him, without holding anything back, while you still can, so that, beyond the day when the silver cord is snapped, you will enter the eternal city where the streets are paved with gold (Revelation 21:21). Have you done that? Will you do that? Will you do that now?

ECCLESIASTES 12

JULY 6

TRANSPARENCY

"You yourselves know how I lived among you the whole time from the first day that I set foot in Asia, serving the Lord with all humility and with tears and with trials that happened to me through the plots of the Jews; how I did not shrink from declaring to you anything that was profitable, and teaching you in public and from house to house." ACTS 20:18-20

In his meeting with the Ephesian elders, Paul reminded his brothers in the faith that the manner of his living and teaching among them had been transparent and sincere. In no way had his conduct resembled that of a dishonest salesman who desperately hopes that you will purchase the used car and drive away from the lot before you notice the rusted floor beneath the mats.

Paul's time in Ephesus wasn't a flying visit by a traveling evangelist who shot into town, endeared himself to the people, and then left again. No, he had spent at least two years there, staying involved, teaching the gospel, and building the church (Acts 19:1 – 20:1). The people in Ephesus had seen him in the streets and in the marketplace. Many of them had had the opportunity to have private conversations with him. They would have known that when he said that he served the Lord with great humility, he was telling the truth. They had seen the tears he'd wept over them and the trials he'd faced among them.

In other words, Paul's ministry and Paul's heart were transparent. There was nothing to hide, and he would never have sought to do so. Paul later wrote to the Corinthian church about the need for transparency, saying, "We have renounced disgraceful, underhanded ways. We refuse to practice cunning or to tamper with God's word, but by the open statement of the truth we would commend ourselves to everyone's conscience in the sight of God" (2 Corinthians 4:2). He also emphasized the great importance of transparency to his protégé, Timothy: "Keep a close watch on yourself and on the teaching" (1 Timothy 4:16).

Paul believed that Christians ought to close the gap between what they say and how they live. The power and effectiveness of God's word can be undermined if there is not transparency on the part of the one bearing the good news.

When you share the hope and truth of the gospel, those who listen should be able to investigate your life and confirm that you genuinely believe the truths that you are proclaiming. Inside and outside the church, the way you live should commend the gospel just as much as the words you say. This doesn't mean you will be without sin; it does mean that your life will reflect that you have been transformed by God's grace. Pray that God would help you, by His grace, to be a living testimony to the truthfulness of the message you proclaim.

ACTS 19:1-20

JULY 7

PRAYING AT ALL TIMES

"Rejoice always, pray without ceasing, give thanks in all circumstances; for this is the will of God in Christ Jesus for you." 1 THESSALONIANS 5:16-18

We are in the midst of a spiritual battle. Warfare might not appear to confront us at every turn, but the fact of the matter is that we continually wrestle against the spiritual forces of evil (Ephesians 6:12). On such a battleground, prayer is absolutely essential—hence the apostle Paul's exhortations to "pray without ceasing."

What does this mean? Paul is not commanding us to drop everything and have a formal prayer meeting every hour, on the hour. Certainly, it is a grand privilege to pray aloud together with other saints. But oftentimes our prayers ring out only in our hearts. The hymn writer captures it well when he provides us with these words:

Prayer is the soul's sincere desire
Uttered or unexpressed;
The motion of a hidden fire
That trembles in the breast.[53]

This is prayer. Whether "uttered or unexpressed," it is fundamentally an engagement with God. And it is to be an unceasing part of our lives, along with thanksgiving, whatever our circumstances.

Lest we fool ourselves into thinking that prayer is simply a nice treat once we get around to it, the calls to continual prayer alert us to just how essential an activity it is. Prayer is not optional; it is vital. Prayer is not an item to check off our to-do list, as though five minutes in the morning will cover us for the rest of the day. It is impossible for anyone to enjoy an intimate relationship with God without walking through their day, and the circumstances it brings, in an attitude of prayer.

To pray, then, is to give voice—even if inaudible—to one of the most essential truths of the Christian faith: *apart from Christ you can do nothing* (John 15:5). The moment you think you can make it through the spiritual skirmishes of life on your own, you are in danger of defeat. But when you abide in Christ through prayer, He promises to cause you to bear much fruit and to fill you with joy as you march on in battle for His kingdom. Today, then, seek to pray and give thanks in all the situations you face; seek to speak to your Father in each moment He leads you through; and rejoice that in Christ, at every moment you have the ear of the Creator of the universe in this way.

JOHN 15:1-11

53 James Montgomery, "Prayer Is the Soul's Sincere Desire" (1818).

JULY 8

UNEXPECTED JUSTICE

"If anyone injures his neighbor, as he has done it shall be done to him, fracture for fracture, eye for eye, tooth for tooth; whatever injury he has given a person shall be given to him." LEVITICUS 24:19-20

Some of us may be tempted to stumble over this sort of statement in the Bible, viewing it as too harsh and vengeful. However, this Old Testament principle is not about gaining unlimited retribution against an enemy. Rather, it is intended to ensure that the punishment for a crime matches, and doesn't supersede, the damage done. It is a protection against going over the top in vengeance while making sure that justice is rendered.

Many parts of the world are bemused by Western culture's failure to match the crime with the punishment. For example, imagine that somebody steals millions of dollars through an elaborate, decades-long scheme. After months of going through the legal system, that person will probably be sentenced to many years in prison. And yet the countless victims of the crime are still without their money. From Scripture's perspective, the criminal should have to work hard until they have paid back to everyone what has been taken. In that way, the punishment would match the crime.

For justice to be served, punishment must take place. And everyone longs for justice of this kind, deep down. Discussing the need in films and dramas for a satisfying ending for flawed protagonists, Sara Colleton, an executive television producer, commented, "Whether you want to call it retribution, which is slightly too biblical for my taste, there is some need for moral judgment that accumulates with these characters, which they cannot escape."[54]

The fact that we know justice needs to be done is an indication that we were created by God as moral beings. We all exist with an internal awareness of "oughtness," no matter how much some might try to deny it.

In the Bible, however, ultimate justice is delivered in a completely unexpected way that satisfies not only our desire for justice but our desire for acceptance. Though we are the criminals deserving judgment, someone else took all our rags of moral unrighteousness, corruption, and religious indifference. The fitting punishment for our crime was death—yet Jesus Christ, the Son of God, bore that punishment in our place and instead clothed us with the credentials necessary to live as His ambassadors and die as His friends.

If you have laid hold of those righteous robes, never forget that you don't deserve them. Today, rejoice anew in God's grace. His righteous vengeance has been satisfied through Christ. As you have done, so it was done to Jesus. His punishment fit your crime. And so now your Judge gathers you up in His loving embrace and calls you His child. The Christian can never be anything other than deeply humble, and yet the Christian need never feel anything other than secure and loved.

GALATIANS 3:10-14

---

54 John Jurgensen, "How 'Breaking Bad' Finale Can Stick the Landing," *Wall Street Journal*, September 27, 2013, https://www.wsj.com/articles/SB10001424052702304526204579097430735706624.

JULY 9

A RELIGIOUS PROBLEM

"There are many who are insubordinate, empty talkers and deceivers ... They profess to know God, but they deny him by their works." TITUS 1:10, 16

Sometimes our greatest problems come from within the church, not outside it. Such was the case in Crete, where Paul had left Titus to place the churches on solid foundations with godly leadership (Titus 1:5). Paul's primary concern in his letter to Titus was not the rampant atheism, agnosticism, syncretism, or humanism that was present in the surrounding culture. A careful reading of Titus, and indeed of church history, indicates that the greatest threat to the church emerges from people inside the church who claim to know the Lord but deceive both themselves and others. Paul describes some people within this church as those who "profess to know God, but they deny him by their works." They had a creed, but their conduct did not match it. They could say the right words, but there was no fruit to be seen in their lives.

Cretans as a whole had a reputation of being "liars, evil beasts, lazy gluttons" (Titus 1:12). And the problem appears to have been that several who professed faith within the Cretan church and who had some influence over others looked no different from the surrounding culture. And when professing believers have a lot of "God talk" but very little godly living, their behavior not only matches that of the society outside but undermines the witness of the church to the society outside.

A church can be a dangerous place. If we're not careful, churches can provide opportunities for people to make a few superficial changes while continuing to live just the same as everyone around them. They may believe that they have given their lives to Christ but in fact they are not willing to accept His lordship over any area of their life where change would be socially costly. In Crete, perhaps it should have been truth-telling, working hard, and moderation with food that would have set the church apart. For us, perhaps, it will be not making an idol of our kids' education, eschewing materialism, and refusing to treat politics as the solution to everything.

We can easily go from being irreligious to being religious without actually being transformed by God's grace. The danger is that religion itself may actually be what keeps someone from fully embracing the truth about Jesus. We ought to ask ourselves: *Do my works give credence to my profession of faith in Christ? Or are they indistinguishable from those of my neighbors who make no claim to be Christians?*

What is the antidote to such empty religiosity? It is to recognize that true Christianity not only gives us a new creed but will also change our conduct. And it is to understand that our lives are transformed from the inside out rather than the outside in—not necessarily all at once but certainly in a way that, over time, cannot be mistaken. It is as we look at God's mercy in Christ that we are moved to offer our lives in worship (Romans 12:1).

GALATIANS 3:1-9

Bible Through The Year: Obadiah; Acts 8:1-25

JULY 10

THE PARADOX OF FREEDOM IN CHRIST

"The law of the LORD is perfect, reviving the soul; the testimony of the LORD is sure, making wise the simple; the precepts of the LORD are right, rejoicing the heart; the commandment of the LORD is pure, enlightening the eyes ... Moreover, by them is your servant warned; in keeping them there is great reward." PSALM 19:7-8, 11

Christians often seem to have a paradoxical relationship with God's law.

Sometimes, we misapply Paul's teaching that we're not under law but under grace (Romans 6:14) to suggest that all of the law was only for Old Testament times. Back then, the error goes, God's people did as they were told and obeyed the Ten Commandments; now, we can do whatever we want because we live in freedom. But with such a perspective, it's difficult to understand the psalmist's *love* for God's law. He didn't see the law only as something that had to be done—as a means to an end—but recognized it in itself as a source of restoration, joy, and blessing. That should be no less the case for believers today. It is true that we're no longer under law as a means of *acceptance with* God; but we are still to see the law as a means of *living for* God. We have been redeemed so that we might be the firstfruits of God's new creation, dedicated to God by doing His will—and we find His will in His law!

Jesus told us, "If you abide in my word, you are truly my disciples, and you will know the truth, and the truth will set you free" (John 8:31-32). The liberating power of God's word will only do its work when we hold on to the truth in obedience to what Jesus said.

The apostle James described God's law as perfect, giving us freedom (James 1:25). In Christ, this law is no longer external to us, written on tablets of stone. It is now written on our hearts: "The Holy Spirit also bears witness to us ... 'This is the covenant that I will make with them after those days, declares the Lord: I will put my laws on their hearts, and write them on their minds'" (Hebrews 10:15-16).

This is the paradox: our freedom in Christ is tied directly to our obedience. Disobedient people think they're free, but really they're in bondage to sin. Obedient people may at times feel constrained, but they're in freedom, no longer enslaved to the impulses of a sinful nature. The greater our obedience, the greater our freedom, for the more we obey our Creator who told His image-bearers to enjoy being blessed (Genesis 1:28), the more we are living in line with the people we were made to be.

The psalmist recognized this paradox and therefore could rejoice in God's law. So should we. If you want to know freedom from guilt, lust, fear, loneliness, aimlessness, and emptiness, you must abide in the truth. As you walk in obedience to God's law, you will discover true freedom that revives your soul, bringing unending joy and unimaginable blessing along the way. In what way are you struggling to live under God's law today? That will be the place where you can experience the paradoxical freedom of obedience.

JEREMIAH 31:31-34

JULY 11

LIFTING SIN'S BURDEN

"The next day he saw Jesus coming toward him, and said, 'Behold, the Lamb of God, who takes away the sin of the world! This is he of whom I said, "After me comes a man who ranks before me, because he was before me."'" JOHN 1:29-30

Are you weary, beleaguered, and weighed down today by the burden of your sin? Do you lack assurance of your forgiveness before God? If so, there is only one sure antidote: to fix your gaze humbly and believingly on the Lord Jesus Christ. Anyone or anything else is insufficient to deal with the oppressive weight of sin.

In reading the Old Testament, we discover that the substitution of the innocent for the guilty is the divine principle of dealing with sin. The sacrificial system and its requirements were put in place by God in order to address His people's disobedience. But as the story of God's people unfolds, it becomes apparent that the sacrificial system was not sufficient in and of itself. Neither the priests nor the animals were enough. They couldn't take away sin. They couldn't save. They couldn't justify. And they couldn't make the people holy.

But the sacrificial system was absolutely necessary, in one important respect: it anticipated and explained the arrival of the perfect Lamb. As the writer to the Hebrews explains, "If that first covenant had been faultless, there would have been no occasion to look for a second" (Hebrews 8:7). So when John the Baptist saw Jesus and declared, "Behold, the Lamb of God, who takes away the sin of the world!" he was proclaiming the truth that Jesus was the one who had come to offer His very life for sin, once and for all, for anyone who might believe.

In Jesus we have not only this willing and spotless sacrificial Lamb but also a perfect "high priest" who "entered once for all into the holy places, not by means of the blood of goats and calves but by means of his own blood, thus securing an eternal redemption" (Hebrews 9:11, 12). In contrast to the priests of old, who could never sit down on account of the fact that their work was never done, Jesus was able to say "It is finished" and sit down at God's right hand (John 19:30; Hebrews 10:12).

Oh, the joy and freedom that are ours when we place our trust in Jesus as the final sacrifice for our sin! What peace and rest for our weary souls! In Him our burden is lifted and we are forgiven, freeing us to sing forever:

I need no other argument,
I need no other plea,
It is enough that Jesus died,
And that He died for me.[55]

LEVITICUS 16

55 Eliza E. Hewitt, "My Faith Has Found a Resting Place" (1890).

JULY 12

GOD, GIDEON, AND GLORY

"The LORD said to Gideon, 'The people with you are too many for me to give the Midianites into their hand, lest Israel boast over me, saying, "My own hand has saved me." ... And the LORD said to Gideon, 'With the 300 men who lapped I will save you and give the Midianites into your hand, and let all the others go every man to his home.'" JUDGES 7:2, 7

The annals of history contain many men of military genius—men like George Washington, Napoleon, or Julius Caesar, whose strategic acumen led them to world-shaping victories. The Bible's account of Gideon is memorable for a number of reasons, but displays of military genius is not one of them. In fact, much of his story is intended to convey the exact point that Gideon's victory owed *nothing* to his strength or strategy.

Think of the scene: Israel was facing oppression by the Midianites, and the Lord called Gideon, with all his self-doubt, to bring deliverance. The foe was massive, "like locusts in abundance, and their camels were without number" (Judges 7:12). Gideon summoned his own force of 32,000—a substantial but undermanned army. Nothing could have prepared Gideon's ears for what the Lord said next: "The people with you are too many." Even after he sent 22,000 home, it was still too many.

The story gets even stranger when we read God's method for whittling the number of troops from 10,000 down to a final tally of 300: whoever used his hands to drink was allowed to stay and fight, while the rest were sent home. Some have explained this water-lapping test as God's way of identifying the right kind of warrior for the battle, but that misses the point. God wasn't looking for a particular *kind* of person; it was a particular *number* that He was after. He was getting the army down to a number so small, so clearly incapable, that when the victory came, all 300 and the whole of Israel would know that *God did this*.

And that is how it unfolded. Gideon spurred his men to battle, and God gave the victory. Reading the story, it's clear that this conquest required no military skill whatsoever. In fact, the battle was won without a single Israelite using his sword (Judges 7:22). All that was required was the favor of God.

Do you find it strange that God would use such unlikely methods to accomplish His purposes? Consider your own life. God's purpose for you is to conform you to Christ's image, to glorify Himself through you, and to use you for the spread of the gospel. As you look back over your life, has it not been the case that God has used some unlikely methods to accomplish these purposes? God used 300 men to defeat the Midianites because the weakness of the army put His might on display. In the same way, He uses our weakness, suffering, and fumbling efforts to demonstrate His gracious power. God has always been about the business of using the weak things of the world to shame the strong (1 Corinthians 1:27)—and your life is no exception. Let the story of the 300 give you boldness to obey God without fear or compromise—not in your own strength, but because of His.

JUDGES 6:11-16

JULY 13

A SHADOW WITHOUT SUBSTANCE

"'Death is swallowed up in victory.' 'O death, where is your victory? O death, where is your sting?' The sting of death is sin, and the power of sin is the law. But thanks be to God, who gives us the victory through our Lord Jesus Christ."
1 CORINTHIANS 15:54-57

In these verses, the apostle Paul is openly taunting death. How can he do so? Death is so horrible. It's so tragic. It's so sad. It seems so final. What did Paul know that enabled him to flout its terrible tyranny with such confidence?

It is because death has lost its sting.

To illustrate Paul's point, imagine this scene: A young girl is gleefully playing with her father in the backyard. A bee starts buzzing around. When it flies into view of the little girl, she shouts, "Oh, keep that bee away from me! I don't want to get stung! Daddy, please do something!" As the bee draws closer, the father begins to swat at it—and as he reaches out, the bee fastens on him and drops its stinger right into the father's arm. The father takes the sting and experiences the pain. The bee's sting is drawn, and the little girl is safe.

On the cross, Jesus Christ bore the sting of death. Sin leads to death, and death stings because of sin, for sin must lead to judgment. But Christ bore the judgment for sin in His own body on the tree so that all who trust in Him will never face judgment (Galatians 3:13). We may still walk through "the valley of the shadow of death" (Psalm 23:4), but because of what Christ has done, that is all death is: a shadow without substance. This is the very reason that Jesus took on humanity. Our Lord took on flesh and blood for this purpose: "that through death he might destroy the one who has the power of death, that is, the devil, and deliver all those who through fear of death were subject to lifelong slavery" (Hebrews 2:14-15).

You no longer have to live in that kind of slavery or walk in that fear. By His own death and resurrection, Jesus has abolished true death forever. He took death's sting so that you would never have to face its power over sinners. Instead, you can walk in freedom today and every day, knowing that God has already given you decisive victory over sin and death through your Lord, Jesus Christ. So you can look at death and say, "Horrible, tragic, sad though you are, you have lost your sting." And you can look at the one who drew the sting for you and say:

Thine be the glory, risen conquering Son—
Endless is the victory Thou oe'r death hast won![56]

HEBREWS 2:10-18

56 Edmond Budry, "Thine Be the Glory" (trans. Richard Birch Hoyle, 1923).

JULY 14

HUMBLE FAITH

"Behold, his soul is puffed up; it is not upright within him, but the righteous shall live by his faith." HABAKKUK 2:4

We're often preoccupied with understanding great things. We focus our attention on scientists, scholars, and experts—and, of course, we often need their insights! But, as believers, we must remember that ultimately we live by faith, not by human insight.

The Bible describes individuals who believe that they can handle life and death on their own as "puffed up." Such people regard the idea of bowing down before God as ridiculous, unnecessary, and unhelpful—and they're prepared to scorn those who choose to do so. In contrast, the righteous don't look to themselves to find all of the answers; they humbly "live by ... faith." They believe what God says simply and solely because God said it.

We see this verse's principle referenced on several occasions in the New Testament. Paul, for example, in writing to the Ephesian church about what it means to know God, reached back to Habakkuk. He made it clear that God gives His righteousness as a gift of grace through faith, not as something we earn by our good deeds or religious works (Ephesians 2:8-9). His epistle to the Romans can be seen as an exposition of this text from Habakkuk: in the gospel, he told the Roman church, "the righteousness of God is revealed from faith for faith, as it is written, 'The righteous shall live by faith'" (Romans 1:17).

Jesus addressed our need for humble faith in His parable of the Pharisee and the tax collector (Luke 18:9-14). The Pharisee gloated that he was not like other people: "God, I thank you that I am not like other men, extortioners, unjust, adulterers, or even like this tax collector" (v 11). His soul was puffed up. But the tax collector recognized that he was a sinner and sought God's mercy. Jesus said, "This man went down to his house justified, rather than the other. For everyone who exalts himself will be humbled, but the one who humbles himself will be exalted" (v 14).

The puffed-up soul pictured in this parable and in Habakkuk's prophecy can so easily be a portrait of you and me. We find it easier to live by human wisdom and effort than by faith in God. Our natural state is to puff ourselves up, not to humble ourselves at the foot of the cross. When we suffer from big views of ourselves and small views of God, we need to remember that humility of heart comes from an awareness of who God really is:

O worship the King all-glorious above,
O gratefully sing His power and His love:
Our shield and defender, the Ancient of Days,
Pavilioned in splendor and girded with praise.[57]

Sing more of His greatness than of yours and more of His power than of yours, live for His praise more than for yours, and you will know the glorious freedom and peace of the life of humble faith in the God who loves you, forgives you, and saves you.

ROMANS 1:1-17

57 Robert Grant, "O Worship the King" (1833).

JULY 15

KEEPING NEAR

"Therefore we must pay much closer attention to what we have heard, lest we drift away from it." HEBREWS 2:1

When asked in conversation whether or not they are married, no husband or wife would reach for a photo album or rummage for a legal certificate to support their answer or prove their status. Rather, they would talk about current experiences—the privileges, the joys, perhaps even the challenges and the struggles of life with their spouse. So it is in the Christian faith: our expressions of its reality ought to be directly related to our present experience and not merely our past conversion. Keeping near the heart of God strengthens our relationship with Him and provides us with fresh reminders of His grace and mercy.

This does not happen by accident. Spiritual drift is a constant and often unnoticed danger in our spiritual lives. In order to prevent us from drifting and abandoning the love we had at first (Revelation 2:4), the writer of Hebrews warns and invites us to "pay ... closer attention to what we have heard"—namely, the message of the gospel. When we immerse ourselves daily in the reading and memorizing of God's word, our affections are stirred, and our gaze remains fixed on Jesus' atoning work on the cross.

We must, though, combine the ministry of the word with faith. It is possible to sit under the word of God and yet to remain impervious to its truth. All kinds of information may rattle around in our heads without ever reaching our hearts or commanding our wills. But when we combine gospel truth with faith, then we strengthen and experience our relationship with God, in the present tense.

Committing ourselves to gathering with God's people also encourages daily continuation in the Christian life. Luke tells us that the early church devoted itself to, among other things, "the apostles' teaching and the fellowship" and "the breaking of bread" (Acts 2:42). Why? Because they understood that the gathering of God's people in worship and for the study of the Scriptures is one of the key means that God has ordained to ensure that we don't become spiritual castaways.

If you sense yourself drifting today, do not give in on the one hand to the temptation to believe that all is lost, or on the other hand to the temptation to think that it does not matter. Return again to the Shepherd and Overseer of your soul (1 Peter 2:25), and ask for a fresh outpouring of His Spirit, who is able to strengthen and equip you as you pursue an abiding relationship with the Father through hearing over and over again the glorious truths of the gospel.

ACTS 2:42-47

JULY 16

SEARCHING FOR LOST DONKEYS

"Now the donkeys of Kish, Saul's father, were lost. So Kish said to Saul his son, 'Take one of the young men with you, and arise, go and look for the donkeys.'"
1 SAMUEL 9:3

When Kish sent Saul to look for his lost donkeys, neither father nor son could have known where the search would lead. Behind the scenes as Saul undertook this apparently mundane chore, God was sending him to Samuel. Soon the future king of Israel would meet the prophet of God—all because of some wayward farm animals!

This is a striking illustration of the doctrine of providence. God Almighty acts in and through the apparently random, humdrum bits and pieces of life. It's a great mystery how God accomplishes His plan for creation as we think and act freely—yet the Bible assures us that our liberty does not interfere with His secret will. And although He is the first cause of all things, He routinely uses a variety of means in order to bring about His purpose from all of eternity. This understanding stands in stark contrast to the views of our modern culture, which often sees life as either coldly deterministic or randomly meaningless.

And so, as you drive to the same workplace each day, or perform the same tasks each day, surrounded by the same people each day, recognize this: in at all, God is working out His purposes in your life and guiding you along in your life. Further down the road, with a bit of perception, you will be able to look back and recognize that the situations which were apparently arbitrary or commonplace when they happened were in fact part of God's loving direction of your way (Proverbs 16:9).

In your life, you will have your own version of the frustration of the lost donkeys, the uncertainty of the search, and the surprise of finding a prophet. In all those ups and downs, remember that you are not bobbing around on the sea of chance, nor are you held in the grip of blind deterministic forces; you are being trained in the school of God's providence. The good, the bad, the ugly, the foolish, the disastrous, the wise, the encouraging, the difficult, and the uncertain are all brought under the sovereign control of a God who "has done all things well" (Mark 7:37). How can that transform your perspective on the rest of your day?

1 CORINTHIANS 10:31-33

JULY 17

CARRYING THE CROSS

"As they led him away, they seized one Simon of Cyrene, who was coming in from the country, and laid on him the cross, to carry it behind Jesus." LUKE 23:26

For three years, Jesus had ministered to people, touching and changing lives. But now, the teacher from Galilee who had turned the other cheek (Matthew 5:39), who had walked the second mile (v 41), found Himself being led away outside the city to be crucified. And unbeknown to the onlooking crowd, what was about to happen would be *the* defining moment of all of history.

As they led Him toward Calvary, Jesus stumbled and staggered under the weight of His cross, His appearance marred beyond recognition from the beatings He had suffered (Isaiah 52:14). Concerned that Jesus might not live long enough to be crucified, the Roman soldiers seized an unsuspecting bystander, "one Simon of Cyrene." Before Simon even knew what was happening, they had "laid on him the cross, to carry it behind" the bloodied body of Jesus of Nazareth.

Simon's part in carrying the cross is a reminder of what it means to be forever identified with Jesus, who bore our sins. Indeed, to be united with Christ is to be united with Him in His sufferings (Philippians 3:10). The story of the cross is not "the messy bit" which affords us personal forgiveness and then allows us to forget and move on. If we follow Christ, then, like Simon, we carry a cross (Luke 9:23-24). We are called to give up what is easiest for us in order to do what is obedient to Christ. Jesus' disciples, both then and now, recognize that their lives are to be cross-shaped ones.

Not only that, but our methods and message need to be cross-shaped too. It is only to our shame when we try to present to the world a crossless Christianity, one that esteems success, wealth, comfort, and strength. Such a message is futile, useless, and even dangerous! Jesus' ministry was oriented toward the least and the last, the left-out and the marginalized. He didn't come to put together a group of religious professionals. Rather, He called a people to Himself in order that we might hold out the message of the cross to those who are broken and buffeted, fallen and downhearted—people like you and me.

So, as you see Simon carrying a cross behind the one who would die on the cross for His people, see yourself there too. Will you deny yourself and carry your cross today? Will you hold out the message of the cross to others today? Do so with joy, for the path of your bloodied Savior did not end at His death—and so, following Him, neither will yours.

MARK 8:34-38

JULY 18

ALREADY RICH

"Let the lowly brother boast in his exaltation." JAMES 1:9

It seems like a paradox to say that a "lowly brother" should rejoice and take pride "in his exaltation." We should ask, "What exaltation?" If life is viewed simply from the perspective of time, wealth, and status, then there is no high position for the lowly. But when we view life with godly wisdom, remembering the glorious riches that Jesus provides, we see that the believer who lives precariously on the lowest rung of the socio-economic ladder in fact has a significant and secure position simply because they are in God's care.

Two biblical stories illustrate respectively the danger of viewing low circumstances without wisdom and the blessing of wisdom in the midst of poverty.

In 2 Kings 5:15-27, Gehazi, the servant of the prophet Elisha, chased after the prosperous Naaman, seeking riches for himself. But Elisha confronted Gehazi, essentially challenging him not to despise his position as a servant but to believe that God would look after him. Because of his lack of trust in God, Gehazi and his descendants became lepers. His story reminds us of the peril of greed, envy, and ingratitude.

Ruth, meanwhile, was abjectly poor. After migrating to Bethlehem following the death of her husband, she and her mother-in-law, Naomi, had nothing to eat other than the bits and pieces of grain that Ruth could scrape up from already-harvested fields. When she was shown preferential treatment by Boaz, "she fell on her face, bowing to the ground, and said to him, 'Why have I found favor in your eyes, that you should take notice of me, since I am a foreigner?'" (Ruth 2:10). Because she was clothed with humility before Boaz and—more importantly—before God, she was able to receive Boaz's kindness as the blessing it was, without any presumption. Instead of being quick to seek more material wealth, she was quick to be grateful for what she had been given.

Ruth's story teaches us something else. As Boaz was Ruth's kinsman and redeemer, so Jesus is the Redeemer who shed His blood for men and women like Ruth, who are undervalued and disregarded. Paul reminds us that when we were called, "not many of you were wise according to worldly standards, not many were powerful, not many were of noble birth" (1 Corinthians 1:26). Jesus has come to those who were on the lowest rung of the spiritual ladder—you and me—and has caused us to ask the same question as Ruth: *Why have You shown such interest in me?*

James's message is not that we will become rich by applying wisdom. Rather, he wants us to see that if we think about life from a proper perspective, we will realize that we are *already* rich beyond imagining. The wisdom of God comes to us in our poverty to show us the vastness of all we have in Christ; and it comes to us in our plenty to remind us that the only wealth that matters is what we have in Christ. When you grasp this, you can look at any less-than-desirable circumstances and continue in the journey of faith, with your eyes fixed on all that awaits you in heaven, where your true treasure lies.

JAMES 1:9-15

JULY 19

DEALING WITH DEATH

"When the time drew near that Israel must die, he called his son Joseph and said to him, '... Do not bury me in Egypt, but let me lie with my fathers. Carry me out of Egypt and bury me in their burying place.'" GENESIS 47:29-30

Death will come to us all. Therefore, the great question of life is not so much "How do we face life and live in this world?" but rather "How do we face death and where will we live in the next world?" This life isn't irrelevant; indeed, it's vitally important! But we can't know what it means to live unless we have first learned how to die.

Jacob is a wonderful illustration of how to live and die in light of God's promised plan. He was specific in his requests regarding his death and burial—and his concern over his burial place was primarily about theology, not geography. He recognized that in his death, he was making a statement about his place in the unfolding plan and purpose of God's relationship with His people.

God had made a covenant with Abraham, promising that he would become the father of a great nation in the land of Canaan, the promised land. This promise was passed to Isaac and then to Jacob. Humbled by and entrusted with this promise, Jacob wanted it to be passed on to the coming generations through his final blessing and his burial location. He wanted his descendants to remember they were destined for Canaan, not Egypt, and he wanted them to remember his faith in the certainty of God's plan and purpose.

Joseph honored his father's wishes, and Genesis 49 – 50 describes the elaborate funeral procession from Egypt to Canaan and the mourning that followed. Scripture tells us that the onlooking Canaanites noticed the elaborate ceremony (Genesis 50:11), but they couldn't have known the full depth of its meaning. Similarly, many people do not—because they *cannot*—fully understand why Christians deal with death in the way the Bible says we can. The Christian's perspective on death should be radically different from anything that the world is able to offer. If we simply go through the same motions as other people, with the same subdued ceremonies, the same sentimental music, and the same empty platitudes, we miss a prime opportunity to say in our dying and in our mourning, "Death has no ultimate hold on us. We have been delivered from our sins and therefore from the terrors of death. Thanks be to God for giving us victory through Jesus Christ!" (see 1 Corinthians 15:57).

When the world is watching, the way we deal with death is an opportunity to proclaim that the King of heaven came to earth and transformed how we live *and* die. The covenant that Christ made on the cross cleared the debt of your sin and guarantees you and all believers "an inheritance that is imperishable, undefiled, and unfading" (1 Peter 1:4). Like Jacob and countless other saints who have faithfully gone before you, be sure to proclaim this in the way you speak of death, in the way you grieve for those saints who go before you, and in the way that, one day, you confront your own passing. How does this comfort you today? How does this reframe your own perspective on your future today?

1 THESSALONIANS 4:13-18

JULY 20

WHERE IS GOD?

"Now in the days of Ahasuerus, the Ahasuerus who reigned from India to Ethiopia over 127 provinces, in those days when King Ahasuerus sat on his royal throne in Susa, the citadel, in the third year of his reign he gave a feast for all his officials and servants. The army of Persia and Media and the nobles and governors of the provinces were before him." ESTHER 1:1-3

A natural response for anyone who reads the book of Esther is to wonder, "Where is God in this book?" It is one of only two biblical books that don't mention God by name. (The other is the Song of Solomon.) Why the omission? While commentators and scholars have offered all kinds of explanations, the fundamental reason why God's name does not appear may just be the simplest: because He didn't want it there. But that leads us to an even bigger question: Why would God not want His name in Esther's story?

Perhaps it is because God is wanting to teach us that there will be times in life when He is apparently absent, but He's not. Charles Spurgeon writes, "Although the name of God does not occur in the Book of Esther, the Lord himself is there most conspicuously in every incident which it relates ... I have seen portraits bearing the names of persons for whom they were intended, and they certainly needed them. But we have all seen others which required no name, because they were such striking likenesses that the moment you looked upon them you knew them."[58]

While God's name is missing from Esther, then, His presence is supremely evident. He is at work in the refusal of the Persian queen, Vashti, to accede to her husband's angry demands (Esther 1:12). He is at work in making the young Jewish woman who gives her name to the book, Esther, beautiful (2:7). He is at work in the sleep patterns of the king and in his reading choices (6:1). And He is at work in overruling the hatred of the king's first minister, Haman (8:7-8, 17). Esther lived "in the days of Ahasuerus," the mighty Persian king. But she also lived in the days of the *al*mighty Creator God, who rules on high. And we live in those same days.

Life's unfolding story always reveals to us that God is in the details. The book of Esther makes clear that He is present not only in the "lightning bolts" of His intervention—in the parting of the Red Sea (Exodus 14) or the calming of the storm (Mark 4:35-41)—but also in the humdrum of life. In the everyday events, God is working His purpose out.

Perhaps you find yourself in the midst of deep darkness and circumstances that seek to overwhelm you. If so, pray that God will help you hear His word, which promises, "Never will I leave you; never will I forsake you" (Hebrews 13:5, NIV); which assures us that "all things work together for good, for those who are called according to his purpose" (Romans 8:28); and which calls us to "cast your burden on the LORD, and he will sustain you" (Psalm 55:22). When God appears to be most absent in your life, He is still at work.

PSALM 55

58 "Providence—As Seen in the Book of Esther," *The Metropolitan Tabernacle Pulpit* 20, no. 1201, p 613.

JULY 21

THE KING OF KINGS

"Now in the days of Ahasuerus, the Ahasuerus who reigned from India to Ethiopia over 127 provinces ... in the third year of his reign he gave a feast for all his officials and servants. The army of Persia and Media and the nobles and governors of the provinces were before him, while he showed the riches of his royal glory and the splendor and pomp of his greatness for many days, 180 days."

ESTHER 1:1, 3-4

The book of Esther presents King Ahasuerus to us as a big deal. He is a big deal textually: his name comes up time and time again throughout Esther. He is also a big deal politically: India and Ethiopia, the scope of his reign, represented the extreme boundaries of the then-known world. And the picture of his greatness only builds as he is shown giving a celebration that lasts for six months! The longevity of this party attended by so many nobles was a status symbol. In all of history, under any standards of kings, dominions, authorities, and powers, this king stands out as significant.

Clearly, Ahasuerus was a big deal. But when we take all the notions that describe this king and compare them to Jesus, the King of kings, we see that only Jesus is the *real* deal.

King Ahasuerus "reigned ... over 127 provinces"—quite a lot of territory! Yet our heavenly Father says to the Messiah, "Ask of me, and I will make the nations your heritage, and the ends of the earth your possession" (Psalm 2:8).

King Ahasuerus was seated upon his throne while hundreds of nobles came to give their respect—a significant display of authority. But that fades into obscurity when we read, "And he who was seated on the throne said, 'Behold, I am making all things new ... It is done! I am the Alpha and the Omega, the beginning and the end'" (Revelation 21:5-6). The authority of King Jesus reaches to the ends of the earth, forever and forever.

King Ahasuerus put together a banquet that lasted for 180 days—a party to rival any other in history. But the marriage supper of the Lamb is a banquet that will be eternal (Revelation 19:6-9). In the meantime, He has left us little feasts of remembrance so that we may pause together as His subjects and come to His table to acknowledge that Christ is the King who died in our place (Luke 22:19).

Ahasuerus sat on a splendid earthly throne, but where is all his finery, majesty, and authority now? It's buried. Jesus, meanwhile, continues to be seated at the right hand of the Father in heaven, the ascended King and reigning Lord. The big deals of the world, whether they're from the 5th century BC or the 21st century AD, will eventually bow before His authority. He is the real deal—and yet He invites us to come and meet Him!

It is easy to be captivated, impressed, and directed by those men and women of this world who are a big deal. But take a few moments to reflect on the significance of Jesus. As you come before the presence of the one and only truly great King, bow and acknowledge His worth, and let His majesty and holiness and kindness lead you to submit with joy to His kingly rule.

DANIEL 7:1-14

JULY 22

FOOLISH PASSION

"On the seventh day, when the heart of the king was merry with wine, he commanded Mehuman, Biztha, Harbona, Bigtha and Abagtha, Zethar and Carkas, the seven eunuchs who served in the presence of King Ahasuerus, to bring Queen Vashti before the king with her royal crown, in order to show the peoples and the princes her beauty, for she was lovely to look at. But Queen Vashti refused to come at the king's command delivered by the eunuchs. At this the king became enraged, and his anger burned within him." ESTHER 1:10-12

In a display of pride and bravado, King Ahasuerus issued a command for the presence of his queen. This was not the gesture of a kind, caring husband who wanted his wife to meet his friends. Rather, this was Mr. Big planning a show-and-tell for his friends in which everything was calculated to indicate his majesty, might, and significance. Josephus, the Jewish historian, records that it was a violation of the Persian code of ethics for a man's wife to be the occasion of observation or approbation of any other men.[59] The king, then, was breaking the bounds of propriety in every way.

There was a progression in the king's behavior. The wine had gone to his head, and he made an ill-thought summons to his wife. When she refused to come, he became enraged. He then sought the advice of those around him, who only pandered to his ego. He could have paused to consider if their advice was proper in relation to the laws of the land or to the queen and his esteem for her—but instead, his anger and weak will led him to a quick, foolish decision. Earlier that morning, if someone had told the king that by midnight he would have banished the queen from his life forever, he probably would have thought it impossible. But still he did it. A big ego, too much alcohol, a quick temper, and bad advice led to an outcome he surely never desired.

Three years after he had deposed the queen and fresh off a disappointing military campaign against the Greeks, we read that "the anger of King Ahasuerus had abated," and "he remembered Vashti and what she had done and what had been decreed against her" (Esther 2:1). He was bruised in his ego and saddened by his past—a picture of the empty sorrow of someone who has pursued everyone and everything, and particularly his own agenda, at the expense of the living God (Ecclesiastes 4:7-8). King Ahasuerus' experience serves as a warning to us that in a moment of foolish passion, we, too, can alter and diminish, or even destroy, our lives forever.

There is a path that seems right, but we are told that in the end it leads to emptiness and death (Proverbs 14:12). As you face decisions, be quick to ask yourself whether your ego, your temper, false friends or overconsumption are guiding you; and be equally quick to look to the Savior to guide you in the way of wisdom, along the narrow road that leads to fullness of life (Matthew 7:13-14).

DANIEL 3:1-18

59 *Antiquities of the Jews* 11.6.1.

JULY 23

CITIZENS AND FOREIGNERS

"Now there was a Jew in Susa the citadel whose name was Mordecai, the son of Jair, son of Shimei, son of Kish, a Benjaminite, who had been carried away from Jerusalem among the captives carried away with Jeconiah king of Judah, whom Nebuchadnezzar king of Babylon had carried away." ESTHER 2:5-6

In this world, you are a foreigner.

In this, you and I have something in common with Mordecai. As "a Jew in Susa," Mordecai was from a family that had been carried off into exile during the Babylonian invasion of Jerusalem. A few generations later, and now in Persia, we encounter Mordecai. Enough of an elder to play the role of father, Mordecai had adopted his orphaned cousin Esther (Esther 2:7). He was a pragmatist. Deciding that nothing helpful would come from Esther declaring herself a Jew, he commanded her to conceal her identity when she was taken to the palace (v 10). Mordecai then put himself in the right place to observe what was happening to this cousin he cared for (v 11). And he later discovered an assassination plot which allowed him to gain favor with the king (v 21-23).

It appears that Mordecai, like many second- or third-generation exiles, had a particular interest in his country's welfare. He was removed from his family's homeland, and he was trying to figure out how to be a good Jew *and* a good citizen in Persia. The conditions weren't ideal; he and the other exiles who were with him were in a minority context, in the midst of a majority that was overwhelmingly opposed to them. However, as Jews in this foreign land, their job wasn't to take over Persia or bring down the government. Their job was to learn what it meant for them to affirm their faith in an unfamiliar and difficult situation.

Many Christians in the West need to stop thinking in majority terms. Genuine, Bible-believing, gospel-affirming Christianity is in the minority. (Indeed, it often has been—perhaps more often than we might think!) We are like exiles living in a foreign land. But there is no need for alarm. The story of Esther reminds us that God preserves His people within ungodly environments so that they might be witnesses to His name.

The questions we must consider as believers today, then, are these: How can I be a good Christian *and* a good citizen? How can I live for Jesus and "seek the welfare of the city" where He has sent me (Jeremiah 29:7)?

Paul reassures us that we are indeed a part of God's plans, saying, "In [Jesus] we have obtained an inheritance, having been predestined according to the purpose of him who works all things according to the counsel of his will, so that we who were the first to hope in Christ might be to the praise of his glory" (Ephesians 1:11-12). So, as you attempt to live faithfully for God in this foreign context—and make no mistake, if you are a believer living in this world, you *are* a foreigner!—you still have great reason to hope.

ROMANS 13:1-10

JULY 24

NOT ALWAYS TIDY

"When Esther was taken to King Ahasuerus, into his royal palace … the king loved Esther more than all the women, and she won grace and favor in his sight more than all the virgins, so that he set the royal crown on her head and made her queen instead of Vashti." ESTHER 2:16-17

Hadassah, the Jewish girl who became queen of Persia, is better known to us by her Persian name, Esther, which means "star." She was an orphan, adopted by her cousin, and she was especially attractive (Esther 2:7). When the king held a beauty pageant in search of a new queen, Esther "was taken into the king's palace and put in custody of Hegai, who had charge of the women" (v 8). Up to this point, she had concealed her Jewish nationality (v 10).

Hegai, the eunuch in charge of all the women, was especially pleased with Esther, quickly advancing her, and when it was her turn to go before the king, he coached her accordingly (Esther 2:9, 15). It worked out well, as she won first prize and was made queen. Esther was in a position to help her people—but there's nothing to suggest that her goal was anything greater than wearing the crown.

This story has elements that are awkward and difficult. The average Jewish mother would not have been thrilled to find out that her Hadassah was sleeping with an uncircumcised pagan king. The average Jewish father would not have been thrilled to know that his Hadassah had gone undercover in Persia and refused to let anybody know about her kindred, background, or identity. She may be a heroine of this story, but she was a heroine "of questionable morality and orthodoxy."[60]

It isn't necessary, however, for us to approvingly reflect on the path Esther took. While we recognize that God was providentially in control of the drama that was taking place in her life, we don't need to say that she made good decisions every step of the way. God in His providence granted Esther a little piece in the unfolding drama. But we are to look past Esther and her choices to the true hero of the story: God, who is committed to working out all things for the welfare of His people.

The events of Esther's story were not as tidy as we might perhaps wish. Of course, that's not an excuse to intentionally make decisions that aren't pleasing to God. But it is a reason to be encouraged, because the events of God's providence in our lives are not as tidy as we might wish either. Review your own life, and realize that although not all your decisions have been good ones, not all your plans have been selfless, God in His providence has brought you to this day. As you tell your story, be determined to tell of the true hero: God, who is the First and the Last and is working His purposes out in your life.

JUDGES 13:1-4; 16:23-30

60 Barry G. Webb, *Five Festal Garments: Christian Reflections on the Song of Songs, Ruth, Lamentations, Ecclesiastes, and Esther,* New Studies in Biblical Theology 10, ed. D. A. Carson (IVP Academic, 2000), p 120.

JULY 25

WHAT IS GOD DOING?

"As Mordecai was sitting at the king's gate, Bigthan and Teresh, two of the king's eunuchs, who guarded the threshold, became angry and sought to lay hands on King Ahasuerus. And this came to the knowledge of Mordecai, and he told it to Queen Esther, and Esther told the king in the name of Mordecai. When the affair was investigated and found to be so, the men were both hanged on the gallows. And it was recorded in the book of the chronicles in the presence of the king. After these things King Ahasuerus promoted Haman." ESTHER 2:21 - 3:1

Have you ever done something great at school, at work, or maybe even at church, only to see someone else get the credit?

This was the experience of Mordecai. He had discovered and revealed an assassination plot against King Ahasuerus, and the king promoted... Haman, giving him a throne of his own so that all the royal servants and all those within the government circles were subservient to him. All Mordecai received was a few lines at the bottom of a page.

But Mordecai did not yet understand how significant his recorded actions would prove to be, not only in his life but for the entire Jewish population—indeed, to some extent, for the whole world! For, five years later, at a moment when God's people faced being wiped out at Haman's command, one night the king could not sleep, "and he gave orders to bring the book of memorable deeds, the chronicles ... And it was found written how Mordecai had told about Bigthan and Teresh ... who had sought to lay hands on King Ahasuerus" (Esther 6:1-2). The world would call that a coincidence. The believer knows it to be God's providence.

It is important that we do not try to interpret the events of our lives only in terms of their immediate impact or personal relevance. God's providences are seldom self-interpreting, and if we try to understand all that's going on solely in the immediacy of the moment, we will usually come to the wrong conclusion. We want answers to appear clearly and quickly and the resolutions to come *now*, but God calls us to cast our gaze on Him, trusting that His unfolding plan covers everything that is past, present, and future. We are to live and die in faith, believing that God will fulfill His purposes in every event, both big and small, both those we have dreamed of and those that feel like nightmares.

It is justifiable to wonder what God is doing in your life and in this world. You probably will not get the right answer, though, by trying to analyze things within the frame of your life itself, in terms of the here and now. What God is doing with you, in you, through you, and for you is almost certainly something far more significant than anything you can see. God is a covenant-keeping God who is sovereign over all the details of your life. That is the truth and hope on which to stand.

PROVERBS 16:1-9

JULY 26

GOD IS NOT MOCKED

"After these things King Ahasuerus promoted Haman the Agagite, the son of Hammedatha, and advanced him and set his throne above all the officials who were with him. And all the king's servants who were at the king's gate bowed down and paid homage to Haman, for the king had so commanded concerning him. But Mordecai did not bow down or pay homage." ESTHER 3:1-2

Nothing written in the Bible is accidental or irrelevant. The writer of Esther, for example, introduces Haman to us as "the Agagite, the son of Hammedatha." That description is reinforced later on with the added emphasis "the enemy of the Jews" (Esther 3:10). When such repetition occurs, we should recognize that the writer wants us to understand a piece of information as significant. Some biblical background will help us appreciate the importance of this particular description of Haman.

After leaving Egypt, God's people had been advancing toward Sinai when Amalek came and fought with them. We read that "Joshua overwhelmed Amalek and his people with the sword. Then the LORD said to Moses, 'Write this as a memorial in a book and recite it in the ears of Joshua, that I will utterly blot out the memory of Amalek from under heaven'" (Exodus 17:13-14).

Later, when Saul was made king of Israel, he was given a charge by God to destroy the Amalekites, their king Agag, and all that they had (1 Samuel 15:2-3). In other words, Saul was to enact the judgment of God on those who had lived in active opposition to Him and His people for centuries, refusing to repent. Yet despite the clarity of God's command, "Saul and the people spared Agag ... and all that was good, and would not utterly destroy them" (v 9). Saul later confessed to Samuel, "I have transgressed the commandment of the LORD and your words, because I feared the people and obeyed their voice" (v 24).

In the Persia of the 5th century BC, power resided in the hands of Haman—and the writer wants us to understand that he was "the Agagite," a descendant of Agag. Not only that but Mordecai's grandfather was a "son of Kish" (Esther 2:5). Kish was Saul's father. Mordecai, then, was a Jew whose lineage was connected to Saul, the king who had decided that God's word didn't really matter. As a result of Saul's decision, an old conflict was allowed to keep simmering, and then bubbled up and boiled over as Haman sought to destroy all the Jews (3:6). Mordecai is confronted by the evil of an Agagite who shouldn't exist—but who does exist because of the disobedience of Saul, Mordecai's own ancestor.

God is not mocked when He gives His commands, issues His warnings, and says what He wants done. Failure to obey God always has ramifications. When we listen to the suggestions of others rather than to the directions of God, we will live with the implications for ourselves, and so will those who love us and those who live within our sphere of influence. The wisdom of God is vaster than the wisdom of man. Be quick, then, to obey God's command, that you may live in the blessing of obedience and not store up trouble for yourself or those who follow you.

DEUTERONOMY 11:18-32

JULY 27

DESTRUCTION AND DELIVERANCE

"When Haman saw that Mordecai did not bow down or pay homage to him, Haman was filled with fury. But he disdained to lay hands on Mordecai alone. So, as they had made known to him the people of Mordecai, Haman sought to destroy all the Jews, the people of Mordecai, throughout the whole kingdom of Ahasuerus."
ESTHER 3:5-6

It has been observed that no proud man ever received the respect and regard which he thought was due to him. Such was the case for Haman. It wasn't sufficient for him to have everyone else treating him with reverence when there was a Jew named Mordecai who refused to. Haman's fury was clearly over the top. He had a problem with Mordecai, but his anger was such that even the man's death would not be enough for him. Every one of that man's people also had to be destroyed.

How does one Jew saying "no" result in a desire to destroy the entire Jewish community? Haman's conniving, malicious pursuits represented the activities of his spiritual father, the Evil One (John 8:44). Satan understood that the Deliverer-King, the serpent-crusher promised in Genesis 3:15, would come from the Jews, the descendants of Abraham, and so he was committed to their destruction. This also explains Herod's overreaction centuries later in killing every male child under the age of two (Matthew 2:16). These weren't just the frenzied actions of desperate men; they were Satan's attempts to obliterate the Messiah.

When Haman went to the king with his plot, the king (who made decisions based solely on what pleased him in the moment) was easily manipulated, and the edict was written (Esther 3:8-11). Significantly, it was given on the thirteenth day of the first month—the day before the celebration of the Passover (3:12; Leviticus 23:5). In the shadow of the news of this pogrom that was due to descend on them in twelve months' time, the people of God gathered to remember God's miraculous intervention when they were in an impossible situation in the bondage of Egypt. The edict of Haman pronounced that their destruction was inevitable—yet the terror they faced was an occasion for them to look to Him who had promised that He would keep them to the end. Would they act in mistrust and fear, or faith?

The people of God would eventually discover that the very means planned for their destruction was the means God would use for their deliverance (Esther 7:9-10). This points us forward to the cross of Jesus, where the method by which the Evil One sought to destroy God's purposes was the means God used for the great victory Christ achieved.

At times you may live in the grip of fear because you are in what seems to be an impossible situation. When you do, remember this: "The name of the Lord is a strong tower; the righteous man runs into it and is safe" (Proverbs 18:10). There is not one promise that God has made that He will not keep, whatever the Evil One may seek to do. You can rest in the confidence that comes from knowing that God's word and promises will never pass away, and that the darkest moments are often used by God to bring His greatest victories.

PSALM 7

Bible Through The Year: Psalms 43–45; Acts 19:1-20

JULY 28

FREE TO MOURN

"When Mordecai learned all that had been done, Mordecai tore his clothes and put on sackcloth and ashes, and went out into the midst of the city, and he cried out with a loud and bitter cry. He went up to the entrance of the king's gate, for no one was allowed to enter the king's gate clothed in sackcloth." ESTHER 4:1-2

The outfit these verses describe Mordecai wearing wasn't a fashion statement but a means of conveying the grief which had engulfed his heart. Throughout the Old Testament, tearing clothes and wearing sackcloth and ashes was a common way to publicly display mourning, agitation, and consternation (Job 1:20; Jonah 3:6-9).

This anguish was especially personal to Mordecai because he carried the burden of knowing his people were about to be exterminated on account of his refusal to bow before Haman (Esther 3:2-6). He had done what he thought was right, and he had to leave the rest to God. But that did not mean he glibly walked about, singing of God's providence. No, Mordecai headed for the middle of the city, wailing bitterly. It's a sad picture, and one replicated throughout the provinces as the news spread and others reacted similarly (4:3).

As he cried and mourned, the king's gate was as close to the throne as Mordecai dared to go. If he had gone any closer, he would have been a dead man. Kings generally don't like it when people are grieved by their decrees. At times, we have a similar disdain for sadness within the church. Perhaps you have even heard it said that solid, faithful, believing souls never feel the need to lie on the ground, wail, or mourn. This is an error, foisted foolishly upon believers and owing far more to self-help books than to God's word.

George Lawson writes that "the faith of God's people does not interfere with the exercise of affections suited to mournful dispensations of providence."[61] These "mournful dispensations of providence"—tragedies that take your spouse when you want her to stay living with you, that take your child when you expect him to grow old, that take your health or your security or your dreams—bring with them a tumult of emotion. And we see in Mordecai an honest and understandable reaction which sets many of us free to do the same: to feel and acknowledge and communicate our emotions in a godly way, rather than to suppress or ignore them.

A trust in God and a commitment to the understanding that He overrules everything for the praise of His glory and will bring everything underneath the rule of Christ does not rule out lament over the sinfulness and brokenness of this world. It is legitimate and even good for us to express deep sadness, lament, inquiry, discouragement, disappointment, fearfulness, and faintheartedness when our path leads us through difficulty. As you face such emotions, cry out to God. He does not forsake His people. He does not sneer at your pain or disdain your tears. Indeed, "the LORD is near to the brokenhearted" (Psalm 34:18).

PSALM 34

61 George Lawson, *Discourses on the Whole Book of Esther* (Edinburgh, 1809), p 112.

JULY 29

CALLED TO ACTION

"Mordecai told him all that had happened to him, and the exact sum of money that Haman had promised to pay into the king's treasuries for the destruction of the Jews. Mordecai also gave him a copy of the written decree issued in Susa for their destruction, that he might show it to Esther and explain it to her and command her to go to the king to beg his favor and plead with him on behalf of her people." ESTHER 4:7-8

Mordecai regularly walked up and down the streets outside the entrance to King Ahasuerus's gate in order that he might pick up snippets of information and hear the latest news. What he heard on the day described in these verses, however, was irregularly distressing: the Persian Empire was about to drive the Jewish people to extinction.

His cousin, Queen Esther, wasn't around the city gates. She was isolated in her palace and had no clue about what was going on. When the news reached her that the Jews, including Mordecai, were mourning, fasting, and weeping, she responded with compassion, but she was in the dark as to the nature of the problem (Esther 4:3-5).

Though one understood the gravity of the situation and the other was at this point unaware, both Mordecai and Esther were confronted with weighty questions. How was a man like Mordecai to hold the line as both a believer in God *and* a significant subject of the king? Was he helpless against the tyranny of the Persian Empire, or could he make a difference and change the course of events? How was Esther, who had been taken into the king's bed, to navigate the fact that she had a Persian name *and* a Jewish name? Would she identify with God's people? Or would she choose to live in the splendid isolation that was afforded her in the palace?

Ultimately, Mordecai did not just sit back. He attracted the attention of Esther's companions and helped her to understand what was happening—and the role she could play. Esther chose to sacrifice her comfort, and possibly her life, to risk intervening on behalf of God's people. Both understood that the providence and sovereignty of God do not relieve believers of their responsibility to do what is right and use whatever influence they have on behalf of His people.

As people believing in God's providence, then, how should we live in a world that is opposed to the gospel? At times, we may feel that we are helpless to effect any change in a culture that seeks to undercut our faith. We may also simply prefer the comfort of naivety, isolating ourselves from society by talking only with other believers, reading only Christian books, and watching only "faith-based" movies or TV shows. But God's providence doesn't call for inactivity. It calls for *activity*. For God's providence is often worked out through the bravery of His people, through their refusal to cease striving for what is right and good. Today, as you read your Bible, seek to understand how it relates to the current events of your world. And ask God's Spirit to show you how He might be calling you to step out in faith, take risks, and speak up, for the sake of the gospel and the people of God.

MARK 6:14-29

JULY 30

LEAVING THE SHADOWLANDS

"Mordecai also gave him a copy of the written decree issued in Susa for their destruction, that he might show it to Esther and explain it to her and command her to go to the king to beg his favor and plead with him on behalf of her people." ESTHER 4:8

"Her people." The secret was out. Esther was the woman who won the beauty pageant, became queen to the most powerful king in the known world, and kept her true identity concealed for years. Yet if no one had known before, Hathach the eunuch now knew that the queen was a Jew. She and her family were included in the edict of extermination. Esther's identity had been flushed out, not as a result of God intervening with a burning bush, a miraculous sign, or a dramatic voice from heaven but by a message from her cousin.

The queen was confronted with a situation that called for her to leave the shadowlands behind and reveal who she was, what she believed, and to whom she belonged. In her private world she knew she was a Jew, part of the covenant family of God, but she had been living in a public world where that fact remained undisclosed. Privately she had one identity, but publicly she had another—and now circumstances had brought her to the moment when she would have to determine who she would be. Was her identity primarily in being a queen of Persia or in being a woman of God?

Some of us are confronted by that very same predicament: we've got a private little world, we believe the gospel in our hearts, and we're in church on a Sunday, but there's no one in our office, on our streets, or anywhere around us who knows. And then the moment comes when private and public cannot be kept apart: a note from a friend, a call from your mom, a conversation with your business colleague, or a seemingly random interaction brings you to a moment when you must choose which side of the fence you will live on. The ancient words of Joshua challenge you: "Choose this day whom you will serve" (Joshua 24:15). For ultimately, a private faith that never reveals itself publicly is not a true and living faith at all. If our allegiance to King Jesus is real, it must be public.

So perhaps this verse and this page bring you to your moment of challenge. Perhaps today you find yourself in the shadowlands between two worlds, and you know that you are being challenged to declare boldly, in the place where you have been keeping it private, "This is who I am, this is where I belong, and this is what I believe." Will you do that? God is worthy of nothing less than your full, open devotion.

ACTS 5:17-42

JULY 31

BRINGING OUT THE BEST IN PEOPLE

"Then Esther spoke to Hathach and commanded him to go to Mordecai and say, 'All the king's servants and the people of the king's provinces know that if any man or woman goes to the king inside the inner court without being called, there is but one law—to be put to death, except the one to whom the king holds out the golden scepter so that he may live. But as for me, I have not been called to come in to the king these thirty days.'" ESTHER 4:10-11

Mordecai had made a big request of Esther: "to go to the king to beg his favor and plead with him on behalf of her people" (Esther 4:8). Esther basically responded, *That's easy for you to say! You're not the one doing this!* Many of us respond similarly when there is some great drama before us, adventure awaiting us, or challenge confronting us. We tend to put on the brakes and insist, "Let's not get carried away. Let's use our minds and be sensible."

It was risky for Esther to do what Mordecai was asking of her. The likelihood of Esther losing her head was significant. The only chance of pulling off such a scheme was if the king indicated his approval by holding out his golden scepter—and Esther was not hopeful. She didn't feel she had special access or leverage to go in uninvited, as she had recently slipped down the list of the king's desirables.

Esther recognized that Mordecai and the Jewish people had a major problem, but, at least at first, she didn't see herself included in that problem. She was not going to play the beauty card or the queen card. Frankly, she didn't want to play *any* card. The cost of getting involved was too great.

We can be encouraged by the faintheartedness of Esther. When the word of Haman's plot reached her, she was not enthusiastic about taking the initiative on behalf of God's people. If we're honest, we see our own hearts in her response. Most of us are reluctant to step up and to put our reputations or comforts or incomes (let alone our lives) in jeopardy for the living God and for His people. We tend to echo Esther's instinctive reaction: "I'm not doing *that*. I'm not going *there*."

Nevertheless, God didn't set Esther aside. Esther would go to the king, and Esther would be the means by which God's people would be saved. God brings the best out of people in order to achieve His purposes, even when we say no at the outset. It's remarkable! Be encouraged, then, to go and do what you know God is asking of you, even when—indeed, *especially* when—you feel fainthearted.

ACTS 1:4-11

AUGUST 1

SERVE WHERE HE HAS PLACED YOU

"Do not think to yourself that in the king's palace you will escape any more than all the other Jews. For if you keep silent at this time, relief and deliverance will rise for the Jews from another place, but you and your father's house will perish. And who knows whether you have not come to the kingdom for such a time as this?" ESTHER 4:13-14

When Esther hesitated to speak to King Ahasuerus about Haman's plot against the Jews, Mordecai's response was, to quote one commentator, "grounded in the reality and necessity of God's intervention."[62] He knew that God would keep His covenant promise and could raise up someone else if Esther chose to keep silent. Yet Mordecai also asked Esther to consider whether God had placed her in the right place at the right time to act on behalf of her people. She had won the beauty pageant and become queen, but she hadn't been responsible for putting her nose on her face or determining the color of her eyes or the length of her legs. God had done all of that. Mordecai didn't claim certain inside knowledge of the will of God, but he did realize that God had put Esther in a unique position and that He may well have done so for a unique purpose.

Although it may not always feel like it, God has also put each of us in a unique position for a unique purpose. He has us exactly where He wants us, positioned perfectly for "good works, which God prepared beforehand" (Ephesians 2:10). So, instead of wishing for a new job, location, or abilities so that we can get on with our own big, overarching plan, we need to recognize that God's plan may very well involve simply doing what we're already doing, to His glory.

There is no ideal place in which to serve God except the place where He has set you down—wherever it is. Such a perspective transforms sweeping a floor into divine activity. You may not be a queen like Esther, but your role matters. That's a tremendous liberation from the fear that life is happening somewhere else, and a tremendous motivation to get on with obeying God here and now! Wherever God has placed you, respond today in obedience to His foreordained purposes. As you go to your office, to your school, or throughout your town, neighborhood, or city, let the words of this hymn become your prayer:

Forth in Thy name, O Lord, I go,
My daily labor to pursue,
Thee, only Thee, resolved to know
In all I think, or speak, or do.
The task Thy wisdom hath assigned
O let me cheerfully fulfill,
In all my works Thy presence find,
And prove Thy good and perfect will.[63]

1 CORINTHIANS 7:25-35

62 Iain M. Duguid, *Esther and Ruth*, Reformed Expository Commentary, ed. Richard D. Phillips and Philip Graham Ryken (P&R, 2005), p 49-50.

63 Charles Wesley, "Forth in Thy Name, O Lord" (1749).

AUGUST 2

NO GOOD APART FROM GOD

"Preserve me, O God, for in you I take refuge. I say to the Lord, *'You are my Lord; I have no good apart from you.'"* PSALM 16:1-2

What do you treasure in this life? We all have something that brings us great delight or somewhere that just seems restful and right. Sometimes, though, we catch a glimpse of life without those earthly pleasures. Maybe it's illness or even bereavement that clarifies things for us. What kind of car you drive away from the hospital when you find out that your loved one has been diagnosed with malignant cancer doesn't matter, does it? The same goes for your clothes, your jewelry, your gadgets, your house—all of a sudden, they're not nearly as important as they once seemed.

We can and should enjoy what God has graciously given us. He "richly provides us with everything to enjoy" (1 Timothy 6:17). It's not that the good things of the earth are bad. But what we have in God is so delightful, so rich, that coming to know Him is like discovering a treasure hidden in a field. That treasure so enraptures us that in our joy, we do whatever it takes to get that field and the delights it contains (Matthew 13:44).

Without the treasure we have in God, as Psalm 16 tells us, we ultimately have no other good. When we sit down to a bowl of cereal or oatmeal or whatever breakfast may be, in our minds we ought to be saying, *Apart from You, Lord, I have no good thing. You're the one that made the grain to grow. You're the one who provides my food.* When we get up and walk out of the door, and have health and strength to do so, who makes it possible for us to walk? When we lie on our beds at night and we can enter into the rest of the evening, who makes it possible?

You have no ability even to see these letters, to hold up this book, or to comprehend what you are reading apart from the enabling grace of God. Only He can preserve and sustain us. Only God gives to us "life and breath and everything" (Acts 17:25). In the end, we have no good apart from Him—but He has more than enough goodness to go around. He is the source of all our treasures—and He is Himself our greater treasure. When you see Him as He truly is, your natural response will be to make Him the center of your life, around which revolve your thoughts, decisions, feelings, and actions. That is, you will say to Him, "You are my Lord," for in His presence "there is fullness of joy," and at His right hand are "pleasures forevermore" (Psalm 16:11). Where else would you possibly prefer to take refuge, and what else would you treasure more than Him?

MATTHEW 13:44-46

AUGUST 3

AN ATTITUDE LIKE CHRIST'S

"Do nothing from selfish ambition or conceit, but in humility count others more significant than yourselves. Let each of you look not only to his own interests, but also to the interests of others. Have this mind among yourselves, which is yours in Christ Jesus." PHILIPPIANS 2:3-5

Misplaced words and unkind glances have great potential to cause division. We all know how easy it is for friendships to be torn apart through such seemingly minor offenses. But if we trace the problem to its root, we'll discover that at the center of our disunity is the ugliness of pride and the exaltation of self. How easily we say, "If she thinks I'm going to apologize, she's got to be crazy! If he wants me to say I'm sorry, he's going to have to do something first. I didn't start it; therefore, I don't need to end it."

When Paul wrote to the Christians in Philippi, he was concerned about their attitudes. He wanted to make sure that they would have harmonious relationships and tender hearts toward one another. It was important for them as a church family to enjoy unity of heart, mind, and purpose, particularly as they came under pressure from their culture to renounce Christ or compromise on their obedience to Him.

In seeking to instill a spirit of unity among these Philippian believers, Paul didn't give them something like "seven principles on establishing unity." Rather, he pointed them to the element that is foundational to all harmonious relationships: humility. And what better way to illustrate true humility than to turn their gaze to the Lord Jesus Christ! Paul knew that if only they would consider Jesus, they would see that His humble attitude was the very example and pattern that needed to pervade their minds and their relationships.

Within the church, our prayer should be that people will look at our relationships and say, "There is such a sense of unity and harmony among these people! It seems that they are all for Christ and that they are all for one another. There is a Christlike attitude about them. I wonder how they came to be that way?"

We don't muster up humility from our own resources; we depend upon the Holy Spirit to enable us to be humble as He conforms us to the image of Christ. Read Paul's words to the Philippians and take them to heart, fixing your eyes on your Savior. Reflect on the selfless incarnation and obedient death of the Lord Jesus Christ, and all your selfishness and pride will begin to look so dreadfully ugly. You cannot think about Jesus and simultaneously excuse your self-centeredness. So, look at Christ! There die all your selfish aspirations.

PHILIPPIANS 2:1-6

AUGUST 4

GENUINE SERVICE

"The one who has the bride is the bridegroom. The friend of the bridegroom, who stands and hears him, rejoices greatly at the bridegroom's voice. Therefore this joy of mine is now complete. He must increase, but I must decrease."
JOHN 3:29-30

There are people who claim to be experts at reading body language. They can discern what is being communicated in the ways others position their bodies and hands and by the facial expressions they make. This could be a useful skill, especially for knowing—or at least coming close to knowing—whether someone is being genuine or false.

There are ways, though, that Christians can conduct themselves with inauthenticity that cannot be read by people fluent in body language. It's a sad fact that different motivations drive people to serve in the name of Christ. Some people serve not out of genuine interest in the well-being of others but with self-interest leading the way. They may want to be noticed. They may crave a pat on the back. They may be pursuing a good reputation. Such a motivation may lead to good things being done, but it doesn't produce genuine service. Christian service, in other words, can be fake. From a distance, it looks like the real thing, but get up close and you find it to be wanting.

So how do we know what is authentic? Here are two signs of a genuine heart of service for us to look for in ourselves, as well as in others.

First is the willingness to serve in anonymity. This is the kind of service that delights in doing good regardless of any attention. "Among those born of women none is greater than John," said Jesus Himself (Luke 7:28)—and yet the Baptist longed to see Christ glorified at his own expense, a passion articulated so memorably when he confessed, "He must increase, but I must decrease."

Second is the existence of sincerity. The apostle Paul affirmed that his friend Timothy, for example, was "genuinely concerned" for the Philippians' welfare, unlike those who "seek their own interests" (Philippians 2:20-21). Epaphroditus, too, was "longing for" the good of the Philippian church (v 26). Such longing cannot be faked but arises out of genuine love.

Many years ago, one preacher declared that he was "content to be God's errand boy." Could you say that with integrity? Do you delight in decreasing if that means Christ's glory will increase? Do you have real concern—longing, even—for the good of others? Those around us may not be able to tell what motivates us, but we can be sure that the Savior we claim to serve most certainly can.

Perhaps this is a good opportunity to prayerfully consider the example of Paul, who said, "I do not account my life of any value nor as precious to myself, if only I may finish my course and the ministry that I received from the Lord Jesus" (Acts 20:24). Ask God for the grace to echo these words with sincerity. Who knows what He might do with a life that you have fully surrendered to Him?

1 CORINTHIANS 3:5-15

AUGUST 5

SERVING THE SOVEREIGN

"To whom then will you liken God, or what likeness compare with him? ... It is he who sits above the circle of the earth, and its inhabitants are like grasshoppers; who stretches out the heavens like a curtain, and spreads them like a tent to dwell in; who brings princes to nothing, and makes the rulers of the earth as emptiness." ISAIAH 40:18, 22-23

What ought to be the Christian's relationship to authority?

On the one hand, we ought not to despise human authority because we recognize that God is behind its establishment. We would have to remove large portions of Scripture to come close to the idea that the Bible is a revolutionary tract undermining rulers. Yet, on the other hand, we also understand that no human authority has ultimate or permanent authority. God ordains the rise of leaders and He also orchestrates their demise. No matter how powerful they seem in a moment, for a season, or even during a lifetime, within a relatively short time their power will be gone and in almost every case the world will remember them no more.

We must remember whom we ultimately serve—the sovereign God to whom all other rulers are "grasshoppers." Therefore, when the authority of man seeks to oppose the authority of God, we are to ask, along with the apostles, "whether it is right in the sight of God to listen to [rulers] rather than to God" (Acts 4:19)—and we are to answer as they did.

In Acts 4, the apostles spend a night in prison after healing a lame man. When they are released, they gather with the other believers and regain true perspective by remembering that they serve the sovereign Lord, the Creator of the earth, sea, and everything in it (Acts 4:24-26). Applying this truth, they then recognize that though they are under subjugation by the Roman authorities and facing the persecution of the Jewish religious establishment, these leaders are only doing what God's "hand and ... plan had predestined to take place" (v 28), while they have been commissioned to preach the good news to the ends of the earth by the ascended King, Jesus Himself. With that perspective, they continue to share the gospel boldly and openly.

Can the same be said of us in our age? Will we obey God and share Christ even if those who wield earthly power over us are commanding us to silence or compromise?

What is it that silences us? One answer is surely how quick we are to forget that God is sovereign and that the nations and rulers of the world are under His authority. Having forgotten that, we succumb to a political correctness which makes us increasingly fearful of telling anybody that Jesus Christ is the only Savior. So, have you lost sight of Jesus' kingly rule and reign? Do those who are ultimately grasshoppers to your Lord loom too large in your view of who to listen to and how to live? Then join the early believers in remembering, recognizing, and proclaiming the truths that God is the incomparable Creator of everything and that ultimate authority belongs to Him.

DANIEL 6:1-28

AUGUST 6

THE ATTITUDE THAT FOSTERS UNITY

"Have this mind among yourselves, which is yours in Christ Jesus, who, though he was in the form of God, did not count equality with God a thing to be grasped, but emptied himself, by taking the form of a servant, being born in the likeness of men. And being found in human form, he humbled himself by becoming obedient to the point of death, even death on a cross." PHILIPPIANS 2:5-8

A church is—or should be—a collection of very different people, with different backgrounds, personalities, and experiences. Yet we are also "all one in Christ Jesus" (Galatians 3:28). If that truth is to be an experiential reality rather than a mere slogan, it is vitally important that we pay attention to what the Bible has to say concerning the kind of attitude that will foster unity. Fundamentally, Paul shows us, harmony is won through focusing our attention on the humility of the Son of God.

Paul provides us with the theological underpinnings that will give rise to humility by telling us how Jesus humbled Himself: "Have this mind among yourselves, which is yours in Christ Jesus, who, though he was in the form of God..." Jesus is eternally, totally God. There was never a time when He was not God. By starting here, Paul makes the extent of Christ's humility most apparent. For, although Jesus is fully God, He "did not count equality with God a thing to be grasped." "The highest place that heav'n affords is His by sovereign right,"[64] but He had a greater priority than His own uninterrupted glory: to deliberately and voluntarily set aside the prerogatives which were His as God's equal. Not only that, but Jesus further humbled Himself by making Himself nothing. He did so not by the subtraction of divinity but by the addition of humanity, "taking the form of a servant, being born in the likeness of men." He became as much an earthly servant as He had been the heavenly sovereign.

But even then, His humiliation was not yet complete. He further humbled Himself by "becoming obedient to the point of death, even death on a cross." He chose to be born as a baby, to live as a man, to suffer as an outcast, and to die as a criminal. He exchanged the homage of angels for the hatred of men. Do you realize how distinctive this is in the panorama of world religions? There is nothing like this anywhere else!

At first sight, these details of Jesus' humility may appear to constitute nothing other than impractical, arms-length theology. In fact, though, His humility is transformative for our everyday attitudes and actions within our church families. For, as we see this amazing and unfathomable reality of the Creator of the universe coming down to this world, taking the same humanity that we have, walking with us, and hitting the dusty earth, all for us, we see how we are called to view our fellow believers. "Have this mind among yourselves," God's word commands us. How can you look to the needs of others? How can you think more of them than of yourself? How will that mindset inform the prayers and practical details of your day?

JAMES 2:1-5

64 Thomas Kelly, "The Head That Once Was Crowned with Thorns" (1820).

AUGUST 7

THE WEIGHT OF GLORY

"As soon as he mentioned the ark of God, Eli fell over backward from his seat by the side of the gate, and his neck was broken and he died, for the man was old and heavy. He had judged Israel forty years." 1 SAMUEL 4:18

Not many places in the Bible mention somebody's weight! This verse, then, ought to give us pause as we consider its significance. It may seem that Eli's heaviness is mentioned simply to explain the physical reality of his death. But it's actually more than that.

Earlier, in 1 Samuel 2:12-17, the narrator tells us that Eli's sons had a custom of using a three-pronged fork to dig into the meat offered for sacrifice in order to take a portion for themselves and their family from the meat that belonged to God. They despised the tabernacle—the place that God had appointed for His own dwelling place among His people—deciding that their own earthly longings and selfish preoccupations took precedence over His glory. In one sense, God's glory had been stolen and wrapped around Eli's belly (v 29). His girth was a physical expression of the sin being perpetrated and promoted by the priests at Shiloh.

This is clearer in the writer's original Hebrew, where the word for "heavy" is transliterated *kabed*. It is the verbal form of the word *kabod*, which is translated "glory." The writer is making a play on words, showing that when those who are fastened on themselves and their own significance seek to rob God of His glory, they treat Him as if He is light and may be manipulated. And so, regarding themselves as heavy, they look to take precedence in everything.

Nevertheless, the sun eventually set—or rather events came crashing down—on Eli's life, and he died miserably. He is now one of several individuals in the Bible, particularly in the realm of priestly or pastoral function, who stand as warnings against the presumptuousness captured by Paul's words: "Let anyone who thinks that he stands take heed lest he fall" (1 Corinthians 10:12).

This wisdom is not only for individuals who believe themselves to be unassailable—though it certainly is for them. It is also a striking warning to every assembly of God's people. Let us hate the thought that in our churches we might ever take from the glory that God deserves in order to serve, enrich, or enjoy ourselves. This Sunday, as you head to your church, remember that you are there first and foremost not for yourself but to glorify your majestic, transcendent, glorious Lord and encourage His people.

1 CHRONICLES 16:8-34

AUGUST 8

THE SOURCE OF TRUE WORSHIP

"He said, 'Lord, I believe,' and he worshiped him." JOHN 9:38

When he was first found by Jesus, the blind beggar in John 9 had been helpless and hopeless. Then he had become the object of God's supernatural intervention and had had his sight restored. As a result, his life had become both better and harder; for, as a result of having his sight restored by the Lord, he was denied the support of his parents, challenged by the Pharisees, reviled for his faith, and finally cast out of the synagogue. But when Jesus found and spoke with him, those losses paled in comparison to the one whom he had gained; and so he fell down at his Savior's feet in devoted worship.

The picture at the outset of John 9 is of a man lost in hopelessness and helplessness. Yet the chapter ends with this man as he will always and forever be: a worshiper of Christ, the Messiah, the Savior, the King.

This man is actually a fulfillment of the statement that Jesus made earlier to another person that He'd sought out—the woman at the well. Jesus had told her, "The hour is coming, and is now here, when the true worshipers will worship the Father in spirit and truth, for the Father is seeking such people to worship him" (John 4:23). The blind beggar had been sought out by Jesus, his sight had been restored, his mind had been taught, and his life had been transformed. And what did he become with what he had been given? A worshiper!

Absence of worship comes from absence of faith. The blind beggar said, "Lord, I believe," and then he worshiped. If you are not a worshiper, you won't make yourself one by trying extra hard. Instead, check to see whether you are a believer! If you've come to believe that the Father accepted the sufferings of Christ as the sin offering for all who trust in Him, then you will understand why it is that the man cast himself before Jesus. We are not talking about a style of worship or how well we sing; if you are in Christ, worship is a reflex action, and praise is a genuine reality that permeates every facet of your life.

Men and women who throw themselves down at the feet of Christ do so because they understand who Jesus is, why He came, and what He has done for them. Christ-exalting praise is *not* all about us and the songs we want to sing; it's all about God and giving glory to His name.

Has your love for God grown cold? Is praise and worship a burden for you rather than a delight? When those feelings creep in, the only remedy is to fix your eyes on Christ. Remind yourself afresh of His finished work on the cross, and you, like the blind beggar, will overflow with worship for Christ.

MARK 10:46-52

AUGUST 9

WORK OUT YOUR SALVATION

"Therefore, my beloved, as you have always obeyed, so now, not only as in my presence but much more in my absence, work out your own salvation with fear and trembling." PHILIPPIANS 2:12

Every parent knows what happens when a child receives a gift that comes with a lengthy set of instructions. There the child sits, staring at the pages, trying to discern how to put the thing together. At that moment, the gift has been received; now the thing is to work out what to do with it.

When we come to faith in Jesus Christ, we receive salvation as a gift—and then we spend the rest of our lives learning by God's word what to do with it: how to live as new creations. At times, we wish it were an instantaneous transformation, in which everything would become immediately apparent to us. But that is not how God designed it. Instead, the Christian life is a joyful—and at times painful—voyage of discovery.

And so Paul exhorts us to "work out" our salvation. He is not saying that we are to work *for* our salvation. He is not thinking of good works that we must contribute to gain or maintain salvation but about how we are to respond to the salvation that is already ours in Christ. He is not telling us how to *be* saved people but how to *live as* saved people. Once we understand that, we are in a position to act upon Paul's instruction.

The call to work out our salvation is a call to consistency. Just as we called on the name of the Lord to save us at the start of our Christian lives, so we must continue to call on His name. This takes very ordinary, practical forms in our lives. We continue to come before God in prayer. We continue to gather with fellow believers for worship. We continue to hear from Him in Scripture. We continue to strive to walk in His grace, putting sin to death and growing in spiritual fruit. We work at the Christian life, for we remember that no one matures as a believer by accident.

It is all too common for professing Christians to live however they please six days a week and then to go to church on Sunday to feel better about themselves; or to live obediently in most areas of their lives but reserve one or two for themselves and hold back from placing them under Jesus' lordship. That is not the Christian life. God's grace is not meant to free us to live however we please but to fuel consistent lives of godly character. Grace doesn't relieve us of our responsibility to be obedient; it actually makes our obedience possible. And so it's by this very grace, and in response to the gift of salvation God has given us in Christ, that we work out our salvation, for our everlasting joy and for His eternal glory. Today, you do not need to work *on* your salvation—Christ's finished work has already secured it for you. But today, you are called to work *out* your salvation, so that it shapes you more and more.

COLOSSIANS 2:6-7

AUGUST 10

ALL IN THE FAMILY

"One who heard us was a woman named Lydia, from the city of Thyatira, a seller of purple goods, who was a worshiper of God. The Lord opened her heart to pay attention to what was said by Paul. And after she was baptized, and her household as well, she urged us, saying, 'If you have judged me to be faithful to the Lord, come to my house and stay.' And she prevailed upon us." ACTS 16:14-15

When God redeems someone, He brings him or her into a relationship not only with Himself but also with all the others who call on the Lord. How does He do this? Acts 16 gives us an example in Lydia.

Lydia appears to have been an upstanding lady. As "a worshiper of God," she had some religious interest, and as "a seller of purple goods" she was apparently an astute businesswoman. Her life probably seemed just fine as it was. And yet when she encountered the gospel, she moved from mere religious interest to a genuine relationship with Jesus Christ, which caused her to lovingly use her resources for her new spiritual family.

Here is the life-changing moment: "The Lord opened her heart to pay attention to what was said by Paul." That's it! That's the entire process: the Lord opened her heart to believe, and she believed. In that moment, Lydia joined God's family. And what's more, she immediately began to serve her brothers and sisters in Christ by opening up her home.

Lydia's story reminds us that what begins as an individual call to conversion should always move to participation in the family of God. Romans 8:15-16 points out that each of us is adopted by God upon our coming to him in faith, but it also notes that *together* "we are children of God." Our relationship with one another is founded in the fact that we have a relationship with Jesus, and our relationship with Jesus places us in relationship with one another.

Just as with a physical family, we don't get to choose our spiritual sisters or brothers. (If we're honest, we might like to put some of them back and try again—though, of course, they may say the same of us!) Your fellow church members are who they are based on God's sovereign choice. It is easy to dwell on our differences, but the most important aspect of God's family is not what distinguishes us from one another but what we share: that God has opened our hearts to receive the gospel and now calls us to worship and follow Him together.

If the Lord has opened your heart, then you belong to a new family. By no means is it a perfect family, and feuds and fallouts may happen. But Jesus still calls you to love your brothers and sisters, no matter your differences. After all, He loves them enough to have died for them. And so He calls you to place what you are and what you have in the service of this family. How will you use your time, your home, and your resources in such a way that love for one another increasingly becomes the distinguishing family trait in your church?

1 JOHN 3:11-18

AUGUST 11

A THRONE FOREVER

"Your house and your kingdom shall be made sure forever before me. Your throne shall be established forever." 2 SAMUEL 7:16

God made a covenant with David, promising that his kingdom would last forever. And yet after the reign of David's son Solomon, the kingdom was divided, and within a few hundred years both the northern kingdom and the southern kingdom were destroyed (2 Kings 17 and 25).

For those living in the generations of captivity that followed, God's promise to David must have seemed like a fairy tale. Their experience held no evidence of any great Israelite kingdom or king on the rise. Psalm 89, written during this time, begins with God's faithfulness but ends with the people's troubles: "Lord, where is your steadfast love of old, which by your faithfulness you swore to David? Remember, O Lord, how your servants are mocked, and how I bear in my heart the insults of all the many nations" (Psalm 89:49-50). Speaking into that context of distress and hopelessness, the prophets reminded the people, *Wait a minute! Though it doesn't look like God's promise is still in effect, you can be sure it is, because of His covenant love. There's more to come.* They spoke of the future:

For to us a child is born,
  to us a son is given;
and the government shall be upon his shoulder,
  and his name shall be called
Wonderful Counselor, Mighty God,
  Everlasting Father, Prince of Peace.
Of the increase of his government and of peace
  there will be no end,
on the throne of David and over his kingdom,
  to establish it and to uphold it
with justice and with righteousness
  from this time forth and forevermore.
The zeal of the Lord of hosts will do this. (Isaiah 9:6-7)

There was still, said the prophets, another place, another name, another rest, another kingdom, and another throne to come. The failures of God's people did not mean that God had forgotten His promise. It would all be fulfilled in Jesus.

History repeats itself. Whether because of disease, persecution, politics or grief, we will at times find ourselves in that place of confusion that Psalm 89 gives voice to. In such a time (which is really any time before Jesus returns), we need prophetic voices to remind us of God's covenant faithfulness—that our Lord reigns on His throne both now and forever. So today, take heart. Your failures do not mean that God has forgotten His promise. There is more to come.

PSALM 89

AUGUST 12

AS YOU HAVE ALWAYS OBEYED

"Now, not only as in my presence but much more in my absence, work out your own salvation with fear and trembling, for it is God who works in you, both to will and to work for his good pleasure." PHILIPPIANS 2:12-13

Every schoolteacher would love to have such authority over their class that the students are well-behaved not only when the teacher is present but also when they have walked out of the room and been gone some time. Not many teachers have been able to accomplish that! But it's an understandable desire.

That desire is similar to the one expressed by the apostle Paul when he wrote to the Philippian church, exhorting them to walk in obedience "not only as in my presence but much more in my absence." Paul's concern was not simply that these believers would listen to him but also that they would live in a way that was "worthy of the gospel of Christ" (Philippians 1:27). For Paul, a life worthy of the gospel meant a life marked by obedience to Christ. This was how believers were to "work out" their salvation "with fear and trembling."

The power of Paul's concern becomes clear when we consider the verses leading up to Philippians 2:12. He has just finished describing the humility and exaltation of the Son of God, who became a servant and took on human flesh. When He did this, Jesus "humbled himself by becoming obedient to the point of death, even death on a cross" (v 8). Our Savior had a mission to accomplish: the salvation of sinners. He was fully obedient to that mission, even unto death. And so, having shown them the amazing obedience of Jesus, Paul tells his readers likewise to continue in their own obedience.

They are to do so, he says, "with fear and trembling"—that is, with an understanding of the majesty of the God who has won them and who now works within them. Notions of obedience, fear, and trembling are unwelcome to humanity, but those who want to be identified with Christ are still called to pick up their own crosses and follow Him on the path of humility and obedience. This is not an optional extra in the Christian life; it is intrinsic to it. For a professing Christian to live in persistent and habitual disobedience is not only a sign of immaturity but an absolute absurdity. How can those who belong to our obedient Savior take the matter of obedience lightly?

We should remind ourselves daily that we are always visible. There is never a moment when any word, deed, thought, or motive is not seen by God. Beyond all expectation, despite the fact that God knows and sees us fully, we remain recipients of His love—but this does not lessen the reality that He knows us better than we know ourselves. So, with the fear and trembling which that reality should prompt, we are to take obedience seriously.

About which part (or parts) of your thoughts, your words, or your deeds is the Spirit telling you that you need to change, to obey? Do not forget who saved you and won you, and who it is who sees you and works in you.

MARK 9:2-7

AUGUST 13

NO-NAMES AND GOD'S PLAN

"When they came to the land of Zuph, Saul said to his servant who was with him, 'Come, let us go back, lest my father cease to care about the donkeys and become anxious about us.' But he said to him, 'Behold, there is a man of God in this city, and he is a man who is held in honor; all that he says comes true. So now let us go there. Perhaps he can tell us the way we should go.'" 1 SAMUEL 9:5-6

Saul, the future first king of Israel, had been with his servant for a few days, searching unsuccessfully for his father's missing donkeys. Saul was ready to "go back" home—but his servant was not quite ready to give up. Instead, he suggested they consult with the "man of God" to ask him to "tell us the way we should go." Saul agreed, and soon their search would lead to the encounter with the prophet Samuel in which Saul would be anointed king of Israel (1 Samuel 10:1-8).

We might think that the servant would have been the tired one advocating for a return trip home, while the future king would have proposed the visit to the prophet—yet the opposite was the case. The Bible gives the impression that this servant was sensitized to God's workings and was beginning to recognize that this search for donkeys was turning into something far more substantial.

How wonderful is this! Who was this servant? We don't even know his name. But he was hugely significant in God's unfolding plan.

Indeed, all through the Bible we see God using those who could have been considered insignificant by earthly standards but whose spiritual insight led to important changes. Second Kings 5:1–14, for instance, tells of a little girl who, when the Syrians raided Israel and carried off girls as slaves, was taken to live as a servant in the house of a leprous army commander named Naaman. There, she proved instrumental in Naaman's life, suggesting that he visit the prophet of Israel, Elisha. Eventually, this led to his miraculous healing. Hundreds of years later, it was to a young unmarried girl in an unremarkable provincial town that God gave the privilege of bearing His Son; and it was to shepherds far from the places of power and influence that He gave the task of being the first humans to broadcast the news that the Christ had been born.

For servants of the living God, stories like these remind us that it's not our names or our credentials that matter; it's the task to which God calls us, which He folds into His glorious, eternal purposes. Do not underestimate how a word of encouragement or exhortation or witness from your lips today might be used by our Lord in the unfolding of His purposes.

MARK 12:41-44

AUGUST 14

THE LORD OF ALL NATIONS

"The LORD roars from Zion and utters his voice from Jerusalem … 'I will send a fire upon the house of Hazael … I will break the gate-bar of Damascus.'"

AMOS 1:2, 4-5

The God of the Bible is the God of justice. He sees all, He knows all, and He promises to settle all accounts. This is wonderfully good news for God's people, who can rest knowing that no injustice we endure escapes His eye. As the psalmist writes, "God reigns over the nations; God sits on his holy throne" (Psalm 47:8). All will give account to Him for their conduct. These are truths made powerfully clear through the prophet Amos, through whom the Lord pronounced judgment on six nations.

In Amos 1:3 – 2:3, God begins His pronouncement with Syria and its capital, Damascus, which He says will face judgment for being ruthlessly cruel to the people they conquered. Then comes Gaza, who are involved in trafficking and slavery. Next is Tyre, who are also guilty of human trafficking. He turns then to the people of Edom, whose hatred and wrath condemn them. Next comes Ammon, whose lust for land has led them to barbaric violence. Last is Moab, guilty of cruel vengeance.

From these verses, we not only learn what God thinks of these specific ancient nations and their particular wicked actions; we can also draw conclusions about what He loves and hates more generally. We can be certain that God hates people made in His image being treated as things or property. We can be sure that God will not tolerate unmitigated hatred and violence, especially at the expense of the helpless. We can know that God will call to account those who value profit over people or who do not keep a pledged word.

God has not changed His mind on these matters since Amos declared them. The Lord still hates these sins and will call every nation and every person who proves guilty of them to account. So, when these deeds are committed against God's people, we can be certain that justice will be done. Justice will come in the course of history for some nations and individuals; it will come in eternity for all of them.

This is comforting news when we suffer; but it is also sobering news because we sin. We should ask ourselves whether any trace of these behaviors exists in our own hearts. We may not be guilty of acts of cruel violence or of land lust, but the hatred, anger, greed, selfishness, and pride that lead to such deeds may well find a place within us. It is always wise to ask the Lord to search us and mercifully reveal to us areas where sin remains. As God's people, we can do this not fearing judgment but knowing that our judgment has been endured for us at Calvary by the Lord Jesus Christ. God rules the nations, and God rules eternity. May He reign in your life as well, in how you confront the injustice in this world and repent of the injustice in your heart.

AMOS 2:6-8

AUGUST 15

FROM GRUMBLING TO GRATITUDE

"Do all things without grumbling or disputing, that you may be blameless and innocent, children of God without blemish in the midst of a crooked and twisted generation, among whom you shine as lights in the world." PHILIPPIANS 2:14-15

Ancient Israel had a lot of great moments—crossing the Red Sea, entering the promised land, the reign of King David, and many more. But the Israelites could also be a disaster. Think of what they did just after the exodus. They had seen the wonders of the Lord, had been redeemed from bondage in Egypt, and had been set free from tyranny and slavery. They of all people should have been marked by joy and gratitude. But not long after they left Egypt, the entire community grumbled about food and drink and complained about the leadership and motives of Moses and Aaron (Exodus 16:1-9). It was not a good look for God's people.

Centuries later, Paul wrote to God's people in Philippi to keep them from a similar failure, telling them to "do all things without grumbling." He wanted his readers to understand that the *manner* in which they did something was as vital as *what* they were actually doing. As for them, so for us: it is possible for us to do the right thing but to do it in a spirit that deprives us of joy and is detrimental to all who are around us.

Peter included a similar instruction in his own letters: "Show hospitality to one another without grumbling" (1 Peter 4:9). He could have left it at "Show hospitality to one another," and they (and we!) would have had an easier time keeping the instruction. But those words "without grumbling" show how much Peter understood human nature. God is not concerned with the mere performance of hospitality, or any other good deed, but with the disposition of our hearts as we carry it out.

We can think of all kinds of examples in our lives, can't we? Maybe you have a teenager in your home who does their chores with a less-than-happy heart. Perhaps you have a coworker who seemingly can only complete a task after complaining about it. Or maybe the example is you, silently grumbling about the life God has given you or the acts of service to which He has called you. The sad reality is that we are often more like the Israelites than we care to admit. We, too, forget the great salvation God has accomplished for us, and we, too, would rather determine the course of our lives than entrust ourselves to God. Yet Paul tells us that when we do things without grumbling, God is making us "blameless and innocent, children of God without blemish." Every time we resist the opportunity to grumble, it is evidence of God transforming us.

Today, recall the way God delivered you through the sea of your sin and condemnation, bringing you to the other side and the solid ground of salvation in Christ. You did not deserve it, nor did you achieve your redemption any more than Israel did. Then recognize ways in which you are going about your days with a grumble in your heart, and pray that God would so amaze you with His grace once more that your grumbling against Him would be displaced by a gratitude that praises Him.

PSALM 95

AUGUST 16

SWEET EBENEZERS

"Now, therefore, thus you shall say to my servant David, 'Thus says the LORD of hosts, I took you from the pasture, from following the sheep, that you should be prince over my people Israel. And I have been with you wherever you went and have cut off all your enemies from before you. And I will make for you a great name, like the name of the great ones of the earth.'" 2 SAMUEL 7:8-9

Reminders are vitally important. Again and again in the Scriptures, the word of God to His people is essentially that of Deuteronomy 6:12 and 8:11: "Take care lest you forget the LORD." When we fail to remember, our hearts go astray.

When King David and the kingdom of Israel were at rest, David had proposed to build a house for God—a finer place for the ark of the covenant to dwell than in a humble tent (2 Samuel 7:1-2). But David's ideas weren't part of God's plan (v 6). So instead of leaving David to think about what he might do for God, God sent the prophet Nathan to remind David of what God had done for him—and to reveal what God intended yet to do.

God had taken David from lowly shepherd to exalted king. That wasn't something that David himself had initiated; God had. Everywhere David had been, God had been with him. His enemies were now scattered and David was at rest because God's hand had been on him. David was being reminded, as he sat on the throne, of how far he had come from the field—and who had brought him so far. And in being reminded of this, he was also being assured that God would continue to lead him on. God had begun the process—and when God commits Himself to someone, He brings to completion the good work that He has begun (Philippians 1:6).

In a sense, David was being given an "Ebenezer moment": a reminder that God helps His people. Years previously, the prophet Samuel had given all the people a similar moment when he raised up a stone to remind them of the victories God had given Israel. He "called its name Ebenezer; for he said, 'Till now the LORD has helped us'" (1 Samuel 7:12).

Be careful not to forget how God has helped you. Take time today to remember and reflect on the purposes to which He has called you, His presence along the way, and the ways in which He has rescued and protected you. For as you do so, you will be reminded that the God who has helped you this far will assuredly continue to help you today and every day as He works to bring His good purposes to completion.

His love in time past forbids me to think
He'll leave me at last in trouble to sink;
Each sweet Ebenezer I have in review
Confirms His good pleasure to help me quite through.[65]

1 SAMUEL 7:3-17

65 John Newton, "Begone Unbelief" (1779).

WHERE TO FIND HAPPINESS

"Blessed is the man who walks not in the counsel of the wicked, nor stands in the way of sinners, nor sits in the seat of scoffers; but his delight is in the law of the LORD, *and on his law he meditates day and night."* PSALM 1:1-2

We might expect that by now men and women would have mastered the art of happiness. By now the subject ought to be obsolete, because everybody ought to know what happiness is and how to achieve it. But in fact the evidence points in the opposite direction. You only need to look at the news briefly to recognize that genuine happiness is in short supply.

The Bible concerns itself with our genuine happiness. The word that begins Psalm 1, translated as "blessed," may also be translated as "happy." Likewise, the very first word out of Jesus' mouth in his Sermon on the Mount was a form of the word *happiness*: *Happy,* he essentially said, *are the meek, the merciful, the peacemakers* (Matthew 5:3-11).

According to the opening verses of Psalm 1, one aspect of our happiness relates directly to how we think and how we see. Our thinking about reality shapes our lives, for better or for worse. Therefore, if we desire to live under the smile of God and enjoy the sort of blessed happiness that only He can provide, we must not embrace the godless thought patterns of our world. This "counsel of the wicked" refers to the aims of the ungodly—their maxims, principles, and ensuing patterns of behavior. Such worldly wisdom holds out the promise of happiness and blessing but in reality leaves us chasing the pot of gold at the end of the rainbow; we are ever searching but always coming up empty-handed. Happiness is found in refusing to chase after the wind even as the world calls you to do just that.

Yet the path toward lasting happiness isn't just one of rejecting deceitful counsel; it also involves embracing the beauty of truth. The happy person's "delight is in the law of the LORD." Reading and thinking about the word of God is presented to us not as a task or a duty but as a joy, a delight. Why? Because it leads us into deeper communion with its author: our Creator, Sustainer, and Savior. So, whatever fleeting pleasures this world presents to you, cling to God's word alone as that which can revive your soul (Psalm 19:7). Nothing else can bring true, sincere, lasting joy to your life.

MATTHEW 5:3-11

AUGUST 18

BRIGHT LIGHTS

"Do all things without grumbling or disputing, that you may be blameless and innocent, children of God without blemish in the midst of a crooked and twisted generation, among whom you shine as lights in the world, holding fast to the word of life, so that in the day of Christ I may be proud that I did not run in vain or labor in vain." PHILIPPIANS 2:14-16

We all know people who light up a room when they enter it—men and women who possess qualities that make them compelling and attractive. They lift our spirits. For reasons we can't always articulate, we enjoy being near them.

As Christians, we should strive to have a similar effect on those around us. This is not to say that we must try to morph into something that most of us are not and become the life of every party! Our endeavor as believers isn't about personality, charisma, or a sense of humor. It's about moral purity. This is what Jesus was getting at when He told His disciples that they were "the light of the world": they were to live so that people would see their good works and glorify God (Matthew 5:14-16). This is also what Paul had in mind when he told his Philippian friends that they were to "shine as lights in the world" in the midst of "a crooked and twisted generation." The character of Christian people, in other words, ought to be not only observable but also radiant.

As the people of God, we gather to worship the living God, to be edified by His word and strengthened in His grace—but not so that we might then go home and keep quiet! When the effect of our Christianity stops at the door of the church building, it is of little use to anyone. We step out from corporate worship into a world that is dark and confused in innumerable ways, and we should therefore step out with a determination that we will live in that world with bright, shining faithfulness.

In the ancient world, stars were used as navigational aids. People would walk outside, look up, and, by means of the heavens, determine their course. Paul wanted his readers to be as useful as the stars in the sky, becoming navigational aids for a world that doesn't know which way to turn, pointing to the great lodestar of all of life: the one who made the stars.

In order to live this way, we must *hold fast* to the word of life as a light to our own path. Our own steps must be governed by God's true and authoritative word. We must also *hold forth* this word of life. The good news of Jesus is contained in God's word, and it is therefore His word that we should be ready to offer to our neighbors and friends, knowing that it will not return void (Isaiah 55:11). As stars shine forth light, so we are to hold out gospel life.

If we, by God's grace, resist the temptations of grumbling, impurity, and selfishness, and if we, by God's grace, live with joy, contentment, and hope, all the while holding on to God's word, we will most assuredly shine for the good of our neighbors and the glory of God. You are called to shine in the darkness. Be sure to do so today.

MATTHEW 5:14-16

AUGUST 19

SEEING AND SHARING CHRIST

"Their eyes were opened, and they recognized him. And he vanished from their sight ... They rose that same hour and returned to Jerusalem. And they found the eleven." LUKE 24:31, 33

Good news needs to be shared.

Sometimes, when we have guests in our home whom we know very well, and especially if they are brothers or sisters in the family of faith, we may ask them to pray before we share a meal. It is a request meant to honor the visitor to our table. Luke's Gospel gives us a similar scene, though here the visitor appears to have taken the lead in deciding that He would pray. After Jesus' encounter with two disciples on the road from Jerusalem to Emmaus, He "went in to stay with them" (Luke 24:29), and "when he was at table with them, he took the bread and blessed and broke it and gave it to them" (v 30).

Previously, on their long walk from Jerusalem, when this pair encountered Jesus, "their eyes were kept from recognizing him" (Luke 24:16). But now, as Jesus blessed the meal, they were *made* to see Him. God chose this moment to reveal that they were in the presence of the risen Lord Jesus Christ.

Just as God through His Spirit opened these disciples' eyes to behold the truth of the risen Christ, so He used His word to ignite within their hearts a passion for who Jesus was and is. As soon as they recognized Jesus, and even after He disappeared, "they said to each other, 'Did not our hearts burn within us while he talked to us on the road, while he opened to us the Scriptures?'" (Luke 24:32).

The hour was late, they had walked a long way, and they had just sat down to eat, and yet they could do nothing other than rise and return to Jerusalem to share the amazing news with the eleven disciples. What a night that must have been!

Their enthusiasm is a reminder to us that the news that Jesus is alive wasn't simply their news, or the Eleven's news for that matter. It is news that needs to be shared and that is most enjoyed in company with others who understand its glorious implications. It belongs to all who are the Lord's. And no matter what language we speak, what country we visit, or what journey we take, we are not far from other believers with whom we can rejoice together in a living hope given to us by the resurrection of Jesus Christ from the dead (1 Peter 1:3-5). You can share this joy right where you are, though, with those you live with and worship with by looking them in the eye and, with a smile, saying, "Jesus has risen."

This news needs to be shared. Do you long to see Christ for who He really is and show others the same? Do you desire to see and to help others see Jesus in the humdrum affairs of life? If so, then ask God to do what He did for these disciples, that you may discover afresh and share who Jesus is and what He is to you.

JOHN 1:35-51

AUGUST 20

WHAT TO DO WITH A GUILTY CONSCIENCE

"David arose and stealthily cut off a corner of Saul's robe. And afterward David's heart struck him, because he had cut off a corner of Saul's robe. He said to his men, 'The LORD forbid that I should do this thing to my lord, the LORD's anointed' ... As soon as David had finished speaking ... to Saul, Saul said, 'Is this your voice, my son David?' And Saul lifted up his voice and wept. He said to David, 'You are more righteous than I, for you have repaid me good, whereas I have repaid you evil.'" 1 SAMUEL 24:4-6, 16-17

There is a sense in which the story told in part in these verses can be viewed in terms of conscience—a sensitive conscience, as found in David, and a hardened, seared conscience, as found in Saul.

David knew that although the Spirit of God had departed from Saul, Saul was still the Lord's anointed king, and the anointed of the Lord should never be cursed or killed (Exodus 22:28). Because his conscience was sensitive to God and His law, he was immediately burdened by what he'd done in cutting Saul's robe—even if he could have done much worse. So David repented of his sin before his men and prevented them from attacking Saul (1 Samuel 24:6-7).

After David spoke to Saul openly about his withheld vengeance (1 Samuel 24:8-15), Saul was moved to tears by his kindness. But Saul did not seize this opportunity for reconciliation. As genuine as his tears may have been in the moment, his response was ultimately superficial and short-lived, the result of a hardened and blackened heart. We know this because he continued to hunt David.

The Bible says the conscience is a basic building block of our humanity. The law of God is written into the human heart, whether we have heard His commandments or not (Romans 2:14-15). When we ignore God's law to follow our own way, we experience guilt and shame. In that moment, we are faced with a choice: Will we seek forgiveness and reconciliation? Or will we allow our conscience to be further hardened by pursuing our selfish desires?

A guilty conscience is a heavy burden, but it can also be a gift. Walter J. Chantry writes, "Conscience is a friend to hurry you into the arms of the only Saviour from the broken law and its curse."[66] If you are experiencing the burden of a guilty conscience, do not mistake momentary sorrow for real repentance. Turn to God in repentance, turning from your sin and in His strength resolving to change. That is the way to be forgiven. For if a guilty conscience is the gift that drives you to God, a cleansed conscience is the gift that you will receive from Him.

PSALM 25

66 Walter J. Chantry, *David: Man of Prayer, Man of War* (Banner of Truth, 2007), p 92.

AUGUST 21

FRIENDS IN CHRIST

"I hope in the Lord Jesus to send Timothy to you soon, so that I too may be cheered by news of you. For I have no one like him ... I have thought it necessary to send to you Epaphroditus my brother and fellow worker and fellow soldier, and your messenger and minister to my need." PHILIPPIANS 2:19-20, 25

Do you have someone you would call in a moment of crisis? What qualities make him or her suited for such a responsibility? More than likely, the person you'd decide to call is someone whom you trust, and someone who you know would drop whatever he or she was doing to come to your aid. Such men and women are true friends.

When Paul found himself in need of help, stuck in a Roman jail cell, he knew what friends he could call: Timothy and Epaphroditus. He mentions them by name in Philippians 2 and describes them as beloved co-laborers in Christ. Yet what is most helpful for us to see is not merely that Paul had such trustworthy companions but why they were so.

First, these were men of action. Paul had "no one like" Timothy and said that his "proven worth" was known to all because "he has served with me in the gospel" (Philippians 2:22). Likewise, Epaphroditus was a "fellow worker and fellow soldier," a man who "nearly died for the work of Christ, risking his life" in ministry (v 30). These men embodied Christian action. They weren't merely names on a membership list or numbers on a chart. They were putting their faith to work and showing their worth to the faith. When Paul needed to send someone to Philippi, he knew they would act.

They were also men of availability—not in the sense that they simply kept their calendars clear but in that they were ready to do what was needed, when it was needed. These were not small commitments that Paul asked them to make! But he knew that their dedication to Christ was such that when he called, they would be available.

Could you be described in these ways? When there are ministry needs around you, are you known to be a man or woman of action and availability? It doesn't necessarily, or often, look like signing up for something so dramatic as that which Paul sent his friends to do. The point isn't to serve in grand ways. The Lord doesn't need your labors. But when you commit to acting in His name and being available for His causes, He may be pleased to use you for the good of His people.

Simple, small acts can be significant. What if you determined to pick up the phone twice a week to call a fellow church member and encourage them? What if you regularly visited someone to pray with them? There is no better friend than the one who points others to Jesus. Be sure to surround yourself with those kinds of friends, and work to be such a friend yourself.

PROVERBS 27:5-9

AUGUST 22

STRIVING AFTER THE WIND

"What has a man from all the toil and striving of heart with which he toils beneath the sun?" ECCLESIASTES 2:22

Over the years, I've sat with many parents who were distraught over the potential consequences of their children's wrongful pursuits. Each of these mothers and fathers have been disappointed in their son's or daughter's choices, and as we have talked it has become clear that their disappointment is grounded in their belief that everything would be much better if their child would just be like them. On further probing, it has turned out that by this they have meant that everything would be better if their child would simply give their lives completely to their work.

Scripture's conclusion about a life devoted to labor for its own sake is clear: it's all meaningless and a striving after the wind. This is not to say that work is irrelevant or unhelpful. Work comes from God, so it must be good—but only when pursued rightly. But Solomon warns that when work is the totality of your life, all of your "days are full of sorrow," and "even in the night" your "heart does not rest" (Ecclesiastes 2:23). Workaholics awaken in the night and turn over in their bed. They far too often need pills to get themselves to sleep, pills to wake themselves up, pills to get themselves through the day. And if "pills" is a far-off concept for you, simply replace it with whatever remedy you see people turn to—or find yourself turning to—to help you switch off and to help you switch on.

When life is lived this way, eventually everything will collapse. As time goes on, those who give themselves to their possessions become more and more consumed by them. It's not worth losing one's soul for the sake of stuff. Yet as Jesus taught, there is a way to build your house upon the rock (Matthew 7:24-27). The only solid joys and lasting treasures that may be discovered in life's journey—even in work—are those found in a personal, living faith in God.

So, "choose this day whom you will serve" (Joshua 24:15): the idols of wealth and vain ambition or the God of heaven. Be sure to prepare your heart and make your choice before you sit at your desk or stand in the factory, tempted to give yourself completely to your work. Pray in earnest, "Lord Jesus, I do not want to place my hope in career achievement or wealth accumulation. Lord Jesus, be my Savior and show me how to live today with You as my comfort and my source of contentment." That is the way to work hard at your labors without worshiping them.

ECCLESIASTES 2

AUGUST 23

TRUE POWER IN THE ONE SPIRIT

"Not by might, nor by power, but by my Spirit, says the Lord *of hosts."*
ZECHARIAH 4:6

At one point or another, when we're facing trouble in life, we're all tempted to ask, *What's the point of all of this? Why make the effort to keep going? Why do I face all this difficulty or opposition?* Sometimes it looks as if some 21st-century churches and Christians live and operate primarily out of discouragement rather than being glad and rejoicing in the day the Lord has made (Psalm 118:24).

Some despondency is understandable. But we certainly don't want to live there all the time—nor do we need to. Our discouragement should never lead us to disbelieve that God is still at work. The fact of the matter is that sometimes God's work looks less impressive from a worldly viewpoint than we'd like. But while "some trust in chariots and some in horses," we are to "trust in the name of the Lord our God" (Psalm 20:7). In the heat of battle, combat equipment like chariots and horses sure was intimidating. Yet while it may seem that the side with the most firepower always wins, we must never forget that God is always at work among His people, and He will give victory—not by might nor by power, but by His Spirit.

Nothing—no wealth, no influence, no strategy, no ability—can be a substitute for the work of the Spirit in our lives and in the church. Think back to the leadership of the New Testament church, for example. Its leaders were some bold, proactive men, if for no other reason than because they had had so much facetime with Jesus. And yet, when it came time for the gospel to spread, what did Jesus do? "He ordered them not to depart from Jerusalem, but to wait for the promise of the Father" (Acts 1:4)—that promise, of course, being the Holy Spirit. Without the power of the Spirit, the apostles, however capable or determined they may have been, were going nowhere fast. With the Spirit, they began a movement that changed the world.

In our day, we need to remember that true gains for the kingdom will never come merely from a higher position in society, larger bank accounts, or more power. Instead, we wait on God's Spirit to move where He wills and to work however He chooses. After all, God's thoughts are not our thoughts, neither are our ways His ways. His wisdom is as high above us as the heavens are above the earth (Isaiah 55:8-9). If deep down you are self-reliant, remember this: the kingdom will not advance, in your own life or through your witness and ministry, except by the work of the Spirit. If deep down you are discouraged, remember this: the kingdom will advance, even in your own life and through your witness and ministry, because the Spirit is at work. Do not trust in chariots or in horses, but in the Lord your God.

PSALM 115

AUGUST 24

WHAT ARE YOU WAITING FOR?

"Our citizenship is in heaven, and from it we await a Savior, the Lord Jesus Christ, who will transform our lowly body to be like his glorious body, by the power that enables him even to subject all things to himself."

PHILIPPIANS 3:20-21

Life is filled with waiting. Whether it's waiting for the weekend, for an upcoming vacation, or for the birth of a child or grandchild, we're always waiting for something. And the Christian life itself is a waiting period; Paul says that, as citizens of heaven already, we now "await a Savior, the Lord Jesus Christ."

For Christians, this waiting should be one of the defining features of our lives. There is an otherworldly dimension to our existence—and it's important. We are not to be consumed by, controlled by, constrained by, or riveted to "earthly things" (Philippians 3:19), but we are to "seek the things that are above" (Colossians 3:1) as we eagerly await our Savior and the fullness of the benefits He will shower on us. We are to be a waiting people, not a settling people.

If you have ever been separated from a close loved one for an extended period, perhaps you have felt the pangs of intense longing. You may be just fine for a few days or even a few weeks, but soon you feel as if a part of you is missing. You eagerly anticipate your reunion—and when the day finally draws near, you can hardly stand the wait any longer!

Paul wants us to wait expectantly for our Lord Jesus Christ with the same sort of longing. We will do that as we remember that "the appointed time has grown very short" (1 Corinthians 7:29) and that "salvation is nearer to us now than when we first believed" (Romans 13:11). However long or short the wait is from our perspective, Jesus will return in due time—and when He does, He will transform us to be like Himself, forever.

That reunion may come sooner than you think—and it will certainly come "soon" when compared to the vastness of the eternity that awaits us! But for now, you and I are still left to watch and wait for the return of our King. So, until that day when you are brought into the presence of your Savior forever, be sure not to settle for what this world has to offer, becoming more excited about the "now" than the "not yet." Instead, say with the psalmist, "I wait for the LORD, my soul waits, and in his word I hope; my soul waits for the Lord more than watchmen for the morning, more than watchmen for the morning" (Psalm 130:5-6). However today goes, make it a day of waiting for what is to come.

ROMANS 13:11-14

AUGUST 25

WHERE TO TURN WHEN YOUR THOUGHTS GO DARK

"Then David said in his heart, 'Now I shall perish one day by the hand of Saul. There is nothing better for me than that I should escape to the land of the Philistines. Then Saul will despair of seeking me any longer within the borders of Israel, and I shall escape out of his hand.'" 1 SAMUEL 27:1

Sometimes our thoughts are our greatest enemy.

However difficult his circumstance, David had always placed his confidence in God. Indeed, in the final conversation that ever took place between King Saul and David, David declared to Saul that although he didn't know what would happen, he knew that God would deliver him from his troubles (1 Samuel 26:23-24). David had good reason for such confidence: deliverance had been a theme throughout his life. Whether it was from the lion, the bear, or the Philistine giant (1 Samuel 17:37), or, later, from Saul's murderous pursuit of him, David was quick to attest to God's rescue.

It is surprising, then, that having just avowed his commitment to the delivering hand of God, David then convinced himself in his heart that Saul would eventually kill him. Rather than reflecting on God's goodness and faithfulness, he allowed his thoughts to go to dark places. His confidence gave way to depression and his faith gave way to fear, and so he went to seek security in the company of the enemy (1 Samuel 27:2)—a decision that would lead to a mess of deceit and difficulty (v 8-11).

Our thoughts really matter; they give rise to our actions. An old saying reminds us of this principle: *Sow a thought, reap an action. Sow an action, reap a habit. Sow a habit, reap a character. Sow a character, reap a destiny.*

You may be able to look back on chapters in your own life when, like David, you began to talk nonsense to yourself, made foolish choices, and found yourself trapped. You may be in that place right now, struggling to stop your thoughts spiraling downwards and leading you into a course of action that you know, deep down, is unwise or wrong. David didn't just need saving from threats to his life; he needed saving from *himself*—and so do you and I. But the good news is that we can't exhaust God's kindness and mercy, even if our thoughts have gone in the wrong direction and even if our actions have taken us off course. As God rescued David, so He has rescued us through the cross of Christ. When you find your thoughts turning to dark places, then, remind yourself of God's goodness, deliverance, and faithfulness, and let that shape your heart's response to the difficulties you face, and shape the course you take as you navigate them.

GALATIANS 6:7-10

◇ Bible Through The Year: Psalm 119:1-88; 2 Corinthians 4

AUGUST 26

THE SUBTLE INFLUENCE OF ERROR

"There are many who are insubordinate, empty talkers and deceivers, especially those of the circumcision party. They must be silenced, since they are upsetting whole families by teaching for shameful gain what they ought not to teach."
TITUS 1:10-11

Beware the danger of empty talkers.

The church in Crete was threatened by some within the community of faith who were nevertheless marked by rebellion. They were like those who enlist in the army, report for duty, and put on a uniform, but as soon as battle commences, they refuse to obey their commanding officer.

Such insubordinate individuals are, Paul says, "empty talkers." They talk about nothing, but they make it sound as if it's the most important thing that you've ever heard in your life. They want to deviate from the main things and the plain things of Scripture and get everybody to focus on the sidelines, on their traits. And shockingly, although they are "deceivers," they are able to draw people after them.

Some people are peculiarly susceptible to this kind of nonsense. It's not possible to have a product that sells unless you've got a market that is buying. If a congregation is not well versed in the truth, and if it doesn't have elders like those described in Titus 1:5-9 to safeguard the flock, then it will be vulnerable to individuals who rise from among the believers and seek to draw the faithful away.

The greatest danger is not necessarily an all-out onslaught from outside the body of faith. More often than not, it is creeping and subtle, and it comes from inside. Those who deceive in this way are not necessarily easy to recognize. They won't say, "Follow me, I'm turning away from the truth." Rather, they say, "Follow me, because I know the key teachings that you need to believe. You need to make sure that you're doing these things and not doing those things."

The gospel is the amazing story that through Jesus and His work upon the cross, God completely transforms the lives of His children. Along with this change in our hearts, He gives us the unchanging truth of His word—and that truth is worthy of our prayers for the church and its elders. It is worth defending with all our might. So let Paul's words be a reminder to guard against deceitful empty talkers and to be vigilant as you check your own heart. Listen to those whose words are full of grace and truth, and ensure that your own words are saturated with those two hallmarks of the true Christian life, too.

TITUS 1:5-16

AUGUST 27

WHO SHALL DWELL ON YOUR HOLY HILL?

"O Lord, who shall sojourn in your tent? Who shall dwell on your holy hill? He who walks blamelessly and does what is right and speaks truth in his heart."
PSALM 15:1-2

"Who shall dwell on your holy hill?" The question that David poses in the first verse of this psalm is of utmost importance. It may strike us as a question that's tied only to worship in ancient Israel, but in truth it takes us to the very doorstep of heaven and asks us, *Who will enter these gates?*

While the answer is explained in the rest of Psalm 15, the general point is one we find throughout Scripture. The writer of Hebrews advised his readers to "strive for ... the holiness without which no one will see the Lord" (Hebrews 12:14). The Lord Jesus similarly instructed that "the gate is narrow and the way is hard that leads to life, and those who find it are few" (Matthew 7:14). Those who will stand on the holy hill of the Lord and enjoy His presence for eternity, then, are those who arrive there by the narrow way, striving after holiness.

The sad truth is that too many assume they will dwell on God's holy hill because they once said a prayer, walked down an aisle, or are a member of a church. It is a grave mistake to think that those acts on their own will merit eternal life if they are accompanied with a way of life that gives no evidence of knowing Christ as Lord. Charles Spurgeon once preached, "If the man does not live differently from what he did before ... his repentance needs to be repented of, and his conversion is a fiction."[67]

So, who will ascend the hill of the Lord? It is the one who "walks blamelessly," in a way that cannot be confused with that of an unbeliever, and whose life manifests the reality that God has saved him or her. It is the one whose talk is not marked by slander but who "speaks truth in his heart." This is someone who doesn't merely say what is *correct* but says what is *true*, with no gap between what is said and what is lived.

The combination of reading Psalm 15 and looking honestly at ourselves will very likely be discouraging. Only the Lord Jesus embodies the psalm's portrayal of holiness to perfection; only He deserves to dwell on His Father's holy hill, and only because He chose to die for His people's sins and clothe them with His perfection are we invited to live with Him there. But it is good and right to let the light of God's word shine on our hearts and expose what is there, for it will move us to repentance and to gratitude to our Savior. And those who know they will stand there because of Him will seek to be like Him. Consider your walk and your words, and pray that you would be ever more conformed to the image of Christ until you dwell with Him on God's holy hill.

PSALM 15

67 "What Is It to Win a Soul?," *The Sword and the Trowel* (December 1879), p 561.

AUGUST 28

THE PATH TOWARD REJOICING

"Rejoice in the Lord always; again I will say, rejoice." PHILIPPIANS 4:4

Happiness cannot be turned on like a tap. Joy does not come at the flip of a switch. As Christians, we have highs and lows like anyone else. Sometimes we feel great; other times we feel stuck. So what do we do with a command that tells us to be joyful continually—or, as the text has it, to "rejoice ... always"?

Some people conceive of joy as something that ebbs and flows according to our circumstances. If this were so, the path to joy would be to ensure that our circumstances contain as many good things as possible and that we cut out anything, and anyone, that brings us down. But the apostle Paul offers us a different take. The Christian joy he describes is intended to be steady and stable. Paul clues us in to the source of this joy here: "Rejoice in the Lord always; again I will say, rejoice." The key is the phrase in between "Rejoice" and "always"—"in the Lord." Those three little words make all the difference in the world! If we let our joy ebb and flow with our circumstances, then we're inevitably going to find ourselves in trouble. Hard times will come, sooner or later. But if we rejoice *in the Lord*, who is "the same yesterday and today and forever" (Hebrews 13:8), then our joy is anchored in someone unchanging, and so it will be unfading.

Christian joy is a joy that can coexist with deep sadness. Your circumstances may bring you grief, but they need not extinguish your joy if you find it "in the Lord"—in who He is, how He loves you, and what He has promised you. Place your hope in Him and remind yourself of His unchanging nature and you will be on the path toward rejoicing always, even in hardship. Today, no matter your circumstances, you can find solace, rest, and, yes, even joy in the glorious truth that God is with you through it all and will one day set all things aright.

PSALM 147

AUGUST 29

REMEMBER YOUR CREATOR

"Remember also your Creator in the days of your youth." ECCLESIASTES 12:1

Not everyone ages at the same rate or in the same way. Some people are full of life well on into their twilight years, while others fade long before their time. But all of us, no matter how young or old, no matter how we feel or how frail we are, are moving one day at a time toward the day that the lights finally go out.

It's with that end in mind that the author of Ecclesiastes calls us to remember our Creator while we still have time. But when he says "Remember," he's not calling us to a mechanical exercise such as recalling irregular English verbs or multiplication tables. The call to remember encourages us to drop every sense of self-sufficiency and to cast ourselves unreservedly on God as our Creator and Sustainer. To "remember your Creator" means to know Him, love Him, and serve Him as your highest joy.

The timeframe in which this exhortation is to be responded to is significant: the writer specifically urges his readers to remember God "in the days of your youth." If you are no longer young, don't worry—this may apply to you much more than you think! The Bible is far more flexible concerning youthfulness than we are. Even so, there is no question that those who are younger particularly need to heed these instructions.

We must beware of saying to ourselves, "I'll get around to the serious stuff when the serious time comes." This *is* the serious time! The days will soon come when you will not be able to see as you once saw, hear as you once heard, or walk as you once walked. However fast or slowly, the house of your life is breaking down. How tragic it would be to assume that you can remember your Creator tomorrow, and tomorrow, and tomorrow, but never today, and then find that there is no more tomorrow. Beware of allowing the best years of your life to pass filled with things that will ultimately prove to be worthless. Remember your Creator while you have the opportunity. And if you feel your best years are already behind you, remember this also: God is able to "restore to you the years that the swarming locust has eaten" (Joel 2:25). It is better to remember now than to spend eternity with regret.

LUKE 9:57-62

AUGUST 30

GOD'S PROTECTIVE WORD

"I do not ask that you take them out of the world, but that you keep them from the evil one." JOHN 17:15

When Jesus prayed these words for His disciples, He prayed them aloud. And so this prayer was also an instruction to them about how to interact with the surrounding world. The life that Jesus sets forth here is one that is neither comfortably indistinguishable from the world nor comfortably separate from it.

This is Jesus' vision for His people: to be in the world but distinct from it. This is, in fact, what God's people have always been called to, as a "kingdom of priests and a holy nation" (Exodus 19:6; 1 Peter 2:9-10). The Psalms are abundantly clear that evil is a present danger. People are described as "enemies" and "bloodthirsty men" (Psalm 59:1-2), "evildoers" are all around (94:4), and there are some whose ways can only be described as "crooked" (125:5). Therefore, the great challenge is knowing how to honor Christ's words—how to refrain from being compromised by the evil which surrounds us.

Our greatest form of defense is seen in Jesus' request to the Father: "Keep them from the evil one." Protection is available to all who entrust themselves to God. This truth is articulated in the Psalms too, where we read of God's protection being offered to the needy. The Lord says that "because the needy groan, I will now arise" (Psalm 12:5). In other words, it is not the arrogant and boastful that He protects but those who recognize their dependence on Him. Theirs are the groanings the Lord hears. And the Lord's protection for the needy is also protection from the wicked. David confesses that God "will guard us from this generation forever" (v 7). Wicked people may hurt God's people but they cannot do so in any permanent way, for ultimately they cannot hurt our souls. God will keep us from everlasting harm.

The protection of God is *for* the needy and *from* the wicked, but how does it come to us? *Through* the word of God, which provides a lamp for our feet and a light to our paths (Psalm 119:105). His every word proves true, offering a shield against all foes (18:30). If we want to live faithfully in the world, we must devote ourselves to the Scriptures. To think rightly about the evil around you, then, the word of God must be in your heart, in your mind, and on your tongue. God has given it to you to keep you.

Do you pray for yourself what Jesus prayed for His followers on that night before He died? Consider whether you are more in danger of becoming like the world or of removing yourself from it. Ask the Lord for the love, wisdom, and courage required to live as He did: in the world and yet gloriously distinct from it.

JOHN 17:9-19

AUGUST 31

THE POWER OF PROPER THINKING

"Finally, brothers, whatever is true, whatever is honorable, whatever is just, whatever is pure, whatever is lovely, whatever is commendable, if there is any excellence, if there is anything worthy of praise, think about these things."
PHILIPPIANS 4:8

Many of us begin the day with anxious thoughts. The "peace of God, which surpasses all understanding" (Philippians 4:7) never seems to reach us in the middle of the night or when we first open our eyes. Instead, as the morning comes we say to ourselves, "There is so much to think about. So many things are dancing around in my mind. I've got so many challenges." Thoughts such as these so easily produce anxiety and stultify our commitment to prayer.

Paul helps us to overcome these draining, even crippling feelings by directing our gaze toward those virtues which will liberate our thinking. A mind that is filled with the content described in Philippians 4:8 will have little space for anxiety-producing, peace-disrupting, joy-destroying notions.

What Paul was encouraging his readers to adopt is a distinctly Christian way of thinking. A Christian mind, he taught, is not a mind that is trained to think only about "Christian topics" but one that has learned to think about everything from a Christian perspective. Ultimately, we are what we think about. It is in our minds that our affections are stirred, and it is through our minds that our wills are directed. It is in the mind that we conceive of and produce every action. It is therefore imperative that we learn to think about what is right and godly.

The Bible is not concerned with mere mental reflection for its own sake. The Christian is not called to sit on a high hill and think blessed thoughts in abstraction, removed from the routines of everyday existence. Rather, Paul provides us with a list that will establish us in our motives, our manners, and our morals. Each of us is called to live in the realm of the real, not the phony; the serious, not the frivolous; the right, not the convenient; the clean, not the dirty; the loving, not the discordant; and the helpful, not the critical. In short, we are called to think like Jesus.

Paul is not simply calling you to pull yourself up by your bootstraps, though. This is not a rallying cry to try your best to perform the list. Sanctification by self-effort is not God's agenda. The multifaceted virtue Paul speaks of is the fruit which grows on the tree of salvation. This fruit is brought forth by those whose roots are embedded in grace. So, let your heart be gripped by God's grace, and train your mind to think on that which is truly praiseworthy. When those influences converge, your life will be one that brings glory to God. Aim to make His grace, and this fruit, the first thing you think about when you wake up tomorrow.

LUKE 6:43-49

SEPTEMBER 1

THEOLOGY FOR LIFE

"I would to God that not only you but also all who hear me this day might become such as I am—except for these chains." ACTS 26:29

Paul's beliefs were forged in the furnace of life. When his legs were virtually cut out from underneath him, he learned all the more that God is in control.

It was during Paul's two-year imprisonment in Rome that he wrote letters to the Ephesian, Philippian, and Colossian churches and to his friend Philemon. It was during this season of suffering that God encouraged him to write of Jesus, "In him all things hold together" (Colossians 1:17). When he wrote to the Ephesians, he urged them to see that God, who is sovereign over all, has put all things under Jesus' feet (Ephesians 1:22). These truths were not just theoretical. Paul relied upon them during the most difficult seasons of his life.

Paul's experiences doubtless helped him to understand more deeply that he needed the gospel not just for salvation but for all of life. We, too, need the gospel daily—the good news that Jesus died in the place of sinners, that He was raised for our justification, and that He sent the Spirit to sanctify us and to fill us. The gospel creates within us a confident anticipation of the return of Jesus. It causes us to view the world from a heavenly perspective.

John Stott, who was unparalleled in his ability to synthesize and succinctly condense vast amounts of material, summarized the impact of Paul's imprisonment upon his theology in this way: "Paul's perspective was adjusted, his horizon extended, his vision clarified and his witness enriched."[68] His chains did not become an occasion for disappointment or regret. Rather, his trials, which kept him in a state of weakness and dependency upon God, altered his perspective and shed light on the horizon. He was able to stand before a Roman governor, a king, and a queen, and say, *What you have you cannot keep. What I have I cannot lose. I wish you could become like me—a sinner saved by grace, an heir to eternal life. I would not like for you to share my chains, but I would love for you to share my faith.*

Paul experienced the very truth that he had written to the Romans years earlier: "We know that for those who love God all things work together for good, for those who are called according to his purpose" (Romans 8:28). This was so not only for Paul but is also true for all who have placed their faith in Jesus Christ. Are you facing a discouraging trial? Take courage! You have all you truly need, and you cannot lose it. All the riches and comfort that this world can offer do not compare to what you have in the gospel—"Christ in you, the hope of glory" (Colossians 1:27). Christian theology is not for an ivory tower but for the prison cell, for the trials. Let the truths of the gospel strengthen your soul and shape your perspective as you cling to the hope that Christ has purchased for you.

ACTS 26:1-29

68 *The Message of Acts,* The Bible Speaks Today series (IVP Academic, 1994), p 404.

SEPTEMBER 2

GOSPEL PARADOX

"There is therefore now no condemnation for those who are in Christ Jesus."
ROMANS 8:1

Are you ever disappointed with yourself? Maybe it seems that your journey toward holiness is painstakingly slow. Perhaps it seems that an approximation of Newton's third law somehow applies to your Christian life: for every victory, there is an equal and opposite failure.

You are not alone. Even the great apostle Paul expressed serious disappointment in his ongoing battle with sin: "Wretched man that I am! Who will deliver me from this body of death?" (Romans 7:24). Reading of the depth of Paul's frustration, it is worth considering that perhaps we aren't actually disappointed *enough*. After all, it's probably not typical Bible-study behavior in your church to cry out in lament over your own wickedness!

Yet even in his state of despair Paul knew that sin, however serious, would not—could not—have the final say. In the very next verse, hope breaks in: "Thanks be to God through Jesus Christ our Lord!" (Romans 7:25). Then, after the next sentence restates the problem, we ascend to one of the highest peaks in all of Scripture: Romans 8, which begins with the glorious promise of today's header verse.

Why does Paul respond to his failures by saying, "Thanks be to God"? It is because "there is therefore now no condemnation for those who are in Christ Jesus." *No condemnation, now or forever!* Here we have one of the gospel's most wondrous paradoxes: I am weak, failing, and guilty; but at the same time, in Christ, I am safe, secure, and loved.

How can this be? To answer, we can look back to another great "therefore" in the book of Romans: "Therefore, since we have been justified by faith, we have peace with God through our Lord Jesus Christ" (Romans 5:1). We don't deserve such grace. God could rightfully let us drown in our wretchedness. Instead, through Jesus, He grants us peace and gives us hope. We are justified; Jesus has taken our condemnation so that now, when His Father looks at us, He sees Jesus and all His perfection.

You and I are sinful—yes, dreadfully so, and we remain so. But we are also supremely loved, completely forgiven, and never in any danger of condemnation. Do not suppress or ignore your disappointment at your ongoing flaws and failings. Let it drive you back to Jesus, in gratitude and relief. The more aware we are of our sin, the more wonderful we will realize is the truth that there is not, and never will be, any ounce of divine condemnation for those who are in Christ Jesus.

PSALM 103

SEPTEMBER 3

A TASTE OF HEAVEN

"There is therefore now no condemnation for those who are in Christ Jesus."
ROMANS 8:1

One of the great malignant heresies of our day is the "prosperity gospel." Proponents of this false teaching aim to persuade men and women that great material blessings like health, wealth, and general prosperity await those who just have enough faith or who give them just a little more money. But God never made any such promise. Such promises of prosperity await us in eternity, not necessarily now. Too many lives of faith have been ruined by false teachers promising *right now* what God only promises *in eternity*.

In guarding against the prosperity gospel, however, we must not miss the glorious truth that in Christ, some of heaven's blessings *do* break into our earthly existence. In fact, one of the most bountiful outpourings of God's kindness belongs to us now: "There is therefore *now* no condemnation for those who are in Christ Jesus." Surely there is hardly a more attractive offer than being made right with the Creator of the universe *now*—and for all eternity.

This status of "no condemnation" is not just something we aspire to and reach eventually. Paul says this blessed state is for us immediately. If we are "in Christ Jesus," united to Him by faith, then we have already stepped forward into peace with God. We already stand in grace, not condemnation.

There is no middle territory between standing in grace and standing in condemnation. If we are not justified—if we are not declared righteous on the strength of Christ—we are condemned. Jesus states it plainly for us: "Whoever believes in [me] is not condemned, but whoever does not believe is condemned already, because he has not believed in the name of the only Son of God" (John 3:18). There is no middle ground on which to stand.

But there is no need to seek to stand in any middle ground. For a sinner who turns in repentance and faith to Jesus, their present reality is transformed to a living hope; God moves them from death to life. He plants them in the soil of His grace, where He nourishes them with steadfast hope. They are rooted firmly under the endless smile of His mercy. What greater prosperity could there possibly be?

For most of us, it is easy to see all that we do not have. Perhaps you have reason today to wish that God would give you greater health or wealth, or more time, or different relationships, now. But, for a moment, pause and see what you do have and cannot lose. You enjoy the smile of God. You will never face His condemnation. That is His promise, and it is more precious than anything else this world can offer—and all that He promises, He does.

JOHN 3:10-21

SEPTEMBER 4

NO GREATER VICTORY

"There is therefore now no condemnation for those who are in Christ Jesus."
ROMANS 8:1

One of the perennial misconceptions about Christianity is that God views each of us as a sort of living scoreboard: one side lights up with our sins and failures, the other tallies our good deeds and victories, and so long as the good wins out in the final score, the results will be good enough for God—right?

But the fact of the matter is that if we tally up our sins and compare them to our obedience, we're always losing. It's not even a competition, really. Like when a pro team faces off against a junior varsity squad, it'll be a blowout. Still, too many of us fool ourselves into thinking we have time for a comeback—we can fix ourselves up just enough before the final whistle blows or work hard enough to come out victorious.

Such thinking isn't even on the same playing field as the gospel. And it misses grace entirely.

It is never our own score that helps our standing before God. No, it has to be Christ's. In the words of Paul's letter to the Ephesians, your salvation "is not your own doing; it is the gift of God" (Ephesians 2:8). The gift is Christ's perfect tally in our place. Nothing less than His perfect righteousness will do.

When you really begin to understand the gospel, it sounds too good to be true. What person deserves such extravagant grace? But that is precisely the point. Our salvation is completely a gift, and it is utterly undeserved. We don't deserve it now, nor could we ever. But God grants mercy to us regardless. He declares us victorious—*no condemnation!*—because of Jesus Christ, and only because of Him.

Being a Christian does not immunize you against taking a scoreboard approach to life. Paul's entire letter to the Galatian church was to urge them not to give up on grace. We face a constant battle to remember that it is in Christ, and only ever in Christ and never in our performance, that we enjoy "no condemnation." Have you lost the joy of your salvation? It is likely because you are looking too much at yourself and too little at Jesus. In the Christian life, there is no need for despair and no room for pride because it is never about you; it is always about Him.

In Christ Jesus, God gives you the win. There's no greater gift, no greater victory, and no greater joy.

GALATIANS 4:21 – 5:1

SEPTEMBER 5

SENT AND SENDING

"Jesus said to them again, 'Peace be with you. As the Father has sent me, even so I am sending you.' And when he had said this, he breathed on them and said to them, 'Receive the Holy Spirit.'" JOHN 20:21-22

Jesus came to earth as a man on a mission, and He left earth having called His people to that same mission.

Jesus made it clear from the very beginning that He came to preach good news: "The time is fulfilled, and the kingdom of God is at hand; repent and believe in the gospel" (Mark 1:15). That remains true, and so it makes perfect sense that when His earthly pilgrimage was nearing an end, the Lord sent His disciples out to continue that mission. Appearing to His friends on the evening of that first Easter Sunday, He wasted no time in commissioning them to proclaim the way of forgiveness, while reminding them that the Holy Spirit would help them in His absence.

For the disciples, the previous few days had been overwhelming. Within just 72 hours, they had shared in the first Communion meal together, had watched their Savior and friend be unjustly tried and crucified, and had begun a grieving process that completely engulfed them. But their mourning was unwound by Jesus' return after His resurrection. Now life meant going out to do just as He'd asked: proclaiming this amazing story, good news, forgiveness, and the love of God. These men lived for that—and, in most cases, they died for it.

Only a couple weeks later, we find Peter preaching a sermon. He began:

> Men of Israel, hear these words: Jesus of Nazareth, a man attested to you by God with mighty works and wonders and signs that God did through him in your midst, as you yourselves know—this Jesus, delivered up according to the definite plan and foreknowledge of God, you crucified and killed by the hands of lawless men. God raised him up, loosing the pangs of death, because it was not possible for him to be held by it. (Acts 2:22-24)

Peter directly addressed the situation his listeners were facing: they were rebels unfit for God's goodness, who had rejected the King whom God had sent to live among them and reveal Himself to them. Yet now that same God had punished His only Son instead of sinners and was offering forgiveness to them through the mouth of one of Jesus' followers.

Christ's call for us to share the reason for the hope that is in us (1 Peter 3:15) is no different for us today than it was for His disciples then. We are surrounded by death, despair, emptiness, regret, and fear. All the time, we peer into an unknown future. Those in our circles of influence need to know that only in Jesus can they find pardon and peace. Praise God that His Spirit goes before us. What would change in your words to others if you knew you were sent to them by divine appointment as part of a divine mission? "As the Father has sent me," says Jesus, "even so I am sending you."

JOHN 20:19-21

SEPTEMBER 6

A JOYFUL HEART

"Hannah prayed and said, 'My heart exults in the LORD; my horn is exalted in the LORD. My mouth derides my enemies, because I rejoice in your salvation.'"

1 SAMUEL 2:1

It is impossible to praise God too much or for our hearts to be too filled with joy at His love for His people. We should be quick to praise God when we can see His work in our own lives; but we should also be quick to locate that blessing in the context of His goodness to His people collectively. We see this repeatedly in Scripture. In 1 Samuel, for instance, when Hannah sought the Lord for help, she used phraseology which was related to the people of God, not just to her own personal circumstances: "O LORD of hosts…" (1 Samuel 1:11). Her appeal had been that God would look upon her in the way that He had looked upon His people in the past.

When God gave her the child she had longed for, her thanks echoed the language of Israel on occasions of great deliverance. Soon after God's people were delivered from slavery in Egypt by the power of God, Moses had sung his song, and Miriam had led the way in dancing with her tambourine ensemble (Exodus 15). Hannah, too, had a song to sing—or rather, a prayer of thanksgiving to pray. And her prayer broke the bounds of her particular circumstances. She rejoiced that there was a connection between what God had done for her individually and what He was doing for His people corporately.

As she did so, her heart exulted. When the word "heart" is used in the Bible, it speaks to the very center of our existence, including our minds, wills, and affections. So when Hannah said, "My heart exults in the LORD," she was expressing how the very centrality of her being was caught up in His greatness. Her mouth spoke out of her heart's fullness.

Just as Hannah likely reveled in the example of Miriam, a thousand years on from Hannah's prayer another woman sang to God in similar vein. Mary doubtless knew Hannah's prayer and may even have borrowed some of it, continuing the established pattern of rejoicing in God's mighty acts in the song we know as the Magnificat (Luke 1:46-55).

What about us? Do we respond with similar jubilation when God works in our lives personally and in His people corporately? Or are we in any danger of seeing Hannah's praise as a bit over the top? How would we respond if a "Miriam" stood up and started playing her tambourine? We can sometimes be too measured, or even merely go through the motions, in our praise. We sing in church about the Lord's strength, power, goodness, and kindness, and yet we hardly open our mouths to sing or to smile. We must take care to remember that we're not dealing with a philosophical construct, a concept, or something that we find within ourselves. No, we're singing about and praying to the living God, who acts on behalf of His people!

So, like Miriam, Hannah, and Mary, embrace the purposes and works of God in your life. Be quick to pray, quick to praise, and heartfelt in both. Take time today to let your heart exult in the Lord!

1 SAMUEL 2:1-10

SEPTEMBER 7

YOUR GRACE, YOUR MERCY, AND YOUR PEACE

"Grace, mercy, and peace will be with us, from God the Father and from Jesus Christ the Father's Son, in truth and love." 2 JOHN 3

One of the fundamental and most fantastic truths of the Christian faith is that God gives to us what we do not deserve. As sinners, down to the very last man, woman, and child, we deserve death. And what does God grant us instead? "The free gift of God is eternal life in Christ Jesus our Lord" (Romans 6:23).

This reversal—God giving us what we do *not* deserve and withholding what we *do* deserve—is so precious that we have a special word for it: *grace*. By His grace, God gives the most beautiful gift of life to the least deserving.

And how is it that He can show us such grace, freeing us from sin and guilt and bringing us every benefit in Jesus Christ? Because of His *mercy*. It is God's great mercy that inclines Him to give us what we don't deserve—and by that mercy, He showers us with grace.

Flowing from such grace and mercy is a bounty of *peace*. Peace is the experience of those who have been reconciled to God, of those who are no longer alienated from Him but who now live in fellowship with Him and in community with other recipients of His favor. This peace is such an otherworldly experience of God's grace and mercy that it "surpasses all understanding" (Philippians 4:7).

In a world that can feel fraught with disappointment and danger and sometimes void of meaning and purpose, what more could we ask for than such supernatural grace, mercy, and peace? They are stable. They are durable. They are permanent. And God the Father is always pleased to dispense them generously to all who come to Him through His precious Son, Jesus Christ. If you are trusting Christ, grace, mercy, and peace will be with you. So, pause before moving on and let the meaning and magnitude of those three words sink in. God's grace is yours, God's mercy is yours, God's peace is yours—all through Jesus, your Savior.

2 JOHN

SEPTEMBER 8

NOURISHMENT FOR THE SOUL

"His delight is in the law of the LORD, and on his law he meditates day and night." PSALM 1:2

God's truth will outweigh and outlive all its detractors. As the prophet Isaiah proclaims, "The grass withers, the flower fades, but the word of our God will stand forever" (Isaiah 40:8).

As the Psalter opens, we find that the blessed person—the truly happy one—delights in the enduring truth of God's word. The very words of the Lord are precious to them; each word tastes sweeter than honey (Psalm 19:10). Yet such a person doesn't only *delight* in the law of the Lord; they also *meditate* upon it.

Meditation is akin to the process of digestion. It is possible, in physical terms, just to stick food in your mouth and do nothing with it, but that will add nothing of nutritional value to your body. We risk the same with God's word if we come to it Sunday by Sunday and turn to it day by day without intentional meditation.

Often we feel as if our lives are racing by at 100 miles an hour. Daily time in God's word becomes a chore to complete, just to say we've done it. Instead, we need to find ways to store up God's word in our hearts (Psalm 119:11). We need consciously to take time to chew it over, to ask throughout the day, "What does this verse really mean? How should it shape my thoughts and actions in this situation? What is it showing me about the glory of God? How might God use it to conform me to the image of Christ?"

We are not called to snack on the Scriptures but to feast on them. Since there is no end to God's excellencies, there is no end to the riches of His word. What will it mean for you to meditate on it? By prayer, seek the help of the Spirit of God to harness your heart and mind to the text. Carefully consider what the Bible has to say. Ponder it. Probe it. Chew on it throughout the day to release as many soul-nourishing nutrients as you can. And as you meditate on the law of your Lord, ask God not just to increase your knowledge of Him but also to change you from the inside out to be more like His Son. As you see His word go to work in your heart and mind and life, you will come more and more to delight in reading it and living by it.

ISAIAH 40:6-9

SEPTEMBER 9

THE DANGER OF MISDIRECTED SYMPATHY

"There followed him a great multitude of the people and of women who were mourning and lamenting for him. But turning to them Jesus said, 'Daughters of Jerusalem, do not weep for me, but weep for yourselves and for your children.'"
LUKE 23:27-28

The shouts of "Crucify!" coming from the crowd had abated. Their mission had been successful: Pilate had sent Jesus to His execution. Now, in place of shouts for death, a new sound arose—the sound "of women who were mourning," wailing, and weeping.

It would have been no surprise if the exhausted Jesus had simply glanced in the direction of those "lamenting for him" as He staggered toward the site of His crucifixion, noticing and perhaps acknowledging their sympathy. But He did more than that. He actually stopped, turned to them, and said, "Do not weep for me, but weep for yourselves and for your children." In other words, He told them that their sympathy was misdirected—that instead of feeling pity for *Him*, they should consider the perilous state *they* were in.

Jesus' words were not a stern rebuke, as if it was wrong for these women to mourn. Rather, He wanted them to see that there was something for which they needed to weep with a far greater concern—namely, the judgment that awaited Jerusalem if its inhabitants were to persist in their unbelief and rejection of Him.

Less than a week before, Jesus had spoken about the destruction of Jerusalem: "They [Israel's enemies] will dash you to the ground, you and the children within your walls. They will not leave one stone on another, because you did not recognize the time of God's coming to you" (Luke 19:44, NIV). These women recognized enough to extend their sympathy toward the buffeted and broken body of Jesus. They recognized that this was a sorry sight, a travesty and perversion of justice. But they did not yet recognize the time of God's coming to them. And those who do not recognize that in Jesus God has come to keep His promises and hold out salvation from His judgment will be left to face that judgment. For Jerusalem, a prequel of that final judgment would come when the city was occupied by a Roman army in AD 70, its citizens killed, and its temple razed to the ground.

Now as then, Jesus is not calling us to mere sympathy. He doesn't need it! Jesus is not on a cross today; He is seated at the right hand of the Father on high. Jesus' words to these women then—and to us now—are a warning to those who would rather feel sorry for Him as a victim of injustice than face up to the fact that humanity is facing deserved and terrible judgment. We need to mourn humanity's condition and come to Him in repentance and faith. Because on that final judgment day, there will be no refuge from Him. There is only refuge in Him.

LUKE 19:41-46

SEPTEMBER 10

THE HOPE OF RESURRECTION LIFE

"As was the man of dust, so also are those who are of the dust, and as is the man of heaven, so also are those who are of heaven. Just as we have borne the image of the man of dust, we shall also bear the image of the man of heaven."
1 CORINTHIANS 15:48-49

Even if we muster all our imaginative powers, it's impossible for us fully to conceive of the world as it ought to be—and, indeed, as it *will* be. Can you imagine a world where earthquakes, storms, and tornadoes no longer wreak havoc and destruction? A world in which the word *cancer* strikes fear into nobody's heart? A body without weakness, without infection, without sickness, without sadness, without death?

The fact is, none of us can imagine that. But we do have an image of our hope for resurrection life in our Lord Jesus Christ. In being raised from the dead, He has become the firstfruits of all who trust in Him. What we see in Him is what we are someday to become.

By nature, we are all "in Adam" and destined for death; but to any who are in Christ, God promises renewed hope (1 Corinthians 15:22). By triumphing over death, Christ, "the last Adam" (v 45), has set us on the path to indestructible life in heaven. Once we walked the path of "the man of dust," but now all who are in Christ "bear the image of the man of heaven."

What will life be like when that man of heaven returns to earth and brings heaven with Him? Scripture doesn't lay out all the details. But we do know that instead of being perishable, our bodies will be imperishable. We currently have a limited shelf life, but we have the promise and hope of an eternal life with no expiration date. We will live forever (1 Corinthians 15:42), and every day in that forever will be glorious, for nothing will ever perish, spoil, or fade (1 Peter 1:4, NIV). We also know that God will transform us from a condition of dishonor and weakness to a renewed state of power and glory (1 Corinthians 15:43).

Neither you nor I have the categories to fathom such a resurrection life. Whatever you imagine, the reality will be better! But of this you can be sure: that life does await you, for your risen Lord Jesus Christ has trampled death underfoot once and for all. Death has been swallowed up in His irreversible victory (1 Corinthians 15:54).

Today, you will still see the forces of death at work around you—even *in* you. Perhaps you are very aware of that in one way or another as you read these words. But be assured that the kingdom of light has already prevailed over the domain of darkness. In fact, your citizenship already belongs to the kingdom of resurrection life. At times you may still feel the decay and the dust, but you can yet find hope, knowing that the man of heaven will one day transform your "lowly body to be like his glorious body" (Philippians 3:21)—forever!

1 THESSALONIANS 5:1-11

SEPTEMBER 11

WHAT TO DO WITH LIFE

"The man who had been possessed with demons begged him that he might be with him. And he did not permit him but said to him, 'Go home to your friends and tell them how much the Lord has done for you, and how he has had mercy on you.' And he ... began to proclaim ... how much Jesus had done for him." MARK 5:18-20

If we find it worthwhile to send missionaries into alien environments, and if we praise those who make the decision to leave their homeland and go overseas, then we need to confront the question: "What am I doing to tell others about Jesus? What am I doing about my street, my workplace, and my own spheres of influence? Am I boldly proclaiming the freedom and life promised through Christ?"

Our Christianity can grow too comfortable. We may think, "I'm a fairly decent human being. I show up at church every Sunday. I find inspiration in the Bible. I look after my family." But that is not a description of the transformed life that Christ called us to when He told us to go and make disciples (Matthew 28:18-19). That lifestyle is not what has converted unbelievers across the world throughout history. That complacency sees faith simply as an add-on, a decision made along the way, like someone deciding to join a gym just because they know it's good for them.

Like the man possessed by a demon in Mark 5, before we can passionately proclaim Christ as Lord and Savior, we first must become acutely aware of how helpless we are: held captive by our sin, roaming in the land of death. Only then can we fully realize the freedom, joy, and life to which Jesus Christ has delivered us. If we have grasped what Christ has done for us, then we will not need to be told that such a merciful deliverance should not be kept to ourselves but shared, whether with the ends of the earth or simply with those immediately around us.

You don't need to read books or take a class to share Jesus. You can simply tell others how Christ turned you right side up. Jesus had the man in Mark 5 start with his family and friends. His plan for the gospel to spread throughout this region started with one transformed life. So you may not be able to answer all your friends' questions. You may not know all about the doctrine of the Trinity. But if you are in Christ, you do know that while you were once blind, you now see.

The church is not a pleasure-cruise marina but a lifeboat station. It is our duty, and our privilege, to do as that rescued man did: to go out onto the sea of life to...

Rescue the perishing, care for the dying,
Snatch them in pity from sin and the grave;
Weep o'er the erring one, lift up the fallen,
Tell them of Jesus the mighty to save.[69]

Who is Jesus calling you to go to today?

LUKE 8:26-39

69 Fanny Crosby, "Rescue the Perishing" (1869).

SEPTEMBER 12

DEVOTED TO GOD'S WILL

"Then Esther told them to reply to Mordecai, 'Go, gather all the Jews to be found in Susa, and hold a fast on my behalf, and do not eat or drink for three days, night or day. I and my young women will also fast as you do. Then I will go to the king, though it is against the law, and if I perish, I perish.'"

ESTHER 4:15-16

Only once we are unafraid to die are we free to live.

Up until this point in the book of Esther, Mordecai has been sending the instructions and Esther has mainly been responding. But now Esther decides what she must do. She moves from being passive to being active—and she does so with absolute, resolute commitment. She will go and speak to the king on behalf of her people.

Though she would approach him alone, the queen's endeavor was not going to be a solo effort. Her Jewish community would fast with her on her behalf; they were in this together. The fast was one not of mourning but of declaring their desperate need for God's intervention. Esther recognized that she had to do something, but she didn't want to go to the king haphazardly, hoping to stumble into his presence based on her looks or what she had meant to him. She wanted to go to the king only on the strength of who God is and what He wanted.

Esther's devotion to God's will was evident, and striking: "If I perish, I perish." She was committed to go to the king even though it was against the law and might well result in her death (Esther 4:10-11). While risk was involved, she understood that the demand of God supersedes all other considerations. She knew she must do all she could to act for the good of God's people—and so she was willing to put her life at risk.

Common sense would have told Esther to play it safe—to keep quiet and hope that perhaps the king would invite her into his presence. But common sense and believing faith are not always in accord with one another. After all, common sense would argue that the worst thing that can possibly happen to our life is for us to lose it, while believing faith views death as "gain" and "far better," for it is a departure to be with Christ (Philippians 1:21, 23).

Esther was willing to die to do what was needed. She had decided that it was better to perish obediently than to live disobediently. Only when we get to the point in our own spiritual journeys where we can sincerely say, "If I die, I die," can we go on living for God. The risk may be great, but the reward is infinitely greater. Today, ask God to orient your heart so that you can declare with the psalmist, "A day in your courts is better than a thousand elsewhere. I would rather be a doorkeeper in the house of my God than dwell in the tents of wickedness" (Psalm 84:10). If that is your perspective, you will find courage and obedience come far more easily, and joyfully.

ESTHER 4:1-16

◇ Bible Through The Year: Judges 13–15; John 5:1-24

SEPTEMBER 13

ONLY FOOLS RUSH IN

"When the king saw Queen Esther standing in the court, she won favor in his sight, and he held out to Esther the golden scepter that was in his hand. Then Esther approached and touched the tip of the scepter. And the king said to her, 'What is it, Queen Esther? What is your request? It shall be given you, even to the half of my kingdom.' And Esther said, 'If it please the king, let the king and Haman come today to a feast that I have prepared for the king.'" ESTHER 5:2-4

"Fools rush in where angels fear to tread."[70] Esther seems to have understood this. As she prepared to entreat King Ahasuerus, she was resolved to take the route of obedience to God, even though she might die—but she approached the moment with subtle wisdom. She was simultaneously brave, appropriate, cautious, humble, skillful, delicate, and precise. Her entrance before the king was cleverly designed and carefully planned and executed.

The time for fasting and preparation was over, and Esther appropriately prepared herself by putting on her royal robes (Esther 5:1). She approached the king according to protocol. She recognized that she had entered a peculiarly perilous environment. When Ahasuerus extended his grace toward her, she humbly accepted it by touching the tip of his scepter.

While the king was exaggerating by offering half of his kingdom, he was saying there was little limit to what he was prepared to do for his queen, because she had found favor in his eyes. Esther's answer—to invite the king to dinner—sounds rather anticlimactic! Yet there was skillful wisdom displayed in her invitation to a great banquet. She seemed to understand that the way to this man's heart was through his stomach, so she invited him to eat with her. The king was very pleased with Esther's request. After all, it's one thing to put together a feast for yourself, as Ahasuerus did earlier (Esther 1); it's another thing altogether to be invited to a feast that is prepared in *your* honor.

Esther understood that what she was to ask of the king was no small thing. The king would soon learn Esther's true identity, and she essentially was about to ask him to lose face in front of his entire kingdom. Her plea needed to be delicate yet precise.

For many of us, once we've resolved to do something, we are tempted to just get at it directly, with no concern as to how we might affect or offend anybody else. After all, something needs to be done! But we often find ourselves acting in a way that is entirely unhelpful and unedifying. It is very possible to do the right thing in the wrong way.

Next time you face a situation that demands obedience and courage, take a leaf from Esther's book, and consider not only *what* you must do but *how* best to approach it. It is right to take risks to obey God and share His gospel; it is unwise to increase them in how you go about it. Like this queen, you can be bold—and winsome.

ESTHER 5:1-8

70 Alexander Pope, *An Essay on Criticism* (1711).

SEPTEMBER 14

CONSUMED BY PRIDE

"Haman went out that day joyful and glad of heart. But when Haman saw Mordecai in the king's gate, that he neither rose nor trembled before him, he was filled with wrath against Mordecai." ESTHER 5:9

Haman was the archetypal egomaniac. He surrounded himself with those who would listen to his incessant talking about himself and who would sycophantically acknowledge his significance and greatness. He lived with the mistaken notion that he was the center of the universe. Haman would fit perfectly in contemporary Western culture, where social-media feeds and news outlets are often littered with stories of those who apparently have done little of true significance but who live for, and expect, attention and recognition. (Of course, our hearts are not much different in their proud desire for praise. The difference is often not that we are more godly but that we lack the opportunity to showcase ourselves.)

So it was that after Haman attended the exclusive banquet put on by Queen Esther, he left "joyful and glad of heart" at the elevated position in the kingdom that had seen him invited as the honored guest. Yet all the enjoyment, prestige, and accolades were insufficient to prevent him from becoming entirely destabilized by the fact that Mordecai did not stand when Haman passed by. His joy was so brittle that this one apparent slight caused wrath to consume him.

Pride does that to a person. Nothing can ever satisfy. For the proud person there is always another promotion, another award, another dollar to aim for—something else beyond their reach. King Solomon writes of such a person, "Do you see a man who is wise in his own eyes? There is more hope for a fool than for him" (Proverbs 26:12). This was true in Haman's life. It was pride that drove him to plot murder—even a massacre. It was pride that meant he could not enjoy what he had but could only be angry at what he did not have.

We may shake our heads at Haman's pride. But then we read in God's word of how Jesus, God Himself, "emptied himself, by taking the form of a servant, being born in the likeness of men. And being found in human form, he humbled himself by becoming obedient to the point of death, even death on a cross" (Philippians 2:7-8). And we are forced to ask whether we are more like that or like Haman. When we thoughtfully consider Jesus' pattern of humility, we see the truth of our own prideful hearts.

We would do well to echo the words of George Whitefield: "O that I could always see myself in proper Colours! I believe I should have little reason to fall down and worship myself. *God be merciful to me, a Sinner!*"[71] As we witness Haman's pride and eventual downfall and look inside ourselves, surely we are prompted to cry out for God's mercy to help us walk in humility like Jesus—for "God opposes the proud but gives grace to the humble" (James 4:6).

ESTHER 5:9-14

71 *The Two First Parts of His Life, with His Journals* (W. Strahan, 1756), p 75.

SEPTEMBER 15

HUMBLE FAITHFULNESS

"So Haman came in, and the king said to him, 'What should be done to the man whom the king delights to honor?' And Haman said to himself, 'Whom would the king delight to honor more than me?' ... Then the king said to Haman, 'Hurry; take the robes and the horse, as you have said, and do so to Mordecai the Jew, who sits at the king's gate. Leave out nothing that you have mentioned.'" ESTHER 6:6, 10

Here is one of the Bible's great jaw-dropping moments.

Haman was a proud and presumptuous man, and this led him to make a huge miscalculation. His assumption, upon hearing that there was a "man whom the king delights to honor," was to assume that he must be that man. So he outlined a plan for exaltation involving royal robes, a royal horse, a crown, and public praise with no one in mind other than himself (Esther 6:8-9). We can imagine Haman's heart swelling as he heard the king say to him, "Hurry, take the robes and the horse, as you have said..." And then he heard... "And do so to Mordecai the Jew."

How that name must have struck Haman's heart when he heard it!

Haman had set out that day to hang Mordecai (Esther 6:4). And now he was being told to parade the man through the public square, announcing the king's generous reward for the one person Haman most despised. What a picture! What a performance!

By contrast, the humility and normality of Mordecai's existence is established in just a single sentence: "Then Mordecai returned to the king's gate" (Esther 6:12). Mordecai didn't blow his trumpet as Haman had done when he came from Queen Esther's first banquet (5:11-12). Though he was paraded through the town—an unsought exaltation, an unsought ride on the king's horse—he just went back and sat down where he had always sat.

There's something compelling about humble faithfulness—doing what we do, day in and day out, not in hope of praise but because it is the right thing to do. It doesn't seem like much at the time. Yet often when children and grandchildren reflect on the lives of their faithful parents and grandparents, they say things like "She always did this," "He always sat there," "This is when she always prayed," or "This is where his Bible always was."

Mordecai did what was right because it was right, not because he wanted to be recognized and exalted. Today, let it be enough that you do what is right in God's eyes, whether you're honored by those around you, as Mordecai was, or you're quickly forgotten like so many faithful believers throughout history. One day, all the scales will be reset, and honor will be given where honor is due. In the meantime, set aside any prideful endeavor for distinction, and continue in the normality of your daily routine with faithfulness and humility.

ESTHER 6:1-11

SEPTEMBER 16

DOES GOD NEED US?

"Then Queen Esther answered, 'If I have found favor in your sight, O king, and if it please the king, let my life be granted me for my wish, and my people for my request. For we have been sold, I and my people, to be destroyed, to be killed, and to be annihilated. If we had been sold merely as slaves, men and women, I would have been silent, for our affliction is not to be compared with the loss to the king.'" ESTHER 7:3-4

We take risks and serve our God because our success does not rest on us.

The moment had come for Esther to act on Mordecai's challenge and speak to the king for the sake of God's people (Esther 4). She purposefully used the words of the edict: "destroy," "kill," "annihilate" (3:13). Moreover, Esther didn't plead with the king based on his sense of morality. Instead, she made her appeal on the strength of the king's self-interest—the killing of his favorite queen. Esther skillfully spoke in such a way as to turn the spotlight on Haman without implicating the king. When the king asked, "Who is he, and where is he, who has dared to do this?" (7:5), Esther might have justifiably shown him a mirror—but that would not have been smart!

Through all of this, God was at work in events over which Esther had absolutely no control. And He was also at work in the way in which Esther exercised her wisdom, skill, obedience, and so on—aspects of her personhood over which she *did* have control.

It isn't that God needed Esther so badly that if she didn't act, His plan would have failed. That would be to give too much prominence to human responsibility. But neither is it true that God was going to do whatever He wanted regardless of Esther's involvement. That wrongly divorces His sovereignty from human engagement. This is a great mystery! God may purpose to use human agents, but He can work without us. And even when He *does* use us, success depends upon neither His agents nor what they do.

This is true for us as we endeavor to tell people about Jesus or teach God's word. God could reveal Himself however He sees fit and grow the faith of His people however He wishes, but He gives us a part to play. He tells us to teach, to encourage one another, and to proclaim the gospel. And so we do. But in the end, we know that no heart-and-life transformation is ever achieved apart from the work of the living God. He is the only one who softens hard hearts and opens darkened eyes. He is the only one who can ordain both the means and the end.

And it is because God is sovereign that you have every reason to act in obedience to Him. Though success is not dependent upon you, the God who made the entire universe has chosen to use you. He will complete His good work (Philippians 1:6). He will use His people to reach His people and serve His people. Let this understanding humble you, even as it gives you encouragement to face the tasks to which you have been called, to take risks, and to serve and obey Him as He works in and through you.

ESTHER 6:12 - 7:10

SEPTEMBER 17

WEEPING, PLEADING, AND SPEAKING

"Then Esther spoke again to the king. She fell at his feet and wept and pleaded with him to avert the evil plan of Haman the Agagite and the plot that he had devised against the Jews." ESTHER 8:3

Self-interest is never acceptable for the child of God.

If Esther had only been interested in making sure that Haman received his just deserts and that her own life was saved and her own exalted status secured, then her purpose would have been completed with Haman's death. Her aim, however, encompassed not only Haman's punishment and her own security but the salvation of the whole Jewish nation. For Esther, rescuing herself was not enough as long as her people still faced annihilation.

As Esther "spoke again to the king," it was only a matter of hours since Haman had fallen at Esther's feet, concerned only for himself (Esther 7:7-8). She, by contrast, fell at the king's feet concerned only for her people. She could not bear to see their destruction.

Centuries later, another Jew, when his life was radically grabbed hold of by God, stated, "I have great sorrow and unceasing anguish in my heart. For I could wish that I myself were accursed and cut off from Christ for the sake of my brothers, my kinsmen according to the flesh. They are Israelites, and to them belong the adoption, the glory, the covenants, the giving of the law, the worship, and the promises" (Romans 9:2-4). The apostle Paul wasn't content that he alone had met Jesus on the Damascus road. He longed to see his people come to a saving knowledge of Christ. In this he followed his Lord and Savior, who came from His heavenly throne to the squalor of a stable in order to lift His people from the miry pit and take them to His eternal paradise. The Lord Jesus Himself wept over those who would not see that in His coming, God was offering them peace instead of conflict and rescue instead of judgment (Luke 19:41-44).

When a man or woman comes to know Christ's salvation, not only are they set in a right relationship with God; they also become aware that those who are unconverted are in a wrong relationship with God and are facing judgment and an eternity outside of His loving presence.

We should never be like Haman, concerned only for ourselves. God forgive us when we are. It is right for us to weep as we recognize the calamity that is facing people if they will not find refuge in Christ—our family, friends, and neighbors included. Like Paul, we should care more for their salvation than our own. But, also like Paul, we can do more than cry, for our tears can be accompanied with prayers that those we love would turn to Jesus and embrace Him as their Messiah, and with a proclamation of the gospel, in the hopes that the Lord will use us to divert their path from death to life, just as He used Esther to rescue the Jews. Who will you weep over, pray for, and seek to speak to?

ESTHER 8:1-17

SEPTEMBER 18

THE GOD OF GREAT REVERSALS

"When the king's command and edict were about to be carried out, on the very day when the enemies of the Jews hoped to gain the mastery over them, the reverse occurred: the Jews gained mastery over those who hated them." ESTHER 9:1

Haman and his cronies had been confident that the annihilation of the Jewish population on the thirteenth day of the twelfth month was inescapable. It had been decreed throughout the kingdom. The Jews were going to be obliterated. But when the day dawned, the Jews overpowered their enemies instead. Haman and his friends had taken nearly a year determining what would be the best day for their enemies to be killed (Esther 3:7). No wonder that the author is specific about the date when the great reversal took place: "on the very day" Haman had chosen!

This is just one of several great reversals in the book of Esther. Earlier, Haman had emerged from the banquet with the king and Esther the queen feeling as if he was on top of the world. He had gone home to his wife and friends and "recounted to them the splendor of his riches, the number of his sons" (Esther 5:11). Yet on that day chosen by Haman, all ten of his sons, his crowning glory, were killed (9:7-10). His family plummeted from exaltation to devastation.

Mordecai's experience was just the opposite. He went from obscurity and apparent irrelevance to becoming the most powerful man under the king. He started off as "a Jew in Susa the citadel" who sat at the king's gate (Esther 2:5)—which doesn't sound like much! But by the end of the book, he "was great in the king's house, and his fame spread throughout all the provinces, for the man Mordecai grew more and more powerful" (9:4).

Mordecai and Esther did not gloat over the destruction of their enemies. They did, however, dance and celebrate with their Jewish community (Esther 9:18) because they recognized that these reversals were God's doing, and so they were marvelous in their eyes (Psalm 118:23). We can almost hear them singing the song of deliverance:

> You have turned for me my mourning into dancing;
> you have loosed my sackcloth
> and clothed me with gladness,
> that my glory may sing your praise and not be silent.
> O LORD my God, I will give thanks to you forever! (Psalm 30:11-12)

God is the God of great reversals. He can turn a curse into blessing. He achieves the impossible, the word irreversible means nothing to Him, and no situation is irredeemable for Him. The cross of Calvary stands as the ultimate and eternal evidence of this.

If you are facing circumstances that look hopeless, call out to God for help. Even though you may have to wait through your entire earthly pilgrimage, He promises to deliver you. And if you have already experienced one of God's reversals in your life, take time to give thanks and sing His praise. He is good indeed!

ESTHER 9:1-19

SEPTEMBER 19

A FIRM OBLIGATION

"The Jews firmly obligated themselves and their offspring and all who joined them, that without fail they would keep these two days according to what was written and at the time appointed every year, that these days should be remembered and kept throughout every generation, in every clan, province, and city, and that these days of Purim should never fall into disuse among the Jews, nor should the commemoration of these days cease among their descendants."
ESTHER 9:27-28

"Obligation" is a fairly unfashionable word in contemporary Western culture. People commonly say things like "I don't want to make you feel obligated in any way." But obligation is often necessary and good. I want to be obligated to my wife entirely, and I want her to be obligated to me. When my children were young, I wanted them to be obligated to me in terms of respecting my parental authority. And in fact, the obligations that extend throughout interpersonal relationships are first of all obligations to God Himself.

After being rescued from destruction at the hand of Haman, the Jews "*firmly* obligated themselves" to the task of remembrance. They were not half-heartedly committing to observing their new tradition, only keeping it if it was convenient for them when the time came. They were *definitely* going to follow through. That's the nature of duty.

The Jews not only committed themselves but also obligated their children and "all who joined them." They made this a comprehensive commitment throughout all locations and every generation. And 2,500 years later, the tradition of Purim still goes on. Jewish communities throughout the world continue to celebrate the feast because of the obligation these people made never to allow the generations that followed to forget God's intervention on their behalf in Esther's time and through Esther's bravery.

Our culture tells us that we don't need to obligate ourselves to anyone or anything, that we can just live for ourselves in the here and now, and that most commitments can be rethought in future if we feel they are inconvenient or unsustainable. But in the kingdom of God, obligation matters. After all, God has obligated Himself to save and keep His people. What you commit to and hold to speaks of what matters most to you. So, commit yourself to the celebration of the gospel, including partaking in those great moments that God has given us to remember what He has done for us: the sacraments of baptism and the Lord's Supper. And, so far as you are able, ensure that these things pass from one generation to the next. Even if Christ has not yet returned a thousand years from now, there will be those who know and stand for the gospel because of the obligation we have made in our generation.

ESTHER 9:20-32

SEPTEMBER 20

A MIND FOR OTHERS

"All the acts of his power and might, and the full account of the high honor of Mordecai, to which the king advanced him, are they not written in the Book of the Chronicles of the kings of Media and Persia? For Mordecai the Jew was second in rank to King Ahasuerus, and he was great among the Jews and popular with the multitude of his brothers, for he sought the welfare of his people and spoke peace to all his people." ESTHER 10:2-3

Occasionally in the course of history, a single person has arisen without whose presence everything would be different. One such person was Winston Churchill, the former British prime minister, statesman, and defender of freedom. No student of history is able honestly to disavow that the history of the Second World War and its consequences would have been radically different if Churchill had not stepped forward. Though often the tide of history seems to flow inexorably on regardless of the actions of any one person, you will be able to think of those in your own nation and society who have diverted history's course in a decisive way.

Back in the 5th century BC, Mordecai was one such individual. The events of his life were recorded in the chronicles of Media and Persia because if he had not arisen, things would have been markedly different.

Mordecai wasn't a Persian. He was a Jew and lived as a Jew, honoring a different God (the only true God), living in a different way and keeping different traditions than the Persians. Yet even though he was so obviously different, he was honored by the Persians, not because he spoke out of both sides of his mouth or sought to curry favor with King Ahasuerus but because of his absolute integrity and moral consistency. Mordecai didn't set out to be liked. He set out to do what was right—what God had given him to do.

When someone is given a position of significant influence, they often become unpopular because others are jealous. Mordecai's lasting popularity with his fellow Jews was uncommon. It may have been in part because Mordecai cared about them. He did not become isolated from or disinterested in his people but instead used his position for the welfare of others, rather than the enrichment of himself, and to speak "peace to all his people." As one commentator sums it up, "Mordecai's lasting legacy is that he combined service to the king with service to his people, without compromising on either account. He serves both and speaks up for both, desiring for both their good and their peace."[72]

Learn from Mordecai. Aim to do what is right—what God has given you to do, in the place and the time He has assigned for you. Like Mordecai, let your legacy be one by which people recognize that because you have a mind for God, you also have a mind for others—doing all you can to bring them rest, welfare, peace, and prosperity. Your deeds may or may not make it into the history books of this world—but they will be recorded and celebrated in eternity.

ESTHER 10:1-3

72 Debra Reid, *Esther*, Tyndale Old Testament Commentaries (InterVarsity, 2008).

SEPTEMBER 21

THE PRIVILEGE OF HIS WORD

"His divine power has granted to us all things that pertain to life and godliness, through the knowledge of him who called us to his own glory and excellence."
2 PETER 1:3

When was the last time that you paused to ponder what a privilege it is to have nearly unlimited access to God's word? These days, we can carry it around in our pockets and pull up any chapter and verse or even search the entire Bible in a matter of seconds.

Instant access to all of Scripture feels so commonplace. And yet we ought to be astounded at such an honor! Their Author formed the heavens with His fingers (Psalm 8:3). He breathed the Scriptures out Himself (2 Timothy 3:16). Their contents are more valuable than the finest gold (Psalm 19:10), and their truth will endure forever (1 Peter 1:24). In the Bible, we find all that we need for life and godliness—and nothing we don't. Every paragraph is unique in its addition to the whole, and yet every part contributes to the one grand story. Most of all, it is the means by which the Spirit brings us into a deeper "knowledge of" God—which we could translate "relationship with," since the Greek word Peter uses, *epignosis*, carries the sense of a relational knowing, not a merely intellectual one. It is through the word that we come to know more intimately our Maker, whom we were created to glorify and enjoy forever.[73]

In the longest prayer of our Lord Jesus that Scripture records, He spends much time praying for His people. In one specific petition, He asks this: "Sanctify them in the truth; your word is truth" (John 17:17). Jesus Himself knew the power of God's word. When Satan tempted Him in the wilderness, He responded with scriptural truth. In one instance, he quoted Moses from Deuteronomy 8:3 and reiterated for us that "man shall not live by bread alone, but by every word that comes from the mouth of God" (Matthew 4:4). If Jesus Christ nourished His own soul on the word of God, then how much more do we need its food?

Sometimes constant easy access to something causes us to miss what a privilege it is to have it—like water or electricity, for example. While the shower and the lights are working fine, we hardly give them a second thought. But we certainly do notice when they are gone! Let's not treat God's word the same way. God has gifted us with such unhindered access to His truth. Why not take it up and read? How will you soak in the Scriptures and bask in the rays of truth that contain everything you need for life and godliness?

PSALM 119:33-40

73 Westminster Shorter Catechism, Answer 1.

SEPTEMBER 22

JESUS, YOUR FRIEND

"This is my commandment, that you love one another as I have loved you. Greater love has no one than this, that someone lay down his life for his friends. You are my friends if you do what I command you. No longer do I call you servants, for the servant does not know what his master is doing; but I have called you friends, for all that I have heard from my Father I have made known to you." JOHN 15:12-15

Folk and pop singers often write songs about alienation because it produces such raw emotions. Paul Simon captured it well when he sang of building impenetrable walls in his life and becoming a "rock" and an "island," rejecting love and laughter because "friendship causes pain."[74]

But the truth that all of us know deep down is that friendship is vitally important for each and every one of us. God Almighty has wired us to care for one another. We long for relationships: to be known, to be loved. We know that even one genuine friend makes us truly rich in this world. We don't want to be islands.

Yet while we may have true friends who are loyal, sensitive, and honest, we can only find ultimate friendship in Jesus. He alone is the friend who "is the same yesterday today and forever" (Hebrews 13:8). His brand of friendship extends far beyond the bounds of human friendship; He knew how to be a true friend even to tax collectors and sinners (Matthew 11:19; Luke 7:34). One of the reasons that some find friendship so difficult is because it demands vulnerability and openness. But Jesus is never in a bad mood, never lets us down, never treats us capriciously. And He wants to be friends with us—with you! As you come to Him in faith, the one through whom all things were created delights to call you His friend. Let that sink in a little.

Every friendship requires effort, and friendship with Jesus is no different! That's why Jesus tells us, "You are my friends if you do what I command you." When we receive Jesus as a friend, we also accept Him as our King.

Perhaps you have found human relationships to be hurtful or fleeting. Perhaps you are surrounded with friends, or perhaps you cannot count a single one. In any case, here is the most wonderful friend: the one who knows us completely and loves us all the same. With Him we can have the kind of friend that "sticks closer than a brother" (Proverbs 18:24).

Earthly friends may fail or leave us,
One day soothe, the next day grieve us;
But this Friend will ne'er deceive us:
Oh, how He loves![75]

JOHN 15:12-17

74 Paul Simon, "I Am a Rock" (1965).
75 Marianne Nunn, "One There Is above All Others" (1817).

SEPTEMBER 23

HOW TO OVERCOME JEALOUSY

"Wrath is cruel, anger is overwhelming, but who can stand before jealousy?"
PROVERBS 27:4

Jealousy has been the downfall of humanity since our very beginning.

In Genesis 4 it was Cain's jealousy of his brother Abel that led to murder. While it might be easy to dismiss their story as inapplicable to ourselves, since we probably don't have a criminal record for murder and are not tempted to obtain one, it is possible to bring ruin to those we envy without ever laying a hand on them, through a snide word here and a blessing withheld there. Not only that but jealousy, when left unaddressed in our hearts, will crush us and overwhelm us.

Jealousy flourishes when others receive more or achieve better than we do. It can penetrate our minds even as we observe the lives of people we don't know well, simply because we perceive them to have some form of advantage unavailable to us. When someone else experiences happiness because of success or a good reputation, jealousy may manifest as a kind of sadness for ourselves that excludes any gladness for the other. Consider the parable of the prodigal son (Luke 15:11-32): when the elder brother watched his father celebrate the homecoming of his delinquent younger brother, he refused to cheer along. Why? Because even though he had never lost good standing with his father, he resented the joyous forgiveness and recognition given to another.

Jealousy can make us hostile toward those who have never meant to harm us. When Joseph's brothers observed how their father loved him, "they hated him and could not speak peacefully to him" (Genesis 37:4). Suddenly, at their breakfast table, relationships were broken—and through no fault of Joseph's! He had done nothing by his own design to intentionally harm or hinder his brothers, but they hated him because seeds of jealousy were planted deep in their hearts.

Jealousy also fails to recognize that God knows what He is doing when He apportions gifts. When we are jealous of another's success, we say to God, "You ought to understand that *I* am supposed to be there… *I* should look like her… *I* should have what he has." But shall the potter have to endure such questions from the clay (Isaiah 64:8)? Why do we think we can question God's divine wisdom as He deals with us and with others? He has made us and arranged our circumstances exactly as He desires.

Rare is the man or woman who does not struggle with jealousy for one reason or another, at one time or another. So what is the cure for it? With the Holy Spirit's help, it is to name jealousy for the sin that it is and ask Him to help us daily to root it out, purposefully and ruthlessly. And, again with the Spirit's help, we can consider all that we have in Christ—for as we think about the spiritual blessings that are ours through Him, jealousy withers and contentment grows in its place. Do not let envy grow in your heart today—and if and where it has done so, root it out.

1 TIMOTHY 5:6-10

SEPTEMBER 24

DRAWING NEAR

"Let us draw near with a true heart in full assurance of faith, with our hearts sprinkled clean from an evil conscience and our bodies washed with pure water."
HEBREWS 10:22

For the vast number of God's people living under the old covenant, access to God was only by way of the high priest. Only he was able to physically draw near to God with any sense of intimacy—and this only once a year, on the Day of Atonement! It was therefore dramatic and revolutionary for the writer of Hebrews to exhort his readers to "draw near" to God as they prayed.

What happened to cause such a seismic change in the way people are able to approach God? The answer is, in short, Calvary. When "Jesus cried out ... with a loud voice and yielded up his spirit ... the curtain of the temple was torn in two, from top to bottom" (Matthew 27:50-51). Under the old covenant, this curtain had restricted access to the presence of God—but now the barrier was obliterated. Now it was possible for men and women, on the basis of Christ's atoning death, to make their way directly into God's presence. Now they could draw near to the God who is majestic in His holiness and in whose presence no sinner could live—until Calvary.

How should we respond to the writer's invitation? First, we ought to draw near with confidence. The writer prefaces his exhortation by saying, "Since we have confidence..." (Hebrews 10:19). Whereas previously our approach to God could only ever have been tentative and fearful, now we're able to come confidently in faith and great joy on the basis of "the blood of Jesus" (v 19).

Second, we ought to draw near with gratitude. We should recognize the wonder of being able to come into His presence directly. We are not to draw near haphazardly or flippantly, for it took the death of the Son of God to open "the new and living way" to God (Hebrews 10:20). We are therefore to approach Him in humble and reverent thankfulness.

Whereas the Old Testament way, as Franz Delitzsch puts it, "was simply a lifeless pavement trodden by the high priest, and by him alone,"[76] the way that we now walk is indeed new and living. Thanks be to God that we now draw near through Jesus, fully assured that we are accepted by our Maker. Are you holding back from praying to your almighty Father out of an awareness of your sin? Be sure that the blood of Jesus has covered it. Are you under the impression that you need to clean up your act and bring your good deeds before God if He is to accept you? Be clear that the curtain is torn and Jesus has done it all. Do you skip drawing near to God out of complacency or busyness? Be aware that Jesus died to give you that privilege. Because of Calvary, we can, and should, draw near with confident, grateful joy today.

HEBREWS 12:18-24

76 *Commentary on the Epistle to the Hebrews*, trans. Thomas L. Kingsbury (Edinburgh, 1870), 2:171.

SEPTEMBER 25

BLESSED TRINITY

"It shall come to pass that everyone who calls on the name of the LORD shall be saved." JOEL 2:32

There are "biblical" words that are not, in fact, in the Bible. For example, you will not find the word *substitute* in your Bible, and yet the word conveys the beauty of what happened when the Son of God died in the place of sinners. You will not find the word *Trinity* in the Scriptures either, and yet it represents true teaching about who God is. And the truth it captures is wondrous.

Adding to the wonder of the doctrine of the Trinity is the fact that such a teaching arose from a faith that was utterly committed to the one-ness, the unity, of God. The truth that there is one God was fundamental for Old Testament believers. The passage that articulated the monotheistic heart of the Hebrew faith, and which every Jew knew by heart, declared, "The LORD our God, the LORD is one" (Deuteronomy 6:4). Salvation is found in this one God alone: "Everyone who calls on the name of the LORD shall be saved." It would be impossible to overstate how deeply the truth of God's unity was embedded into the thinking of God's old-covenant people.

This was true when the early church exploded into being in Jerusalem. For men like Peter and Paul, the unity of God was axiomatic. The only way for them to come to understand that the one God exists in three Persons, then, would be for that God to reveal Himself to them. This is precisely what happened in the person of Jesus Christ, who claimed authority to forgive sins and verified that authority by doing what is possible only for God to do (Mark 2:1-12). In this way Jesus revealed Himself to be the divine Son of the divine Father, and together They would send the divine Spirit to Their people (John 14:23-26). Then, before ascending to heaven, this Jesus commissioned His disciples to make disciples of all nations and to baptize them in the one name of God, which is attributed to three Persons: God the Father, God the Son, and God the Holy Spirit (Matthew 28:19-20). The disciples understood that the Lord of the Old Testament had been with them in Jesus. They had been fishing with the Lord, had sat at His feet, and had watched Him work wonders. And they understood that when they urged people to call on the name of the Lord to be saved, they were urging them to call on Jesus Christ (Acts 2:21; Romans 10:13).

For the disciples, this understanding came as the Spirit of God worked in their hearts and minds as they considered what Jesus had taught them and what He had done. For us, it comes as we meditate on the Scriptures and let the Spirit illumine its pages for us. Yet the truth of God's triune nature is not for our mental exercise alone; it also ought to cause our hearts to swell in adoration of our vast, mysterious, and transcendent God, who nevertheless draws near to us. And it ought to fuel us, as it did the disciples, to go into this unbelieving world with confidence that this triune God—Father, Son, and Spirit—will draw people to Himself as the gospel message goes forth.

JOEL 2:21-32

SEPTEMBER 26

THE CROWN OF LIFE

"Blessed is the man who remains steadfast under trial, for when he has stood the test he will receive the crown of life, which God has promised to those who love him." JAMES 1:12

It's easy to want to graduate without taking the required classes. But without taking the classes there's no way to be ready for the tests, and without a test there's no graduation. As in academia, so in our faith: it would be foolish to think that we can graduate to maturity and completeness in the Christian life before taking the courses and going through the tests.

When James writes about the believer who "*has stood* the test," he uses the word *dokimos*, which refers to someone who is tested, tried, and approved. This kind of person has the seal of God's approval on their life, and that becomes clearer and clearer through their perseverance.

The "crown of life," or, more accurately, the crown that *consists* of life, is "a picture of eternal life,"[77] which God promises to His people. It suggests the idea of God welcoming us at the finish line and crowning us with honor, blessing, and life that is everlasting. So the duration of the test is the duration of our lives. Our test lasts until Christ returns or calls us home—and so here is a call to remain steadfast to the end.

It is this perspective and this promise that transform how we meet the most difficult times of our lives. We're often tempted to regard individual trials as intruders rather than welcoming them "as friends" (James 1:2, Phillips). But when we understand that the whole of life is a series of tests, that can reassure us, giving us an opportunity to think seriously and realistically about what we go through. We can know with confidence that ahead of us lies the crown of eternal life with Jesus, and that our trials are opportunities to learn perseverance and grow in Christlikeness, proclaiming to the world that the one whom we are walking toward is sufficient not just for life but also for joy.

The Christian life has no simulation phase to prepare us for the real thing; it is a real-time experience all the time, every day. We're not afforded the opportunity to find out exactly how we will parent our children, deal with the sudden loss of a loved one, or react to whatever else might come our way until these things actually come our way. These are the real-life courses we must take to graduate on to spiritual maturity. What trials are you walking through today? These are the classes, unchosen by you though they may be, which the Lord knows will enable you to persevere and will prepare you for your crown. As, by His grace, you remain steadfast in the storms today, remember that you are "blessed," not with the false blessing of an easy life now but with the eternal blessing of the "crown of life" to come.

JAMES 1:2-4

77. Derek Prime, *From Trials to Triumphs* (Regal, 1982), p 28.

SEPTEMBER 27

MYSTERIOUS PROVIDENCE

"The next day we put in at Sidon. And Julius treated Paul kindly and gave him leave to go to his friends and be cared for." ACTS 27:3

Acts 7:58 records that Saul of Tarsus watched over the coats of those who were stoning Stephen, the first martyr. Soon after this, Saul (later also known as Paul) was at the forefront of the persecution that resulted in Christians being driven out of Jerusalem, scattering them into the regions around it—and spreading the gospel along with them (8:3-4)! And then Saul was converted: Christ brought him to faith and commissioned him as an apostle even as he was "breathing threats and murder against the disciples of the Lord" (9:1).

And so it was that by Acts 27:3, Saul, now always known as Paul, had Christian friends in Sidon—likely members of a community founded in the city at the time of the persecution and dispersion that had followed Stephen's death. The friends that were available to Paul in Sidon were there because Saul of Tarsus had been such a horrible persecutor. God indeed "moves in a mysterious way His wonders to perform."[78]

If we had been among those who were persecuted by Saul, we likely would have joined in their mourning, saying, *O Lord, we're all being spread apart. Our families are being scattered. Our communities are being broken up. Isn't this dreadful and awful?* From their perspective, it certainly appeared so. Even in the midst of such great tragedy, however, we see God's mysterious providence: Paul himself, now a Christian, was on the receiving end of Christian kindness from a church that existed in that city in part because he had been such a determined persecutor.

In due time, the tangled messes of our present lives, of our difficulties and disappointments, will all be put in their proper perspective. We should remember that…

Ill that He blesses is our good,
And unblest good is ill;
And all is right that seems most wrong,
If it be His sweet will![79]

This little anecdote from Paul's life reiterates the truth that Joseph declared to his brothers when they sought his forgiveness for having sold him into Egypt: "As for you, you meant evil against me, but God meant it for good" (Genesis 50:20). God is able to sweep even the evil intentions of people into the unfolding drama of His purposes for His children. He is faithful and unchanging. Take comfort in His mysterious providence, knowing that He will not allow anything to befall you which will not ultimately be used for your good and His glory.

GENESIS 45:4-15

78 William Cowper, "God Moves in a Mysterious Way" (1774).
79 Frederick W. Faber, "I Worship Thee, Sweet Will of God" (1849).

SEPTEMBER 28

GOD'S WISDOM

"This alone I found, that God made man upright, but they have sought out many schemes." ECCLESIASTES 7:29

I once received a letter from a young man who'd been educated at the highest level in both American and British universities. In that letter, he wrote, "I must say, all the education in the world has made me the most stupid and unenlightened man." It's hard to believe that these words came from such a scholar—but truly, he knew enough to recognize that foolishness has nothing to do with mental faculty but everything to do with moral rebellion.

Human foolishness exists because of our disobedience to God, who is the only source of true wisdom and enlightenment. Such rebellion results in alienation from God and others. And since God must punish sin, the foolishness of man leads to condemnation. We are created to be "upright," but we lean into self-sufficient, self-aggrandizing schemes. We are twisted and stunted because we live for ourselves instead of our Creator. So we can know all sorts of things and yet know nothing. Yet in our hopeless state, the wisdom of God can be made known to us in the Lord Jesus Christ (Colossians 2:2-3). This wisdom becomes ours only when we believe in Him as our God and Savior, for "the fear of the Lord is the *beginning* of knowledge" (Proverbs 1:7, emphasis added). God's Spirit enables us to turn from our old way of life and start on a new journey. As we turn to Him in repentance, the Lord will accept us, even in our sinfulness. And then, by His great power, He will take us and change us by His grace.

That is God's wisdom. You can't find it in any self-help book. You can't find it in mere religion or philosophy. You can't find it in the best universities. Those are dead-end streets. You can only find it in Jesus, who offers to become your wisdom and righteousness. In our foolishness, we have all run from the one who made us—yet He has pursued us, made known to us our condition, and chosen to reveal His Son to us. Take time to praise God for His infinite wisdom and amazing grace! And then consider this: Would anything need to change if you made all your decisions and set your direction in life by beginning with "the fear of the Lord" and not with the schemes of man?

COLOSSIANS 2:1-4

SEPTEMBER 29

BETWEEN FAITH AND FEAR

"'See my hands and my feet, that it is I myself. Touch me, and see. For a spirit does not have flesh and bones as you see that I have.' And when he had said this, he showed them his hands and his feet. And while they still disbelieved for joy and were marveling, he said to them, 'Have you anything here to eat?'"

LUKE 24:39-41

The disciples were real people—and they found believing in the resurrection difficult. News of Jesus' resurrection produced a roller coaster of emotions within His disciples. One minute they seemed to be up on the crest, and the next minute they were hurtling toward the ground. Reports of an empty tomb were met with mixed emotions of awe and unbelief. Indeed, they thought the words of the women who had discovered it were "an idle tale, and they did not believe them" (Luke 24:11).

Even when Jesus appeared suddenly and stood among His disciples, their sorrows were not soothed and their fears were not calmed. Instead, we discover that they were still in panic mode. Face-to-face with the resurrected Christ, they "were startled and frightened and thought they saw a spirit" (Luke 24:37). Even after Jesus showed them His hands and feet, they still battled disbelief as it jostled against the dawning joy.

This is a wonderfully honest picture, isn't it? Here we find the group of people who were to be the pillars of the church, all essentially hiding behind couches and coming out of closets, saying, *We thought we saw a ghost!*

The disciples' battle against fear and disbelief is a great encouragement for those who flip between hope and despair. It's one thing to affirm our belief in the resurrection on a fine Sunday morning, surrounded by a crowd of fellow Christians. It is quite another to affirm it on a difficult Tuesday afternoon, surrounded by people who are convinced it is an idle tale, or when we are waiting on test results in the doctor's office or fending off loneliness.

A real Christian is not someone who does not doubt; it is someone who brings their doubts to the fact of the empty tomb and reminds themselves that our faith rests on historical events, and that those historical events are ones which cause us to feel joy and marvel at God. If you find yourself today in a battle against fear and unbelief, cry out to God, praying the prayer of the man in Mark 9: "I believe, help my unbelief!" (v 24). The disciples' doubts and fears did not exclude them from the kingdom; neither did they preclude them from kingdom work. So today, ask God to guard your faith, and walk forwards remembering that Jesus really has risen and really does have work for you to do.

1 CORINTHIANS 15:50-58

SEPTEMBER 30

THE PATHWAY TO HOLINESS

"If you live according to the flesh you will die, but if by the Spirit you put to death the deeds of the body, you will live." ROMANS 8:13

Your holiness matters.

In the Old Testament, the word "holy" doesn't always refer to a moral state; often, it refers to a relationship. Cities are described as holy cities, vessels as holy vessels, and buildings as holy places. This means that they stood in a special relationship to God. And so it is in redemption: we have been placed in a special relationship to God. We have been set apart for a holy use.

If you are married, perhaps you had other relationships before the one you enjoy with your spouse. I was married in the summer of 1975. That day, whatever romantic relationships I had had in my past were all over and done with—finished—because I was united to my wife. I was made new. I came to our wedding as an individual; I left married. My wife and I were set apart for one another through the vows, the covenant commitment, that we made to one another.

We cannot make vows to the Lord Jesus Christ and then just treat Him anyway we want. We simply cannot fool around with holiness. Why not? Because without holiness "no one will see the Lord" (Hebrews 12:14). The apostle Paul goes so far as to say that we must "put to death the deeds of the body." The Puritans called this "the mortification of the flesh." And this mortification doesn't happen automatically. It doesn't happen unconsciously. It's not a process of osmosis. Rather, what we need is the painstaking, day-by-day working out of our own salvation with fear and trembling (Philippians 2:12). We need the Spirit's prompting and enabling to remind us that we have to weep deliberately and consciously over our own sins, repent of them, turn from them, and seek to obey our Lord—and not only with those sins that are clear and obvious but also with inward sins such as envy, pride, malice, hypocrisy, and self-righteousness. It's a wonderful day when God shows us the ugliness of a sin that has been indwelling us and prompts us to tackle it. Here's the way to deal with sin: ruthlessly, immediately, consistently.

When true holiness begins to take root in our lives, it does not make us judgmental or unbending. That is legalism, where we set ourselves apart for rule-keeping pride; it is not holiness, where we are set apart for pleasing God. Instead, holiness manifests itself in graciousness, pleasantness, and goodness. So holiness is attractive. When we see it in others, whether or not we call it holiness, we warm to it and long for it. And holiness is possible, because the Lord Jesus died for the failings of our flesh and sent His Spirit to dwell in us so that we can fight sin and walk toward eternal life.

The pathway to that holiness emerges from thinking upon the wonder of all that Jesus has done for us. Ponder that path. Ask Jesus to make it real to you in a way that it's never been before. And as you walk, keep your eyes fixed on Jesus, "the founder and perfecter of our faith" (Hebrews 12:2).

ROMANS 6:1-11

OCTOBER 1

FATHER, FORGIVE THEM

"Jesus said, 'Father, forgive them, for they know not what they do.' And they cast lots to divide his garments." LUKE 23:34

Of all the cries that have been uttered by victims of unjust execution, surely none has ever been more amazing than this: "Father, forgive them."

The soldiers who nailed Jesus to the cross probably felt that they had experienced everything a man could experience in the carrying out of their duties. Surely they had grown accustomed to threats and vile abuse coming from those condemned and had listened to curses galore. They must have found themselves looking at one another in puzzlement; we can imagine one of them saying, *Did he really say, "Forgive them"?* and the other replying, *Yes... I think he really did.*

Earlier in His ministry, Jesus had instructed His disciples to "love your enemies" and "pray for those who abuse you" (Luke 6:27-28). In His prayer on the cross, Jesus practiced what He preached. Surely this is an example for us—and surely it is also a challenge, for if Jesus could do this as He was hoisted on His cross, is there any situation in which we cannot do the same?

Jesus' words here should make us ask this, though: Was His prayer a blanket expression of forgiveness, unrelated to the response of the hearts of men and women? Clearly not. Consider the context in which these words were said. Jesus was about to give His life expressly to pay the price for sin and to open the gateway into heaven. As Paul tells us in 2 Corinthians 5:19, "In Christ God was reconciling the world to himself, not counting their trespasses against them." God did not choose to ignore sin, to overlook it altogether. He did not count men's sins against *them* because He was counting their sins against *Him*—namely, Jesus. God does not overlook injustice even as He offers forgiveness. Nor does He call us to do so.

So as Jesus prayed to His heavenly Father, asking that those involved in this atrocity—including those who stood by idly and watched—would be forgiven, He was praying that they would see their need of a Savior, would see that *He* is that Savior, and would turn from their sin and discover that their transgressions could be fully pardoned. In other words, Jesus asked that the truth of 2 Corinthians 5:21—that God "made him to be sin who knew no sin, so that in him we might become the righteousness of God"—might take hold of their hearts and lives.

Here in the death of Jesus of Nazareth is the forgiveness of all *your* sin—sin that is no longer counted against you because it was counted against Him. When the reality and truth of Jesus' death and Jesus' prayer dawns on your mind and stirs your heart, then you shift from a generic awareness of the potential for forgiveness to a personal experience. And so you pray that God would seek out those around you with such forgiveness even as you seek to hold out such forgiveness in your own life.

MATTHEW 26:26-29

OCTOBER 2

FUEL FOR CHEERFUL GIVING

"The point is this: whoever sows sparingly will also reap sparingly, and whoever sows bountifully will also reap bountifully. Each one must give as he has decided in his heart, not reluctantly or under compulsion, for God loves a cheerful giver … You will be enriched in every way to be generous in every way, which through us will produce thanksgiving to God." 2 CORINTHIANS 9:6-7, 11

God loves a cheerful giver. One reason for this is that *He* is a cheerful giver, gladly and generously giving Himself and every good gift to His people. And one of the good gifts that God has given us is a series of promises and proverbs to fuel our cheer as we give. 2 Corinthians 9 provides an abundance of such fuel.

Paul teaches that "whoever sows sparingly will also reap sparingly, and whoever sows bountifully will also reap bountifully." This is essentially a proverb, like those we read in the Old Testament: "One gives freely, yet grows all the richer; another withholds what he should give, and only suffers want" (Proverbs 11:24). The thing about proverbs, though, is that they should be read for what they are—general truths—rather than what they are not: categorical promises. Paul is not giving us a formula: *If you put in a certain amount, you will receive a larger amount.* Instead, he is encouraging his readers to sow gladly and liberally because there are benefits to be had when we do so. Generous giving brings its own rewards, which the stingy will never know. If you scatter only a few seeds of your favorite flower and expect a beautiful display in a few weeks, you will be disappointed. If you sow handful after handful, the result will be glorious to behold.

More fuel for our giving comes a few verses later, where Paul says that those who are generous "will be enriched in every way." Sadly, it is common for people to stop right there, concluding that God will make them wealthy once they've given away some money. He may do just that, but it comes with the purpose revealed in the rest of the verse: "You will be enriched in every way *to be generous in every way*." God may indeed enrich you, but the enrichment is intended for greater generosity, which in turn will "produce thanksgiving to God." What a promise this is, that God will repay our generosity *so that we might continue to be generous*! As we give away, God gives us more to give away. Who could ever be tight-fisted in the face of such lavish promises?

It is a tragedy that so many have abused these promises and proverbs, using them to bait well-intentioned people into giving for the wrong reasons. There is no need or excuse for false assurances of prosperity or manipulative calls that tug at our heart strings; we have so many good, God-honoring reasons to be generous! The truths and promises of God's word are rich enough, and they alone will fuel genuine Christian cheer as we give. Dwell on these truths, and on our Savior, who "though he was rich, yet for your sake … became poor, so that you by his poverty might become rich" (2 Corinthians 8:9). That is the only way to give in a way that truly honors God: to give both sacrificially and cheerfully.

2 CORINTHIANS 9:6-15

OCTOBER 3

HE KNOWS

"Talk no more so very proudly, let not arrogance come from your mouth; for the LORD *is a God of knowledge, and by him actions are weighed."* 1 SAMUEL 2:3

Contemporary society is full of examples of what it looks like to celebrate self-assertiveness, human achievement, and a preoccupation with the "I/me/my" focus of our age that pays scant, if any, attention to God. *He does not see,* is the assumption; and if He does see, He does not mind. As believers we are not immune from any of this, for by nature our hearts love to assume that we ourselves are the fount of all knowledge—that we know best how we should think.

An inclination toward self-sufficiency and pride leads to some downplaying or even denying elements of biblical truth in their teaching and thinking. In the church today, God's judgment and justice are surely such elements. They're not easy to hear about or to proclaim, but they are central to the truth of the Bible. Paul writes that God will judge "the secrets of men by Christ Jesus" (Romans 2:16). We cannot hide anything from Him, though we are tempted to believe we can. He knows our hearts, and by this Lord of knowledge "actions are weighed."

In Daniel 5, we see how the Babylonian king Belshazzar discovered the folly of an arrogance that caused him to exalt himself above the God of knowledge. In the middle of a great feast celebrating himself, using drinking vessels that had been stolen from the Lord's temple, a hand was sent from the presence of God, appearing on a wall and writing words of judgment—and Belshazzar was reduced to a shaking mass. Daniel interpreted the message for him, saying, "The Most High God rules the kingdom of mankind and sets over it whom he will. And you his son, Belshazzar, have not humbled your heart, though you knew all this, but you have lifted up yourself against the Lord of heaven ... And you have praised the gods of silver and gold, of bronze, iron, wood, and stone, which do not see or hear or know, but the God in whose hand is your breath, and whose are all your ways, you have not honored" (Daniel 5:21-23). In the end, Belshazzar had "been weighed in the balances and found wanting" (v 27), and "that very night" he "was killed" (v 30). He thought he knew best. He did not.

It is folly to imagine that God does not see, does not know, and will not act. He knows everything about us, and He weighs our actions. As Hannah knew and Belshazzar discovered too late, self-exaltation leads to judgment; but humility before the Lord is the way to life. So, be careful not to pridefully declare that you want things your own way in one area or another and therefore refuse Jesus' kingship over that aspect of your life. Be careful not to live as though God does not know, and therefore refrain from humble repentance. Instead, humble yourself before the Lord, confessing to Him what He already knows and asking forgiveness for proud thoughts or selfish actions—and "he will exalt you" (James 4:10).

DANIEL 5:1-6, 17-31

OCTOBER 4

MODELS OF CHRISTIAN MATURITY

"Older men are to be sober-minded, dignified, self-controlled, sound in faith, in love, and in steadfastness. Older women likewise are to be reverent in behavior, not slanderers or slaves to much wine. They are to teach what is good, and so train the young women to love their husbands and children, to be self-controlled, pure, working at home, kind, and submissive to their own husbands, that the word of God may not be reviled." TITUS 2:2-5

When life gets difficult, you won't need a three-ring binder full of notes or a self-help guide to life. No, you'll need an arm around your shoulder. You'll need the tender eyes of an older Christian who understands. You'll need compassion. Such ministry in a church is not programmatic; it is relational. It is as a result of knowing people. It is a result of being able to open up to people.

This is why every church needs older men and older women who are marked by maturity, who are not coasting but growing in faith toward God, in love toward others, and in steadfastness in the face of trials.

Titus's role in the congregation to which he ministered was to encourage and exhort the older men to be sober-minded, dignified, self-controlled, and healthy in their faith. He was to be no less concerned with the spiritual health of the church's older women. Just as older men have a significant role in the life of a developing congregation, so the older women are absolutely vital. Churches need older men and women that have run the race and kept the faith to model for younger generations what it looks like to live for Christ.

The church needs older men and women because they can "teach what is good" to those who are younger. The teaching here is lifestyle teaching before it is any other kind of teaching. When Paul wrote these words, he wasn't anticipating a classroom setting with textbooks. This kind of instruction takes place in casual yet intentional conversations as well as arranged meetings, and simply in rubbing shoulders with one another in day-to-day life.

Where are you going to go when your marriage begins to struggle? Who are you going to talk to when your teenager goes into "I don't ever want to talk to you again" mode? Where will you turn when you don't know where to turn? You can visit your pastor, who can pray with you and give you some guidance, but you'll also need an older man or woman who has walked the same path and can say, "Let me tell you how I lived through it. Let me tell you what I did. Let me tell you how I prayed. Let me tell you about the grace of God. Let me encourage you."

Most of us can be such an "older man" or "older woman" to someone of a younger age and earlier stage in life than us. Intentionally make yourself available in this way. And most of us can find someone older and wiser than us and ask them to pray with us, counsel us, and be there for us. Intentionally seek out that kind of friendship, for it is one of the greatest blessings that the church of God gives us.

TITUS 2:1-10

OCTOBER 5

CLING TO THE ROCK

"As for me, my feet had almost stumbled, my steps had nearly slipped. For I was envious of the arrogant when I saw the prosperity of the wicked." PSALM 73:2-3

When we consider the activities and successes of the self-important who seem to be so carefree and uninhibited, it's easy for our minds, our hearts, and eventually our lives to go off in the wrong direction.

We can relate to the psalmist's angst when those who are so apparently opposed to God, to His word, and to anything that is morally right appear to flourish. They seem to do well financially. They seem to do well physically. They always look good. They travel in the right way. They use the right moisturizer. They look magnificent. Meanwhile, we're trying to do the God thing, the Jesus thing—and nothing seems to go right. It can all feel so futile.

When he looked at the prosperity of the wicked, the psalmist began to entertain the idea that he had followed God in vain (Psalm 73:13)—until he adjusted his perspective:

"I went into the sanctuary of God;
  then I discerned their end.
Truly you set them in slippery places;
  you make them fall to ruin.
How they are destroyed in a moment,
  swept away utterly by terrors!" (Psalm 73:17-19)

As we learn to sit in God's presence and have a view of this world that takes account of His divinity and our eternity, we come to understand, along with the psalmist, that there is a higher throne than all the thrones of this world. Justice will be served, though not in the courts of this world's kingdoms, which will all be mere footnotes in history.

Do not become discouraged by those who seem to prosper unduly. Jesus Christ is King. He's in charge of the great reversals, turning us from darkness to light, from sadness to joy, from death to life. God will achieve His purposes. He is holding you and guiding you—and, one day, you will stand with Him in glory (Psalm 73:23-24). There is nothing this world can offer that compares to Him and no reason to envy those who have everything here but nothing of ultimate value. When you are slipping into envy, look at Him, adjust your perspective, and say with the psalmist:

"Whom have I in heaven but you?
  And there is nothing on earth that I desire besides you.
My flesh and my heart may fail,
  but God is the strength of my heart and my portion forever." (Psalm 73:25-26)

PSALM 73

OCTOBER 6

KINGDOM-SHAPED PRAYERS

"Pray without ceasing." 1 THESSALONIANS 5:17

We have no good apart from God. "Every good gift and every perfect gift is from above, coming down from the Father of lights," James tells us (James 1:17). Similarly, Paul asks, "What do you have that you did not receive?" (1 Corinthians 4:7). The resounding response, of course, is nothing whatsoever. All that we have, we have from God.

If that is all true and we can do nothing of lasting value apart from Christ (John 15:5), then what makes us think we could make it through any day without praying to the one whose strength and sustenance we so desperately need? This doesn't mean we need to host prayer meetings 24/7 (although perhaps more times of extended corporate prayer would benefit us all!). But it does mean that we should never attempt to make it through a single day without expressing our dependence on our heavenly Father in prayer.

The reality is that it's easy to get stale in our praying. But that happens most often when our prayer times turn into personal shopping lists, focused more on things that we want than what we and the world around us really *need*. We ought to "let [our] requests be made known to God" (Philippians 4:6)—whatever those requests may be, great or small. But we ought also to pray for grand things. The greatest cries of the people of God should be the greatest concerns of the kingdom.

For example, we can pray for:

- world missions, praying as we send people out of our congregations and around the world
- the teaching of the Bible in places near and far
- the cause of Christ to be established in the world
- God to hold back His hand of judgment and shower us with blessing and mercy
- the faithfulness and growth of the church and our witness around the globe
- our government and its leaders, from the local level upwards
- the homeless, downtrodden, and hungry
- points of light to spring up around your city as testimonies to the gospel of Jesus Christ

This is just a sample, of course. A kingdom-focused list could continue far further! Whatever you end up praying for specifically today and in the coming days, though, ask God for His kingdom to come. Ask Him for His will to be done. What a joy that He calls you to keep on praying, and then answers your prayers to build His kingdom!

MATTHEW 6:9-11

OCTOBER 7

I WILL STRENGTHEN YOU

"I will strengthen you, I will help you, I will uphold you with my righteous right hand." ISAIAH 41:10

People who are very confident in their own abilities and what they've achieved seldom know much of God. Before we can discover God's power and strength in all of its fullness, we must be brought face to face with our own inability and weakness.

We will all go through times in our lives that we'd rather avoid. Like the apostle Paul, we will ask the Lord to remove difficulty from our lives, and we may receive the answer that, if we're honest, we don't always desire to hear: "My grace is sufficient for you, for my power is made perfect in weakness" (2 Corinthians 12:9).

Many of us spend our lives trying to be strong for others, to press on and to hold it together for those we care about. We may even begin to believe that we can do that—but we can't. Even on our best days, we discover that we have limits that we can't overcome on our own. Yet if we will only acknowledge how desperately weak we are, we will be amazed to see the power of God unleashed within our lives. The way to be truly strong for others is to lean on the Lord's strength, rather than to rely on our own.

Perhaps as you read this you are physically, emotionally, or spiritually drained—and if you are not, the time for feeling that way will come. In your moments of weakness, you will be faced with a choice: you can ask God to give you strength, or you can turn to idols. Your natural inclination will not be to turn to God but to rejuvenate and reassure yourself by other means—your possessions, your intellect, your energy, your past achievements. Yet the prophet pursues us with these words: "Thus says the LORD: 'Let not the wise man boast in his wisdom, let not the mighty man boast in his might, let not the rich man boast in his riches, but let him who boasts boast in this, that he understands and knows me'" (Jeremiah 9:23-24).

Instead of trying to press on in your own strength today, allow the Holy Spirit to minister this truth to your soul: God supplies His strength for your weakness. He says, "I will strengthen you, I will help you, I will uphold you with my righteous right hand." You serve a God who has eyes that see you, knees that stoop to help you, and hands that reach out to embrace you. Humbly turn to Him in your weakness and be prepared for Him to meet you with His strength.

ISAIAH 40:27-31

Bible Through The Year: Ezekiel 42–44; John 19:1-22

OCTOBER 8

IT'S GOOD NEWS FOR ALL

"For God so loved the world, that he gave his only Son, that whoever believes in him should not perish but have eternal life." JOHN 3:16

This is perhaps the best-known and best-loved verse in the Bible. It comes in the context of a conversation between Jesus and a devout Jew, Nicodemus. It is then put into action in the following chapter of John, when Jesus converses with a woman on the opposite end of the social, moral, and religious spectrum. This teaches us something important: that the good news of Christ's coming is not limited to pious people, like Nicodemus, but breaks boundaries to extend even to the dejected and rejected, like the woman at the well.

The contrast between these two individuals is stark. Nicodemus was learned, powerful, respected, and theologically trained. The woman was uneducated, without influence, despised, and immoral. Jesus' interactions with both, however, display that all humans need a Savior. Nicodemus's meeting with Christ makes it clear that we can never do enough good to save ourselves. Conversely, the Samaritan woman's experience makes clear that no one can ever do enough bad to be beyond Christ's reach. We all live under God's wrath and judgment until we welcome the light of Christ's salvation—whether you're a Nicodemus, a Samaritan woman, or somewhere in between. The whole world needs God's Son; and God has given the whole world His Son.

Because the gospel of Jesus does not discriminate, neither should we in proclaiming it. While both Nicodemus and the woman at the well needed to hear the same good news, Jesus masterfully shared it with each of them in a personalized way. He did not engage them with the same formulaic conversation; He met them where they were. He simply asked questions that revealed their sinful hearts and God's loving heart for them.

Just as God invites all to hear His gospel, so He invites all who are changed by this gospel to be the agents of change for others. After her conversation with Jesus, the Samaritan woman ran back to her town, telling everyone of how He knew everything she had ever done (John 4:39). The people then responded to her words and sought Jesus out. This should encourage all of us, and especially those of us who lack confidence in extending the gospel invitation to others. When God is at work, we'll be amazed at what happens!

"For God so loved the world..." Such love has come to live in any who believe. It empowers you to do what is necessary to live as God commands. It saves you from the chains that tie you to your past—be it a past of piety and pride, like Nicodemus's, or a past of sordid decisions and shame, like the Samaritan woman's. It spurs you to share this gospel of Son-giving, life-bringing love with those around you. Whoever believes will have eternal life.

JOHN 4:31-42

OCTOBER 9

PRAYING IN JESUS' NAME

"Let us then with confidence draw near to the throne of grace, that we may receive mercy and find grace to help in time of need." HEBREWS 4:16

Just before we close a prayer with an amen, most Christians will say something like "in Jesus' name" or "for Jesus' sake." What are we actually doing when we say that? Is it anything more than just a nice way to close things off?

To pray in Jesus' name is to trust the saving work of the Lord Jesus as the sole ground of our access to God. We could never go to God just in our own name. We couldn't go to God and plead based on our own merits. No, we go to God in Jesus' name—and it is a tremendous privilege to do so! Only because we have a sympathetic High Priest can we "draw near to the throne of grace" with confidence that God Most High will receive us.

Because of our Lord Jesus Christ, we can cast our burdens, our fears, our failures, our expectations, and all our hopes and dreams upon our heavenly Father. No request is too great for Him.

The hymn writer put the opportunity of prayer wonderfully well:

Approach, my soul, the mercy seat
Where Jesus answers prayer;
There humbly fall before His feet,
For none can perish there.

Thy promise is my only plea;
With this I venture nigh:
Thou callest burdened souls to Thee,
And such, O Lord, am I.[80]

Coming to God with such an approach is not just one way among many; it is the only way He will hear our pleas as a Father listening to His children. So whenever you pray, come to your Father in the name of His Son, trusting that His Spirit will guide you.

HEBREWS 4:14 – 5:9

80 John Newton, "Approach, My Soul, the Mercy Seat" (1779).

OCTOBER 10

STAND UP FOR JESUS!

"The Philistines stood on the mountain on the one side, and Israel stood on the mountain on the other side, with a valley between them. And there came out from the camp of the Philistines a champion named Goliath of Gath, whose height was six cubits and a span. ... And the Philistine said, 'I defy the ranks of Israel this day. Give me a man, that we may fight together.' When Saul and all Israel heard these words of the Philistine, they were dismayed and greatly afraid." 1 SAMUEL 17:3-4, 10-11

It should shock us to find the army of Israel in the position described here. After all, they were the army of the living God. Within living memory they had seen God give them great victories as they trusted in Him. You would think that they would have been quite prepared to take on this giant Philistine challenger.

Instead, we see a sorry sight: the army of God, including their king, cowering on the mountainside for over six weeks, waiting for someone else to do their job (1 Samuel 17:2, 16). To Goliath and the Philistine army, Israel's God can't have seemed very mighty to save. The problem, however, was not the Lord. The problem was the army. Because they were attempting to fight in their own strength, they were cowed by Goliath.

As with Israel's armies, the problem in much of the church today is not that our God lacks power over all the events of our world. No, He is omnipotent. Rather, the problem is that the church too often sits on the sidelines, waiting for somebody else to take action while the world looks on and shakes its head and concludes that our God is not mighty to save.

At this point in history, there's a wonderful opportunity for the church to *be* the church. Christ has already won the battle for us. There is no need for His people to be marginalized by worldly "giants" who taunt and intimidate, deterring us from sharing the message of Jesus' triumph over sin and death. Jesus has won, and there is nothing in this world to be afraid of. The gospel is worthy of our courage and, as the hymn writer reminds us, Christ Himself is guiding us: "Stand up, stand up for Jesus! ... From victory unto victory His army shall He lead."[81] It is time for you and me—who, by placing our faith in Him, have already enlisted in His army—to get off the sidelines, to charge down the hill, and to proclaim the victory that is Christ's.

1 SAMUEL 17:48-53

81 George Duffield, Jr., "Stand Up, Stand Up for Jesus" (1858).

OCTOBER 11

OUR HELP COMES FROM THE LORD

"And David said to Saul, 'Let no man's heart fail because of him. Your servant will go and fight with this Philistine ... Your servant has struck down both lions and bears, and this uncircumcised Philistine shall be like one of them, for he has defied the armies of the living God.' And David said, 'The LORD *who delivered me from the paw of the lion and from the paw of the bear will deliver me from the hand of this Philistine.' And Saul said to David, 'Go, and the* LORD *be with you!'"* 1 SAMUEL 17:32, 36-37

When David arrived at the scene of the great standoff between Goliath and God's people, he boldly told King Saul that there was no need for fear—which was quite remarkable when the entire Israelite army had been completely paralyzed by the giant! When they saw Goliath, they ran away. He kept challenging them, but they had no answer. Then up came David, a mere shepherd boy, who simply said, *No one needs to be afraid. I will fight him.*

When Saul understandably questioned David's ability to face Goliath, David neither gave up nor suggested that he was tougher than he looked. Instead, he testified to the Lord's enabling. In caring for his father's sheep, David had dealt with bears and lions, and he knew that such successes had come from God. Now he was confident that that same God would give him success again, this time against this Philistine who had defiantly mocked God's people.

Perhaps David had in mind the amazing scene from Exodus 14, when the Israelites' backs were against the Red Sea and all the balance of power was on the side of the onrushing Egyptian army. Back then, when the people had cried out in fear, Moses had replied, "Fear not, stand firm, and see the salvation of the LORD, which he will work for you today. For the Egyptians whom you see today, you shall never see again. The LORD will fight for you, and you have only to be silent" (Exodus 14:13-14). And that is exactly what God did. Yahweh, the living God who had delivered His people, was the same Lord who would deliver David.

Later, when David penned his poems and provided songs for worshipers, he recollected, "If it had not been the LORD who was on our side when people rose up against us, then they would have swallowed us up alive, when their anger was kindled against us" (Psalm 124:2-3). He then concluded with this great hope-filled declaration: "Our help is in the name of the LORD, who made heaven and earth" (v 8).

On what basis are you able to take on all that comes against you like a giant in the day or a monster in your sleeplessness at night? How do you know that you will succeed? If your courage is founded on your ability, sooner or later you will meet your match. Rather, let your confidence be in the Lord—because the Lord has delivered, and the Lord *will* deliver. And if God is for us, who, ultimately, can be against us (Romans 8:31)?

PSALM 124

OCTOBER 12

NO NEED FOR THIS ARMOR

"Then Saul clothed David with his armor. He put a helmet of bronze on his head and clothed him with a coat of mail, and David strapped his sword over his armor. And he tried in vain to go, for he had not tested them. Then David said to Saul, 'I cannot go with these, for I have not tested them.' So David put them off." 1 SAMUEL 17:38-39

It's the type of helpful reminder that many mothers give younger children on a snowy day or older children before an interview: "Make sure you're properly dressed." For King Saul, being properly dressed was the difference between victory and demise. Thus, when David volunteered to face Goliath on Israel's behalf, the first order of business was for him to suit up. The king rested all his hope in his armor—and so here is a memorable scene, both comic and tragic, of a failed king and a boy who was so weighed down that he could not move.

King Saul was convinced that if he could dig out his old armor and put it on this boy, it might just be adequate enough to see David through, despite the odds that were so clearly against him. Yet Saul was a big guy (1 Samuel 10:23), and David was only a youth (17:33). It was never going to work. Besides, if the armor was not sufficient for Saul to go out against Goliath and win, why did he think a shepherd boy in ill-fitting armor would stand a chance? Saul was a failed king, and the wearing or not wearing of armor had nothing to do with it.

David recognized that far from helping him, this heavy, ill-fitting armor would only hamper his efforts—so he cast it aside. He knew that he didn't need to be made into someone else, because God would help him. He knew that he didn't need to rely on anything else, because God was with him.

It's a sad picture, really. King Saul wasn't even a shadow of the person he had been. There he stood, absent God's Spirit, losing sight of God's glory, his courage gone—and with it his joy, his peace, and the security of his mind. We can imagine his gaze as it follows David heading off toward the brook in the valley and pausing to pick up five stones—the tragic gaze of a depleted king, his shadow growing long in the light of his setting reign.

Let this picture of Saul invite you to consider: Are you relying on "armor" as security in your life? In what ways have you rested your hope on human methods that do not fit and have not worked in a way that will last? Like David, look to the God who helps you and is with you. Then you will be able to cast such "armor" aside and trust in God to lead you. Then you can face the day, every day, with joy, peace, and courage.

PSALM 28

OCTOBER 13

THERE IS NO OTHER

"When the Philistine looked and saw David, he disdained him … 'Am I a dog, that you come to me with sticks?' And the Philistine cursed David by his gods. … Then David said to the Philistine, 'You come to me with a sword and with a spear and with a javelin, but I come to you in the name of the LORD of hosts, the God of the armies of Israel, whom you have defied. This day the LORD will deliver you into my hand.'" 1 SAMUEL 17:42-43, 45-46

Talking trash to your opponent is a practice dating back to long before professional sports. When Goliath, for instance, was insulted by a mere boy being sent to fight him, he began the talk smack—*and* he "cursed David by his gods."

Goliath's cursing is significant. Through it, the giant unwittingly acknowledged that what was about to take place was far more significant than a conflict between two people or two armies or two nations. By invoking his gods, he demonstrated that the battle was ultimately between the so-called gods of the Philistines and the living God, the God of Israel.

A moment's reflection would have reminded all the Israelites that the gods of the Philistines were not an impressive group. Like all false gods, they had to be carried around and couldn't act on their own. Previously, the Philistines had had to set up their god Dagon after he had toppled over—and eventually, his head had even fallen clean off (1 Samuel 5:3-4)!

It makes sense, then, that Goliath's insults or mention of his gods didn't scare David. The shepherd boy recognized that the giant was terrifyingly large and came at him with many great weapons. But he also knew the giant was right about one thing: it *was* a much bigger event than a one-to-one combat—and David knew that the living God whom he served could save him and Israel.

David understood that Goliath's defeat was not about making a name for himself; it would be so that "all the earth may know that there is a God in Israel" (1 Samuel 17:46). The victory was to be a testimony to the assembled crowd on both sides of the valley that God was alive and powerful to save.

The battle today is likewise ultimately between the living God and the non-gods of our age (Ephesians 6:12). Press your friends kindly, and ask how their gods—gods of ambition, politics, education, and so on—are working for them. Do they have peace? Do they have lasting confidence? Do they have contentment? Do they have joy?

Thankfully, we have something that gives all these things and more. We have the God who doesn't topple and who needs nothing from us. We know the living God who has been faithful for a thousand generations and who tells us, "I have made, and I will bear; I will carry and will save" (Isaiah 46:4). Let the world around you see and hear who it is you serve today.

1 SAMUEL 5:1-7

OCTOBER 14

THE MAN IN BETWEEN

"So David prevailed over the Philistine with a sling and with a stone, and struck the Philistine and killed him. There was no sword in the hand of David."
1 SAMUEL 17:50

This is one of the most familiar moments in Scripture, but do not let that blind you to the extraordinary nature of the victory it describes. A mere shepherd boy with his staff, five stones, and a sling brought down an experienced man of war, a giant, who came after him with mighty weapons. It is a victory the fame of which has not dimmed through the centuries.

At stake in David's astonishing battle against Goliath was Israel's future. The army didn't fight. Neither did their failed king, Saul. They only watched as their future hung on the shoulders of David, who was chosen by God to be "the man in between." David was the anointed, appointed servant of God—and in that respect, he was the prototype of Jesus.

Like that of Israel's army, the future of every man and woman hangs in the balance. Our ultimate defeat is by death, when the life we've imagined and built for ourselves comes to a halt. Death terrifies us because it is the punishment for sin (Romans 6:23), which none of us are without (3:23). The law of God demands perfection, yet none of us are perfect (v 10). Death, then, is the undefeatable giant before whom we can but tremble. We need someone to stand in between us and death. We need somebody to step forward.

And He did. Just as David stood between the army of Israel and their defeat, so Jesus stood between us and ours. His victory is the greatest news the world has ever known. The demands of the law were met by His perfect life. The penalty of the law was carried out in His death in place of us, who deserved to die. And the power of death was defeated by His resurrection as He triumphed over it. As David in the Valley of Elah won victory not only for himself but for the whole of Israel, so Jesus at Calvary and the empty tomb won victory for all who are united with Him by faith. No wonder Paul declared, "Thanks be to God, who gives us the victory through our Lord Jesus Christ" (1 Corinthians 15:57)!

As you look upon the cross of Christ and the triumph of His resurrection today, you are looking at the victory that has been won, and won for you. Pause to rejoice, singing songs of praise and thanksgiving because you have victory through Him. Then go out into a world that is fractured and broken and scared to death of death, and declare that people need not fear, for in faith they too can take hold of Jesus, our victorious champion.

2 TIMOTHY 1:8-13

OCTOBER 15

CONFIDENCE THROUGH SUFFERING

"Recall the former days when, after you were enlightened, you endured a hard struggle with sufferings, sometimes being publicly exposed to reproach and affliction, and sometimes being partners with those so treated. For you had compassion on those in prison, and you joyfully accepted the plundering of your property, since you knew that you yourselves had a better possession and an abiding one. Therefore do not throw away your confidence, which has a great reward." HEBREWS 10:32-35

Here is a word of encouragement for those who grieve and for those who seek to comfort them.

Perhaps you or someone you know has faced personal tragedy recently. Perhaps you've lost a loved one, and the pain of the loss is so great, so overwhelming, that you're ready to quit. Perhaps you're feeling helpless and burdened as you watch your brother or sister in Christ walk the painful road of suffering.

Prolonged and intense suffering often causes us to question our faith and commitment. But the author of Hebrews encourages us to remain steadfast as we call to mind our endurance through former hardship. "Recall," he says, "the former days when, after you were enlightened, you endured a hard struggle with sufferings." And in light of this recollection, we must also avoid the temptation to "throw away … confidence," knowing that our perseverance will be greatly rewarded. The longer we go on in the Christian life, the more trials we come through by God's grace, and the more we can look back on them and think, "If I persevered through that, then I can keep going through this."

You may be thinking, though, "This is too much—perseverance is beyond me this time." If so, know this: it is in moments of great weakness that the Spirit strengthens us and helps us (Romans 8:26-28). Even when we do not know what to pray for or how to endure, the Holy Spirit intercedes for us and enables us to do the will of God (v 26).

The writer to the Hebrews exhorts us, as members of God's family, united in Christ, to stand side by side and partner with those who are suffering. Indeed, we are called to actively extend sympathy as we identify with our brothers and sisters in their affliction. Such partnership may come at a cost; early believers even endured the "plundering of … property" as a result of their compassion for those already imprisoned. Yet we must not let its costliness deter us.

In sorrow and in sympathy, we persevere because the Lord stands by us to strengthen and uphold us with His righteous right hand (Isaiah 41:10). As you face life's toils and troubles, don't throw away your confidence or shrink back into the shadows. Fix your eyes, and encourage those around you to fix their eyes, on a "better possession and an abiding one": the glory of eternity with Christ, who has walked the path of suffering before us and now beckons us on, on toward home.

HEBREWS 10:36 – 11:3

OCTOBER 16

PREACHING THE KINGDOM OF GOD

"And he entered the synagogue and for three months spoke boldly, reasoning and persuading them about the kingdom of God." ACTS 19:8

It was impossible to be in Paul's company for very long without hearing from him about one subject: the kingdom of God. When he arrived at a new city and, as was his custom, sought out a Jewish synagogue in which to begin his proclamation of Jesus Christ, it was the kingdom that was his theme. When he was under house arrest in Rome, he welcomed visitors and seized the opportunity to talk to them (Acts 28:30-31). In this, Paul was following his Lord, who, when He began His public ministry, preached, "The kingdom of God is at hand; repent and believe in the gospel" (Mark 1:15).

But what is the "kingdom of God"? When thinking about this kingdom, the Jewish mind looked for the overthrow of their Roman oppressors, the rebuilding of the Jerusalem temple, and the establishing of justice. Yet Paul knew that wasn't the story. He knew that the kingdom of God had been realized in the kingship of the Lord Jesus Christ. The oppressor He had defeated was far worse than the Romans. The access to God He had secured was far more wonderful than that enjoyed at the temple. The justice He guaranteed was greater than anything yet seen in this world, and it lay in the future, awaiting His return to make all things new. Yet the kingdom was and remains not only a future reality but a present one in the lives of those who have bowed the knee to its King.

Paul routinely spoke about the kingdom of God to people who were concerned about oppression and justice. If we're not careful, we can present people with the claims of Jesus in such a way that we give the impression that we don't, and He doesn't, actually care about any of the issues of our day. But people *should* have real questions about the troubles of this world—and we should have answers.

When faced with such questions, we shouldn't respond with superficial, triumphalist statements. Simplistic Christianese platitudes aren't going to cut it. Our answer should be to say, "Yes, I am concerned about oppression. Yes, I am concerned that people in the world are subjugated. Yes, I am concerned about justice. The Bible has a lot to say about these things." Then we need to show people that the answer to our world's frictions and fractures is ultimately found in King Jesus, who overturns oppression and sets captives free and abolishes the dividing wall of hostility and makes a new people who are committed to justice in this world without forgetting that there is a world to come—one of perfect justice and one that has only one entry point: faith in Jesus Christ.

Is your view of the kingdom big enough? Do you see it not just as a future reality but also as a present one, changing everything as it transforms what men and women believe and how men and women live? Will you live as a member of that kingdom, and proclaim that kingdom, as Paul did?

LUKE 6:20-23

OCTOBER 17

REMEMBERED NO MORE

"In the spring of the year, the time when kings go out to battle, Joab led out the army and ravaged the country of the Ammonites and came and besieged Rabbah. But David remained at Jerusalem. And Joab struck down Rabbah and overthrew it." 1 CHRONICLES 20:1

If you were asked to write a biography of David, how many pages would you devote to his affair with Bathsheba? Would you give a chapter or more to the adultery, the scheming, and the murder, and how God was displeased and sent his prophet to expose the sin and call the king to repentance?

Naturally, we would answer yes (and so would the writer of 2 Samuel!). So we may therefore find it quite astonishing that the writer of 1 and 2 Chronicles passes over this incident entirely in his record of David's life. He includes not a single word about David's sins against Bathsheba and Uriah. A friend once told me, "I'd like to think that the Chronicler took so seriously the fact that the Lord had taken away David's sin that he could tell the story of David's life without even mentioning it." Then he added, "I'd like the Chronicler to be my biographer as well!"

Think about it for a moment. The Chronicler wrote his account knowing that David had repented and that God had forgiven David's sins. Why, then, would there be a need to continue mentioning it? Here we have a wonderful reminder that the Lord has completely covered the sins of His people.

As you read about the rest of David's life, you find that his adultery with Bathsheba brought with it a bitter legacy. It cast a dark cloud over the entire remainder of his reign. David was indeed forgiven and restored, for the divine surgery was complete—but scars remained. God's grace can cover even our greatest sins, but this does not remove their consequences in this life. Yet although David sinned greatly and reaped the bitter fruit in this life, the Chronicler's biography of David reminds us of God's amazing grace. God had so removed his sin that the Chronicler could write about David without making any mention of it.

Only the Evil One encourages you to delve into the garbage cans of past sins that you have repented of and that have therefore long been forgiven. Only the Accuser tells you that your sins need to weigh on you or be made up for. Take a moment to thank God for His great mercy and kindness toward you. In Christ, all of your misdeeds have been pardoned. If God remembers yours sins no more, then surely there is no need for you to dwell upon past failures. They have been covered over by His grace. They do not define you and need not dominate you, either today or for eternity.

HEBREWS 9:11-14

OCTOBER 18

IN THIS WORLD FOR GOOD

"Always seek to do good to one another and to everyone." 1 THESSALONIANS 5:15

Do you ever think that the Bible's commands seem impossibly all-encompassing? Paul's first letter to the Thessalonians 5 is chock-full of such directives: "Rejoice always" (1 Thessalonians 5:16). "Pray without ceasing" (v 17). Sometimes verses like these seem to raise more questions than provide answers. A bit of detail or a few caveats couldn't hurt, could they? And what about the command in verse 15? "Seek to do good." For whom? "Everyone." When? "Always." That's a lot of good to a lot of people a lot of the time!

But perhaps instead of thinking of a command like this as impossibly general, a better way to think of it is that it is *abundantly generous.*

We have a God who gives and gives and keeps on giving. No matter how many times we fail Him, He still meets us with kindness. Along with Paul, we should ask ourselves, "What do you have that you did not receive?" (1 Corinthians 4:7). The answer, of course, is absolutely nothing. It is simply in God's nature and disposition to overflow with kindness, mercy, and grace—and as His children, we should be learning to imitate Him as best we can.

We all have bad days, of course. Inevitably, we will displease, or even hurt, someone at some point. But what if we went through today or tomorrow with the aim of always seeking to do good to everyone? What do you think would change? How would others respond? Perhaps instead of seeing others as obstacles or roadblocks, we'd see them more as men and women with dignity, who are worthy of love and respect. Or perhaps instead of us treating some people like enemies, we would begin to understand their positions and even genuinely begin to appreciate them.

Whatever the specific situations you encounter, God has placed you in this world for good. It is your privilege and your pleasure to share His kindness and His goodness with anyone and everyone you can.

1 THESSALONIANS 5:12-24

OCTOBER 19

RECIPIENTS OF GOD'S GRACE

"The grace of the Lord Jesus Christ and the love of God and the fellowship of the Holy Spirit be with you all." 2 CORINTHIANS 13:14

John Newton, the man who wrote the hymn "Amazing Grace," never lost sight of how amazing grace truly is. A former slave trader, Newton never forgot the way sin had reigned in his life before he came to Christ, and he was aware of the sin that remained in his life after his conversion. This is why, toward the end of his life, he said, "I remember two things: that I am a great sinner, and that Christ is a great Saviour."[82]

We, too, do well to remember our sinful state apart from Christ; for if we do not know ourselves to be sinful, then the story and wonder of the grace of our Lord Jesus will be significantly minimized.

One of the challenges of the Christian life is that while we never outgrow our need for God's grace, our folly can convince us otherwise. It was with this concern that Paul closed his second letter to Corinthians with this blessing: "The grace of the Lord Jesus Christ ... be with you all." What is the grace to which Paul is referring? Perhaps the finest distillation of its glorious truth comes earlier in the same letter when Paul tells his readers, "For you know the grace of our Lord Jesus Christ, that though he was rich, yet for your sake he became poor, so that you by his poverty might become rich" (2 Corinthians 8:9).

The Scriptures never humble us by confronting us with the reality of our sin without lifting us by comforting us with the reality of God's grace. We do well to remember the truth of our salvation in Christ. He left the realms of glory to come in flesh and walk among us. He came to live as a man and to do so without sin. He lived in absolute perfection and in total obedience to God's holy law. And yet, rather than receive the honor He deserved, "bearing shame and scoffing rude, in my place condemned He stood."[83]

The one who gave Himself on the cross will not seem worthy of our worship if we do not recognize that it was *our* sin that made it necessary and that it was *His* love that made it happen. Christ Himself had no debt to pay, no punishment to bear. What He endured was what we deserve—and He did it for us. Only when the reality of our sinfulness becomes apparent to us will the wonder of His salvation become marvelous to us.

Take some moments to consider anew the sins you've committed, which Christ has paid for—not to wallow in them or to feel some sense of self-loathing but to remind yourself that you were not and will never be a worthy recipient of the grace of God in Christ—and yet He gives it anyway. You are a great sinner, and Christ is a great Savior. Oh, what amazing grace!

ISAIAH 1:12-18

82 John Pollock, *Amazing Grace: John Newton's Story* (Harper and Row, 1981), p 182.
83 Philip P. Bliss, "'Man of Sorrows,' What a Name" (1875).

OCTOBER 20

LIFE UNDER THE SUN

"I have seen everything that is done under the sun, and behold, all is vanity and a striving after wind." ECCLESIASTES 1:14

The book of Ecclesiastes shows us what life is like "under the sun"—and what it shows us is very discouraging. Each one of us pursues satisfaction in this world, but no matter how hard we try or how close we think we may come to it, it eludes us. We have an innate appetite for that which is new and better because we think it will bring us the satisfaction that we are seeking, but ultimately our efforts always come up empty. You're as likely to catch fulfillment as you are to chase down the wind.

Consider the places to which you have turned for satisfaction. Have you tried to find meaning in your life by filling it with relationships? Then you've probably discovered that there isn't a person on the face of the earth who can fulfill your deepest longings. Have you been trying to satisfy yourself in intellectual pursuits? Then perhaps you've learned that there's not a theorem you can ponder that will ultimately sate your curiosity. Have you been seeking satisfaction in experiences and travel? There is not a journey you can take that will answer your yearnings for sights of beauty and majesty. Or maybe it is something else for you. But whatever we turn to for satisfaction cannot bear the weight of our hopes. Sooner or later, we always end up feeling empty once more.

Is this pessimism? No! This is life "under the sun." It's like a Rubik's Cube with two blocks missing: no matter how many times you spin it, you won't be able to get all the colors where they need to be because it's inherently flawed.

If you have been able to put the Rubik's Cube of your life together so that you can make sense of why no earthly thing you pursue brings you satisfaction, it's only by the grace of God. There's only one worldview that is able to make sense of life—only one that answers the questions that are in your mind when you lie awake in the middle of the night.

Your search for satisfaction—your deepest longings and questions—can only be addressed by God Himself. The 5th-century theologian Augustine once declared of God, "You have made us for Yourself, and our hearts are restless until they rest in You."[84] This deep soul-rest is available to you at any time; it can always be found in the all-satisfying God. Whatever you do or don't have, whatever you're wishing for or working for "under the sun," be sure to find your deepest sense of satisfaction in knowing and serving the Lord. With Him all strivings cease, for in Him all longings are met.

MATTHEW 11:25-30

84 Augustine, Confessions 1.1.1.

OCTOBER 21

A GOSPEL CHURCH

"As he was getting into the boat, the man who had been possessed with demons begged him that he might be with him. And he did not permit him but said to him, 'Go home to your friends and tell them how much the Lord has done for you, and how he has had mercy on you.'" MARK 5:18-19

What does it mean to be a "gospel church"? What does Christ call churches to be? And how do we ensure that our churches live out that calling and refuse to be diverted from it?

When a church is drifting, it's usually only when it looks over its shoulder that it realizes that, often unwittingly, it has lost its gospel focus. Over time, perhaps quickly, perhaps slowly and imperceptibly, that church has become turned in on itself. The congregation has grown comfortable and content with empty seats in their services, or with seats that are full for the wrong reasons. It is very possible for a church to slowly drift, become self-satisfied, and eventually lose its way.

An individual church will only remain devoted to its mission when its members constantly maintain an outward gaze. Jesus encouraged this very mindset after He healed the man who was possessed by demons in Mark 5. When this man asked Jesus if he could stay with Him, Jesus told him no—which may come as a surprise, given that some of Jesus' first words in Mark's Gospel were "Follow me" (Mark 1:17). But Jesus was telling this man that following involved going—going home to his friends and family and telling them "how much the Lord has done for you." Jesus did not want him to rest content with the knowledge of Christ that he had received. He wanted him to make the good news about Christ known to those around him.

As with this man, God calls us to His Son, He calls us to be the followers of His Son—and that involves us going out and spreading the news about His Son. For Jesus never calls anyone to follow Him without also making them "fishers of men" (Mark 1:17). If we have truly come to Him, then we will go and share Him.

On the cross, Jesus declared, "It is finished" (John 19:30). The work of redemption is indeed a finished work that was and remains accomplished by Christ alone. Yet Christ includes His followers in His unfinished work of bringing the news of this amazing and wonderful story to the world. There are plenty of important elements of church life that should never be ignored, but when we neglect evangelism, pursuing these other things becomes like rearranging furniture in a house that's on fire.

Have you received the mercy that is found in Christ alone? Do you know others who have yet to believe the gospel? Then Christ calls you, too, to "go home to your friends and tell them how much the Lord has done for you." He calls your church to be a place that welcomes anyone and everyone who wants to meet the man who has made such a difference in your life and the life of others in your church. Will you accept His calling? This week, with whom are you going to share the one who has done so much for you?

ACTS 11:19-26

OCTOBER 22

THE WONDERFUL CROSS

"Grace to you and peace from God our Father and the Lord Jesus Christ, who gave himself for our sins to deliver us from the present evil age, according to the will of our God and Father, to whom be the glory forever and ever. Amen."

GALATIANS 1:3-5

It is an inescapable fact of the human experience that we all face death. We have to live through the deaths of loved ones, and then, eventually, we have to face our own end. It has been this way since Adam and Eve ate the fruit of the forbidden tree. So it is that one in every one dies, and every death marks the end of someone's ability actively to affect the course of history.

Yet there is one death that has altered and defined the history of the entire world.

The death of Jesus Christ stands in distinction from all others. First, unlike most people, He faced death willingly. He declared, "I lay down my life that I may take it up again. No one takes it from me, but I lay it down of my own accord" (John 10:17-18). The Lord Jesus was no helpless victim. He went to the cross neither as a result of cruel fate nor because He lacked the power to do anything about it. He could have called legions of angels to His defense had He so chosen, but instead He faced His grim execution and "gave himself" courageously and willingly.

Second, His death was purposeful. Jesus died "for our sins to deliver us from the present evil age." The cross represents the appeasement of God's wrath at sin by God's love for sinners through God's gift of His Son. He alone determines how sinful people can be declared righteous in His holy presence. He knew that it could be not the result of their endeavors, their observance of the law, or all of their triumphs put together; but He determined that it would be as a result of Christ's death on the cross.

Third, then, and utterly uniquely, this death was saving. There is no other way for sinners to be made right with God. If there were, then Christ would have died for nothing. No, when Christ died on the cross, it did not serve merely as an example or as a display of God's love—although it was those things too. Most fundamentally, when Christ died, it accomplished salvation for sinners.

The ignoble death of a 1st-century Galilean man did all of this—what a wonder! And yet, that is not the greatest marvel of all. The greatest astonishment is not that it was done but that it was done *for you and for me*. We will never grasp the depth of it—the magnitude of the love that brought Him to that cross—and so we joyfully confess with Paul that on the cross, the Son of God "loved me and gave himself for me" (Galatians 2:20). We must never grow cold to the central truth of Christianity, and of eternity: that "Jesus … gave himself for our sins to deliver us from this present evil age." We will be giving God glory for this salvation forever; be sure you give Him glory today, too.

PSALM 22

OCTOBER 23

DEEP COMFORT

"The steadfast love of the Lord *never ceases; his mercies never come to an end; they are new every morning; great is your faithfulness."* LAMENTATIONS 3:22-23

The expression of God's faithfulness found in this verse is familiar to many of us. It's the kind of text that is routinely put on mirrors or on nice pictures with the sea and sky in the background. We may well, then, be used to seeing this verse in a very comfortable setting. In reality, though, it actually comes from quite a dark place. If it were set to music, it would be set in a minor key.

The book of Lamentations is situated in an uncomfortable setting, for it is the reflections of the prophet Jeremiah upon the circumstances of God's people when Jerusalem was taken by Babylon and they were carried off into exile. Lamentations is exactly what its title suggests: a series of poems that express the people's sorrow for what has taken place.

Lamentations begins in absolute desolation: "How lonely sits the city that was full of people!" (Lamentations 1:1). In the face of such catastrophe, it's common to think that evil has defeated good or that God has given up on sinners. But in the case of Jerusalem's fall, nothing could have been further from the truth. God was still in charge. It was He who allowed the powers of Babylon to rise in order that His people would become aware of their sinfulness and neediness and cry out to God in repentance.

The Lord afflicted His people "on the day of his fierce anger" (Lamentations 1:12). Yet in the midst of their deep sorrow, He also brought a deeply comforting word. His people may have been brought low, but they had not been forsaken. They had experienced the ending of many things: the end of peace, the end of security, and the end of home. But two things they would never experience the end of: God's steadfast love and God's undeserved mercies. Those were new, and sufficient, every morning. The people would learn far more about their God in the place of exile than they ever had in the comfort of home.

Indeed, it is often in our darkest moments that the faithful character of God shines most brightly to us. When things are going well, we're tempted to think we're sufficient on our own. But in moments of despair, we can cling to God's faithfulness, and in times of failure, we can appreciate His mercy.

You may someday find yourself in a similar situation to that of the citizens of the ransacked Jerusalem—a situation in which all the wheels have come off and you feel bereft of joy. Perhaps you find yourself in that place today. In moments like these, when life is set in a minor key, you need this deeply comforting reminder: the steadfast love of the Lord never ceases. His mercy will never run dry. His faithfulness toward you will never fail. In those moments when we have lost much, we can rely on this: we will never lose His love, and we will never lose His mercy.

LAMENTATIONS 3:49-58

OCTOBER 24

A SOLID CONVICTION

"We know that for those who love God all things work together for good, for those who are called according to his purpose." ROMANS 8:28

The way we respond to life's circumstances reveals a lot about us. Some look at life and think, "I'm stuck in a dead-end job. I eat the same lunch almost every day. My relationships usually bring me down more than they build me up. And I'm supposed to believe this is good—that this is the gift of God? I don't see it."

Yet if we are in Christ, then we are assured that God's perfect plan is unfolding exactly as He intends. And we are taught that we exist for a purpose far greater than "just" driving a bus, being a teacher, or being a parent. An occupation is never meant just to pay the bills. A hobby is never meant just to entertain or pass the time. The content we consume with our eyes and ears is never meant just to distract our minds from life's stresses. Everything we do is an opportunity to honor God, to become more like His Son, and to point others to Him. It is when we lose sight of this that even the most satisfying moments of life will eventually leave us feeling empty, and the worst times in life will cause us to question His presence or goodness.

When we look at life with a Romans 8:28-shaped perspective, everything changes. Sure, many of our circumstances stay the same. We face many of the challenges that we've always had—but we face them with a new heart and with the great hope of eternal life. God may see fit to leave you in the same situation you've been in for years, but He will never leave you alone in it. He has promised a Helper (John 14:16-17), and He has no abandoned projects. He has no forsaken children. You live within the framework of His unfailing providential care.

When God's word reminds you that "for those who love God all things work together for good," it points you away from your own view of things, away from the world's view of things, and toward God's unseen hand stitching together all the events of your life—including those you would never have chosen—to work for good. And what is that good? "To be conformed to the image of his Son" (Romans 8:29). In everything, God is shaping you to be more like Jesus, ready for the day when you have the joy of seeing Jesus.

Remember, then, that all of your circumstances, from the highest of highs to the lowest of lows, are instruments of divine mercy that God is using to accomplish His eternal purpose. What a comfort to trust Him every day! What a motivation to serve Him today!

JOHN 14:15-27

◇ Bible Through The Year: 1 Samuel 30–31; 1 Timothy 4

OCTOBER 25

TRUTH TRANSFORMS

"You, O Lord, are a shield about me, my glory, and the lifter of my head. I cried aloud to the Lord, and he answered me from his holy hill. I lay down and slept; I woke again, for the Lord sustained me." PSALM 3:3-5

There is a direct correlation between thinking properly and doing wisely. It is as true in living the Christian life as it is anywhere else.

Take David in Psalm 3, for example. First, he calls to mind truths about God: "You, O Lord, are a shield about me, my glory, and the lifter of my head." Then, out of that truth, he "crie[s] aloud to the Lord." There's a lesson in the order of those verses: we have to know and believe the truth about God before we can call out to Him and confidently expect His help.

Sometimes, as we hear God's word being read and taught, we might think to ourselves, "I don't need to know more stuff about God! Just tell me how to work in my office. Just tell me how to be a good wife. Just tell me how to get through my schooling." But the reality is that you must know truth about God first. Then, and only then, what you know about God will empower you to press on, no matter your circumstances. It is truth that transforms us.

Truth also offers us rest. We know from the inscription of Psalm 3 ("A Psalm of David, when he fled from Absalom his son") and from verse 1 ("O Lord, how many are my foes!") that David was writing at a time when he faced great trouble. His son had rebelled against him and was threatening to take the kingdom from him. Yet, in this moment when all seemed lost and the temptation to despair must have been strong, David was able to say, "I lay down and slept; I woke again, for the Lord sustained me." Sleep in itself is a gift—God "*gives* to his beloved sleep" (Psalm 127:2, emphasis added). But to sleep when you are faced with an insurrection led by a member of your own family—that is a phenomenal testament to God's comforting grace.

David probably felt like doing a million things in an attempt to remedy his trouble. Nevertheless, he found rest because he knew God would watch over him. He knew the truth that ultimately, regardless of how dire his circumstances seemed, "salvation belongs to the Lord" (Psalm 3:8). Likewise, whatever your circumstances, the very same truth that transformed David and gave him rest is yours today. Will you believe it? For it is in knowing that the Lord saves and sustains you that you will find peace in the midst of life's storms, and that you will find yourself able to rest even on the hardest of days. We can sleep because He does not.

PSALM 3

OCTOBER 26

HE HAS MERCY FOR YOU

"The tax collector, standing far off, would not even lift up his eyes to heaven, but beat his breast, saying, 'God, be merciful to me, a sinner!'" LUKE 18:13

One of our world's great tragedies is that churches sometimes perpetrate falsehoods about God. This happens whenever a person or an institution confuses the gospel of grace with religious routine.

Perhaps you've heard before, or have been given the impression, that what you need to do is get yourself as fit as you possibly can in order to approach God: that God will not accept you unless you come acceptably to Him, unless you have something good you can show for yourself. Nothing could be further from the truth! All the fitness that God requires is that you see and confess your need of Him.

By our very nature, we do not see our need for God. Instead, we resist Him: "No one seeks for God ... No one does good, not even one" (Romans 3:11-12). It is therefore a great and glorious experience when suddenly, perhaps taking even ourselves by surprise, we find ourselves saying, *You know, this wonderful offer of salvation in Jesus is exactly the thing that I need.* To see, to know, to feel, and to experience the depth of our insufficiency and then begin to see the light of God's mercy is nothing short of a miracle.

When Jesus told the parable of the Pharisee and the tax collector who came to the temple, He had exactly this sort of humble self-recognition in mind. The Pharisee pleads his righteousness and is proud that he is "not like other men, extortioners, unjust, adulterers, or even like this tax collector" (Luke 18:11). The tax collector, however, takes an utterly different approach. He has no confidence in himself and no sense that he deserves an audience with a holy God. All he can muster are these precious words: "God, be merciful to me, a sinner!" And yet it is this man, the tax collector, who Jesus says "went down to his house justified, rather than the other" (v 14).

This parable is a wonderful invitation to those of us who know we have messed up in life. It is also a great challenge to those of us who have been Christians for years—for the devil loves to point us to our good works and suggest that we now deserve acceptance from God. As the religious expert, the Pharisee should have known better, but his religious uprightness blinded him to grace. Don't be fooled as he was. In the end, all that you ever bring to God is an empty cup for Him to fill. You are never anything other than a sinner in need of mercy—but you need never be anything other than that, for God loves to be merciful to sinners. Come freely. Come with empty hands. Come without worry. He has mercy for you.

LUKE 18:9-14

OCTOBER 27

ACCESS TO GOD

"Through the greater and more perfect tent (not made with hands, that is, not of his creation) he entered once for all into the holy places, not by means of the blood of goats and calves but by means of his own blood, thus securing an eternal redemption." HEBREWS 9:11-12

The wonder of the Bible's story is that God—seeing us in our inability to know Him, to love Him, to understand Him, and to serve Him—came to redeem and restore us. God secured our redemption through a series of mighty acts, culminating in the Lord Jesus Christ, whom He sent in order to bring us back into relationship with Himself. In bridging the chasm between God and us, Jesus fulfills His role as our Great High Priest.

As Jewish Christians, the first recipients of the letter to the Hebrews had experienced tremendous changes as a result of following Jesus, particularly in their worship. Their devotion was no longer marked by the grandeur of the temple and all of its accompanying sights, sounds, and fragrances, and they no longer participated in witnessing the high priest coming out on the Day of Atonement.

All of this had changed when Jesus, by His death on the cross, became both the sacrifice and the scapegoat for sins. In the same way that the high priest had previously emerged from behind the temple curtain as an indication that God had accepted the people's sacrifice for sin, the Lord Jesus had come forth from the tomb to declare His sacrifice accepted by the Father. The curtain had been torn (Matthew 27:51; Mark 15:38; Luke 23:45). The door of heavenly access was now open.

By fulfilling the priestly role, Jesus has secured our access to God once and for all. There is no need for repetition—no need for another sacrifice. In contrast to the Old Testament high priests, who stood daily, "offering repeatedly the same sacrifices, which can never take away sins," Christ "offered for all time a single sacrifice for sins," and then "he sat down at the right hand of God" (Hebrews 10:11-12).

The wonder in this, of course, is that Jesus did what no one else could do. He was the priest who made the offering and at the same time He *was* the offering. He voluntarily bore the punishment that was due to us on account of our sin, in order that we might enjoy full pardon from and reconciliation with God.

What difference does this make to us? First, it inspires constancy in our hearts. The first readers of the letter to the Hebrews seem to have been tempted to turn back to their Jewish rites. But Jesus is the ultimate and final High Priest and sacrifice. There is no need to go anywhere else, and there is nowhere else to go. Second, it brings confidence to our prayers. For as we approach God on His throne through Christ, we do so without fear, knowing we are forgiven and are speaking to our heavenly Father. Do you struggle with constancy or with confidence? See Jesus, your High Priest, who has entered into the presence of God, in the heavenly tent—and know that in Him, and Him alone, you have all you need.

HEBREWS 3:1-6

OCTOBER 28

THE ONLY FAITHFUL ONE

"Your steadfast love, O Lord, extends to the heavens, your faithfulness to the clouds." PSALM 36:5

If you do a little digging, you'll find plenty of articles that ask the question, "Is anyone faithful anymore?" Usually, they refer to marriage, but the question is applicable to almost any sphere of life. When I talk to members of my congregation who work in business, for example, they often tell me of workers who appear to be very committed to the team and the mission at the beginning, but then, all of a sudden, they're nowhere to be found. Loyalty to the company or the task at hand frequently dissipates very, very quickly.

It's rare to find people known for steady devotion and consistency, who let their yes be yes and their no be no (Matthew 5:37). And when we do find someone who makes a promise and keeps it, even when it's difficult, it's quite striking.

The only perfect standard of faithfulness that we have—of total loyalty and of complete commitment to keeping a promise—is God. The psalmists continually reflect upon it. As high as you can see, Psalm 36 tells us, that is how far God's faithfulness stretches. There are no ends to which He will not go to remain loyal to His people; there is nothing that will prevent Him keeping His word. Moses continually reminded the people of Israel of God's faithfulness: "Know … that the Lord your God is God, the faithful God who keeps covenant" (Deuteronomy 7:9). James, too, describes God's faithfulness by saying that in Him "there is no variation or shadow due to change" (James 1:17). God's faithfulness is one aspect of the absolute perfection of His character. Given that every believer has staked their eternal future on Him keeping His word, this is very good news!

Other people, as well as the gods of your own creation, will inevitably let you down—be it through their flaws or their frailty. The only promise that can utterly be relied upon is that of the eternal, righteous God, who has revealed Himself in creation and who has confirmed His truthfulness in the person of His Son. He is 100-percent reliable all of the time, for all of eternity—including for all that you are facing today.

PSALM 36

OCTOBER 29

THE DEVIL DEFANGED

"The reason the Son of God appeared was to destroy the works of the devil."
1 JOHN 3:8

By grace, every believer in Christ has been transferred from the domain of darkness into the kingdom of God's beloved Son (Colossians 1:13). We live in the world now as children of light and endeavor to bear the fruit of that light (Ephesians 5:8-9). Yet as glorious as this may be, we know that darkness is not yet fully eradicated from our lives.

The truth is that everyone who becomes a citizen of Christ's kingdom is caught up in a cosmic conflict of eternal significance. Praise the Lord, the Evil One has been powerless to prevent God's adopted children from knowing salvation—but having tasted that measure of defeat, he now seeks to do everything in his power to prevent us from *living* as true heirs of our Father's eternal kingdom. He is totally committed to disrupting and destroying what it means for us to "be imitators of God" (Ephesians 5:1) and to "walk as children of light" (v 8). His one great aim is to stop you trusting in Christ—to knock you off the narrow road before you reach the gates of glory.

We should not ignore the alarming terms which Scripture uses to describe the devil and the urgent terms in which we are urged to withstand him. Peter urges us to "be sober-minded" and "watchful" because our "adversary the devil prowls around like a roaring lion, seeking someone to devour" (1 Peter 5:8). Satan is a real and a vicious enemy. He trades in doubt, division, and destruction. He comes at us both morally and intellectually. With the ferocity of a supernaturally empowered beast, he seeks to maul us and shred our faith to pieces.

What is a Christian to do when faced with such a vicious enemy? The good news for us is this: "The reason the Son of God appeared was to destroy the works of the devil." Though he may still prowl, his defanging has already begun, and ultimately, he will be cast into the lake of fire (Revelation 20:10).

Defeat is certain for the devil and his minions—and, through Christ, victory over him is yours, Christian. In Christ, God has given you the spiritual power to "stand against the schemes of the devil" (Ephesians 6:11). He offers you indestructible armor in the gospel and His very word as your sword (v 11-17). When you fall, you are forgiven. The devil has no power over you. James puts our charge succinctly: "Resist the devil, and he will flee from you" (James 4:7).

So, where is the battle for you? Is it against a particular sin or in a certain trial? Take up the means of grace God offers you in Christ—including your company of fellow soldiers—and, by simply believing the gospel of God, force the prowling lion to retreat!

1 JOHN 3:7-10

OCTOBER 30

THE POWER AND MYSTERY OF OBEDIENCE

"The LORD said to Samuel, 'How long will you grieve over Saul, since I have rejected him from being king over Israel? Fill your horn with oil, and go. I will send you to Jesse the Bethlehemite, for I have provided for myself a king among his sons' ... Samuel did what the LORD commanded and came to Bethlehem."

1 SAMUEL 16:1, 4

Samuel stands out in the pages of biblical history but neither on account of the originality of his ideas nor because he was an initiative-taker. No, his distinction is that he was a man who simply did what God told him. After Saul's rebellion against God, the Lord rejected Saul as king—and Samuel was the one who was told to inform the king of this. So he did (1 Samuel 15:10, 26-29). God then told Samuel that the season of grieving was over and that it was time for him to move on to his next assignment: anointing the next king of Israel. So he did. God said it, and Samuel did it.

The instruction given to the prophet to prepare some oil, go to the small, insignificant town of Bethlehem, and meet with a man called Jesse probably didn't seem incredibly spectacular to Samuel. But he could never have understood the extent to which his obedience would bring him into the heart of a climactic moment in the ongoing story of God's salvation of His people.

It was in the town of Bethlehem that, decades earlier, God had provided a husband for the young widow Ruth. Her grandson Jesse was the man that God sent Samuel to meet, and her great-grandson, David, was the boy whom God would tell Samuel to anoint as king. A thousand years later, in Bethlehem, God would bring forth His Anointed One, Jesus—a descendant of David (Matthew 1:1, 5-6), whom Samuel anointed that day—to be ruler and shepherd over all His people (2:6). Samuel's obedience to all that God told him to do put him on the stage as this next scene of God's sovereign plan unfolded. But Samuel did not know any of that as he filled his horn with oil and began his journey to Bethlehem.

Most of the commands of God don't involve any impressive deeds or great drama. Many of us will not understand the significance of our obedience. Often we will obey not because we can see what God is doing but simply because we have committed ourselves to obeying Him. We may live our lives never knowing what a particular act of obedience has meant in His plans. Be careful, then, to faithfully obey even the seemingly inconsequential instructions of God, for obedience to His command is always right, and you never know beforehand how He will use it.

MARK 14:3-9

OCTOBER 31

THE PURPOSE OF THE CROSS

"When they came to the place that is called The Skull, there they crucified him, and the criminals, one on his right and one on his left." LUKE 23:33

The Gospel writers, without exception, do not dwell on the manner in which Jesus was crucified. Indeed, if you search the Gospels, you will discover that there are very few details concerning Christ's physical suffering. Given the exceptionally brutal manner in which He was executed and the fact that all of Scripture moves us toward the cross, this absence of detail should give us pause, causing us to wonder why the Savior's death is captured only in that simple phrase "There they crucified him."

Presumably, the Gospel writers understood that if they focused on the physical sufferings of Jesus, then we could very easily stop at that. We might mistakenly think that once we have been gripped, stirred, and moved by this dreadful scene, we have come to terms with it. In point of fact, though, to focus on the outward aspects—the physicality—of this terrible event is to miss the purpose of the cross altogether.

For this reason, the Gospel writers did not explain much of what Jesus' physical suffering was like but rather point to what was happening to Him spiritually as He hung there. Their focus is more on the *purpose* of the cross than on the cross itself.

Throughout Scripture—indeed, from the very beginning of it all, in the book of Genesis—the greatest need of humanity is atonement. As soon as the first man and woman turned their backs on God in the Garden of Eden, they were alienated from Him on account of their disobedience. Ever since, humanity has followed in our first ancestors' steps: we, too, turn our backs on God and live in His world in rebellion against Him. This sin, this alienation, must be atoned for, and no amount or doing or trying on our part can reconcile us to God.

But in Jesus, "the righteousness of God has been manifested" to us (Romans 3:21), and we are reconciled to the Father through faith in the Son, "whom God put forward as a propitiation by his blood, to be received by faith" (Romans 3:25). This is atonement. This is the place where the Father's wrath over sin was turned away from sinners and onto another—onto His own Son. This is the purpose, the great and wondrous achievement, of the cross.

There is all the difference in the world between sympathy for Jesus as the perfect sufferer and faith in Christ as our personal Savior. Stop and consider what He hung on the cross to do. Reflect on His spiritual suffering—the agony of bearing the judgment of His Father. Do not gaze on Him so that you feel sorry for Him, but until you are worshiping Him.

MARK 15:33-39

NOVEMBER 1

THE LAW OF LOVE

"If you really fulfill the royal law according to the Scripture, 'You shall love your neighbor as yourself,' you are doing well." JAMES 2:8

The last time you said you loved someone or something, what did you mean?

In our age, we often equate love with a certain emotional experience. People declare "love" based on how they feel. It's no surprise, then, that the idea of acting lovingly out of a sense of duty sounds strange to our ears. Surely if an action is dutiful, it cannot be done out of love?

The book of James offers quite a different view of the relationship between love and duty. When James wants to summarize the law of God, he does so with the words "You shall love your neighbor as yourself." The law, in other words, is fulfilled by love. We must therefore make it a priority to understand what love is and what it is not.

James does *not* mean that the law is fulfilled when we feel a certain way about our neighbors. Anyone who has read James—or much of the Bible at all, for that matter—knows this cannot be the case. For one thing, the Ten Commandments, which are the heart of the Old Testament law, say very little about how we ought to feel but quite a lot about what we ought to do. The commands against murder, adultery, lying, and stealing are aimed at our actions. And laws like these, says James, can be summarized as "Love your neighbor." How do we love our neighbor, then? By doing the right thing.

Consider also the significance of James' phrase "as yourself." How often do any of us *feel* really great about ourselves and find ourselves truly and wholly lovely? Rarely, I would guess. And yet, despite how we feel about ourselves, we most likely see to it that we are cared for. Our love for others ought to be in this way as well. The absence of emotional intensity does not excuse us from obedience.

This does not mean that the right response is to be content with a cold heart as long as we are gritting our teeth and doing the right thing. We should *want* our affections toward others to match our actions, and we ought to pray toward that end. But we should also understand the role our emotions play in our love. Emotions make a great servant but a poor master. They can serve us in doing the right things, but they cannot be our guide for what we should and shouldn't do. Indeed, sometimes it is only once we have decided to act in love that our feelings catch up. Pray today, then, for your affections to be pleasing to God, *and* for you to fulfill His royal law as you act in love toward your neighbors by obeying Him.

JAMES 2:8-17

NOVEMBER 2

GOSPEL ABC

"I am the bread of life; whoever comes to me shall not hunger, and whoever believes in me shall never thirst." JOHN 6:35

Has your church ever done a community outreach event? Perhaps you've been part of one of these that has offered people free food, along with games for children and a chance to bounce around on inflatables. That's all wonderful. We certainly want people in our neighborhoods to know we are friendly, perhaps even likable. But, quite frankly, any group of people—believers or not—can put on an event like that.

We must want more for our friends and neighbors than that. We must long for them to have an encounter with the risen Jesus and to find life in Him.

The best reason for a church to convene a community day, then, is the same reason for it to convene any gathering: so that men, women, and children might have a direct encounter with the living God through the gospel of Jesus Christ. Ultimately, we want unbelieving people around us to become committed followers of Jesus.

One way to conceive of sharing the good news is by reciting the ABCs of the gospel:

A – *Admit*: We all have something to admit. We have sinned, every last one of us. We have fallen short of the glory of God (Romans 3:23). And though "the wages of sin is death, … the free gift of God is eternal life in Christ Jesus" (6:23). Unless we *admit* our need, we will never know the remedy.

B – *Believe*: There is something to believe. Jesus Christ died in the place of sinners like us. The good news of the gospel is not about what we're able to do in order to make ourselves acceptable to God; it is the wonder of what God has already done in Jesus. The message is that "while we were still sinners, Christ died for us" (Romans 5:8). We must *believe* it.

C – *Come*: We must come to Jesus. We can have a sense of our sinfulness and even know that Christ died in our place, but unless we entrust ourselves to Him, we remain lost. Jesus says, "*Come* to me, all who labor and are heavy laden, and I will give you rest" (Matthew 11:28, emphasis added).

Sometimes people get stuck between B and C and, despite knowing they're sinners and understanding the gospel, have never actually *come* to the Lord Jesus. It is worth checking that this does not describe you. If it does, it's appropriate to ask, *What are you waiting for?* The Lord Jesus Himself said, "Whoever comes to me shall not hunger, and whoever believes in me shall never thirst." When you sense pangs and longings in your soul that nothing else seems to satisfy, then come to Jesus. Full and everlasting satisfaction awaits.

If you have come to Jesus and found life in Him, then do not keep quiet about Him. The "bread of life" is for offering around! So by all means let us and our churches show gospel kindness in our acts of love. But we are called to do more, too: to share gospel truth in what we say. To whom will you offer the "bread of life" this week?

JOHN 6:53-69

NOVEMBER 3

SHOULD CHRISTIANS TITHE?

"The earth is the L*ORD's and the fullness thereof, the world and those who dwell therein."* PSALM 24:1

When the topic of biblical stewardship and finances comes up, what is one guiding principle that quickly comes to mind? The most common answer is almost certainly "tithing." And yet, for a word that historically has been used so often in the language of church life, there's a good deal of misunderstanding about what it actually means to tithe. So what does the Bible teach about tithing and the Christian's relationship to it?

First, the *tithe* (the word simply means "a tenth") was the basic principle of giving in the Old Testament. From the beginning, the Jewish people were to bring tithes of their crops and livestock to the Lord (Leviticus 27:30). These tithes were brought to the Levites (temple workers), who would then give a tenth of the tithe to the priests. This pattern was established firmly and fairly in the law of Moses, but as spiritual indifference set in among the people, the practice fell into disuse. For example, we read of Nehemiah's dismay when he "found out that the portions of the Levites had not been given to them … So I confronted the officials and said, 'Why is the house of God forsaken?'" (Nehemiah 13:10-11).

Second, while tithing is the pattern of giving in the Old Testament, it is not stated as an obligation in the New Testament. There we are confronted by an eloquent silence on this subject. This must be significant. We would expect that someone like Paul, with his intimate knowledge of the law, would have affirmed the Old Testament pattern, or at least alluded to it as a principle to be applied in the church. But he does not.

How, then, is a Christian to respond to these two observations? Should we tithe in the way the Israelites were commanded to do, or do we ignore that principle in the way the New Testament seems to? Well, it is true that the tithe is not explicitly commanded in the New Testament—but neither is it explicitly rejected. So while we are not to offer tithes as a matter of obedience to the Old Testament law, neither should we simply ignore the principle. The idea of giving ten percent could be a good starting point for Christians, but it is a starting point and no more. For if we are not careful, the principle of the tithe can be used to alleviate our conscience as we give the bare minimum and try to keep God out of our business. The problem with that kind of approach is that, as the psalmist writes, the earth and all its fullness is the Lord's—including every last cent and possession we claim as ours! We think of ourselves as "giving" to God, but, in truth, He owns it all.

The relationship of the Christian to the principle of tithing, then, is not a neat and clean one. Ten percent may be far too much for you at the moment—or it may be far too comfortable! So perhaps the best way forward is to use that number as your starting point and then to ask God for wisdom and integrity as you look at your finances and at your heart. Let Him reveal how you can most faithfully use your finances—which, in truth, are *His* finances—for His glory.

2 CORINTHIANS 8:8-15

NOVEMBER 4

A GREAT LIE ABOUT THE CHRISTIAN LIFE

"As for the rich in this present age, charge them not to be haughty, nor to set their hopes on the uncertainty of riches, but on God, who richly provides us with everything to enjoy." 1 TIMOTHY 6:17

There is a great lie about the gospel that is common in our culture and that sometimes we, as churches and individual believers, help to promote. The fatal fabrication is this: *Coming to Jesus and believing the gospel means no more fun. The Christian life is a dull life, a lesser life—a disappointing life, even.* Thank God, nothing could be further from the truth!

Scripture describes God as a Father who gives good gifts to His children (Matthew 7:11), and as the one who "richly provides us with everything to enjoy" and who will refuse "no good thing" to "those who walk uprightly" (Psalm 84:11). We must be clear: the testimony of Scripture does not suggest that we can do whatever we want, nor does it imply that God will give us whatever we want. It does, however, repeatedly tell us that we have a generous Father who wants His children to enjoy His many blessings.

Paul's first letter to his protégé Timothy declares that "everything created by God is good, and nothing is to be rejected if it is received with thanksgiving, for it is made holy by the word of God and prayer" (1 Timothy 4:4-5). So the Christian standard is not one of austerity or asceticism, nor consumption or consumerism. No, we are guided by God's word to set our hopes on God and to enjoy all He gives us as good gifts from Him. This approach to life leads us to a wellspring of unending joy.

Inevitably, this revelation of our Father's character as the great Giver and our greatest treasure will lead us to a different kind of lifestyle than those of many of our neighbors. As we learn that "it is more blessed to give than to receive" (Acts 20:35), we don't quite keep as much to ourselves. As we realize that "godliness with contentment is great gain" (1 Timothy 6:6), we don't require the latest gadget or shiniest car to temporarily boost our happiness.

The Christian life is not drab, nor dull, nor ever pale. While our faith may lead us to forgo certain creature comforts in this life, untold riches await all who give their lives to Jesus. And what's more, those riches in heaven stretch back from heaven to bless us now with supernatural peace and sturdy joy as we delight in good gifts from our heavenly Father's hand. Be sure not to believe the lie that a life following Jesus gives you less than you would otherwise have enjoyed. Be sure not to promote that falsehood to those around you, either.

1 THESSALONIANS 1:2-10

NOVEMBER 5

HIS HANDS RAISED HIGH

"He led them out as far as Bethany, and lifting up his hands he blessed them. While he blessed them, he parted from them and was carried up into heaven."
LUKE 24:50-51

Jesus' earthly pilgrimage can be thought of as a journey towards His departure; having left heaven and come to earth to be born as a baby, He lived as a man, taught, performed miracles, called His people to follow Him, died as their Savior, rose to life—and then, at the appointed time, He went back to the Father and to glory. In a sense, this moment was what everything else had been leading up to.

Scripture clearly teaches that the moment of Jesus' departure was fixed in eternity past (1 Peter 1:19-20). Luke, for instance, records for us that when Jesus "went up on the mountain to pray" (Luke 9:28), two men, Moses and Elijah, "appeared in glory and spoke of his departure, which he was about to accomplish at Jerusalem" (v 31). Later in the same chapter, we read that "when the days drew near for him to be taken up," Jesus "set his face to go to Jerusalem" (v 51). Both the time and manner of Jesus' departure were determined by God, for our good and for His glory.

The fact that Jesus left decisively should encourage us. If His post-resurrection appearances had just grown fewer and fewer and then petered out, nobody would have really known what was going on. Confusion, chaos, and discord would have reigned. But instead, as we read, Jesus visibly ascended to heaven in front of His disciples, leaving no one in any doubt that He had accomplished His purpose.

As He departed, Jesus lifted His hands in blessing. These early believers would have understood this gesture in a way that most of us do not today. At that time, it was customary for people of stature and significance not simply to walk out the door and leave but to bestow a blessing upon those who were under their care. Jesus' disciples must surely have found it meaningful and deeply reassuring, then, that their final view of their beloved Master was the sight of Him making this familiar gesture. He would no longer be with them; but His blessing would be. They were His people, under His care, even as He returned to reign from heaven.

What a wonderful Lord we have, who lifted up His hands to be nailed to the cross and who now loves to lift His hands up in blessing His own. Jesus is far more willing to bless us than we are even to take the time to ask Him to bless us. He loves to do this. Is that the picture you have of Christ, with His hands raised in blessing on your life? You can. You should!

NUMBERS 6:24-26

NOVEMBER 6

THE HEART THAT GOD ACCEPTS

"Then David arose from the earth and washed and anointed himself and changed his clothes. And he went into the house of the Lord *and worshiped."*

2 SAMUEL 12:20

When David's child, born as a result of his adultery with Bathsheba, was afflicted with sickness, it awakened within the king a spiritual zeal that had been dormant. David began to seek God, and he prayed desperately that God might spare his little boy. He refused to eat, and he no longer lived his life as usual while his child's life hung in the balance.

David had previously attempted to cover over his sin by trying to pawn off his child on the unsuspecting Uriah, whose wife he had slept with. But when God, in His mercy, confronted David with his sin, the king's posture completely changed. David sought God because God had first sought David and softened his heart. Such a change could only be brought about by the work of God.

Then came the dreadful news: the child had died. The late theologian Alec Motyer compared repentance to gathering back a stone that has been thrown into a pool: you can get the stone back, but the ripples upon the water will continue to spread.[85] David repented of his abuse and adultery, and God, in His mercy, accepted David's repentance. But God did not stop the ripples.

Yet God was still able to use this tragedy to form David into the man that he needed to be. David responded in a strange and unexpected way: he arose, cleaned himself up, and went into the house of the Lord. The one who had been hiding from God now went to meet with God. The tragic death of David's son did not lead David to stay at arm's length from God. No, it led him into an even deeper relationship with Him.

When he entered the house of the Lord, David would have needed to bring a lamb without blemish as a sacrifice. But that was not the only sacrifice he brought. He also offered the only damaged sacrifice that is acceptable to bring into God's house: as David later wrote, "The sacrifices of God are a broken spirit; a broken and contrite heart, O God, you will not despise" (Psalm 51:17).

God did not leave David to cover up his sin, and He did not leave him alone in dealing with the consequences of his sin. God's treatment of David reveals that He cares deeply about the state of His children's hearts. He will go to great lengths to bring you back when you wander away from Him. More than anything else, God wants you to have a broken and contrite heart before Him. When He makes you confront your sin, or afflicts you, or doesn't give you what you desire, don't assume that it is because He doesn't love you. It is because He is graciously drawing you closer to Himself.

2 SAMUEL 12:1-10

85 *Treasures of the King: Psalms from the Life of David* (InterVarsity UK, 2007), ch. 13.

NOVEMBER 7

DELIGHTING IN GOD'S WILL

"Behold, the days are coming, declares the Lord, when I will establish a new covenant with the house of Israel and with the house of Judah, not like the covenant that I made with their fathers on the day when I took them by the hand to bring them out of the land of Egypt." HEBREWS 8:8-9

When God's people cannot rise to the heights of His standards, the Lord does not lower His standards to match their abilities. Instead, He determines to transform His people through the person and work of His Son, Jesus.

According to Old Testament practices, every high priest was appointed to offer both gifts and sacrifices on behalf of the people. However, when Jesus came to fulfill the role of our Great High Priest, He ushered in the new and perfect covenant by offering Himself as the final sacrifice. By His death and resurrection, Jesus secured a covenant that cannot be broken—a covenant that these words had looked forward to when the prophet Jeremiah first spoke them (Jeremiah 31:31-32); a covenant that transforms the hearts of those with whom it is made. But how does this transformation take place?

Following His resurrection, Jesus ascended into heaven and sat down "at the right hand of the throne of the Majesty in heaven" (Hebrews 8:1). This decisive act not only signified that His work was complete but also initiated the coming of the Holy Spirit. Prior to His death and resurrection, Jesus essentially told His disciples, *It is necessary for Me to go away. If I'm here, I'm just here, in this body and in this place. But when I go, when I send the Holy Spirit in all of His fullness, He will not only be with you, but He will be in you—all of you, wherever you are. And He will take the things that are Mine, and He will make them precious to you.*

It's the ministry of the Holy Spirit, then, to transform and renew our hearts so that God's law will be written on them and so that it will be our delight to do His will (Jeremiah 31:33). Previously, God's ways were irksome to us. Previously, His law was only condemnation to us. But now it has become a joyful reality. To live in purity, wholeness, and faithfulness has now become our delight.

The new covenant also enables us to know God through His word. Our knowledge of God doesn't come primarily through sacraments, a hierarchy of priests, or teachers and pastors. Instead, all of us, from the least to the greatest, can know God (Hebrews 8:11). When we know God personally and intimately, we are assured of our forgiveness; and when we see Christ personally and intimately in His word, we are transformed by the Spirit to become more like Him (2 Corinthians 3:18).

This is the wonder of what Jesus has done as our Great High Priest. He has secured our forgiveness, and He has sent His Spirit. In what ways are you struggling to obey God, or even really to *want* to obey Him? Ask Him to work through you, by His Spirit, to transform your view of His law and to enable your obedience of it. What you could never do on your own, you can do as you keep in step with Him.

JOHN 16:5-15

NOVEMBER 8

PROPHECY FULFILLED

"It was the will of the LORD to crush him; he has put him to grief… Out of the anguish of his soul he shall see and be satisfied; by his knowledge shall the righteous one, my servant, make many to be accounted righteous, and he shall bear their iniquities." ISAIAH 53:10-11

One of the most powerful aspects of the Gospel accounts of the crucifixion of Christ is the way that again and again and again they record how the events of the day fulfilled Old Testament prophecies made hundreds of years before.

When the chief priests and scribes delivered Jesus to Pilate, the Roman governor was perplexed at His choice not to publicly defend Himself. When Pilate asked, "Are you the King of the Jews?" Jesus replied enigmatically, "You have said so" (Matthew 27:11). When the religious leaders continued making accusations, Pilate asked again, "Have you no answer to make? See how many charges they bring against you" (Mark 15:4-5). Yet Christ did exactly as Isaiah 53:7 had foretold: He "opened not his mouth," but instead waited in silence to be sentenced to death.

Later that day, only hours before Jesus breathed His last, the noonday sun was suddenly and dramatically swallowed up in darkness (Matthew 27:45). The Jewish people who were present ought to have understood the significance of that event from what had happened at the first Passover. They knew that in Egypt, the ninth plague, which preceded the death of the firstborn, was the plague of darkness (Exodus 10:21-29). The darkness on the day of crucifixion mirrored that very plague, identifying the need for blood to be shed, for a lamb to be slain, and for provision of shelter from the judgment of which the darkness itself spoke.

The Gospels show us that Jesus knew He was the one who had been promised, the one who would bear our sin to win our salvation. He lived out the prophetic words of Isaiah 53, and He operated of His own will according to the plan of Almighty God, expressing God's love and sacrificing everything for those who deserve nothing except judgment.

As Old Testament prophecy was fulfilled before their eyes on the day that Christ was crucified, the biggest question that Pilate and the Jews each faced was essentially "What shall I do with Jesus?" And that is the great question that we all face every day. By our very nature, we neglect His wisdom, rebel against His authority, and doubt His goodness. That is why "it was the will of the LORD to crush him," for God had purposed that He Himself would "bear [our] iniquities." The realization that God had planned His Son's sin-bearing death centuries before He hung on the cross—in fact, had planned it before the creation of the world—ought to bring us to our knees in awe, not just at the sovereignty of God's plan but also at the love that brought it into being, the love that wrought its climax at Calvary. Christ remained silent as He stood before Pilate; there is no reason or excuse for us to remain silent as we kneel before Him and consider all He has done for us.

LUKE 4:16-21

NOVEMBER 9

GLAD SUBMISSION TO GOD

"But he gives more grace. Therefore it says, 'God opposes the proud but gives grace to the humble.' Submit yourselves therefore to God." JAMES 4:6-7

It seems hard to imagine now, but there was a time in the not-so-distant past when people hardly ever wore seat belts, and children weren't required to have the sort of car seats they must have now. Without belts and latches to restrain them, it could prove rather difficult to get children to sit and stay sitting. The story is told of a young boy who found himself in the car with his mother. He was in the back seat, and, as boys tend to do, he found himself getting restless, so he was up and down and moving around. His mother, of course, told him he needed to sit. Finally, after repeated requests and repeated refusals, his mother felt the need to stop the car and exercise appropriate discipline. She then got him back in his seat and set off down the road again. A few seconds later, the boy mumbled from the back seat, "I may be sitting down on the outside, but I am standing up on the inside."

That little story is likely to prompt us to smile—but it also sounds something of a warning for us. This boy, while outwardly obeying, was inwardly rebelling. How often might that characterize our own behavior toward God? Perhaps we outwardly do and say the right things, especially when we are in public and most of all in church, but inwardly we are thinking and feeling just the opposite. As innocent and normal as the scenario may seem, it was pride rearing up in that small boy's heart that provoked that defiant comment—and it is pride that is rearing up in our own hearts when we sit down outwardly but stand up internally. And God sees all.

Real submission to God is the outworking of a truly humble heart. To submit to God is to align ourselves under His authority. By nature, we oppose authority and do not like to be told what to do. But obedience to God ought never to be grudging. We should submit with a joyful, happy abandonment to God's will as it is revealed to us in His word. It is our delight to discover His truth and act accordingly.

Such joyful submission is possible because of the nature of the one to whom we submit. When we submit to the Lord Jesus Christ, we give ourselves to true freedom (Galatians 5:1). We yield to a light burden and an easy yoke (Matthew 11:30). So, take a close look at your own life and heart today. Are there ways in which you are sitting down on the outside but standing up on the inside—obeying God but grumbling about it and begrudging having to do it? There is always more grace for such pride, but it does need to be humbly repented of. What is it that you need to remember about God in order to do that, and then to submit willingly, joyfully, and wholly to His will for you?

ROMANS 6:15-23

NOVEMBER 10

DEAD-END STREETS

"I said in my heart, 'Come now, I will test you with pleasure; enjoy yourself.' But behold, this also was vanity." ECCLESIASTES 2:1

Ecclesiastes is an ancient book, yet its words are compellingly relevant. Although it was written around 3,000 years ago, you might think that the author had his finger on the pulse of our contemporary life. And indeed, as you read, you find yourself being walked down a number of dead-end streets representing the common paths we often tread in our search for satisfaction.

One route through which we try to find meaning in life is education. Experts constantly assert that the problems of substance abuse, sexual abuse and misconduct, and other societal ills can be solved if only people can be better educated. Yet experience shows us that mere information cannot in and of itself satisfy the needs of the heart, nor is it capable of taming the unruliness of the soul. Judged by many yardsticks, Western nations are the best-educated in human history, but they do not appear to be the happiest, and they may well be those that most thirst for instant gratification.

So if education doesn't satisfy us, we might turn down the pathway of pleasure. We decide to let the good times roll. At first, we might find something resembling happiness—but we eventually discover that the pleasure it brings is only fleeting. It turns out to be a form of escapism, luring us into a make-believe, rose-colored, self-focused life that sounds great but is empty.

Much of the world that surrounds us is set up to call us down dead-end streets like these. Now, it would be a dreadful misunderstanding to think that Christianity is disinterested in education and pleasure. Nothing could be further from the truth! Yet the author of Ecclesiastes shows us that none of these pursuits will in and of themselves make sense of our lives or answer our deepest longings. Only when we come to know the true and living God does the enjoyment of life's blessings feed into lasting joy.

These dead-end streets contain some hope, however—for Christ can break through and save us, drawing us onto the narrow path that leads to life (Matthew 7:13-14). Maybe that's exactly what happened for you. Or perhaps you're tempted to resist the warning of Ecclesiastes and go down one of these paths instead of the road of faithful obedience to the Lord—or you are tempted to implicitly or explicitly encourage your loved ones to go down them. If the temptation to see education or enjoyment as the one thing you must have calls your name, remember this: one day you will stand before the throne of God, and you will have to give an account. Which path will you walk along?

MATTHEW 7:13-14

NOVEMBER 11

THE GIFT OF REMEMBRANCE

"He took bread, and when he had given thanks, he broke it and gave it to them, saying, 'This is my body, which is given for you. Do this in remembrance of me.'" LUKE 22:19

Most of us find it far easier to forget than to remember. That is why nations feel the need to build war memorials, monuments, and museums—so that, as generation follows generation, the significance of an event is not lost over time. Thus we often hear the phrase "Lest we forget."

Many times throughout the Bible the people of God are called to remember events and put in place certain memorials to aid with that recollection. When the Israelites crossed the Jordan into the promised land, Joshua gave instructions to set up stones in the middle of the river. It likely seemed a strange thing to do, but Joshua told the people that it was to be a sign: "When your children ask in time to come, 'What do those stones mean to you?' then you shall tell them that the waters of the Jordan were cut off before the ark of the covenant of the Lord. When it passed over the Jordan, the waters of the Jordan were cut off. So these stones shall be to the people of Israel a memorial forever" (Joshua 4:6-7). Simply looking at these stones would help God's people recall His faithfulness and provision as He led them into the spacious land He had promised and prepared for them.

Centuries later, as the book of Esther explains, Mordecai established Purim—the Feast of Lots—in order to commemorate "the days on which the Jews got relief from their enemies, and as the month that had been turned for them from sorrow into gladness and from mourning into a holiday" (Esther 9:22). The Jews were to rejoice in their deliverance by sending provision to one another as an indication of God's kindness and as a way of passing on some of His generosity to those who needed God's gracious compassion.

We, too, are given a practice of memorialization. Jesus not only bore the punishment we deserved and opened the way for us to enjoy eternal life, but He also gave to His followers a simple meal to help us remember what He has done. Every time we celebrate the sacrament of the Lord's Supper, we do so in remembrance of Jesus, who has faithfully provided our salvation and has turned our sorrow into gladness. If we don't celebrate the feast—if we don't keep this memorial as part and parcel of our history—then we lose the ability to reflect upon eternal realities. Indeed, it is as we share in the Lord's Supper and remember His death and the feast that we are invited to in glory that the Spirit feeds our hearts, strengthening our faith.

The Lord's Supper must never become a dry ritual, something we perform just because it is what we do. It must always point us away from itself, and away from ourselves, to the great rescue at the cross. And in between our celebrations of the Supper, we are still called to remember, for the more we call Jesus' loving atoning death to mind, the more we will remember who we are and whose we are, and the more joyful and worshipful we will be. So, how will you remember today that you have a Lord whose body was broken for you?

1 CORINTHIANS 11:23-26

NOVEMBER 12

CHRIST KNOWS YOUR WORKS

"To the angel of the church in Ephesus write: 'The words of him who holds the seven stars in his right hand, who walks among the seven golden lampstands. I know your works.'" REVELATION 2:1-2

Jesus knows you.

The letter to the church in Ephesus is the first of Christ's seven letters to the first-century churches in Revelation 2 – 3, and each begins, "I know…" Jesus knew and understood these early believers' circumstances. When it came to their successes and their struggles, their trials and their tribulations, He was deeply aware and concerned, and He wrote to each church specifically about the context in which it found itself (Revelation 2:9, 13, 19; 3:1, 8, 15).

Pause for a minute and think about the nature of that phrase, "I know your works." Who knows you? Perhaps you might think of your spouse, your children, or your boss. But ultimately, "Who knows a person's thoughts except the spirit of that person, which is in him?" (1 Corinthians 2:11). The only one who truly knows is the one who, through the apostle John, wrote this letter.

The psalmist, understanding this, marveled:

O Lord, you have searched me and known me!
  You know when I sit down and when I rise up;
  you discern my thoughts from afar …
Even before a word is on my tongue,
  behold, O Lord, you know it altogether …
Such knowledge is too wonderful for me;
  it is high; I cannot attain it. (Psalm 139:1-2, 4, 6)

Christ's letters to the first-century churches are historical, written to real churches in real places, with real men, women, and families living at a certain point in time. Yet the specific issues which the Lord addressed are timeless: believers enjoying a sense of triumphant expectation or dealing with failures in their Christian pilgrimage; struggling converts who had begun well but had slidden into laziness; congregations that were once known for their vibrancy and genuine commitment to Christ and His people becoming dreadfully complacent. These specifics are not unfamiliar to us; neither are they unknown to Jesus.

There is an awesomeness about the simplicity of this phrase, "I know your works," that is relevant to the gatherings of God's people in which we find ourselves today. The risen Christ looks upon us, and He says, *I know.* Come before Jesus today, then, with honesty and openness. He already understands, and, through His word, He wants to speak directly with you about the situation in which you, too, find yourself.

PSALM 139:1-16

NOVEMBER 13

COMMITTED TO TRUTH

"I know your works, your toil and your patient endurance, and how you cannot bear with those who are evil, but have tested those who call themselves apostles and are not, and found them to be false. I know you are enduring patiently and bearing up for my name's sake, and you have not grown weary."
REVELATION 2:2-3

The 1980s British prime minister Margaret Thatcher was nothing if not determined. Whatever view we take of her politics, she was certainly a woman of conviction, famously declaring at a moment when many of her political allies were telling her to change course, "You turn if you want to. The lady's not for turning."

That kind of fortitude and conviction was also evident in the first-century church in Ephesus. When Jesus commended them, it was primarily on account of their principled dedication. They were committed to the task, persevering in it and dedicated to the truth.

The word used for "works" is the complete opposite of idleness and inactivity. Jesus recognized that these Ephesian believers weren't intimidated by the challenges that came from living out the faith of the gospel. They were prepared to extend themselves again and again for the name of Christ.

Twice in the space of just a few words, Jesus also speaks of their endurance or enduring—their perseverance. The Ephesian church wasn't afraid of hard work, but they were also sticking with that work and seeing it through, steadfast and immovable. As William Barclay writes, their toughness was "the courageous gallantry which accepts suffering and hardship and loss and turns them into grace and glory."[86]

Further, these believers were also committed to the truth. They weren't susceptible to every passing wind of doctrine but were prepared to test those who came with new claims, willing to reject them if they proved to be spurious. They stood steadfastly for the truth even against a heretical group that attempted to offer religious experiences that wouldn't impinge upon self-indulgent lifestyles (Revelation 2:6).

What would Jesus say about us today? How committed are we as a 21st-century church? Are we strong, steadfast, and persevering? Do we have enough courage and conviction to stand for the truth and say, *I hate these practices, for I know that Jesus does too*? Or are we in danger of growing "weary of doing good" (Galatians 6:9)? When others suggest compromise in our commitment or obedience to Christ, are we willing to say, "You turn if you want to. I am not for turning"?

As Jesus looks upon you, as He does, may He have much to commend in you as a follower who models spiritual conviction, perseverance, and a determination to live in the real world with a dedicated love for Christ.

2 TIMOTHY 3:1-9

86 Quoted in Leon Morris, *Revelation: An Introduction and Commentary*, The Tyndale New Testament Commentaries (Eerdmans, 2002), p 59.

NOVEMBER 14

REKINDLING LOST LOVE

"I have this against you, that you have abandoned the love you had at first. Remember therefore from where you have fallen; repent, and do the works you did at first. If not, I will come to you and remove your lampstand from its place, unless you repent." REVELATION 2:4-5

It's tragic to see a marriage in which the spouses have grown cold toward each other. Though they're still together, loneliness and isolation abound. There's a rigid, lifeless formality to it, seen in their eyes and understood in their expressions. The vibrancy and fresh discoveries that marked their early love are missing, having slipped away with the passing years.

The Ephesian church was a task-oriented, tough-minded, truth-telling fellowship, and for this they were commended (Revelation 2:2-3). But in His words to them, Jesus revealed their Achilles' heel: though they were seeking to hold fast to the truth, they had abandoned love. One commentator writes, "If the price paid by the Ephesians for the preservation of true Christianity was the loss of love, the price was too high, for Christianity without love is a perverted faith."[87]

Was it that they had lost their love for Christ? For each other? For the unbelieving community around them? It isn't necessary to choose between those options. For when love for Christ is not as it should be, then our love for all else will be affected.

For those of us who are committed to doctrinal faithfulness, here is a challenging reminder that the ultimate measure of a church is found not in its programs, achievements, reputation, or doctrinal orthodoxy but in its love. Christianity, as the Puritan Thomas Chalmers eloquently put it, is about "the expulsive power of a new affection"—about falling in love with Christ, about a sense of the immensity of His pursuing, energizing, loving grace. If that love for Jesus begins to wane, we will begin to look a lot like the church in Ephesus: impressive from the outside but internally loveless. And Jesus warns that this is no small matter; removing the Ephesian church's lampstand means removing His recognition of them as His church, His people. A loveless church is, in truth, not a church at all.

Perhaps you realize that you do not love God the way you once did. This can creep up on us so easily, our eyes growing dry, our prayers growing cold. What can we do?

Jesus says the remedy for lost love is first to "remember." We need to recall what it was about Jesus that caused us to love Him in the first place and then use that as a spur for forward momentum. We need to restore our commitment to the things we did at first—which typically means going back to the basics. In short, we need to look again at Jesus, lifting our eyes from what we do—our programs, our efforts, our ministries—to the beauty and love of the one who died for us and who dwells in us. Love is rekindled by looking at that which is lovely. So if your love has grown cold, gaze at Jesus as He reveals Himself to you in His word—and joy and vibrancy will surely return.

HEBREWS 1:1-13

87 G. R. Beasley-Murray, *The Book of Revelation* (Wipf and Stock, 2010), p 75.

NOVEMBER 15

EMBRACED BY CHRIST

"And to the angel of the church in Smyrna write: 'The words of the first and the last, who died and came to life. I know your tribulation and your poverty (but you are rich) and the slander of those who say that they are Jews and are not, but are a synagogue of Satan. Do not fear what you are about to suffer. Behold, the devil is about to throw some of you into prison, that you may be tested, and for ten days you will have tribulation. Be faithful unto death, and I will give you the crown of life.'" REVELATION 2:8-10

Jesus is the first and the last, the Alpha and Omega, the one who is from everlasting to everlasting. Kingdoms rise and fall, and dynasties crumble, but the Lord Jesus is without beginning and without end, for even death could not hold Him. He precedes us and will continue after us.

The beleaguered people in Smyrna needed to hear this description of their Lord so that they could be reminded of and encouraged by it. Faced with the prospect of suffering, even to the point of death, they felt themselves to be anything other than triumphant. Therefore, to know that they had been included in Christ—to know that He was their Savior, their companion, and their friend—made all the difference to the challenges they faced.

Smyrna was the home of Polycarp, one of the most famous Christian martyrs of all time, who, as the city's bishop, was bound and burned at the stake around AD 155. Polycarp may not have been in leadership at the time the church received this letter from John, but he might well have been a young listener as it was read. At the very least, these words would surely have become very familiar to him as he grew in faith. We see their impact on full display when he was urged to renounce his faith in Christ in order to save his life. Instead of recanting, Polycarp replied, "Eighty and six years have I served Him, and He never did me any injury. How then can I blaspheme my King and my Savior?"[88]

It is tempting to blend so perfectly with the surrounding culture that there is never a possibility of being on the receiving end of animosity and persecution because there is never anything different and challenging about us. But the Lord Jesus does not tell us to avoid suffering in His cause; He tells us not to fear it. If we are prepared to stand strong concerning the exclusivity of the claims of Christ, the purity that is represented in following Christ, and the sufficiency and authority of the word of Christ, then we will need to remember Christ's words: "Do not fear those who kill the body but cannot kill the soul" (Matthew 10:28). Your calling is the same as that to the church in Smyrna: to be faithful to the end, no matter the cost. You have been embraced by Christ, and He is as real, alive, vibrant, and committed to His kingdom and to His people as He was in the days of Polycarp. How will you stand for Him today?

REVELATION 2:8-11

---

88 *The Martyrdom of Polycarp*, ch. 9 (author unknown).

NOVEMBER 16

LIGHTS IN THE DARKNESS

"I know where you dwell, where Satan's throne is. Yet you hold fast my name, and you did not deny my faith even in the days of Antipas my faithful witness, who was killed among you, where Satan dwells." REVELATION 2:13

The city of Pergamum was built on a cone-shaped hill that rose sharply to a height of a thousand feet. It was a strong center of paganism, with a variety of temples and shrines built on the pinnacle; Zeus, Athena, Dionysus, and Asclepius were all represented. Additionally, Pergamum had become the first city to establish a shrine to a living ruler, the Roman emperor, making it the official Asian center of the imperial cult. Spiritually speaking, it was a dark place—so dark that Christ refers to it as the place where Satan made his home.

It was in this place of darkness, pluralism, and idolatry that the church in Pergamum defiantly expressed their loyalty to Christ's name. Being true to the name of the Lord Jesus Christ was an indication that these believers were faithful to all that He had revealed Himself to be—the incarnate Lord, the resurrected King, God Himself. It was no small feat to hold fast to Jesus in a place where people would have been happy to include Him in the pantheon of gods, as just another religious figure among many, but who would not tolerate the claim that He is the King, that beside Him there is no other, and that no one else—not even Caesar—is worthy of the worship that belongs only to Him.

This loyalty to Christ's name was epitomized by a believer named Antipas. Evidently, he wouldn't render to Caesar a title that belonged to Jesus Christ alone. And so he refused to compromise, even as it cost him his life.

The pluralism that was represented in Pergamum marks much of modern Western culture today, which often grants the same credence to all religious claims, giving them equal weight to the claims of Christ. Such a worldview is perfectly happy if we simply add Jesus to the group, but it cannot tolerate Jesus' statement that "no one comes to the Father except through me" (John 14:6). Jesus may be *a* way, but He cannot be *the* way, goes Western 21st-century thinking. And so we are surrounded by the "shrines" of pluralism and by those who worship anything and everything except the living God. We, God's people, have been planted in their midst. Those who remain true to Christ's name will, at some point and in some way, feel the vice-like grip of our surroundings seeking to squeeze the life out of us. Will we match the loyalty of those in Pergamum? Only if we are convinced of what they were convinced of: that Jesus alone is worthy of our commitment and our worship—no matter the cost.

REVELATION 2:12-17

NOVEMBER 17

TROUBLE WITHIN

"I have a few things against you: you have some there who hold the teaching of Balaam, who taught Balak to put a stumbling block before the sons of Israel, so that they might eat food sacrificed to idols and practice sexual immorality." REVELATION 2:14

External pressure to conform is not the only danger to our faith that we face.

The church in Pergamum had been successful in resisting the lures of Satan and of pluralism (Revelation 2:13). They had failed, however, to take care of their own internal problems. Despite the loyalty of some, these believers were guilty of tolerating a heresy that combined idolatry and sexual immorality. The reference to "the teaching of Balaam" here does not refer to some book or body of doctrine. Rather, it is intended to call to mind the activity of the false prophet Balaam in the Old Testament. He advised the Midianite women on how to seduce the Israelites and thereby infiltrate and cause destruction among God's people (Numbers 31:16). One commentator notes that Balaam's clever idea was to break down Israel's power by an indirect attack on their morality: "Pagan food and pagan women were his powerful tools against the rigidity of the Mosaic Law."[89]

Balaam therefore serves as a prototype of all the corrupt teachers who followed his example, promoting an "antinomian" approach to life. *Antinomian* is from the Greek *anti*, "against," and *nomos*, "law"—"against the law"; it describes a libertine, licentious way of thinking that sets aside all that the Bible has to say about holiness, purity, and the fear of the Lord being the beginning of wisdom (Psalm 111:10; Proverbs 1:7; 9:10).

While some believers in Pergamum had fully embraced such teaching, others within the fellowship merely tolerated it—yet in allowing it, they were as culpable as the rest. John Stott writes that "the risen Christ, the Chief Shepherd of His flock, was grieved both by the waywardness of the minority and by the nonchalance of the majority."[90] In failing to act, they made it possible for heresy to spread, to the great harm of God's people. And so, though the majority were commended for holding fast to their right belief, they were also rebuked for failing to deal seriously with those who were guilty of wrong behavior.

If Satan cannot wreak havoc in a church as a result of external challenges, he will seek to do it by the insidious work of internal compromise. So, be on guard. It will always be easy to find a "spiritual guide" who is more than willing to tell you that it's fine to indulge your desires and follow your heart. That is not true Christianity, which not only believes correctly but also behaves properly, exalting Christ and promoting holiness. And it will be even easier to stay quiet rather than humbly challenge those in your church who are putting their desires above their holiness. So ask yourself: *What stumbling block may have been placed in my own path of obedience? And what stumbling block may the Lord be calling me to help another identify?* Our church's holiness, as well as our own, is to be our concern.

JUDE 17-25

89 E.M. Blaiklock, *The Seven Churches: An Exposition of Revelation, Chapters Two and Three* (The Institute Printing and Publishing Society, n.d.), p 35.

90 *What Christ Thinks of the Church* (Harold Shaw, 1990), p 44.

NOVEMBER 18

JEZEBEL'S ROAD

"I have this against you, that you tolerate that woman Jezebel, who calls herself a prophetess and is teaching and seducing my servants to practice sexual immorality and to eat food sacrificed to idols ... But to the rest of you in Thyatira, who do not hold this teaching ... to you I say, I do not lay on you any other burden. Only hold fast what you have until I come. The one who conquers and keeps my works until the end, to him I will give authority over the nations."

REVELATION 2:20, 24-26

The longest of Jesus' letters to the churches in Revelation 2 – 3 was to the least politically influential city of the group. Thyatira was commercial rather than political—a bustling, thriving community populated with many tradespeople, a great place to go shopping. Unlike some of the other churches to whom Jesus addressed messages, the believers there had gotten off to a great start and continued with clear progress.

Yet among the church's many positive traits of "love and faith and service and patient endurance" (Revelation 2:19), a poisonous weed had been allowed to establish itself. Jesus refers to the leader of this clan as "Jezebel," comparing her activity to that of the queen of Israel almost a thousand years earlier. Queen Jezebel had contaminated Israel with a system of thought that divorced religion from morality, suggesting to the people of her time that it was good to live with that dichotomy. In Thyatira, it seems, the same was happening. This woman, a self-described "prophetess," claimed to speak with inspired authority and told believers that they could indulge in idolatry and immorality while still remaining followers of Jesus.

Thankfully, though, not everyone in Thyatira had gone down Jezebel's road. For those who had resisted the temptation, Jesus' encouragement was to cling to what they had: life that was "truly life" (1 Timothy 6:19). He ended with a simple promise: "The one who conquers and who keeps my works until the end, to him I will give authority over the nations" (Revelation 2:26; see Psalm 2:8).

Imagine that being read out in the congregation in Thyatira. Picture the wool merchants and leather workers, their fingers full of needle pricks and big lumps, standing there, concerned, wondering if they could continue to function despite the challenges of immorality and idolatry—and then Christ Himself offers this simple exhortation: "Hold fast."

The promise and exhortation are for you as well. Though you may feel beleaguered, hopeless, and helpless in the face of the immorality and idolatry around you, in Christ you can cling to life that is truly life. He is coming, and He will welcome you to rule the world with Him. As you "hold fast" and continue on toward eternity, remember that the perseverance of the saints is really the perseverance of God Himself: He can keep you till that glorious day.

REVELATION 2:18-29

NOVEMBER 19

WAKE UP!

"To the angel of the church in Sardis write: 'The words of him who has the seven spirits of God and the seven stars. I know your works. You have the reputation of being alive, but you are dead. Wake up, and strengthen what remains and is about to die, for I have not found your works complete in the sight of my God ... If you will not wake up, I will come like a thief, and you will not know at what hour I will come against you.'" REVELATION 3:1-3

The city of Sardis thought it was impregnable because of the way it was built. In fact, it was never taken by a direct assault on the gates and walls of the city—but twice it was taken by stealth, under the cover of darkness. Its very sense of security worked against it.

Apparently, this attitude had crept into the church in Sardis when it came to the Christian life. Clearly, it had a reputation for having a vibrant ministry. Perhaps it was known for its size and influence, or for the way in which it was able to put its programs together and develop certain strategies. But things were not as they appeared. Moral laxity and spiritual complacency had seeped into the congregation.

The risen Christ saw that it was all a sham, because the church lacked the proper spiritual orientation. So He issued a warning: *You'd better wake up! Your city was overtaken by stealth. Your church may be overtaken in the same way.* He then encouraged the church in Sardis to find incentive by looking to the few who were still awake—the faithful ones who were still living pure lives (Revelation 3:4-5).

Moral laxity can be found in contemporary Christianity, including in our own lives, more often than we might care to admit. It is easy to assume we are doing well, and so we don't stop to take real stock of our spiritual health. It is easy to ignore a small compromise here and a habitual sin there—especially when others are doing the same.

Don't let the vibrancy of your singing, the intensity of your preaching, or the consistency of your attendance ever become a cover for an absence of spiritual vitality. If you find you have become complacent or lax in your determination to obey Christ in every part of your life, His instruction for you is clear: *Rouse yourself from your slumbers! Strengthen what remains! Remember what you received! Repent and obey!*

And what if you are discouraged because you are seeking to live all-in for Jesus and find the compromises and half-heartedness of others hard to bear? Jesus has promised you, "The one who conquers will be clothed thus in white garments, and I will never blot his name out of the book of life" (Revelation 3:5). That promise is surely worth living for and trusting in.

REVELATION 3:1-6

NOVEMBER 20

THE OPEN DOOR

"To the angel of the church in Philadelphia write: 'The words of the holy one, the true one, who has the key of David, who opens and no one will shut, who shuts and no one opens. I know your works. Behold, I have set before you an open door, which no one is able to shut. I know that you have but little power, and yet you have kept my word and have not denied my name'"

REVELATION 3:7-8

In the book of Revelation, the key is a symbol of Christ's authority and the door is a symbol of an opportunity. So as He writes to the Philadelphian church, Jesus is declaring Himself to be the holder of the key that opens the door *in* to salvation and opens the door *out* to service. In other words, once we have walked through the narrow gate that leads to life, we discover that life to be a life of service.

The Philadelphians had entered the door into salvation but now were confronted by opposition and the threat of future tribulation. So far, they had "not denied [Christ's] name"—they had not shrunk from declaring the truth about their Lord and Savior in the city He had placed them in. Yet, recognizing that the storm clouds were now gathering, they may have been tempted to simply circle the wagons, sound the retreat, and decide that it was not a good time for evangelism. Considering all that confronted them, they easily could have concluded that such a life of service would need to wait for a more opportune moment.

Christ, however, urged them not to turn back from their calling. The door was open; now they had to go through it! While they would not be spared from suffering, He promised to uphold them when they faced it. He told these hard-pressed believers that if they would boldly march through the door and be faithful to their calling, they would see converts from among those who opposed them (Revelation 3:9).

What about us? Are we prepared to walk through the door of opportunity, knowing that Jesus calls people to saving faith through the words of those who refuse to deny His name? Are we willing to say, "Lord Jesus Christ, I feel I have little strength, but anywhere, anytime, anyone, I'm ready to speak"?

Pray that when you meet the moment of opportunity, you *will* say and do something. Pray that you would be imaginative and creative, with one foot in the Bible and the other foot in the culture, so that you speak the truth about Jesus in a way that connects with those who are listening. If you do not shrink back but rather continue sharing the gospel imaginatively, humbly, sensitively, and creatively, then by the power of His Spirit and the might of His word, those who today see you as an enemy may one day become your brothers and sisters.

REVELATION 3:7-13

Bible Through The Year: 1 Chronicles 28–29; Luke 4:31-44

NOVEMBER 21

THE DANGER OF BEING LUKEWARM

"I know your works: you are neither cold nor hot. Would that you were either cold or hot! So, because you are lukewarm, and neither hot nor cold, I will spit you out of my mouth. For you say, I am rich, I have prospered, and I need nothing, not realizing that you are wretched, pitiable, poor, blind, and naked ... Behold, I stand at the door and knock. If anyone hears my voice and opens the door, I will come in to him and eat with him, and he with me." REVELATION 3:15-17, 20

Laodicea was a financial center, and it had all the confidence and opulence that goes with wealth. It also was famous for its sheep and their soft, black wool, which was woven into expensive garments. Not only that but the city was known for its medical school, which had developed a salve that was useful for treating certain forms of eye conditions.

It was in this environment that the Laodicean church lived: in a financially prosperous city, skillful in its business practices and known for its medical facility. God had placed His people in the heart of that to reflect His light in the diversity of Laodicean life. But the church had been absorbed by the culture. They had lost their cutting edge and were compromised and self-deceived. Instead of reflecting their Savior, they reflected their society.

It is unsurprising, then, that when the Son of Man looked at the church in Laodicea, He found little to His liking. They were stagnant. Wealth had bred in them a sense of self-sufficiency. They wore nice clothes but were oblivious to their spiritual nakedness. While their city's physicians could help restore physical sight, the members of its church were spiritually blind.

Yet was Christ about to abandon them? Not yet. His assessment was not good, the prognosis was poor, and the warning was real. But He didn't send them away. Instead, He invited them to dinner: "If anyone hears my voice and opens the door, I will come in to him and eat with him, and he with me." The word used here for "eat" is *deipnēsō*, which refers not to a meal eaten on the fly but to a full dining experience, where you sit for a long time as an expression of companionship, enjoyment, friendship, and fellowship.

Do you ever congratulate yourself on your prosperity? Do you think about your material possessions more than your Lord's appraisal of your life? Be careful! A lukewarm faith that goes through the motions while embracing materialism and holding Christ at arm's length is, in fact, no faith at all. But be encouraged, too: the Lord is knocking, and He is inviting you into a deeper fellowship with Him, a closeness that will fire your heart once more so that you will sing again:

Riches I heed not, nor vain, empty praise
Thou mine inheritance, now and always
Thou and Thou only first in my heart
High King of heaven, my treasure Thou art.[91]

REVELATION 3:14-22

91 Trans. Mary Elizabeth Byrne, "Be Thou My Vision" (1905).

NOVEMBER 22

BLIND FROM BIRTH

"Some of the Pharisees near him heard these things, and said to him, 'Are we also blind?'" JOHN 9:40

The great, and tragic, irony of the episode John recounts in chapter 9 of his Gospel is that while a blind man receives his sight, many of those who began with two working eyes reveal themselves to be utterly spiritually blind.

John included this event because it is one of the signs that has been "written so that you may believe that Jesus is the Christ, the Son of God, and that by believing you may have life in his name" (John 20:31). As Jesus gave the blind man sight, so Jesus can give us life. Just as surely as He opened this man's eyes physically, so Jesus can open the spiritual eyes of men and women.

And Jesus must open men and women's eyes spiritually because, as the Bible teaches uncompromisingly, men and women are spiritually blind from birth. We may think we see truth clearly, but in rejecting Jesus, we show ourselves to be blind in the only sense that eternally matters. Sin has robbed us of our vision, and we are unable to make ourselves see spiritually any more than the blind beggar could overcome his lack of physical sight. Unless we are made aware of the true nature of our condition from the Bible—until our blind eyes are opened to see our true state and until our deaf ears are unstopped to hear this story—the proclamation of any antidote is irrelevant.

When the Bible says we are blind, it speaks to the awful way in which sin has permeated our condition. Sin affects our emotions, will, affections, and intellect. There is no little citadel in our experience to which we may go to find refuge from our fallen state.

We must not be lulled into thinking that the Bible doesn't really mean what it says, that people aren't *really* totally blind. The friends and neighbors to whom we go and tell the gospel are not living in some middle territory between belief and unbelief, between sight and blindness. They neither see truly nor even know what it *means* to do so. For this, they need divine intervention, just as we once did.

By nature, the gospel story is foolishness to us. We are born deaf to its appeal and blind to its wonder. Only the God who opened the eyes of the blind man can open our eyes too. What a wonder, and a cause for gratitude, that we are able to say with the blind beggar, "Though I was blind, now I see" (John 9:25). And what an encouragement for us to share all that God can do, for there is no greater joy than to speak of Jesus and then watch Him open blind eyes to see who He is and what He has done.

MATTHEW 9:27-31

NOVEMBER 23

TRANSFORMING GRACE

"The grace of God has appeared, bringing salvation for all people, training us to renounce ungodliness and worldly passions, and to live self-controlled, upright, and godly lives in the present age." TITUS 2:11-12

We are to live our lives from the inside out.

When Paul wrote to Titus, he didn't provide him with a mere manual for how to teach people to live properly in their various roles in society. The book of Titus *does* contain numerous commands for how Christians are to live—and that is why, if we are not careful, we can easily read it as a moralistic how-to book. Indeed, when reading God's word as a whole it is possible to slip into reading it as a list of commands that we are to keep in order to gain or maintain God's favor. We need reminding, again and again, that all the Scriptures, including this letter of Paul's, show us the grace of God, and then they show those who have understood the grace of God how to live from the inside out.

The Bible's story is the story of God, who created humans and put them in His company in the Garden of Eden. They were privileged to enjoy His presence and everything He had made. But they rebelled against God, and we too, following those ancestors, have rejected His rule, have adopted a skewed view of the world, and don't seek after Him. Because of our sinful nature, we live life upside down. But when we believe in Christ, our upside-down lives are rectified. We begin to stand the right way up, and we are put back together by the power of Jesus. We are then to live our lives from the inside out, so that what God has accomplished *in* us by His grace is the driving force for what He is now going to accomplish *through* us for His glory.

Paul tells us that "the grace of God has appeared, bringing salvation." In Titus 3:7, he reminds those of us who have trusted in Christ that we have been "justified by his grace," becoming "heirs according to the hope of eternal life." And in 3:8, Paul teaches that these gospel truths are trustworthy things that must be insisted on, "so that those who have *believed* in God may be careful to devote themselves to good works" (emphasis added). This progression is absolutely crucial to grasp. It's not that we are to devote ourselves to doing good works so that we might be accepted by God; it is that because we have *believed* in God and are accepted through the person and work of His Son, we devote ourselves to doing good works. The good works flow from His grace, inspired by that grace. The grace of God is what trains us to live for the God of grace.

Do you desire to be distinct from the world? Do you hope to live a life worthy of God—one that honors Him in all you do? That is a mark of His grace at work in you. Remember that what you do is never what saves you; in Christ, His grace appeared and was poured out on you. Focus not on what *you* are to do for God but on what *He* has done to transform you by His grace. As you do so, you will find your heart and mind trained to live in the way that pleases Him.

TITUS 2:11 – 3:2

NOVEMBER 24

YOUR PRIMARY CALLING: FAITHFULNESS

"They have gone out for the sake of the name, accepting nothing from the Gentiles. Therefore we ought to support people like these, that we may be fellow workers for the truth." 3 JOHN 7-8

About 10 to 15 miles off the coast of France lies a cluster of landmasses called the Channel Islands. In 1940, Germany invaded and occupied them. Among the tunnels the Germans built on one of them, Jersey, there is a plaque that details the generous labor of a few women from the occupied island who bravely sent mittens, socks, flying helmets, sweaters, and more to the United Kingdom's Royal Air Force. Because of their generosity, as some brave airmen flew against the German airplanes to resist Nazi Germany's attempt to take over Europe, they were warmed by the products of those women's compassion.

You might ask, *What's the big deal? These women were just knitting.* But try telling that to an airman who had to brave freezing temperatures in the heat of battle! For him, there was nothing insignificant about socks and mittens. Those women from Jersey made a significant contribution to the Allied war effort by meeting a serious need. In this sense, without ever flying a plane, they were "fellow workers" with the RAF airmen.

The New Testament speaks over and over again of believers laboring alongside each other as "fellow workers." In Philippians 2:25, Paul even speaks of Epaphroditus as his "fellow soldier." The apostle Paul was arguably the most capable missionary and church planter who ever lived—and yet he could not have successfully completed anything without such "fellow workers for the truth," as John calls them.

Every single one of us in the body of Christ has an important function. In wartime terms, some of us are pilots, others of us are mechanics, and some are knitters—and still others of us may be the sheep farmers who provide the wool! Perhaps society would have us grade these contributions, creating a hierarchy of sorts. Perhaps you are tempted to think that your contributions are insignificant. But this is not how things work in the economy of God. As Paul wrote, "The parts of the body that seem to be weaker are indispensable, and on those parts of the body that we think less honorable we bestow the greater honor" (1 Corinthians 12:22-23).

God chooses whom He will to fulfill each function in His body—and what matters to Him most is that we are faithful wherever He has placed us. Stay faithful, and the Lord will strengthen you for whatever role He's calling you to—whether knitting or flying—for the glory of Christ. Do what you can, for what you can do He will use.

3 JOHN

NOVEMBER 25

IT IS THE LORD WHO JUDGES ME

"It is required of stewards that they be found faithful. But with me it is a very small thing that I should be judged by you or by any human court. In fact, I do not even judge myself. For I am not aware of anything against myself, but I am not thereby acquitted. It is the Lord who judges me." 1 CORINTHIANS 4:2-4

Anyone who has ever been a leader knows the vulnerability that comes with the position. Whether a schoolteacher, politician, scientist, team captain, or CEO, anyone who attempts to lead others will learn that there is a spotlight on them due to their position and that they are susceptible to misunderstandings and to false accusations.

When Paul described good stewards—leaders—to the Corinthian church, he said nothing of their popularity, giftedness, influence, or even success. No, the real test of this kind of biblical leadership was "that they be found faithful." Faithfulness was the yardstick and faithfulness was his anchor. Paul was basically saying, *I'm not going to allow my life to be carried along on the emotional rollercoaster of undue compliments on the one hand and undue criticism on the other. Only one opinion, one judgment, matters.*

Paul recognized that he couldn't even adequately evaluate the purity of his own motives. He did not judge himself, in the sense of seeing his own self-assessment as accurate. "It is the Lord who judges me," he knew. He recognized that God was gazing into the very core of his being and that His requirement was faithfulness. This realization allowed him to press forward without being distracted by the adulation of some or the envy and opposition of others.

When you find inept leadership in any organization, you will likely be able to trace the incompetence back to a leader who became less concerned about leading people and more concerned about being liked by them, or who became less concerned about putting others first and more concerned about their own prestige. So, as a result of desperately wanting to be liked by everyone or be honored by everyone, the leader lost the ability to lead anyone meaningfully—to say what must be said or to listen to what must be heard.

Throughout life, if you are always measuring yourself by the approval ratings bestowed by others, you won't be able to function. Since human knowledge of the facts is always imperfect, compliments and criticism are also always imperfect. So don't allow yourself to be knocked off balance by premature and imperfect judgments—including your own! It is good and right for you to examine yourself—but, having done so, you must remember that there is only one judgment that ultimately matters. God is looking for faithfulness to His word and His people. Let that be the liberating yardstick of how you conduct yourself as a leader, a parent, a spouse, a friend—a Christian.

1 CORINTHIANS 4:1-7

NOVEMBER 26

A SONG OF FAITH

"Your work, O Lord, do I fear. In the midst of the years revive it; in the midst of the years make it known ... Though the fig tree should not blossom, nor fruit be on the vines, the produce of the olive fail and the fields yield no food, the flock be cut off from the fold and there be no herd in the stalls, yet I will rejoice in the Lord; I will take joy in the God of my salvation." HABAKKUK 3:2, 17-18

No matter how committed to God we consider ourselves to be, Habakkuk's prayer in these verses is probably not what springs to our minds when we are faced with terrible circumstances, as he was. But his prayer was not for himself alone! Indeed, it was to be accompanied by a choir and instruments and prayed by God's people (Habakkuk 3:19).

Habakkuk was imagining a situation that would amount to great devastation for an agricultural society. No fruit, produce, yields, flocks, or herds meant a completely broken economy and a chronic shortage of food. Yet Habakkuk says that even if confronted with that scenario, our greatest concern should be neither pestilence nor plague but that the work of God would be revived. Ultimately, Habakkuk said he would be found singing, trusting the sovereign work of the Lord. The God of salvation was all he needed for joy (Habakkuk 3:18).

How is Habakkuk able to say, and pray, this? Throughout his prayer, the prophet also recounts God's great works throughout history (Habakkuk 3:3-16). These serve as a reminder to him that God is sovereign, God is good, and God is always to be trusted. Even the darkest of days gives way to the dawn in God's sovereign purposes; and though the dawn sometimes tarries, it does not fail to arrive. Habakkuk knows that God saves His people, and that is sufficient cause for joy. And it is the same for us. God's dealings and deliverance of His people through the Old Testament foreshadow His ultimate deliverance in Jesus. It is in Jesus' life, death, and resurrection that God remembers mercy in wrath and the believer is safely brought through death to life. We're not exempt from calamity—but because of God's great work, we can still rejoice. The dawn of salvation will come, however dark the moment.

As we consider Habakkuk's prayerful song, we should ask ourselves two questions: Am I as concerned as the prophet for the reviving and fulfillment of God's work? And is God alone sufficient for me? May the prayer of the prophet become yours as you seek to further God's purposes among His people in this time. And when the world appears to crumble around you, you can still find joy in the God of your salvation. By faith you can sing:

'Tis what I know of Thee, my Lord and God,
That fills my soul with peace, my lips with song;
Thou art my health, my joy, my staff and rod;
Leaning on Thee, in weakness I am strong.[92]

HABAKKUK 3:3-16

92 Horatius Bonar, "Not What I Am, O Lord" (1861).

NOVEMBER 27

VICTORY IS THE LORD'S

"Arise, O Lord! Save me, O my God! For you strike all my enemies on the cheek; you break the teeth of the wicked. Salvation belongs to the Lord; your blessing be on your people!" PSALM 3:7-8

Does trouble drive you *to* God or *from* God?

In Psalm 3, King David is facing a severe trial: the apparently successful insurrection of his son Absalom. He has had to flee his palace and his capital. Many men he counted as friends have turned against him.

What does David do? He takes his trial straight to the Lord. He recognizes—and we ought to be humble enough to recognize with him—that any life-transforming change, any ultimate solution, any lasting success is owing ultimately and finally to the Lord.

Who can bring deliverance from the enslavement of habitual sin? Who can set captives free? Who can take the burdens from people's backs? Only and ultimately the Lord. Whether we're bothered by a mere nuisance or we've been struck by awful tragedy, God alone brings deliverance.

Even when David's foes surround him, he doesn't try to take vengeance into his own hands. He recognizes that God strikes the winning blow, because it is God who is the one true source of lasting victory. So David cries out, "Arise, O Lord! Save me, O my God!" because he knows that "salvation belongs to the Lord."

Notice, too, that David has more than deliverance for himself in view: "Your blessing be on *your people*," he prays. Trials have a tendency to drive us in on ourselves—away from God and away from others. It's so easy only to pray for ourselves when we are struggling. But David reminds us that even in life's valleys, we are traveling together and need to keep our brothers and sisters in mind and in our prayers—and not only those who already believe, for God's salvation is for any who would cry out to Jesus for help. Our neighbors, our colleagues, the stranger in line with us as we wait for our coffee—they all need this deliverance just as much as any of us.

If you desire victory in your life, you must first recognize, like David, that you can have none apart from God's help. And if you are going be an instrument of grace to the people God has placed around you, you must also look beyond your own needs and call out for their blessing and deliverance to the only one who is mighty enough to grant it. He alone is our eternal hope, our great gift of salvation, the source of satisfaction for our every longing—in the valleys as much as on the mountaintops.

1 CHRONICLES 29:10-14

NOVEMBER 28

YOU WILL EXIT THE BOX

"I am the resurrection and the life. Whoever believes in me, though he die, yet shall he live." JOHN 11:25

In my years as a pastor, I've conducted countless funeral services. I remember one in particular, though, for the lesson that it taught me.

When I arrived at the funeral home, I was asked to wait in a side room. Being an inquisitive soul, I looked around and realized that I was sitting beside miniature coffins—models with their ends sawn off so that you could see what the inside of each coffin looked like.

As I was sitting there, I began to think of what it would be like not just to look inside but to be inside. I became greatly disturbed. I said to myself, "I am a Christian. I believe in the resurrection of the body. I believe that I will die and go to heaven." And yet, I still looked at the coffin and thought to myself, "I don't want to go in one of these things!"

Then the thought came to me: "What comes to the unbeliever's mind when he or she thinks of death and dying?"

In the late 1960s, the United Kingdom introduced grids painted on the roads at particularly busy intersections, called box junctions, accompanied by signs that read, "Do not enter the box unless your exit is clear." The purpose of these grids and signs was to help aid traffic flow. But that day in the funeral home, what entered my mind was how apt that sign's warning is when we consider that we will all be dead and lie in a coffin. Though my body will one day be in a box, my soul will have departed—and my exit must then be clear.

Everybody knows that death is coming. The statistics are clear: one out of one dies. The affairs of life lead inescapably toward the end. Yet God the Son, who existed "before the foundation of the world" (1 Peter 1:20) has come into time in order that we may know a Savior, a Friend, and a Lord and so that we might be prepared for—and even long for!—all that eternity will bring.

You may be one of many who are prepared for just about everything that might possibly happen—except for your exit from the box. But that exit is the one thing for which you must be prepared. You *will* stand before God. You *will* give an account for your life. But the message of the gospel is that you do not need to fear that day, provided that you are trusting in Christ to bring you through. And if you are, then you can look at a coffin and speak to your fears, for though your earthly flesh may end up in one, your soul will not; and you will enjoy a resurrection body that never sees the inside of a wooden box. "Do not enter the box unless your exit is clear"—but, gloriously, your route through is signposted with the blood of Christ and your heavenly destination awaits. Have no fear.

JOHN 11:17-44

NOVEMBER 29

TEACHING WITH INTEGRITY

"I did not shrink from declaring to you anything that was profitable, and teaching you in public and from house to house." ACTS 20:20

Paul never succumbed to the temptation to shape his message to cater to his hearers' tastes, and neither must we.

It is always tempting to temper what we say to avoid the prejudices or tickle the fancies of those we're speaking to, whether we're speaking from a platform or over a meal table. But if we are going to be honest stewards of the message given to us in the Bible, then our teaching and speaking about it needs to be marked by integrity.

Faithfulness to all of Scripture's teaching is crucial. Scripture itself warns us that false teachers will arise and tell people what their itching ears want to hear (2 Timothy 4:3). Times will come when people turn away from sound teaching, instead seeking out voices that don't challenge them with biblical truth but simply reinforce their own views.

Paul spent more than two years teaching among the Ephesians, publicly and privately, and his message was always pure, open, and straightforward. It didn't matter where he was or who his hearers were; what he knew to be profitable—the proclamation and application of God's word—was what he brought.

If someone had come from one of Paul's addresses and was asked, "What did Paul say today?" the response must always have included sentences like these: "He said that we're supposed to turn in repentance toward God. We need to forsake our sins. We are to trust in Jesus as our only Savior. He really challenged me, but he really encouraged me." No matter where you met him and no matter when you heard him, Paul always got to the heart of the gospel. His life and ministry were gospel-centered. He was not willfully offensive or obnoxious, but at the same time, he did not shrink from saying hard but necessary things.

The day will come, if it has not already, when you will be tempted to soften the message of God's word—tempted to loosen your convictions in order to make the warnings, promises, and commands of Scripture seem more palatable to those in your hearing. How will you respond when this day comes? Will you shrink from declaring God's message, as so many around Paul did? Or will you follow the example of the apostle by declaring the truth plainly, trusting that it will bring glory and honor to the Lord, and remembering that what people want to hear is not always or often the same as what they need to hear—what is profitable to them?

2 TIMOTHY 4:1-5

NOVEMBER 30

NOW IS THE TIME

"Now is the favorable time; behold, now is the day of salvation."
2 CORINTHIANS 6:2

Nothing confronts us with our creatureliness quite like the watch that we wear on our wrist or the clock that ticks on our wall. Try and think about *no time.* It's virtually impossible for us to do. God, who is outside of time, created time so that we might live each moment that He has given to us for His glory.

We don't like to face it, but Scripture frequently calls us to face life's brevity. It tells us that our life is "a mist that appears for a little time and then vanishes" (James 4:14). The Bible confronts us with transience in this way not to manipulate us or crush us but in order that we might be sensible. We need to be reminded of how quickly time passes, especially when we are young, because we tend to think that we have more time than we really do.

The Bible almost always addresses us in the now: "*Now* is the favorable time; behold, *now* is the day of salvation." *Now*, in other words, is the time to be reconciled to God. *Now* is the time to take heed—not someday over the horizon. *Now* is the time to hold out the gospel message to those around you. You are not to live dominated by the regrets of yesterday or the anxieties of tomorrow. You are not to live as though you will always have a tomorrow in which to do what you should be doing today. You are to face the fact squarely, head on, that the future comes in at the rate of 60 seconds a minute.

The time that God has allotted you is quickly passing by. If you are not careful, it will be gone before you realize it. In Psalm 90, the psalmist prays, "Teach us to number our days that we may get a heart of wisdom" (Psalm 90:12). May this prayer become your own, and may God enable you to be a good steward of the time that He has given to you. Today is a great day to enjoy your salvation and to speak of it. Now is the time. Be sure to use it.

EPHESIANS 5:15-20

DECEMBER 1

THE PURPOSE OF CHRIST'S ADVENT

"Everyone who makes a practice of sinning also practices lawlessness; sin is lawlessness. You know that he appeared in order to take away sins, and in him there is no sin. No one who abides in him keeps on sinning; no one who keeps on sinning has either seen him or known him." 1 JOHN 3:4-6

Why do we anticipate Christmas with such relish? For the believer, the answer must surely lie, above all, in the awareness that Jesus Christ appeared to take away our sins.

When we read the Gospel writers, we discover this truth at the very heart of their Christmas message. Matthew recorded the words of the angel to Joseph: "[Mary] will bear a son, and you shall call his name Jesus, for he will save his people from their sins" (Matthew 1:21). Ahead of what might be regarded as the first ever Christmas concert, the message the angel gave to the shepherds was similar: "I bring you good news of great joy that will be for all the people. For unto you is born this day in the city of David a Savior, who is Christ the Lord" (Luke 2:10-11). John began from a different vantage point. As he highlighted the commencement of Jesus' earthly ministry, having raised our gaze to the eternal Word becoming flesh (John 1:14), he gave us the words of John the Baptist: "Behold, the Lamb of God, who takes away the sin of the world!" (v 29). And Mark records nothing of Jesus' birth or childhood, but in his Gospel Jesus' first words are an announcement that in Him the kingdom of God has come near to people like us (Mark 1:15), and in one of His first miracles Jesus assures a paralyzed man, "Son, your sins are forgiven" (2:5).

If we say that God has shown His love for us in the incarnation, that is accurate but insufficient. God demonstrated His love for us not simply by sending Jesus as a baby in Bethlehem; rather, His own word tells us that "God shows his love for us in that while we were still sinners, Christ *died* for us" (Romans 5:8, emphasis added).

Of course, if we understand that Christ came to take away our sins, then it's only logical to conclude that we have sins which need to be taken away. Rare is the man or woman who would say that he or she has never done wrong! We all have impure thoughts. We all speak bitter words. We all know what it is to live an unholy life. But the word of God comes to us and says, *Here is the good news: Christ appeared in this world to take away your sins.*

Today, lay hold of this message with renewed joy and gratitude. Let these eight words be the most precious part of your Christmas season: "He appeared in order to take away sins." Your friends, coworkers, and neighbors may be more open to the gospel message during the holiday season; make it your aim, then, not to further the misguided perception that Christmas is nothing more than a sentimental emblem of God's love, as though His Son lay gurgling in the manger but never hung in agony on the cross. God's love can only be fully explained in the purpose of Christ's coming: to take away our sins. This, and this above all, is what gives our hearts bountiful cause for celebration!

MATTHEW 1:18-25

DECEMBER 2

ON THEM HAS LIGHT SHONE

"The people who walked in darkness have seen a great light; those who dwelt in a land of deep darkness, on them has light shone." ISAIAH 9:2

The Bible never disguises just how dark life can get. The Scriptures are clear that when sins multiply, when evil is celebrated, when God is left out, darkness ensues. And yet, over and over in the Bible's storyline, we are reminded that God is not afraid of or defeated by such darkness. In fact, He makes a habit of drawing near and turning it into light.

We see Him drawing near in the third chapter of Genesis. Sin had entered the world; the only two people alive had rebelled against their Maker, and they were hiding in shame. It would have been completely understandable for God to have shown up in Eden, dropped a hammer of judgment on Adam and Eve, and started over with another man and woman. But that's not what He did. He arrived in the garden and asked, "Where are you?" (Genesis 3:9). And when He found them naked and ashamed, He provided a covering for them and gave a promise to them (v 21, 15).

So, too, with His people Israel. By the time Isaiah began his ministry, there was an established history of the people forgetting God and ignoring His prophets. As a result, they labored under the wicked kings they deserved and found themselves "greatly distressed and hungry," leading them to "speak contemptuously against their king and their God" (Isaiah 8:21). Again, it would have been reasonable for the Lord to have done away with His people at this point, leaving them to experience the "distress and darkness, the gloom of anguish" (v 22), without hope or future. They didn't want Him. Why should He have stuck around?

But the next chapter begins with a glorious reversal: "There will be no more gloom for her who was in anguish" (Isaiah 9:1). The Lord would not leave His people, and He would not allow them to remain in misery. No, for these people in darkness, "on them has light shone." The light of grace was breaking into the self-inflicted gloom of sin.

Centuries after Isaiah, the people of God again found themselves in anguish. There were foreign rulers over them, and no prophetic word had been heard for many, many years. *Perhaps He's really done it this time,* the people may have thought. *Maybe the Lord has finally had enough.*

But we know better. We know that into this darkness a child was born. A light shone in the sky, leading to the baby who would prove to be the light of the whole world. The question for us this Advent season, and in any season, is whether the light has dawned in our own hearts or whether we have let the darkness of sin creep in. The good news of Christmas is that the God of the Bible is the God of grace, who comes into the darkness and emptiness of our hearts to bring His light, His joy, and His peace. Are you walking in darkness today, whether that is the darkness of your own sin or the darkness caused by the sin of others? God is neither afraid of nor defeated by these things. In Jesus, He has drawn near. By His Spirit, He can bring light to the dark. Look to Him and walk in His light.

MATTHEW 3:12-22

DECEMBER 3

WONDERFUL COUNSELOR, WONDERFUL CHILD

"For to us a child is born, to us a son is given; and the government shall be upon his shoulder, and his name shall be called Wonderful Counselor, Mighty God, Everlasting Father, Prince of Peace." ISAIAH 9:6

If it was in your power, how would you go about redressing the tyranny, oppression, and suffering that marks and mars our world? What would your solution look like? We all have our ideas—but here is God's: His definitive answer to all of the world's darkness was to send a child.

The people of Israel had long been awaiting the arrival of the one who would embody all of their hopes. The prophets had been declaring the coming of a Messiah, and the expectation of such a deliverer steadily grew. Isaiah added significant fuel to the fire of this longing, declaring that the Messiah would come as "a child," "a son," and that "the government shall be upon his shoulder, and his name shall be called Wonderful Counselor, Mighty God, Everlasting Father, Prince of Peace."

Who could possibly fill this description? Surely no one had yet come who lived up to such language. But it was this child—who came not in military might or with flashes of lightning but in a trough, surrounded by animals and shepherds at His birth—who was God's answer to sin and death. He alone would rule His kingdom "with justice and with righteousness from this time forth and forevermore" (Isaiah 9:7).

Isaiah says the child-king would be called "Wonderful Counselor." Kings were known in some measure by their counselors. The extent of their authority and rule was made apparent by the number of advisers they could call upon for guidance. And yet this King would have none. He Himself *is* the Wonderful Counselor; He has no need of any outside wisdom in order to rule with absolute perfection as well as total authority.

This same Wonderful Counselor is the sole remedy for all expressions of suffering and evil in the world—including those in your life. Are you joyfully submitting to His plans and are you bowing your knee to His rule? Have you entrusted all your ways and all your concerns to His counsel? When His ways and yours are not the same, do you accept that He knows better than you and walk the way He calls you to? God's gift to His world is no ordinary child. This is Christ the Lord, your wonderful Savior!

ISAIAH 8:18 – 9:7

DECEMBER 4

DON'T KID YOURSELF!

"But be doers of the word, and not hearers only, deceiving yourselves."
JAMES 1:22

There was a man on a golf practice range who was, by any standards, an appalling player. When he occasionally connected with the ball, it was with wild slashing movements that sent it in every direction but seldom where he intended. His drives were ineffectual and weak, and he consistently dribbled the iron shots along the ground.

In the middle of this sorry display, he took a call on his cell phone that went something like this: "Yes, I'm on the driving range. Actually, very good. Driving it to the far end of the range. My irons? Oh, straight as arrows, and incredibly long." Those observing wanted to exclaim to him, "Don't kid yourself!"

James is warning us here not to kid ourselves when it comes to the issues of the Bible, faith, believing, and behaving. He has already warned against being deceived in general (James 1:16). Here, though, he makes it personal, identifying a crucial area of jeopardy: the danger of being self-deceived.

To illustrate his point, James uses an amusing analogy, imagining a person who looks into a mirror and then forgets what he looks like (James 1:23-24). This word picture helps us understand our peril. If we have just put on mismatching shoes or have smudges of dirt on our face, a mirror is useful not so that we can congratulate ourselves but in order that we can see our predicament and do what is necessary to fix it. Self-deception, in other words, can prevent us from seeing grave shortcomings that need to be addressed.

The Bible is our mirror. Its purpose is not to congratulate us but to challenge us. When we look into it, we find out things that we wouldn't know had we not looked there. But if we discover them and then do nothing about them, we are self-deceived and remain in our predicament.

If the Bible is going to be effective in our lives, we must listen to it, receive it, and apply it. Treating God's word properly does not mean merely reading it, understanding it, and agreeing with it. It means doing what it says.

As you look into the mirror of God's word today, tomorrow, and every day, notice what is reflected back to you. Then be careful: do not walk away and kid yourself but act on what you have seen, allowing the Bible to be a transforming word in your life, as well as in all the lives that God calls you to touch. Be a doer, not a self-deceiver.

PSALM 119:41-48

DECEMBER 5

REAPING THE HARVEST

"The disciples said to one another, 'Has anyone brought him something to eat?' Jesus said to them, 'My food is to do the will of him who sent me and to accomplish his work ... Look, I tell you, lift up your eyes, and see that the fields are white for harvest.'" JOHN 4:33-35

Today it is harvest time, and we are called to be at work.

In the Gospel of John, it's not uncommon for Jesus' teachings to sound literal but turn out to be figurative. In John 2, for example, He uses the imagery of the temple's destruction and rebuilding to refer to His death and resurrection, but His hearers take Him literally (John 2:19-22). In John 3, He describes salvation in terms of being figuratively "born again," but Nicodemus can think only of physical rebirth (3:3-4). With the Samaritan woman, Jesus uses a physical drink of water at the well to illustrate the eternal satisfaction found in relationship with God, but she mistakes His meaning and asks Him for a literal drink (4:7-14).

It should not surprise us, then, that in these verses Jesus again employs this method, this time with His own disciples. As they encourage Him to eat, Jesus speaks of a different and figurative food—about His mission, and about ours. Jesus' "food," or mission, was "to do the will of him who sent me and to accomplish his work" (see also John 5:30; 6:38). On the cross, we see that work completed as He declares, "It is finished" (19:30). Christ died in the place of sinners so that He can offer grace to sinners. Anyone can be forgiven if they respond with faith to the offer of the gospel. But to respond, they must first be told.

So when the crowd from the Samaritan town approached them and the disciples became concerned about Jesus having something to eat, He called them to "look," to see what was really going on—something much more exciting than a lunch plan! There were men and women who needed to hear the good news that He had come to offer forgiveness. There was a harvest ready to be reaped. We, too, often need such a wake-up call. We so easily miss what is in front of us, failing to notice the opportunities we have to share Christ with the people we meet who are hungry to hear of Him. We so easily make excuses, thinking no one will be interested in the gospel message, thinking we'll take God's mission seriously when we enter a different phase of life, when things are less busy.

Beware of persuading yourself that there is no harvest or that circumstances allow you to sidestep the call to be at work to gather it in. Christ's work is indeed finished, but we are invited to share in His missional harvest, continuing to bring the good news of that finished salvation to lost souls. Do we see this harvest awaiting? Or are we preoccupied with shuffling soil in worldly garden patches which will never bear true spiritual fruit? Perhaps what you need is a perspective shift, an opening of your eyes. Who are the people around you? In what field have you been placed? Will you do the wonderful work of sharing Jesus with them? "The harvest is plentiful, but the laborers are few" (Matthew 9:37). Today it is harvest time, and you are called to be at work.

MARK 4:1-20

DECEMBER 6

ANYTHING BUT ORDINARY

"There was a certain man of Ramathaim-zophim of the hill country of Ephraim whose name was Elkanah the son of Jeroham, son of Elihu, son of Tohu, son of Zuph, an Ephrathite. He had two wives. The name of the one was Hannah, and the name of the other, Peninnah. And Peninnah had children, but Hannah had no children." 1 SAMUEL 1:1-2

Marked by social, political, and religious chaos, the biblical era described in the book of Judges was not dissimilar to our own times. The chaos was summarized and explained in this way: "In those days there was no king in Israel. Everyone did what was right in his own eyes" (Judges 21:25). For people living in Israel at that point in history, around 1000 BC, it was almost as if the world were upside down. To many, it seemed that an earthly king was the only remedy for their problems.

In the midst of all this, we find the spotlight of Scripture alighting on the domestic circumstances of one man, Elkanah. His wife Hannah (presumably his first) was childless, while his second wife had many sons and daughters. Since God had promised that Abraham's family, Israel, would grow to be countless and that it would be through a child born in Israel that He would bless the world, childlessness was more than a matter of personal sadness; it meant being unable to be a part of the way God was keeping His promises to His people. Small wonder, then, that Hannah was hopeless and helpless (1 Samuel 1:7-8). The simple statement that "Hannah had no children" describes a life of deep anguish. And yet through her, God would once again do what He had done throughout the history of His people: reach into the ordinary life of a family and, through His intervention, not only impact them but also direct the course of human history.

Hannah would surely have wondered, month by disappointing month and more and more with every passing year, "Why is this happening to me?" She could not have known that in the withholding, and then in the giving, of a child, God was doing something that would not only answer her own need but would begin to address Israel's need. For her son, Samuel, would one day be the prophet who would anoint David, Old Testament Israel's greatest king.

At times we may feel that we don't fit in the grand scheme of things. Our situations, too, can appear hopeless and helpless. We, too, wonder, "Why is this happening to me?" But as with Hannah, the answer to our question may be in neither the "this" or the "me." The ways of God are vast and beyond our ability to comprehend—and in many cases it will only be in glory that we will get past the surface of understanding how He works in our lives. For now, the story of Hannah reminds us that we can trust God to be at work, to keep His promises, and to reach into the ordinariness of life and intervene in ways that are beyond imagination.

PSALMS 42 – 43

DECEMBER 7

ONCE SAVED, ALWAYS SAVED?

"Take care, brothers, lest there be in any of you an evil, unbelieving heart, leading you to fall away from the living God." HEBREWS 3:12

You may have heard of the doctrinal teaching that some people have come to call "the perseverance of the saints." It is a beautiful doctrine that attempts to capture the keeping power of God over His chosen ones. Jesus said, for example, "My sheep hear my voice, and I know them, and they follow me. I give them eternal life, and they will never perish, and no one will snatch them out of my hand" (John 10:27-28). Romans 8:29-30 similarly offers to us what some have called "the golden chain of salvation," affirming that anyone whom God "predestined he also called, and those whom he called he also justified, and those whom he justified he also glorified." God's promised to glorify those He has chosen is so certain that Paul speaks of it in the past tense.

Sometimes, however, this precious doctrine gets reduced to a dogmatic mantra: Once saved, always saved. Too often, this slogan is misconstrued to mean that as long as someone has prayed the right prayer or said precisely the right thing, they are heaven-bound, no matter how they live. This way lies a complacency that the same Scripture which tells us that no one can snatch a believer from Jesus' hand warns us against: "Take care," the writer to the Hebrews warns church members—"brothers"—because it is possible to have an unbelieving heart that leads us to "fall away from the living God."

How do we hold this assurance and this warning together? By understanding that it is actually *as we persevere* through the Spirit's power that God continues His work of salvation in us.

The ground of our salvation is always the work of Jesus Christ, never our own. But the evidence that we are truly in Christ is the fact that we continue to the end. Christ Himself said that it is "the one who endures to the end" who "will be saved" (Matthew 10:22; 24:13; Mark 13:13). And how do we continue to the end? Only by God's persevering grace, which He has given to us in Christ through His Spirit and which is bolstered in us by the "means of grace"—the Scriptures, prayer, the fellowship of other believers, and so on.

Today, if you find yourself believing that "Once saved, always saved" means you don't have to obey God or pay attention to the Bible's warnings, know this: that is nothing more than a parody of Christian assurance. It is those who heed the warnings who are those the Lord is keeping. Yes, there will be struggles along the way. But be sure always to take care to cling closely to Christ and lay claim to whatever means He has given you to enable you to endure to the very end.

HEBREWS 3:7 – 4:1

DECEMBER 8

ETERNAL PEACE

"Jesus himself stood among them, and said to them, 'Peace to you!' But they were startled and frightened and thought they saw a spirit." LUKE 24:36-37

We might use many words to sum up the achievement of the gospel and our experience of the gospel. One phrase which deserves meditation and inspires worship is simply this: the gospel is a "gospel of peace" (Ephesians 6:15).

When the risen Jesus appeared to the disciples three days after His death, they were understandably frightened. So Jesus spoke to them. What He said was a typical greeting: "Shalom!" or "Peace to you!" But it was also a necessary greeting to calm His disciples' fear. And His words offered His followers far more than just temporary relief. They also pointed to a deeper, eternal peace.

Throughout the Gospel of Luke, *peace* and *salvation* are almost synonymous. At the start of Luke, Simeon had responded to the news of Jesus' coming birth by praying, "Lord, now you are letting your servant depart *in peace*, according to your word; for my eyes have seen your salvation" (Luke 2:29-30, emphasis added). When Jesus was grown, He'd told the woman who had anointed His feet with her tears, "Your faith has saved you; go *in peace*" (7:50, emphasis added). When the risen Jesus spoke peace to His disciples, then, He was using familiar terminology—but in a whole new context.

Jesus' promise of peace can be a stumbling block for those new to Christianity. At Christmastime, people hear phrases like "Peace on earth and good will to men" and perhaps say to themselves, *Well, clearly such peace isn't happening. There seem to be more wars, factions, and disagreements today than there have ever been.* So what did Jesus mean in promising His disciples peace?

Notice that His declaration of peace was followed by an invitation to see His hands and His feet—evidence of His crucifixion. And what was His crucifixion? It was His substitutionary death on behalf of sinners in order to make "peace by the blood of his cross" (Colossians 1:20).

If what Jesus meant by peace was the instant end of all bloodshed and the inhumanity of man to man, then yes, Christianity is a dud. If He was referring to a kind of valium-enhanced tranquility whereby we just drift through our days with nothing able to cloud our vision or bother us, then Christianity is a failure. But if He was speaking of the peace which would be established between the holy God and sinful humankind through His blood shed on the cross, then the gospel truly is the greatest story ever told.

Just as Jesus appeared to His unsettled disciples amid their emotional turmoil, so He comes to us and promises us peace unlike any other. Indeed, He says specifically, "*My* peace I give to you" (John 14:27, emphasis added). Do not be troubled or afraid, then. For you are at peace with your Creator, loved in the only eyes that matter. Your faith has saved you; go in peace.

LUKE 2:25-32

DECEMBER 9

CONFIDENCE IN GOD'S PROMISE

"This very night there stood before me an angel of the God to whom I belong and whom I worship, and he said, 'Do not be afraid, Paul; you must stand before Caesar. And behold, God has granted you all those who sail with you.' So take heart, men, for I have faith in God that it will be exactly as I have been told."

ACTS 27:23-25

As Paul traveled as a prisoner on a boat to Rome, a debate broke out concerning the right course of action for their trip. During the debate, Paul gave a warning (Acts 27:9-10). Apparently, he had already identified himself by his character and leadership, and when it came to sea voyaging, he had wisdom to share. So Paul advised against continuing the voyage on the basis of what he knew about the sea and the season, and from his personal experience of being shipwrecked (2 Corinthians 11:25).

Paul's warning was disregarded, but time proved him right. Suddenly, seemingly out of nowhere, the ship was driven along by a storm of hurricane force "called the northeaster" (Acts 27:14). The effect of the wind was so dramatic that in a moment, a calm sea became devastating, and the vessel was so buffeted that the lives of all on board the ship were threatened. At some point, those who had dismissed Paul's warning had to look into one another's eyes and say, *You know, it's all over. We are clearly not going to get out of here.*

Yet while everything indicated that this was the end for Paul and all on the ship, the apostle still had the promise of God. In Acts 23:11, the Lord had stood by him and told him, "Take courage, for as you have testified to the facts about me in Jerusalem, so you must testify also in Rome." Paul's life may have been threatened by the turbulence, but God's promise was sufficient—and it was a promise that His angel repeated to Paul at the moment of crisis on the ship. Despite appearances, there was no need to fear, for the promise had been made and would be kept. Therefore, Paul told those around him, they could take heart, for the God to whom Paul belonged does exactly as He has said.

In our daily lives, our experiences and feelings don't always appear to agree with God's promises. We know that He has assured us, "I will never leave you nor forsake you" (Hebrews 13:5)—but that vow can feel empty or remote. We know He has promised us that He will always be at work for the good of those who love Him (Romans 8:28)—but that can feel unlikely. We know He has said that His children will see Him face-to-face (Revelation 22:3-4)—but that can feel impossibly distant. Any of us can trust God's promises when the sun is out and when the band's playing. The challenge is to trust Him in the dark and in the silence—or, as in Paul's case, in the midst of the raging storm.

When the fulfillment of God's promise seems least likely, remember Paul. Even when your circumstances and God's promises do not seem to align, know that as He has done repeatedly in the past, God will always keep His word. When wave after wave seems to be crashing upon you, you can trust that the God to whom you belong and whom you serve has promised to bring you safely to the golden shore and the eternal city.

ACTS 27:21-44

DECEMBER 10

A SUFFICIENT TEST

"If anyone thinks he is religious and does not bridle his tongue but deceives his heart, this person's religion is worthless. Religion that is pure and undefiled before God the Father is this: to visit orphans and widows in their affliction, and to keep oneself unstained from the world." JAMES 1:26-27

If someone asked you, "How can I know if my faith is genuine?" how would you respond? What metrics would you suggest for self-evaluation? Perhaps the fruit of the Spirit or the virtues commended in the Sermon on the Mount? There are many from which to choose. Yet the aim of such a test, of course, is not to find *perfection* but to measure whether we are, by God's grace, heading in the right *direction*. And so, when James gives us just such a test, he highlights three specific areas of conduct.

The first part of the test concerns a controlled tongue. All believers run the risk of being precise and orthodox in our praise of God and articulation of the truths of the faith yet all the while being guilty of thoughtless tongue-wagging. The ways to transgress with our tongue are many and common, including slander, gossip, lies, and filthy speech. If we are not seeking to bring our speech into alignment with our claim to know Christ, we may need to inquire if our hearts are deceived.

The second part of the test deals with our compassion. Compassion should mark Christians because it is an attribute of our heavenly Father, who is "Father of the fatherless and protector of widows" (Psalm 68:5). If we belong to Him, then we, too, should have genuine concern for those who are helpless. If our hearts do not break at the plight of the needy, then we ought to ask ourselves whether our religion is indeed pure.

The final part of James' test asks whether our lives are marked by purity. We dare not be socially involved and practically helpful at the expense of our own personal holiness. James therefore urges spiritual watchfulness. The world we inhabit is actively opposed to the purposes of God, and we need to be careful, lest we are carried off by the tide. Keeping in mind the fundamental conflict between the kingdom of Christ and the world will help keep us "unstained from the world." If we instead befriend the world and its values, we will find ourselves practicing a defiled religion.

While the test these three areas constitute is not comprehensive, it is sufficient. None of us pass it perfectly, but we should ask ourselves whether we are headed in the right direction in our speech, compassion, and purity. Perhaps as you read these verses the Spirit of God is pricking your conscience and revealing an area on which you ought to focus some prayerful energy. If that is so, take heart, for true religion is that which is repentant, which looks to the cross for salvation, and which asks the same Spirit who reveals to us our weaknesses to give us the strength to pursue a religious life of controlled speech, genuine concern, and a pursuit of purity.

1 PETER 1:22 – 2:3

DECEMBER 11

GOD'S WAY

"But you, O Bethlehem Ephrathah, who are too little to be among the clans of Judah, from you shall come forth for me one who is to be ruler in Israel, whose coming forth is from of old, from ancient days." MICAH 5:2

When the prophet Micah announced hope for the discouraged people of God, he opened with a surprising statement: he revealed that the promised Messiah would come not from Jerusalem—the royal city from which most of his original Jewish hearers would have anticipated a king to hail—but from Bethlehem. It was in this small, unexpected town that God's work would unfold before His people.

Jerusalem was the most prominent city in Israel. It was the city of the great King David, the location of the temple, and the primary focus of God's people. Bethlehem would not have been on anyone's radar. It was "too little to be among the clans of Judah." It wouldn't have made their Top 100 list, and it certainly wouldn't have been in their Top 10. Yet the significance of Bethlehem is found in its insignificance.

Thinking about the rest of the Bible story, we realize that this makes perfect sense. This is how God works! When Goliath taunted the people of Israel, the strong and brave soldiers of Israel fled. Instead of using these "great" soldiers, God used a small, insignificant shepherd boy—from Bethlehem, of all places!—with five stones and a sling to deliver God's people. When the good news of the Messiah's birth came, we might have expected that the cultural elite of the day would have been the first to hear of it, but instead, God brought the news to a few insignificant shepherds. This is God's way.

Those who dismiss the message of the Bible often stumble over the fact that God's answer for the world lay in a baby who was born in obscurity. This is not a message that anyone would ever invent! Yet it was into this insignificant place that the Messiah came to rule. The one who lay in a Bethlehem food trough was the one with a neverending kingdom which surpasses all other kingdoms.

Recognizing the pattern of God's ways in ancient days enables us to recognize the Messiah now that He has come. It readies us for the reality that the one upon whom all God's promises rested would die a humiliating death on a cross. It reminds us that this is God's way and always has been. And it therefore changes the way we look at our lives. If you consider yourself of significance, beware: for such a view is often the precursor to being humbled. But if you consider yourself of little import, little ability, and little influence, then be encouraged, for God works through insignificant people in insignificant places. So be of no doubt that today God can do great things through you. That has always been His way.

MICAH 5:2-9

◇ Bible Through The Year: Joshua 1–3; Luke 14:25-35

DECEMBER 12

PEACE IN THE CHAOS

"I have said these things to you, that in me you may have peace. In the world you will have tribulation. But take heart; I have overcome the world."
JOHN 16:33

Jesus never promised His followers the absence of trouble. Nowhere does He say to us that as a result of His coming, dying, rising, and ascending, the world is going to be a more peaceful place or that our place in it is going to be more comfortable. In fact, what He says to us is this: "In the world you will have tribulation."

Sometimes we want to import to *now* that which is promised only for *then*—that is, for the eternal future of which Christ has assured us. We might want to claim for ourselves today those promises—wealth, healing, or absence of tribulation—that God intends to bring to fruition during the age to come. Yes, His kingdom has broken into our world with the advent of Christ. But we still await its full benefits. And if we make the mistake of thinking that God has promised us today what He has in fact only promised us in eternity, then we will certainly be disappointed, and we run the risk of turning our backs on Him on the basis that He did not deliver what He had never actually promised us.

But though we can expect to encounter trouble and tribulation right now simply because we follow Jesus as our King, we still have hope for true peace in this world. Paul writes, "Since we have been justified by faith, *we have peace with God* through our Lord Jesus Christ" (Romans 5:1, emphasis added). This is a peace with God that we can claim now as our own. It is freedom from the fear of judgment and death, from recrimination, and from the dredging up of all the vileness that Christ has already dealt with on the cross.

The gospel is the "good news of peace through Jesus Christ" (Acts 10:36). We still have trials. We will groan and suffer under the weight of sin—both our own and that of others. But in the good news of the gospel we have a true and steady peace, even in turbulent times. "Let not your hearts be troubled," says Jesus, "neither let them be afraid" (John 14:27). You may not feel like it's true today, but your Lord Jesus has already overcome the world and all its troubles. The day is not yet here when He will dry all the tears from your eyes, but you can know that that day will arrive, for there is nothing in all the world that can prevent Jesus bringing His final victory. And, in the meantime, you can know that Jesus stands with you by His Spirit, no matter what trouble meets you. What tribulation faces you today? Be sure that Jesus is with you in it and that Jesus will bring you through it—for He has overcome the world. Take heart!

JOHN 16:25-33

DECEMBER 13

WHAT'S THE POINT OF SUFFERING?

"God is treating you as sons. For what son is there whom his father does not discipline? If you are left without discipline, in which all have participated, then you are illegitimate children and not sons." HEBREWS 12:7-8

Suffering does not necessarily lead us into a deeper relationship with God. Prolonged trials can tempt us to give in to rebellion and distrust. But when we're prepared to bow under God's sovereign purposes, He enables us to endure suffering to the end.

The Bible clearly teaches that God is in control over *all* of our lives—the blessings *and* the trials. For example, in Job 1 we find Satan slandering Job, accusing him of loving God solely because of the blessings he has enjoyed (Job 1:9-10). In response, God commands Satan, "All that he has is in your hand. Only against him do not stretch out your hand" (v 12). God's sovereign rule extended over Job's affliction *and* Satan's jurisdiction.

What then can we say with biblical certainty concerning the purposes of God in our suffering? First, God uses hardship in our lives to *assure us of our sonship*. The experiences of discipline that He brings into our lives prove us to be His true sons and daughters: "If you are left without discipline … then you are illegitimate children and not sons." Second, God uses trials to *develop our dependence* on Him. Paul realized that it was "to keep me from becoming conceited" that "a thorn was given me in the flesh" (2 Corinthians 12:7). Pride can lead to a total downfall. God therefore may mercifully ordain experiences of deep pain in order to instill in us that sense of depending on Him. That humility is the soil in which all the seeds of His grace grow to maturity. Third, God uses suffering to *keep us on track spiritually*. It's easy to wander when everything is going smoothly. But have you noticed how your prayer life can change with one visit to the doctor, or how your desire to call out to God can be strengthened by a shadow looming on the horizon? The psalmist noted this tendency when he confessed, "Before I was afflicted I went astray, but now I keep your word" (Psalm 119:67).

As God's child, you can live with the confidence that your heavenly Father knows best and is in control. When the present feels overwhelming and the days ahead seem unsure, you can trust that there is a purpose, hidden though it may be, and you can say:

Though Satan should buffet, though trials should come,
Let this blest assurance control:
That Christ has regarded my helpless estate,
And has shed his own blood for my soul.
It is well with my soul;
It is well, it is well with my soul.[93]

HEBREWS 12:3-11

93 Horatio Gates Spafford, "It Is Well With My Soul" (1873).

DECEMBER 14

THIS IS THE KING

"The people stood by, watching, but the rulers scoffed at him, saying, 'He saved others; let him save himself, if he is the Christ of God, his Chosen One!' The soldiers also mocked him, coming up and offering him sour wine and saying, 'If you are the King of the Jews, save yourself!' There was also an inscription over him, 'This is the King of the Jews.'" LUKE 23:35-38

In Roman-occupied Judea, it was customary for an executed individual to have a sign hanging around his neck declaring the crime he had committed. But with Jesus, there was a problem: Jesus was completely innocent of any wrongdoing.

Why, then, did Pilate put a sign on Jesus' cross that read "This is the King of the Jews"?

The answer comes in John's Gospel. John reminds us that Jesus was the heralded Messiah. Here was the Chosen One of Israel. And Pilate, aware of these prophecies, aware of all the hope and expectation surrounding Jesus, wanted to force the Jews to wrestle with the reality that their apparent king was no king at all—that here he was, a disfigured body hanging on a bitter cross.

Therefore, John records, the Jewish leaders came to Pilate and asked him to change the sign. They wanted it to read, "This man said, I am King of the Jews." But Pilate retorted, "What I have written I have written" (John 19:21-22). His decision was final. And so it was that Jesus died under a sign proclaiming His true identity.

Yet in response to the sign, in response to Jesus' kingship, "the rulers scoffed at him" and "the soldiers also mocked him." From the top of society to the bottom, from the most refined to the roughest, the reaction was the same: rejection. Rulers and soldiers alike took the view that a genuine Messiah would deliver Himself. In other words, they assumed they would know that Jesus really was the Messiah if He saved Himself. It is a tragic irony, for it is actually because Jesus *didn't* save Himself that He is able to save those who come to God through Him. God's ways are not man's ways. The proof of Jesus' identity, and of His love, is that He chose to die under that sign.

It is easy to assume that we do not scoff and mock like those around the cross. Yet sometimes we think and act just like the rulers and soldiers, waiting for God to do something that makes perfect sense to us, refusing to trust that His ways are always good and loving, and then failing to see His perfect plan unfold right in front of us. When such temptation creeps in, remember just how accurate Pilate's inscription was. Christ was and is the King of the Jews. Indeed, He is the "King of kings and Lord of lords" (Revelation 19:16), worthy of all our trust, praise, and adoration.

REVELATION 19:11-16

DECEMBER 15

THE WISDOM OUR WORLD NEEDS

"Who is wise and understanding among you? By his good conduct let him show his works in the meekness of wisdom." JAMES 3:13

It's easy to confuse wisdom and intelligence. If someone has all the right answers and an encyclopedic knowledge of seemingly every subject, and particularly of Bible verses, we may be prone to assume that they are wise—and they very well could be. But equally, they may well not be, for raw intellectual ability and the capacity to retain a vast number of facts don't necessarily equate with wisdom.

In his epistle, James links wisdom not with knowledge but with good conduct and meekness. The one who is truly wise in God's sight will act in a way that accords with the humility (Philippians 2:3-4), gentleness (Ephesians 4:2), and joy (1 Thessalonians 5:16) that God asks of His people. God, who needs no counselor (Romans 11:34), doesn't need us either to impress Him with what we know. Rather, God tells us that what draws His appreciative gaze is the man or woman, girl or boy, who is "humble and contrite in spirit and trembles at my word" (Isaiah 66:2). James has a memorable phrase for this approach to ourselves and to life: "the meekness of wisdom."

A genuinely wise person knows how much they don't know. They know that however much they know, it is only a tiny portion of the vastness of the knowledge that God has. Intelligence marked by wisdom will not be polluted by showy displays of verbosity or railroad others with intellectual vigor. Instead, it will be marked by a humility that always aims to build others up with whatever we have—be that physical, intellectual, spiritual, or emotional strength. Wisdom echoes the prophet Isaiah, who acknowledged, "The Lord God has given me the tongue of those who are taught, that I may know how to sustain with a word him who is weary" (Isaiah 50:4).

The truly wise maintain a high view of God, a sober view of themselves, and a generous view of other people. How do I know if I have a high view of God? If I am constantly aware of just how much I depend on Him for everything. How will I know if I have a sober view of myself? If I am aware of my own shortcomings and understand that all I have is only what I have received from God—if I am in the habit of pointing away from myself instead of toward myself. How do I know if I have a generous view of other people? If I am routinely building them up instead of cutting them down.

This is the sort of wisdom that pleases God and which the world so desperately needs from you—a gentle wisdom that demonstrates itself in good conduct and consistent meekness. How does this challenge you? How will you pursue living with this true wisdom today?

JAMES 3:13-18

DECEMBER 16

SEEING THE LIGHT

"Philip said to him, 'Lord, show us the Father, and it is enough for us.' Jesus said to him, 'Have I been with you so long, and you still do not know me, Philip? Whoever has seen me has seen the Father.'" JOHN 14:8-9

One day in an art class, as the teacher was going around the various paintings to look at what the children were doing, she asked a boy what it was he was painting. The wee boy said to her, "I'm painting a picture of God." "But we don't know what God looks like," the teacher replied. "Well," said the boy, "come back when I've finished and you'll find out!"

With the arrival of the Lord Jesus in Bethlehem, God took a brush and painted on the canvas of history what He Himself was really like. When Christ appeared, He rendered obsolete all previous guesses about God's nature, and He rendered arrogant all subsequent ones.

The writer to the Hebrews put it this way: "At many times and in many ways, God spoke to our fathers by the prophets, but in these last days he has spoken to us by his Son" (Hebrews 1:1-2). In other words, through the prophets of old, God had spoken a multifaceted and varied word, weaving His character and His nature all through the pages of the Old Testament. But in Bethlehem, God spoke in a personified Word. The long-awaited Messiah, the Light of the nations, appeared—and in that tiny little baby, God made manifest His reality.

Just think: in that Bethlehem manger lay God… wiggling His toes! The baby that nursed at the breast of Mary and was rocked to sleep in the arms of Joseph was God, and He remains God. Is it any wonder that the shepherds went out and spread the word? Is it any wonder that the wise men of His day bowed in worship before Him?

Jesus came to make the Father known. May our hearts be so humbled by the incarnation that we come to know God personally, not merely intellectually. Like the shepherds, we have the message of Christ's advent to share with our society. As we spread the good news of Jesus' coming as the Messiah, as the one who is God and has come to make God known, pray that the wisdom of our world may bow before His glory. Do you know Jesus as your Lord? Then—praise God—you have seen, and you know, His Father.

JOHN 14:1-11

Bible Through The Year: Joshua 16–18; Luke 17:20-37

DECEMBER 17

YOU CAN FACE TOMORROW

"If Christ has not been raised, your faith is futile and you are still in your sins. Then those also who have fallen asleep in Christ have perished. If in Christ we have hope in this life only, we are of all people most to be pitied. But in fact Christ has been raised." 1 CORINTHIANS 15:17-20

Every once in a while, someone comes along and claims that we don't need to believe in the bodily resurrection of Jesus Christ. We can still be Christians without the miraculous or supernatural elements of the Christian faith, they say. But the tragedy for them and anyone who follows such a claim is that the implications of there being no resurrection don't just make the Christian life difficult; they make it ridiculous.

If there is no resurrection, Paul pointed out, then those who have died trusting Jesus have utterly perished, and there is no hope of ever seeing them again. If we try to live a Christian life without the resurrection, then "we are of all people most to be pitied." In fact, Paul says, "If the dead are not raised, 'Let us eat and drink, for tomorrow we die'" (1 Corinthians 15:32). If we don't believe in the resurrection, then we ought to buy into all the clichés that so many say (but few truly believe)— "This life is what you make it" and "He who dies with the most toys wins!"

Enticing as such platitudes may be, we all have a sneaking suspicion that death is not the end. God has put eternity into our hearts (Ecclesiastes 3:11), and there is no scraping it out—no matter what force of rational skepticism or indulgent hedonism we apply to it. We know, by design, that there is more to life than life itself.

We also know that tomorrow, and in every tomorrow, there will be sadness, pain, loss, fear, and disappointment. How can anyone cope? Without the resurrection, we can't. That is why Paul reminded the Ephesians that before being brought near to Christ, they had "no hope" and were "without God in the world" (Ephesians 2:12).

"But Christ has been raised." And those five words make all the difference, not only to eternal life but also to life today. If you take God at His word and trust Him in faith, then there is never any reason for hopelessness. You have "a living hope through the resurrection of Jesus Christ from the dead" (1 Peter 1:3). No matter what difficulties await you—and today, and tomorrow, there will be some—you will always have "an inheritance that is imperishable, undefiled, and unfading, kept in heaven for you" (v 4). "Because he lives, I can face tomorrow," goes the song.[94] So can you—and you can do so with joy.

EPHESIANS 2:11-22

94 Bill Gaither and Gloria Gaither, "Because He Lives" (1971).

DECEMBER 18

ENTRUST YOURSELF TO GOD

"Behold, this day your eyes have seen how the LORD gave you today into my hand in the cave. And some told me to kill you, but I spared you. I said, 'I will not put out my hand against my lord, for he is the LORD's anointed' . . . May the LORD judge between me and you, may the LORD avenge me against you, but my hand shall not be against you." 1 SAMUEL 24:10, 12

The verb *to grab* means to seize something forcibly or roughly or to get something by unscrupulous methods. When we were young, most of us would have been taught by our parents not to grab something but instead to wait until it was handed to us. This is not just good behavior for children; it is biblical living for believers.

After God rejected King Saul, David was anointed as the next king over Israel. The throne would eventually be his when Saul died. In the meantime, however, Saul chased David for years, attempting to kill him. David knew that all it would take for him to be able to leave the wilderness and sit on the throne was Saul's death. And then the opportunity to end Saul's life—to take hold of safety, security, and the kingdom he had been promised—presented itself (1 Samuel 24:2-4).

Yet David refused to end Saul's life and take hold of the throne. He did not succumb to the temptation to grab something which was only God's to give.

David's pathway to the throne was a long and winding road, but he chose not to take matters into his own hands or try to speed up the process. Instead, he was prepared to wait for God's time and to rest in His providence.

Imagine how hard that must have been! But this is a faithful response—not to grab a shortcut out of difficulty but instead to serve God in the situation He has placed us in. It's the way of David. It's the way of Jesus, who entrusted Himself "to him who judges justly," even unto death (1 Peter 2:23).

How are you handling the circumstances that seem to threaten your security, satisfaction, or prosperity? How are you responding to people who challenge you? To use the words of Jesus, will you seek first the kingdom of God and His righteousness (Matthew 6:33), trusting that all your preoccupations and passions will be taken care of by God? Make it your aim not to grab at those things which seem to be yours by right or to grasp at a shortcut out of a hard situation. Rather, like David, leave God to order your life, knowing that He has promised you eternity with Him and called you to serve Him along the way.

1 PETER 2:21-25

Bible Through The Year: Joshua 22–24; Luke 18:18-43

DECEMBER 19

WHAT LOVE REQUIRES

"This is love, that we walk according to his commandments; this is the commandment, just as you have heard from the beginning, so that you should walk in it." 2 JOHN 6

Genuine Christian love involves much more than warm feelings, affectionate hugs, and tender affection. While love may very well include emotions and stir our feelings, the love that the Bible calls us to is first and foremost an act of the will.

When the apostle John exhorted his readers to love, he linked that call directly to what God commands. Jesus spoke of love in the same way when he said, "If you love me, you will keep my commandments" (John 14:15). So to express biblical love is to do what God has commanded. The world tells us that love means affirming and admiring; the Scriptures do not. In fact, love means obeying our Creator's commands. Perhaps heeding God's commands will sometimes require us to give a hug—as when we "rejoice with those who rejoice" or "weep with those who weep" (Romans 12:15). But at other times, genuine Christian love may call for correction, admonition, rebuke, or exhortation.

One key to understanding this love is to consider the manner in which Jesus called His followers to love one another. "This is my commandment," He said, "that you love one another *as I have loved you*" (John 15:12, emphasis added). Then He added, "Greater love has no one than this, that someone lay down his life for his friends" (v 13). The call to love, then, is ultimately a call for us to give as Jesus gave. It is a call for us to resolve, no matter what, to seek the good of others—even when that pursuit comes at great risk or cost to ourselves.

We know that Jesus endured the cross "for the joy that was set before him" (Hebrews 12:2). That joy, however, was not immediate. We need only look to Gethsemane or Christ's cry of forsaken anguish from the cross for evidence of that. Likewise, there is an eternal joy set before us, and we need not doubt that every act of costly love "will be repaid at the resurrection of the just" (Luke 14:14). But for now, to love well will often take a toll. It will require us to press on with loving someone when we don't necessarily feel like doing so. It will demand that we give when we just don't want to anymore.

But the good news is that "we love because he first loved us" (1 John 4:19). Not only is Christ your example, but, by His Spirit, He will empower you to walk with Him on the sacrificial path of love. Ask yourself, then, whom the Lord has given you to love today. And then ask yourself what loving them in the way that obeys God's commandments will look like. For that is real love, and it is that love that we are called to walk in each day.

1 JOHN 4:7-12

DECEMBER 20

WONDER AND MYSTERY

"'Behold, you will conceive in your womb and bear a son, and you shall call his name Jesus ...' And Mary said to the angel, 'How will this be, since I am a virgin?' And the angel answered her, 'The Holy Spirit will come upon you, and the power of the Most High will overshadow you; therefore the child to be born will be called holy—the Son of God.'" LUKE 1:31, 34-35

It is not Jesus' birth which is so remarkable but His conception. When the angel announced that although she was a virgin, Mary would have a baby who would rule the entire universe, she simply asked the sensible question: "How?" And with that question we arrive at the very heart of the Christian story.

How was this child to be conceived? God was going to make it happen. He would do it. The language of being "overshadowed" reminds us of God's divine presence being symbolized to the Israelites by a great cloud (Exodus 40:34-38). The conception, in other words, would be supernatural, able to be accomplished by God alone.

As Paul worked through the theology of the incarnation, he wrote, "When the fullness of time had come, God sent forth his Son, born of woman, born under the law, to redeem those who were under the law, so that we might receive adoption as sons" (Galatians 4:4-5). He emphasized that the Redeemer had to be human so that He would be of the same nature as those whom He came to save: a man dying for mankind. But it was equally imperative that the Redeemer should be perfectly holy, because no sinful person could effect atonement for the sins of others. He *had* to be Immanuel—God with us—and He *had* to be man.

The early Christians hammered out the incarnation's implications and came up with ways to describe the one who was conceived by the Spirit in Mary's womb, coming to the convictions that have passed down to us in the early creeds. Our spiritual forefathers identified the wonder of the incarnation, bowed before the mystery of it, and affirmed that Jesus was, and remains, very God and very man.

The idea that God would supernaturally invade this world shouldn't surprise or discomfort us. It takes a supernatural invasion of God into individuals' lives, after all, to bring them to living faith, just as God sovereignly worked a miracle in Mary's womb in order to bring us the Redeemer. Jesus told Nicodemus that unless someone is born from above—a birth brought about by God through His Spirit—they would not see God's kingdom (John 3:3). If we have been brought to salvation, it is only because God has done it. You did no more to save yourself than Mary did to become pregnant with your Savior. The "How?" of salvation is always answered only by "God did it."

So, bow today before the wonder and mystery of God taking on flesh. And bow today before the wonder and mystery of God redeeming you. For that, no less than the virgin birth of the Son of God, is the supernatural work of God.

LUKE 1:26-38

DECEMBER 21

WAITING ON GOD

"Wait for the Lord; be strong, and let your heart take courage; wait for the Lord!" PSALM 27:14

Do you enjoy waiting? Most of us, if we're prepared to be honest, would answer with an emphatic "No!" We need only to sit and wait for somebody to reverse out of a parking space to be reminded of how impatient we really are. Usually, we desire that our needs be met according to our timetable, and modern life teaches us that this is a fair demand. And yet this lack of patience poses a major problem for the Christian—because if we find it difficult to wait, we're going to find it very difficult to walk by faith.

In the Bible, we often see faith demonstrated as men and women wait on the promises of God. (See, for instance, Romans 4.) Indeed, God's "precious and very great promises" (2 Peter 1:4) are seldom given with any kind of time guarantee. This makes all the difference in the world. Most of us can muster up the ability to wait if we know that we only have to wait until next Friday, or until five o'clock, or whenever. But that is not waiting in faith. Rather, Scripture exhorts us to wait not on a specific time but on the faithfulness of the one who promises—namely, God Himself.

If we are in need of strength—strength to endure illness, to resist temptation, to show kindness to a challenging coworker—and we turn to the Scriptures for encouragement, we discover that "they who wait for the Lord shall renew their strength" (Isaiah 40:31). Likewise, at the birth of the church, the word of Christ to the disciples was that they should wait in Jerusalem "for the promise of the Father" (Acts 1:4). In the same way, we are called to wait "for our blessed hope, the appearing of the glory of our great God and Savior Jesus Christ" (Titus 2:13). The Bible tells us to wait, to watch, to pray, to look, and to be ready, not with a knowledge of the timeframe but with the knowledge that God is faithful.

You likely know what it is to have your character tested in faith's waiting room. Remember that genuine faith involves waiting, and it requires that we wait not on external circumstances but on our God, who sees His people and who "acts for those who wait for him" (Isaiah 64:4). Let that build patience within you, both for the waiting times in this life and as you wait for the Lord to return and bring you into the glory of your eternal life.

ROMANS 4:13-25

DECEMBER 22

CHANGED IN THE BLINK OF AN EYE

"I tell you this, brothers: flesh and blood cannot inherit the kingdom of God, nor does the perishable inherit the imperishable." 1 CORINTHIANS 15:50

We cannot enter God's presence in heaven. We simply cannot do it—not as we are now, anyway. Our perishable, decaying bodies are not suited for an imperishable, undefiled kingdom.

By way of the new birth, we have already entered God's kingdom spiritually (John 3:1-8). But ultimately, God will bring His kingdom in all its fullness, and He will reign forever over a new heaven and a new earth (Revelation 21:1). And, says Paul, we can't get there as we are. We can't simply show up there like this, for "flesh and blood cannot inherit the kingdom of God." We must be changed, not unlike a seed (1 Corinthians 15:42-49). When the seed is planted in the ground, it retains its identity, but it comes out radically and wonderfully different.

What does this mean? How will it happen? It is a "mystery," Paul acknowledges (1 Corinthians 15:51). We cannot fully (or even mainly!) understand it. But we can identify at least three aspects of this change from this glorious chapter.

First, God will transform us *instantly*—"in the twinkling of an eye" (1 Corinthians 15:52). This will not be a process but a supernatural transformation, an instantaneous re-creation from one state to another. In that glorious moment, only as long as it takes us to blink, we—whether we are waiting in heaven with Christ or alive on earth (1 Thessalonians 4:15-17)—will be changed for the better, forever.

Second, God will change us *radically*: we "will be raised imperishable" (1 Corinthians 15:52). The one certainty of our life here is that it will end. All our earthly days were written in God's book before one of them came to be (Psalm 139:16). But in the instant God transforms us, He will radically change us, such that death and decay will be replaced with imperishability.

Third, God will refashion us *eternally*: we will "put on immortality" (1 Corinthians 15:53). There will be no risk of reverting to our former condition. "Death shall be no more" (Revelation 21:4), and our present state of decay will become but a memory.

Dwell on this truth for a moment: one day, God will transform you in an instant. He will change you radically. He will refashion you for eternity. He will wipe away every tear from your eyes. Mourning, crying, and pain will all fade from view. It may be hard to imagine now, but in faith you can trust that your God will cause all the former things to pass away. And once He does that, you will dwell with Him forever in unending bliss. That is a truth that can enable you to smile on the hardest of days.

REVELATION 22:1-5

DECEMBER 23

KNOWING WITH CERTAINTY

"In those days a decree went out from Caesar Augustus that all the world should be registered. This was the first registration when Quirinius was governor of Syria. And all went to be registered, each to his own town. And Joseph also went up from Galilee, from the town of Nazareth, to Judea, to the city of David, which is called Bethlehem, because he was of the house and lineage of David, to be registered with Mary, his betrothed who was with child." LUKE 2:1-5

In our day and age, it is trendy to be seeking truth but taboo to say we have found it. Our culture would have us believe that while it's ok to have a concept or an idea, we shouldn't say we have certainty. Luke was different. He wasn't satisfied with anything less than knowing with certainty—for himself and for others. Indeed, it was a key part of his very purpose in writing his Gospel (Luke 1:3-4).

In his account of Jesus' birth, Luke provides us with political, social, geographical, and historical observations that may seem quite mundane. But they all matter. We are being shown that within the sociological context and in obedience to the political structures of his time, Joseph, along with Mary, made a geographical journey to his ancestral home. All of this took place in real, historical time.

While people back then didn't have Google or social media, someone easily could have gone to the record of public registration and looked up Joseph's name. The Gospel writer was not providing a philosophy, an idea, or even a religion. He was delivering an honest account of actual events—events which centered upon the child who was in Mary's womb and who would be born in the city of David, his great ancestor whose triumphs and reign were a mere shadow of the victories this baby would one day win for His people. Luke, with every word and every detail, made it very clear that Jesus' story doesn't exist in a vacuum.

First- and second-century historians were in no doubt concerning Jesus' historicity. Tacitus, a Roman historian who was writing in the early second century, had no interest in supporting the claims of Christ but was absolutely convinced that Jesus was not mythological.[95] Josephus, a Jewish historian writing in AD 93, affirmed the fact that the life, death, and resurrection of Jesus were proclaimed by His followers.[96]

The New Testament doesn't call any of us into the realm of blind faith or to take a leap into the dark. No, it invites us to take a step into the light of absolute truth. In this supernatural space where God took on human flesh, you and I can be certain about the life, death, resurrection, and ascension of Jesus of Nazareth. And in that certainty of what took place in those days you will discover hope, peace, joy, and purpose for your day today.

LUKE 1:1-4

95 *Annals,* 15.44.
96 *Antiquities of the Jews,* 18.3.3.

DECEMBER 24

REJOICE WITH THE ANGELS

"Joseph also went up from Galilee, from the town of Nazareth, to Judea, to the city of David, which is called Bethlehem, because he was of the house and lineage of David, to be registered with Mary, his betrothed, who was with child." LUKE 2:4-5

Jesus' birthplace had a rich biblical history before ever it was visited by angels. It was Bethlehem that had once been stirred at the return of a woman who had left with her husband and two sons. Her name was Naomi. She and her family had gone in search of bread, from "the town of bread" (the meaning of "Bethlehem"), because of famine. While away, she'd lost her husband and both her sons. After this triple bereavement, she returned to the town with one of her daughters-in-law, a woman called Ruth, who gives her name to the Old Testament book that tells their story. This grieving foreigner would one day become a part of the lineage of the Messiah (Matthew 1:1-6).

It was also in the fields surrounding Bethlehem that a shepherd boy, David, looked after his father's sheep. Bethlehem was the place where Samuel arrived in obedience to God's word to find a replacement for King Saul. He asked Jesse to bring his sons out because one of them was going to be the king. They all came. None of them were chosen. The prophet then asked if there were any others, and the one who just looked after the sheep was brought in—and soon became the shepherd king of Israel (1 Samuel 16:1-12).

Then, 1,000 years later, a man named Joseph returned to his ancestral home of Bethlehem to be registered for a census with his betrothed, Mary. In this now-familiar and ordinary yet historically significant place, it was time for the arrival of the promised and long-anticipated Messiah. For some 600 years previously, the prophet Micah had recorded these words:

> But you, O Bethlehem Ephrathah,
> who are too little to be among the clans of Judah,
> from you shall come forth for me
> one who is to be ruler in Israel,
> whose coming forth is from of old,
> from ancient days. (Micah 5:2)

Once again in Bethlehem, presumably in those same surrounding fields where David had once watched over his father's sheep, there would be a stirring as the skies filled up with angelic visitation and echoed to salvation's songs (Luke 2:8-14).

As you approach this familiar territory during the Christmas season, may your heart be stirred afresh in the presence of God's Son, our Messiah. May His Spirit move you to consider with awe the centuries-long complexity of the preparation for that moment when your King lay in a manger. And may He cause you to rejoice with the angels in God's great salvation, knowing that our great God uses the small and ordinary things in life—even a little town like Bethlehem—to accomplish His great and glorious purposes.

LUKE 2:8-14

DECEMBER 25

SUPERNATURAL HISTORY

"While they were there, the time came for her to give birth. And she gave birth to her firstborn son and wrapped him in swaddling cloths and laid him in a manger, because there was no place for them in the inn." LUKE 2:6-7

In the Gospel of Luke, no sooner has the author introduced himself as a detail-oriented historian (Luke 1:1-4) than we are immediately ushered into an environment filled with supernatural occurrences (v 11-17). The story of Jesus' birth is filled with angels, predictions, and miracles (1:26 – 2:21)—and when Luke reports these events, he offers them not as imaginative stories or poetical speculations but as they are: real history.

When we read that Mary laid her firstborn son—the very Son of God—in a manger, it's because she did. When we read that the child she gave birth to was conceived through the power of the Holy Spirit (Luke 1:31-35), it's because He was. Rather than being superfluous, these supernatural elements are an intrinsic part of the Gospel's account.

There are those who have concluded that Jesus' birth narrative appears so dramatically supernatural as to be implausible. They don't believe it themselves or teach it to anybody else. They have decided that the story would be more acceptable to everybody if we simply removed anything miraculous.

But that cannot be done. The story of the gospel is supernatural *in its entirety*, and not just at its beginning, because it is the story of the Creator of the universe entering into time, revealing Himself as Savior and King. Surely it would be more bizarre if the almighty God did not enter and exit the world in entirely supernatural ways that made mere mortals scratch their heads in amazement! Indeed, in each of the supernatural incidents Luke recorded, there were faithful people who had reflected on the Scriptures and were keenly anticipating that God would break into their environment in a way that had never happened before and would never happen again. When God came, these were the people who were ready for God to come and do what only He could do; these were the people who responded in faith.

Christianity is ultimately meaningless apart from the almighty, miraculous intervention of God in time. God has come to meet us, but not at the top of the towers that we have created on the strength of our ideas and investigation into what is plausible. He came to meet us in a cattle shed in Bethlehem. He came to meet us on a Roman cross at Calvary. He works in ways that we cannot explain and cannot predict.

As you reflect on God's word during this Advent season, consider His divine work, which has already been accomplished, and the ways He continues to move today. In doing so, your heart will once again be stirred by the wonder of the triune God's supernatural love for you, and your eyes will be prepared to see surprising ways that God is at work in and around you—ways that you cannot explain, and had not predicted, but love to enjoy and to praise Him for.

GALATIANS 4:4-7

DECEMBER 26

RESPONSES TO THE KING

"He inquired of them where the Christ was to be born. They told him, 'In Bethlehem of Judea, for so it is written by the prophet.'" MATTHEW 2:4-5

When Jesus was born, seven centuries after the prophet Micah had prophesied where He would appear, His arrival was met with a variety of different reactions—and those responses are the same today as they were then: hostility, indifference, or faith.

King Herod was the epitome of hostility toward Jesus. He stands for everyone who says to themselves, "I don't mind some religious person sitting quietly in the back seat, but I don't want anybody driving the car of my life." A religious leader who keeps quiet is acceptable; one who makes claims on a person's life and who does not agree with what they already think is not. Herod did all he could to ensure there would be no king to rival him (Matthew 2:16-18). And many do so still today.

Jerusalem's religious professionals responded to the arrival of Jesus with indifference. When Herod asked them about the coming of the Christ, they were able to answer his questions with great specificity. They were *aware* that Micah had prophesied that He would be born in Bethlehem; but they simply didn't *care*. They wouldn't even take the time to make a six-mile journey to meet and worship the newly born, long-awaited King of the Jews. They completely disregarded Him. They were too busy with their religion to make time for their rescuing King.

Then there were the wise men, this group of foreign astrologers who saw a star in the heavens, worked out what it was announcing, packed their bags, and responded to Jesus in faith. What moved men who were authorities in their field to bow down at the cradle of a child? How does that happen? Only by the power of God. And it was they, and not Herod or the priests, who were the ones who "rejoiced exceedingly with great joy" (Matthew 2:10).

There is only one true dividing line between people. It has nothing to do with skin color, intellect, or social status. It is the dividing line between unbelief—whether that unbelief manifests itself as hostility or indifference—and unbelief. We may note that the Western world grows in hostility to a God who insists on ruling His world, but we should also note that "religious" people are also at risk of unbelief: the unbelief of indifference. Those of us who have heard the Christmas story countless times, who know our Old Testaments, and who are in church Sunday by Sunday are not immune to the indifference that is seen in a lack of joy over the Lord and a lack of response to His word when it calls us to change our plans. And whoever we are, if we won't have Jesus as our King in this life, we won't live in His kingdom on the other side of death. If you choose to ask Jesus to leave you alone, either in your hostility or in your religiosity, He will leave you alone—forever. Your response to Jesus has eternal significance. Look on Him who came to die for hostile and indifferent sinners, then, and allow His great love to soften your heart so that you respond to Him in real, joyful, obedient faith, today and every day.

MATTHEW 2:1-11

DECEMBER 27

THE GREATEST DISCOVERY

"Going into the house, they saw the child with Mary his mother, and they fell down and worshiped him. Then, opening their treasures, they offered him gifts, gold and frankincense and myrrh." MATTHEW 2:11

When the wise men came to Jerusalem in search of the King of the Jews at the end of what was likely an 800-mile journey, they quickly discovered that they had arrived in the wrong place. They came to the king's palace in Jerusalem because of an entirely logical deduction: they thought the palace in the capital city would be the best place to begin. Yet they soon realized that they were going to need more guidance than the stars could provide.

When King Herod heard that the wise men were inquiring about the birth of a new king, he assembled the chief priests and scribes, who determined that the Christ was to be born "in Bethlehem of Judea, for so it is written by the prophet" (Matthew 2:5). The religious specialists were themselves indifferent to this great knowledge, but they demonstrated to the wise men that they needed the Scriptures to point them in the right direction. God may employ all kinds of extraordinary means to draw people to Himself, but He *always* brings them to His word, the Bible, in order that they might encounter the living Word, His Son. There is no other way to God except by the Christ of God, who is revealed to us in the word of God.

Having been led by the Scriptures to Jesus, the wise men then made their greatest discovery: worshiping Christ was the only appropriate response. When they finally encountered Jesus, they fell down, worshiped Him, and offered Him gifts. In the same way, whatever God may use to trigger our thinking and investigation of the truth, whenever He finally brings us to Jesus, we don't arrive before Him as arrogant researchers. No, when our eyes are opened to the majesty of King Jesus, we bow before Him in humility, wonder, and awe.

In your search for the truth, have you yet discovered that the Bible is the surest guide? And, having discovered Christ, have you also discovered that mere knowledge of Him is insufficient—that the only right response is worship, laying before Him the best of all you have: your time, your possessions, your energies, your heart? You know you have grasped the message of the first Christmas if you have sensed that there is a God who is at work, if you have met with Jesus His Son through His word… and if you have bowed down before Him and now offer Him your life daily.

PSALM 29

DECEMBER 28

SHOW NO PARTIALITY

"My brothers, show no partiality as you hold the faith in our Lord Jesus Christ, the Lord of glory." JAMES 2:1

A living faith is not only a listening faith but also a doing faith. True belief manifests itself in action—and, in some cases, in inaction. In other words, true faith is known not only by what it *does* but also by what it *doesn't* do—for example, as James points out, by *not* showing partiality.

Partiality—the sin of treating people differently due to their outward appearance, status, or usefulness—was a clear and present danger in James' day, and it remains so in our own. James was not condemning all acknowledgment of distinctions, or even preferential treatment for legitimate reasons. A young man who gives up his bus seat for an elderly woman is not running foul of James' teaching! Rather, what James was making absolutely clear is this: external characteristics, and especially those that indicate wealth, in and of themselves do not mean that someone deserves honor.

This is the point of the illustration in James 2: if two men enter our gathering, one in fine clothing and the other in shabby, and the wealthy man gets the place of honor while the poor man gets shoved aside, then we are guilty of the sin of partiality. To give such preferential treatment to the wealthy would be to make "distinctions among yourselves and become judges with evil thoughts" (v 4). God does not judge us by such distinctions, and so neither should we judge others in this way.

In His life and ministry, Jesus displayed how impartiality ought to look. He was willing to allow a woman of ill repute to weep over Him and for her tears to wash His feet (Luke 7:36-50). And He was just as prepared to call a rich man down from a tree to take Him to his house (19:1-10). Why? Because He knew that great wealth and worldly honor do not and cannot make someone more valuable in God's eyes. He was well-acquainted with both the richest of riches and the lowest circumstances imaginable. In descending from heaven, exchanging honor for humility, Jesus set aside the glory which was His due in order to draw near to and save sinners like us—rich and poor alike.

When we grasp the wonder of this reality, we begin to see the true ugliness of judging others on the basis of the external and superficial. Partiality should have no place among the people of God because if we know God at all, it is because *He dealt with us impartially.* Be honest with yourself, then, and ask the Lord for the grace to see others in the way He does and to show others the mercy and grace He has shown you.

LUKE 7:36-50

DECEMBER 29

THE BLOOD THAT FREES TO SERVE

"If the blood of goats and bulls … sanctify for the purification of the flesh, how much more will the blood of Christ, who through the eternal Spirit offered himself without blemish to God, purify our conscience from dead works to serve the living God." HEBREWS 9:13-14

The uncomfortable truth is that by nature we are slaves to sin. We serve ourselves, we glory in our folly, and none of us seek after God (Romans 3:11). But there is hope: "God, being rich in mercy, because of the great love with which he loved us … made us alive together with Christ" (Ephesians 2:4-5). And when we are united with Christ by faith, "we have redemption through his blood" (1:7).

Our redemption was secured at the highest cost: the shed blood of the Lord Jesus Christ. John Murray, the Scottish theologian of old, noted, "Christ did not come to put men in a redeemable position but to redeem to himself a people."[97]

The redemption which God the Father has planned, the Son has procured, and the Spirit has applied encompasses all the wonder of a life changed. It is in this eternal redemption that our consciences are purified "from dead works." That is, we are cleansed from our sinful actions, including those of religious self-reliance, which lead to death.

The "blood of Christ" frees us from our slavery to sin to make us slaves all over again—only now we are gladly and joyfully bound to the Lord Jesus Christ, who is our Master and our Guide. Jesus did not go to the extent of redeeming us from all ungodliness so that we could just run around and please ourselves. He did not redeem us so that we might treat Him with scant regard. No, He ransomed our lives in order that we might serve the living God!

What a privilege it is to serve God and to pursue the good works which He has prepared for those who are in Christ (Ephesians 2:10). What joy should fill our souls as we marvel at His redeeming love: that from all of eternity, the triune God entered into a covenant of redemption and planned to secure a people that belong exclusively to Him and who are called to serve and honor Him in all they do.

Perhaps today you are stuck in patterns of unhelpful introspection. Maybe you have been neglecting the fact that you have been redeemed at great cost in order that you might be sanctified in His service. Consider Christ and all He has done for you. Remember that He has enabled you to do what He calls you to do: to live a life of glad obedience.

PSALM 20

97 *Redemption—Accomplished and Applied,* p 63, quoted in Geoffrey B. Wilson, *New Testament Commentaries,* Vol. 2, *Philippians to Hebrews and Revelation* (Banner of Truth, 2005), p 402.

DECEMBER 30

A TASK UNFINISHED

"You are witnesses of these things. And behold, I am sending the promise of my Father upon you. But stay in the city until you are clothed with power from on high." LUKE 24:48-49

We are called to a task that we cannot accomplish alone: to be witnesses to Christ. Following His death and resurrection, Jesus appeared to His disciples, dispelling their fear and doubt by revealing the nail marks in His hands and His feet (Luke 24:39), reminding them of all that had been written concerning Him (v 44), and opening their minds to the truth of Scripture (v 45). And before He returned to His heavenly throne He gave them a task: to witness to what they had seen Him do and heard Him teach. The truth about Him needed to be proclaimed "to all nations" (v 47).

Since that task is as yet unfinished, God's people today are called to witness no less than God's people that day were. We may not be able to go out and say with the apostle John, "That which ... we have heard, which we have seen with our eyes, which we looked upon and have touched with our hands, concerning the word of life ... we proclaim also to you" (1 John 1:1, 3). But in the Bible we have God's very word, which we are called not only to believe but also to proclaim.

Yet we are so limited! One minute we're believing; the next minute our minds are filled with uncertainty. We often step back in fear rather than forward in faith. We find ourselves not quite knowing what we should say about the gospel to those around us.

Jesus, the Good Shepherd, knows this. He knows His sheep—He knows our propensity for fear and timidity—and He assures us that we do not have to speak or act merely by our own power. No, we have received what Jesus told those first disciples to wait for: "the promise of the Father," His Holy Spirit, so that we are "clothed with power from on high."

Jesus gives us His Spirit in order that we might be involved in kingdom business—in order that we might take the good news to the nations and to the ends of the earth (Acts 1:8). Don't give in to fear and timidity. What you cannot accomplish alone you can do in the power He has given you. So, go out in dependence on the Spirit of God, and prayerfully commit to playing your part in the great, unfinished task of proclaiming the name and glory of Jesus Christ to the nations near and far:

Facing a task unfinished that drives us to our knees,
A need that, undiminished, rebukes our slothful ease,
We who rejoice to know Thee renew before Thy throne
The solemn pledge we owe Thee to go and make Thee known.[98]

MATTHEW 28:16-20

98 Frank Houghton, "Facing a Task Unfinished" (1931).

DECEMBER 31

A PRAYER FOR PROSPERITY

"Beloved, I pray that all may go well with you and that you may be in good health, as it goes well with your soul." 3 JOHN 2

Does God desire that you prosper? Does He want you to succeed? Does He want you to do well?

Those are controversial, and complicated, questions—and in large part the answers depend on how we define prosperity and success. We are rightly at pains, on the strength of biblical warrant, to refute every notion of the "prosperity gospel." God is not our personal vending machine, Jesus Christ is not our butler, and the Holy Spirit is not our genie. God has not promised us that faith leads to health and wealth in this world. We should never forget that Jesus, who Himself had nowhere to lay His head in this world (Luke 9:58), said, "If anyone would come after me, let him deny himself and take up his cross and follow me" (Mark 8:34).

On the other hand, the apostle John prays openly and sincerely for prosperity for the addressee of his third letter. What the ESV translates as "go well" and "goes well" is actually a Greek word that means "to prosper"—though we should take care to note that John offers a disclaimer of sorts: "as it goes well *with your soul*." It's a subtle but crucial reminder that health and material prosperity are not disconnected from the spiritual.

Perhaps we might even say that it is only insofar as we prosper spiritually that we can genuinely prosper in any other way. In the words of our Lord Jesus, "What does it profit a man to gain the whole world and forfeit his soul?" (Mark 8:36). Your portfolio can burst at the seams, and you can have the endurance of a triathlete, but unless your soul is fit, then your monetary and physical prosperity amounts to nothing in the end.

So what might John's prayer for prosperity mean for us practically? Many of us, I imagine, will be quite content and happy to pray that all may be well with the souls of our brothers and sisters. But perhaps we may hesitate slightly to pray such prayers as these:

- "May it all go phenomenally well with my dear brother's business."
- "May it all go exceptionally well with my sister's children."
- "May my good friend enjoy the prosperity of God crowning all of his endeavors."

We must remember that these issues are not ultimate—but that doesn't mean they aren't important! As we rightly guard against the "prosperity gospel," we must at the same time never allow our love and care for one another to become stilted. Selfless love always desires the best for others—in the soul, absolutely and primarily, but also in their vocation, relationships, and in any other engagements and transactions in which a Christian participates in a way that is obedient to their Lord.

Perhaps now would be a good moment to boldly lift up some prayers for the right kind of prosperity for others in your church, asking that the Giver might be glorified through all that He gives.

EPHESIANS 3:20-21

ACKNOWLEDGMENTS

As with the first volume of this devotional, my greatest thanks go to the team at the Truth For Life daily Bible teaching program and ministry organization, and in particular to Ryan Loague for overseeing the development of each day's devotional with such theological acuity; Adam Marshall for his careful eye and expertise throughout the process; and Alyssa Scheck, Kate Nees, Hunter Hanson, and Matt Damico for their help with the writing. Bob Butts, who leads the day-to-day work at Truth For Life, provided both encouragement to make this whole project happen and helpful feedback along the way.

As ever, I'm also grateful to my publisher, The Good Book Company, and my editor, Carl Laferton. It remains a great joy to work alongside these brothers and sisters.

SCRIPTURE INDEX

Entries in **bold** refer to the main verse or passage for that date's devotional

PROVERBS

ECCLESIASTES